RESISTING RADICALISATION?

Resisting Radicalisation?

Understanding Young People's Journeys through Radicalising Milieus

❖ ❖ ❖

Edited by
Hilary Pilkington

berghahn
NEW YORK · OXFORD
www.berghahnbooks.com

First published in 2024 by
Berghahn Books
www.berghahnbooks.com

Library of Congress Cataloging-in-Publication Data

A C.I.P. cataloging record is available from the Library of Congress

Library of Congress Cataloging in Publication Control Number: 2023042558

British Library Cataloguing in Publication Data

A catalogue record for this book is available from the British Library

ISBN 978-1-80539-008-4 hardback
ISBN 978-1-80539-012-1 paperback
ISBN 978-1-80539-386-3 epub
ISBN 978-1-80539-009-1 web pdf

https://doi.org/10.3167/9781805390084

The electronic open access publication of *Resisting Radicalisation? Understanding
Young People's Journeys through Radicalising Milieus* has been made possible
through the generous financial support of The University of Manchester.

CONTENTS

....

Part III. Situational and Interactional Dynamics of (Non)Radicalisation

ILLUSTRATIONS

....

Figures

Tables

ACKNOWLEDGEMENTS

This book is one outcome of a collaborative research project bringing together researchers from across Europe and its neighbouring countries. The Dialogue about Radicalisation and Equality (DARE) project received funding from the European Union's Horizon 2020 research and innovation programme (Grant Agreement No. 725349), and we would like to acknowledge the financial support of the European Commission and the very human support of our Project Adviser, Kerstin Wilde, over four and a half years of intense work. Those years included two years of coping with the constantly shifting parameters of possibility, for travel, fieldwork – or any work at all – as we all coped with our own personal and national contexts of the COVID-19 pandemic. The support and patience from the European Commission and the dedication and resilience of the whole research team through this difficult period was incredible. I would like to thank also Diana Chase and Charlotte Jones for their amazing project management skills and above all their kindness, support and humour at the most difficult points in the project.

Only a fraction of the research and a small number of researchers from the whole project are represented in this volume. However, these contributions would not have been possible without the work done by the whole team, either on country-level case studies or on strands of the research that inform, but are not the main focus of, this volume. This book is thus more than a collection of articles by individual researchers; it is a product of the whole research collective. The authors are indebted to the analytic insight and commitment of all the researchers from all countries involved.

Our thanks are expressed also to all the research participants, mainly young people, who agreed to take part in the empirical research conducted for the project. We thank them for their time but above all their trust that we would engage critically but honestly with what they told us. We hope we have fulfilled this commitment.

Finally, we would like to thank Tony Mason and Tom Bonnington at Berghahn for their enthusiasm and support in preparation of the book and the anonymous peer reviewers for their extremely helpful suggestions and comments on both the proposal and the manuscript. Given the polarisation in debate often encountered when researching in this field, we are particularly appreciative of their constructive engagement with this project.

Beyond Endpoints
Rethinking How and Why to Study Radicalisation

Hilary Pilkington

Definitions of radicalisation as the process by which actors come to engage in, or support the use of, violence to achieve their political aims are accompanied invariably by the acknowledgement that only a small proportion of those who hold radical ideas go on to commit acts of violence (see, *inter alia*, Borum 2011a: 9; Horgan 2012; Neumann 2013: 879). Given the implications of violent extremism for public safety, it is understandable that researchers prioritise the study of those who cross the violence threshold, even where they explicitly distinguish violent from non-violent radicalisation (Dalgard-Nielsen 2010; Borum 2011a: 8; McCauley and Moskalenko 2017; Lindekilde, Malthaner and O'Connor 2019: 23). In academic terms, by setting an endpoint – be it cognitive or behavioural extremism – the target population for study becomes more clearly defined and their trajectories to that point can be potentially traced, understood and modelled. As the many complex models to emerge over the last two decades demonstrate, this endpoint focus does not necessarily diminish the complexity of our understanding of radicalisation as a multi-dimensional and multi-factoral process (see, for example, Sageman 2004; Wiktorowicz 2005; Moghaddam 2005; Gill 2007; McCauley and Moskalenko 2008, 2017; Dawson 2017; Kruglanski et al. 2017; Bouhana 2019). That the study of radicalisation trajectories pivots on this endpoint, however, somewhat paradoxically works to undermine the important distinction between acts of terrorism/violent extremism and the process of radicalisation; the 'how' that the concept of radicalisation ostensibly prioritises. As Borum (2011c: 2) recognises, his own employment of the term 'radicalisation into violent extremism' risks conflating the concepts of radicalisation and violent extremism (terrorism) between which he intends to distinguish. At the same time, his reframing of 'radicalisation' as 'the array of processes by which people come to adopt beliefs that not only justify violence but compel it, and how they progress – *or not* [my emphasis] – from thinking to action' invites us to think about how trajectories stop, stall or divert away from behavioural extremism.

So why have relatively few researchers to date taken up the invitation to study those who embark on this journey but never reach its final destination? The relative neglect of the study of 'non-radicalisation' (Cragin 2014) or 'non-involvement in terrorist violence' (Schuurman 2020) might be explained by the difficulty of identifying, and accessing, an appropriate control group (Wiktorowicz 2005: 32) against which to study trajectories into violent extremism. Alternatively, as Dechesne (this volume) suggests, it might signal the difficulty of studying empirically something that exists only in relation to what it is not. Arguing below for the importance of understanding such journeys, we propose approaching non-radicalisation not as the absence of radicalisation (characteristic of a 'normal' control group against which the 'radicalised' may be compared) but as radicalisation that falls short of the endpoint to which the concept remains tied. In this sense, we might think of it as taking a number of forms – partial, stalled or partially reversed radicalisation – and combining different positions on the cognitive and behavioural radicalisation 'pyramids' (McCauley and Moskalenko 2017) underpinned by varying levels of resistance or resilience to ideas or behaviours associated with extremism. Radicalisation along one dimension may even constrain radicalisation on another; developing radical ideas or grievances directed at an 'other' may lead individuals towards people or movements with more extreme ideas or action repertoires, which repulse them or cause reflection that stalls or even reverses radicalisation (see Pilkington and Vestel, this volume; Pilkington, this volume). Thus, while defining radicalisation as a process determined by an end state of violent extremism helps determine a clear empirical object of study, we make the case for understanding, and studying, radicalisation and non-radicalisation rather as a continuum along which individuals shift, in both directions, and whose journeys may be started, paused or reversed at multiple points along it.

Adopting such an approach is challenging empirically; it requires the study of a much wider variety of radicalisation pathways in contemporaneous settings. Drawing firm conclusions based on the study of contextually very different journeys, not to mention journeys that are still in progress, is difficult and any implications that can be drawn from findings must remain tentative. At the same time, we suggest, this approach allows us to ask the most important question of all, that is, *what stops people radicalising*? It also enables us to answer this question not through inference (the absence of those factors found to be present in pathways to violent extremism) but from observing and listening to those engaged in radical(ising) milieus as to what protective factors and strategies are at work and how they might be strengthened. This volume consists of contributors' empirically grounded reflections on the process of non-progression to violent extremism based on research conducted as part of a single, transnational project (Dialogue about Radicalisation and Equality – DARE) on young people's trajectories through radical(ising) milieus shaped by ideologies that we refer to as 'Islamist', on the one hand, and 'extreme-right', on the other. These terms are used in this volume in inverted commas to reflect their problematic, disputed and potentially offensive nature. We recognise this and that using these terms risks misrecognising the very phenomena – indeed, the individuals – that we seek to understand by collapsing a wide spectrum of positions and the core beliefs to which they are anchored. Despite extensive discussion with colleagues within and beyond the project, however, we have not found other terms that more adequately capture the wide range (and contexts) of milieus included in our study (see Appendix) while retaining the bridge between etic[1] and emic concepts necessary if the critical approach to radicalisation that we develop through this volume is to resonate beyond those already similarly disposed. The spectrum of views and behaviours included under these umbrella terms in this project is outlined briefly below and in Chapters 1 and 2. In this introductory chapter, the theoretical framework and methodological rationale for the project as a whole are set out, including how these terms are employed, and an outline of the structure of the book and individual contributions to it is provided.

Studying Radicalisation and Non-Radicalisation as Process and in Process

The wealth of critical reviews of radicalisation studies (see, *inter alia*, Dalgaard-Nielsen 2010; Sedgwick 2010; Borum 2011a, 2011b; Christmann 2012; Kundnani 2012; Neumann 2013; Schmid 2013; Sageman 2014; Grossman et al. 2016; Horgan 2017; Malthaner 2017; Gøtzsche-Astrup 2018) permit us to forego summarising the field in favour of a more partial explication of the key issues of concern to this volume. To this end, we outline briefly our rationale for engaging with radicalisation discourse and for following 'trajectories' (routes) rather than seeking the 'roots' of radicalisation within a wider understanding of radicalisation as a relational, contextual and situational phenomenon. We explain how this is operationalised empirically through a focus on radical(ising) milieus and the multiple pathways young people take through them. We consider the difficulties of studying a 'non' phenomenon and situate our approach within attempts to date to model 'non-radicalisation', understand the factors that protect or generate resilience or resistance to radicalisation and suggest how studying non-radicalisation outcomes among young people in radical(ising) milieus might inform policy and practice in countering violent extremism.

Why Study Radicalisation?

Why – given the extensive critique of the concept of radicalisation – engage in the discourse of radicalisation at all? Conceptually, Sedgwick (2010: 491) argues, 'radicalisation' has brought confusion rather than clarification to the study of political extremism. Since markers of 'moderate' and 'radical' shift across different national contexts, policy spheres and in relation to different extremisms, while it is rarely made clear what the continuum of radicalism being referred to is or the location of what is seen as 'moderate' and 'extreme' on that continuum, he proposes, 'radicalisation' is best deployed as a relative or relational concept. We agree both with Sedgwick's critique and his conclusion. This does not necessarily invalidate the concept, however, but rather confirms the importance of adopting a relational approach to radicalisation. At the same time, Sedgwick's critique indicates the need for radicalisation to be studied in context (see also Crenshaw 2007; Ravn, Coolaset and Sauer 2019), including with explicit reference to what constitutes 'moderate' and 'extreme' in that context and, we propose additionally, for both etic and emic understandings of these to be taken into account.

Such contextualisation includes recognising the extensive body of work that critically deconstructs the political framing of notions of 'extremism' and 'radicalisation'. The contemporary use of 'radicalisation' is intrinsically associated with a specific – 'Islamist' – terrorism and situated in attempts to understand, and counter, an apparent new security threat in the wake of the 9/11 attacks (2001) (Neumann 2013: 878), the emergence of 'home-grown' terrorism in Western Europe (2004–05) and the departure (and now return) of 'foreign fighters' to support ISIS/IS. As a result, della Porta (2018: 462) states, 'radicalization has become a master signifier for the "war on terror"'. As documented in numerous studies, Muslim communities have been the primary target of counter-terrorism legislation initiated in the wake of this war (Choudhury and Fenwick 2011;

Hardy 2015; Kapoor 2018; Kundnani 2014; McGhee 2008), underpinned by elements of radicalisation scholarship, which, once taken up by law enforcement agencies, 'becomes a prospectus for mass surveillance of Muslim populations' (Kundnani 2012: 19). Processes of 'suspectification' (Hickman et al. 2012), through which counter-terrorism practices police the everyday lives of communities rendered 'suspect', are not only externally imposed but draw on the pro-active involvement of Muslims in their own policing (Ragazzi 2016: 729), leading to a fracturing of relations within Muslim communities as individuals internalise fears of state targeting (Abbas 2019: 261). In addition to the societal harm inflicted by such misrecognition, the deployment of a concept of radicalisation rooted in a state-led securitising discourse, alongside the exclusion of emic understandings, inhibits the conceptual purchase of the concept and its ability to inform dialogic counter-extremism interventions (see Kühle and Lindekilde 2012; Pilkington 2022).

The concept of radicalisation has been used increasingly in relation to the right-wing spectrum over the recent period due to a revival of militant right-wing extremist groups and associated political violence, the growth in anti-migrant and Islamophobic sentiment and hate crime, the ongoing evolution of an active extreme-right online milieu and evidence of the transnational organisation of extreme-right groups (see, *inter alia*, Koehler 2016; Lee and Knott 2022). Recent studies have suggested that 'far-right radicalization' is spread through a social contagion process in which social media use and group membership enhance the spread of right-wing extremist ideology (Youngblood 2020), while actors narrate their own radicalisation as a process of gradual awakening as they move through increasingly extreme ideological stances and identities (Lee and Knott 2022: 230). However, the most recent systematic reviews of academic studies continue to show a persistent under-representation of right-wing radicalisation in the literature; between 8% (Franc and Pavlović 2021: 5) and 11% (Ahmed and Lynch 2021: 6) of academic publications in relevant fields were focused on the 'far-right'.[2] The reasons for this are most likely a compound effect of a number of characteristics of right-wing extremism and its relation to political violence that tend towards the exclusion of manifestations of right-wing extremism from the discussion of radicalisation. These include the tendency towards individual (lone actor), rather than organised group, perpetration of right-wing extremist violence (Ahmed and Lynch 2021: 2–3; Ravndal 2016: 7) and the internal ideological heterogeneity within extreme-right milieus leading to their characterisation as being comprised of 'freelance extremists' (Ahmed and Lynch 2021: 15). They also include the apparently low incidence of right-wing terrorism; TE-SAT (Terrorism Situation and Trend) reports, which monitor terrorist attacks (completed, foiled and failed) in the EU, show that over the period 2019–21, just nine of 127 (7%) of such attacks were related to right-wing terrorism (Europol 2022: 8).[3] However, as Bjørgo and Ravndal (2019: 7) note, these data reflect the wide variation in how countries record 'terrorist' offences; right-wing offences are often registered as hate crime, right-wing extremist violence or ordinary violence rather than terrorism. For example, arson attacks on buildings accommodating refugees, where they do not lead to fatalities, often do not reach the threshold to be considered terrorism (ibid.: 8). Thus TE-SAT reporting is indicative of the wider problem of assessing the significance of right-wing violent extremism and, in particular, determining the relationship between hate crime and terrorism. For some, hate crimes are close to, if not precursors of, terrorism since they do not target specific behaviours but are directed at out-groups and seek to instil fear across a wide section of the community, while for others such crimes lack key characteristics of terrorist acts in that they target discriminated minorities rather than those in power, they are mainly unplanned and may not be publicity-seeking (Koehler 2016: 89). These differences in the manifestation, and understanding, of radicalisation across different forms of extremism confirm the importance of its deployment as a relational and relative concept.

Notwithstanding these important critiques, the concept of radicalisation retains value in its capacity to understand violent extremism as the outcome of a *process*. As such, it has helped propel a shift in research away from largely failed attempts to identify shared socio-demographic profiles of violent extremists in order to target prevention measures towards 'at risk' individuals (Dalgaard-Nielsen 2010: 810; Borum 2011a: 14; Horgan 2008: 80; Beck 2015: 26–30; Sageman 2014: 620). While initially the literature focused on processes of cognitive and ideological transformation at the individual level – the role of social ties and small-group dynamics (Sageman 2004), personal and political grievances that preface cognitive openings to radical ways of thinking (Wiktorowicz 2005), gradual intensification of engagement with extremist movements or actors accompanied by withdrawal from earlier networks and bonds and, finally, acceptance of alternative values and readiness to engage in violent action (Moghaddam 2005) – there is a more recent recognition of the importance of contextualising these processes by understanding them in relation to radical movements and the wider societal and political environment (Malthaner 2017: 370, 379–82). This shift is encapsulated by Horgan's (2008) call for a search for the 'roots' of violent extremism to be replaced by understanding 'routes' to violent extremism and underpins a trajectories-based approach to radicalisation. This has facilitated the identification of stages through which individual actors progress towards terrorism (ibid.) and important transitions or turning points in radicalisation (or deradicalisation) journeys (Sieckelinck et al. 2019). However, mapping such trajectories demonstrates there are multiple pathways into extremism (Linden and Klandermans 2007; McCauley and Moskalenko 2008: 429) and different people on a shared pathway have varying outcomes (Borum 2011b: 57). Moreover, the retention of the endpoint of violent extremism as the defining characteristic of a radicalisation pathway can lead to linear interpretations of radicalisation models – such as the 'staircase to terrorism' (Moghaddam 2005) or 'pyramid model' (McCauley and Moskalenko 2008) – and thus to a 'conveyor belt' understanding of how people become involved in political violence (Moskalenko and McCauley 2009: 241). Throughout this volume, we also are primarily concerned with the trajectories of young people (rather than their socioeconomic backgrounds or psychological dispositions). However, we trace pathways through radical milieus not in the abstract, but in situ, and with the starting assumption that individuals will move both towards and away from more extreme positions and that most will never reach the 'endpoint' of either attitudinal or behavioural radicalisation.

How Should We Study Radicalisation?

The premise of our approach is that radicalisation is best understood as a profoundly societal phenomenon. This is articulated neatly by Lindekilde, Malthaner and O'Connor (2019: 23) in describing their own theoretical framework as 'based on a notion of radicalization as a fundamentally social process, shaped by patterns of interaction with, exposure to, and participation in specific social settings or radical groups'. At the individual level, this means we see the interaction between political, social and cultural context and an individual's cognitive development as crucial to understanding the radicalisation process and the pathways leading individuals towards extremist behaviour (Costanza 2015: 3). Thus, while we do not engage in socio-demographic or social-psychological profiling of those we study, we consider their life histories and experiences as central to understanding their trajectories. At the social level, we capture this interaction through a focus on radical milieus as the settings in which trajectories of radicalisation and non-radicalisation are played out. Radical milieus are social formations through which collective identities and solidarities are constructed and take a multitude of forms (religious, ethnic or political) (Malthaner and Waldmann 2014), may be territorially rooted (or not) and display varying degrees of cohesiveness. They provide the immediate social environments from within which those engaged in violent activity can gain affirmation for their actions but, more routinely, provide an environment in which 'grievance' narratives and 'rejected' or 'stigmatised' knowledge are shared and come to form the basis of internal cultures (Malthaner 2017: 389). In this sense they share features of the 'cultic milieu' (Campbell 1972, 2012) in which 'proscribed and/or forbidden knowledge is the coin of the realm' (Kaplan and Lööw 2002: 3) albeit that, in conditions of increasing heterodoxy of mainstream culture, the non-orthodox 'truths' they find may lie in complex conspiracy theories rather than the worlds of the occult, spiritualism and mysticism. Thus, milieus may be both physical and virtual (usually both) and not only ideological but also emotional spaces providing opportunities for voicing anger at perceived injustice, identifying 'like minds' or shared hurts and giving meaning to, and making sense of, life. They are also sites where important bonds are forged with others; bonds that are particularly important for individuals whose family or peer relationships have been either lacking or traumatising.

Of key importance to our concern in this volume is the recognition that radical milieus are not only sites of encounter with radical(ising) messages and agents, encouraging and exacerbating violence, but are often diverse and multi-dimensional social environments in which individuals may criticise or challenge the narratives, frames and violent behaviours encountered (Malthaner and Waldmann 2014: 994). As Malthaner and Waldmann (ibid.) have argued, radical milieus may not only contribute to radicalisation but also constrain it by offering alternative (non-militant) forms of activism. Thus, central to our approach is understanding the interplay between trajectories and milieus. Radical milieus are not static 'contexts', 'factors' or 'sites' of radicalisation; the milieu is rather an evolving relational and emotional field of activity (ibid.: 983) that underpins and envelops radical ideas and behaviours. Moreover, radicalisation does not take place in a single, stable environment but 'in a dynamic constellation of multiple spaces and social relationships that change over time' (Lindekilde, Malthaner and O'Connor 2019: 23–24). Thus, by studying young people's lived experience in selected milieus, we are able to gain a critical window onto life trajectories as they unfold in a context in which often narrow arrays of life options funnel individuals towards more radicalised belief systems (Costanza 2015: 2–3). In methodological terms this means following young people into the everyday contexts and milieus in which they encounter radical(ising) messages and agents and respond to them (see below) rather than analysing retrospectively reconstructed trajectories based on secondary sources documenting life stories of terrorists or through biographical interviews with 'former' violent extremists. By adopting a relational, contextual and situational approach to understanding radicalisation, operationalised through a milieu-based research design affording extended engagement with young people, we are able to study radicalisation not only *as* process but *in* process.

Conceptually, the observation of, and listening to, individuals' reflections on how, and in what context, they experience encounters with radical(ising) messages, and how they receive and respond to them, requires attention not only to context, situation and interaction, but also to agency. As Lindekilde, Malthaner and O'Connor (2019: 23–24) note, 'Individuals are not passive objects of radicalizing influences but actively engage in interactions, formation of new social ties, and evaluation of radicalizing teachings'. Indeed, while all the milieus studied as part of the DARE project were selected as sites where young people encounter radical(ising) actors and messages, we found that most individual trajectories through these milieus involved choices not to engage in, or support, political violence to achieve their aims (even where others in the wider milieu did so). Thus, while these young people's engagement in the milieus might reflect a relative shift towards more extremist positions – embarkation on a radicalisation pathway – the fact that only a few crossed the threshold into violent extremism makes clear the need for more complex ways of understanding those trajectories as ones of partial, stalled, reversed or non-radicalisation. In seeking to understand specifically why and how people do not engage in political violence, despite significant and often justified grievances and in contexts (or milieus) in which others do turn to violence, two emergent concepts in debates about what stops radicalisation are important: non-radicalisation and resilience to radicalisation.

What Stops Radicalisation?

'Non-radicalisation' was first identified by Cragin (2014) from a study of secondary data sources indicating a series of factors important in dissuading individuals from joining terrorist groups (resistance), on the one hand, and leaving such organisations (desistance), on the other. These factors might be broadly summarised as relating to: the costs of participation; the perceived efficacy of violence; social ties to the organisation; and moral (non)acceptability of violent action.[4] The model of non-radicalisation derived was subsequently empirically tested by Cragin and colleagues through a study involving semi-structured interviews with a small number of Palestinian political activists (associated with groups pursuing a violent agenda) and a survey of six hundred Palestinian young people (aged eighteen to thirty) living in the West Bank (Cragin et al. 2015). Although the DARE research design and fieldwork contexts are quite different from their study, some core logics are shared. This relates, first and foremost, to our concern with young people who have been exposed to, or considered, radical ideologies or violence but (mainly) rejected violence. Underlying this is a shared interest in understanding non-radicalisation in contexts in which encounters with radical(ising) messages are an everyday experience. Such contexts problematise how we measure levels of radicalisation, or willingness to engage in violence, especially through the use of survey methods, which differentiate too simply between those who justify political violence and those who are attitudinally opposed to it (Cragin et al. 2015: 16; see also Pilkington, Chapter 6, this volume). Secondly, in both cases, a clear distinction is made between attitudinal and behavioural radicalisation while non-radicalisation is used to refer to resistance to either extremist ideas or behaviour, or a combination of both (Cragin 2014: 338). Thirdly, both see non-radicalisation, like radicalisation, as best understood as a process characterised by a series of stages in which 'individuals weigh their various options or choices between violent and nonviolent pathways' (Cragin et al. 2015: 11). While this is a conclusion of the Cragin et al. (ibid.) study, in the DARE research it constitutes the starting point and, in conjunction with its ethnographic and trajectory-based research design, means its findings can illuminate this process. It does so by revealing how similar factors work differently in different contexts and trajectories, identifying when and how young people make key choices and elaborating an understanding of shifts towards and away from extremism beyond binary outcomes of radicalisation or non-radicalisation (see Pilkington and Vestel, this volume; Pilkington, Chapter 6, this volume).

The study of this kind of non-radicalised 'control group', Cragin (2014: 350) suggests, opens the way to reconsidering the current emphasis on pre-empting[5] radicalisation in policy and practice debates; it might be more effective, she argues, 'to instead encourage non-radicalization'. Indeed the discussion of 'resilience'[6] in debates on countering extremism as 'when people are exposed to one or more of the predisposing or enabling conditions for radicalisation but do not make the transition into violent extremism or terrorism' (Council of Europe 2018: 11) suggests it is a quality or capacity that underpins non-radicalisation outcomes. Notions of resilience and resilience building, at individual and community levels, are central to 'whole-of-society' (Grossman 2021: 293–95) or 'holistic' (Barzegar, Powers and El Karhili 2016: 7) approaches to countering violent extremism (CVE) and have been subject to similar criticism to that levelled at societal approaches to understanding radicalisation. This is that, without a clear delimitation of the object of intervention (violent extremism or terrorism), CVE might come to encompass an 'unreasonably wide scope of activity' and produce 'unintended consequences' (Berger 2016: 8, 34

cited in Grossman 2021: 294). The opportunistic and inconsistent deployment of the notion of resilience to violent extremism by governments can
reinforce a sense among some communities of securitisation by stealth
(see, for example, Hardy 2015; Rosand 2018: 74). However, 'resilience'
has proven to be of ongoing interest to CVE policy makers and practitioners for thinking about how equipped society is to recover from the
after-effects of terrorist attacks and/or how resilience to extremist ideologies might be fostered long-term in communities that may be vulnerable
to, or targeted by, such messaging (see Kerst, this volume).

Discussion of the wider conceptualisation of resilience and its application to the CVE field is beyond the scope of this volume (see Hardy 2015;
Stephens and Sieckelinck 2021; Grossman 2021). Its emphasis on *the
capacity* of an individual or community to survive external shock through
a process of change and transformation, however, offers a way to shift
focus from 'risk' and 'vulnerability' to capacities of (often marginalised)
individuals or communities to cope with, and respond positively to, adversity – albeit at the risk of shifting responsibility for managing structurally
generated, and unequally distributed, risk and harm from government
to those communities or individuals (Hardy 2015: 82). Individual resilience to violent extremism has been identified as enabled by psychological traits such as, *inter alia*, empathy, self-control, value complexity,
self-esteem, tolerance of diversity and ambiguity (Sieckelinck and Gielen
2017: 4; Grossman 2021: 298). It can also be generated by interactions
between individual and societal institutions and processes, which create
positive emotional and educational environments, open-mindedness and
resources and strategies for coping with adversity (ibid.). Approaches to
building resilience that move beyond a binary understanding of resilience
as risk versus protective factors are of particular value; they allow a more
social-ecological understanding that differentiates between risks (as adverse circumstances or environments affecting entire groups or communities), vulnerabilities (as specific challenges or difficulties that enhance
risks) and protection (as factors that mitigate vulnerabilities and risks)
(Grossman 2021: 303). Social-ecological paradigms of resilience, which
stress the interdependence between individuals and social systems and
institutions, potentially provide a pro-social and less security-driven approach to countering radicalisation, which mirrors existing approaches
in other policy areas (such as disaster preparedness and recovery and
public health) and avoids targeting particular communities as vulnerable, deficient or suspect (ibid.: 301–302). In so doing, they mirror some
of the most promising developments in understandings of radicalisation
emanating from multi-level 'ecological' approaches (Dawson 2017: 3;
Bouhana 2019).

Engaging with the debate on resilience – notwithstanding its potential for responsibilisation of individuals and communities noted above – is important not least because of its capacity to see individuals not only as perpetrators or victims. This is important especially in relation to young people, who tend to be positioned as vulnerable to, or at risk of, radicalisation. The empirical tracing of complex, multi-directional pathways to partial, stalled or non-radicalisation, which are charted according to choices young people make (albeit structurally and situationally shaped choices), we argue, is crucial to understanding how exposure to calls to extremist ideas and behaviour are resisted in everyday contexts and thus to developing strength- rather than risk-based approaches to resilience building. Crucial to such strength-based approaches is the recognition that protective factors are not simply inferred from (as the inverse of) risk factors – and thus found wanting among those groups deemed 'at risk' – but that individual resilience is strengthened by developing attitudes and behaviours that empower individuals and provide resources that mitigate risk. The development of these protective factors is facilitated, moreover, by a range of promotive factors – such as dialogue, inclusion, care, vigilance, social safety and education – which underpin societal resilience (Sieckelinck and Gielen 2017: 4–6; see also Council of Europe 2018: 111–14). While this may not allow for the measurement of effectiveness against specific counter-extremism targets, it is a logical outcome of the recognition that radicalisation and extremism are societal, not narrowly security-related, phenomena. As Ezekiel (2002: 60) so powerfully attests, in seeking to resolve the same social structural issues and life crises, relatively few people join racist or violent extremist groups; the more usual outcomes are ordinary coping, numbness, malaise, alcoholism, chronic anger and individual violence. If a broad, strength-based resilience approach empowers those who might take these routes instead, this does not indicate the failure of the resilience-building measure to target extremism but its success in protecting against multiple individual and social harms.

The DARE research project, and the contributions to this volume that draw on its findings, starts from an understanding of radicalisation as a societal phenomenon whose processes can, and should, be studied empirically not only through retrospectively constructed narratives of those who have reached its 'endpoint' (manifest in support for or participation in political violence) but through engagement with individuals at different points in their journeys via social settings where radical(ising) messages and agents are encountered. By seeking to explain involvement in political violence by studying only those who have committed such acts – while excluding those who move in the same milieu but do not become violent extremists – violence always appears as the radicalisation endpoint or apex of the pyramid (Pilkington 2017; Schuurman 2020: 16). In practice, the majority of those moving through radical milieus engage with, appropriate some and reject other ideas and behaviours that they encounter there. This leads to trajectories not only of radicalisation but partial, stalled, reversed or non-radicalisation. While we take seriously concerns that such an extension of the notion of radicalisation could lead to further securitisation and stigmatisation of those who engage with radical milieus or ideas, we argue that, on the contrary, understanding such engagement as a societal rather than security-focused issue allows us to draw on a wider range of theories and strength-based approaches to understanding not only risk and protection factors but the agency of individuals and capacities of communities to resist extremism (see Kewley 2017). By moving beyond a gateway theory – that engagement with radical ideas and participation in radical milieus leads to violent extremism – we are able to release the potential of resilience-based whole-of-society approaches to CVE from the logics of securitisation. Moreover, engaging directly with those in radical(ising) milieus who have non-radicalisation trajectories provides insight into how peer practices and informal settings can be mobilised to recognise, and draw individuals back from, extremism.

The DARE Project: Design and Methods

The contributions to this volume stem from the EU Horizon 2020 DARE (Dialogue about Radicalisation and Equality) project (2017–21).[7] The project set out with the overall objective of shifting how we address radicalisation through understanding it as a societal rather than purely security-related phenomenon. Its research programme focused on 'Islamist' and 'extreme-right' radicalisation, specifically young people's encounters with forces, messages and agents of radicalisation and the choices they make in response to them. Empirical research was carried out in twelve countries: Belgium, France, Germany, Greece, Malta, the Netherlands, Norway, Poland, Russia, Tunisia, Turkey and the United Kingdom (UK). The target population of 'youth' was defined very broadly as those between the ages of twelve and thirty, although in practice most of the empirical research was conducted with the participation of those aged eighteen to thirty-five.

The terms 'Islamist' and 'extreme-right' were employed as umbrella terms to indicate the broad range of milieus with which we engaged, which were characterised by significant internal diversity as well as very different national and regional settings (see Appendix for a brief overview of these milieus). 'Islamist' is used to indicate a wide range of ideological positions rooted in the interaction between Islam and politics in distinction from 'Islamic', understood as relating to Islam as a body of religious thought. We draw here on the much more nuanced discussion of differentiations within and between Islamic worldviews and violent and non-violent Islamist ideologies such as that developed by Wilkinson et al. (2021: 5–6) and on the relationship of these to the conceptualisation of radicalism and extremism (see Schmid 2014: 15–18). However, the ascription of more nuanced categorisations is problematic in our case due the particular focus of the DARE study on young people who, in the milieus studied, were still working through their own positions in relation to mainstream Islamic worldviews and Islamist ideologies rather than having clearly established positions. Thus, the term 'Islamist' is used very loosely, to capture a broad spectrum of individual pathways, from those encountering Islamist ideas through to those convicted of Islamist-inspired terrorist offences. The terms 'extreme-right' or 'right-wing extremism' are used as a short-hand to refer to an extremely wide range of political ideologies broadly characterised by authoritarianism, opposition to democracy and exclusionary nationalism (including biological and cultural racism), although most young people in the milieus studied would not identify themselves with these positions and, with some notable exceptions, did not oppose democratic governance. Some milieus, or elements of them, might be more accurately characterised as 'anti-Islamist' rather than 'extreme-right', that is, as engaged in active opposition to what their participants refer to as 'radical Islam' or the 'Islamification' of Western societies but often reflecting a general antipathy towards Islam or all Muslims. These terms – 'Islamist' and 'extreme-right' – are deeply contested and, in many cases, are descriptors that are consciously rejected and viewed as stigmatising by those to whom they are applied. Thus, where ethnographic material is drawn on, these terms are modified in some contributions to reflect country- or region-specific debates and/or used in quotation marks to indicate that these are terms applied to these milieus in public discourse but are not how actors in the milieus identify themselves.

The framework for the project, its main strands of work, approach and methodologies are outlined below to contextualise the more specific questions addressed and methods used, which are detailed in the individual contributions to the volume. The project employed a multi-method approach including meta-analysis, online data analysis, an experimental survey and historical and ethnographic studies of radical(ising) milieus in the course of pursuing four main strands of work. These research foci are outlined below, including a more detailed description of the ethno-

graphic studies of trajectories through radical(ising) milieus as most contributions to this volume draw on empirical findings from that dimension
of the research.

Inequality and Radicalisation

The research focusing on inequality and radicalisation involved a systematic review of 141 quantitative studies and a meta-ethnographic synthesis
of ninety-four qualitative empirical studies (published between 1 January
2001 and 31 December 2017) on the relationship between inequality and
radicalisation. These reviews analysed what the evidence to date tells us
about the presence and consistency of any relationship between inequality at the individual and societal levels and established the need to distinguish between objective and subjective measures of inequality when
considering that relationship (see Franc and Pavlović 2021; Poli and Arun
2019; Franc, Poli and Pavlović, this volume). The relationship between
inequality and radicalisation was explored also through secondary quantitative data analysis of seven European survey data sets (Storm, Pavlović
and Franc 2020) and a survey experiment among representative online
panel samples of 18–35-year-olds in three countries, which explored the
relationship between perceived inequality, negative intergroup attitudes
and activist and radicalised intentions (Pavlović, Storm and Franc 2021).

  This strand of work has also been informed by the ethnographic studies
conducted on young people's trajectories through radical(ising) milieus
(see below), which confirm the finding from the systematic review that there
is a relationship between perceived socio-political and socio-economic inequalities and injustices and pathways to extremism, but it is neither linear
nor consistent. These ethnographic studies found that perceived socio-
political inequalities were more readily articulated as drivers of radicalisation than perceived socio-economic inequalities. The perceived socio-
political inequalities referred to by actors in both 'extreme-right' and 'Islamist' milieus were expressed as a series of grievances, which are subjectively experienced as systematically unfair treatment. They do not
consistently explain radicalisation but they help understand how feelings
of victimisation, a sense of injustice and lack of human rights protection
may play a role in radicalisation, both at individual and group level.

Online Radicalisation

A study of radicalisation through social media participation in 'Islamist'
and 'extreme-right' milieus was conducted in seven European countries
(Belgium, France, Greece, Germany, Norway, the Netherlands and the

UK). Data were analysed from just under six hundred Twitter accounts and showed that, over the period studied (2010–19), 'right-wing extremist' Twitter activity increased while 'Islamist' extremist Twitter activity was scattered.[8] The content and use of Twitter also differed across the two types of milieus. 'Extreme-right' accounts demonstrated a set of shared ideological positions, were more radical in their messaging and more engaged with one another (through sharing materials or retweeting). The 'Islamist' accounts appeared more as a 'store front' to reroute users to other online platforms and content, mainly promoted religious fundamentalist beliefs and associated lifestyles and displayed low levels of sharing or retweeting content.

The ethnographic studies of young people's radicalisation trajectories also considered encounters with radical(ising) messages online. Online spaces were found to be a significant source of such messages and to contribute to a sense of injustice or victimhood as well as lead to invitations to join extremist movements. At the same time, offline relationships – with those in the milieu, friends and family members – were found to be of continuing importance, and friends, family and authority figures within the milieu were said not only to encourage radical views or actions but also to constrain them. The complex interweaving of online and offline channels of radicalisation are explored in a number of the contributions to this volume (see, for example, Dechesne; Pilkington and Vestel; and Poliakov).

Historical and Interactional Radicalisation

Reflecting recent policy concerns with the potential for 'cumulative extremism' to occur as opposing movements (e.g. 'Islamist' and 'extreme-right' movements) interact, five case studies were conducted (in France, Germany, Greece, Turkey and the UK) tracing the dynamics of radicalisation in the context of contests between opposing movements and the state.[9] The findings suggest interactional radicalisation is far from a binary process, involving two opposing groups; it is shaped by multiple actors, including the state and media agencies, as well as the context within which groups are operating. It was also found that violent contestation between opposing groups does not necessarily lead to more violence; de-escalation and non-escalation, leading away from violence, also occur. Such multi-directionality challenges the 'spiral' narrative of cumulative radicalisation, the outcomes of which, we argue, are better visualised as a series of 'spikes'.[10] Internal group culture was also found to be important in understanding the likelihood of a group escalating to violence or responding in a non-violent manner; non-violence is often the outcome where there is non-equivalent interaction, that is, where one actor is concerned with the other but this concern is not reciprocated. Our findings confirm that 'extreme-right' actors are more concerned with 'Islamist' actors than 'Islamist' actors are with 'extreme-right' actors (see also Sakellariou, this volume). The studies also found that the 'state' can be an active actor in the radicalisation process. In the same five countries, historical case studies of radicalisation were conducted also and a number of key themes were identified. The first was the important role of historical 'counter memory' in radical milieus – in particular narratives of grievance and humiliation – in understanding the construction of the ideological prism through which individuals in the milieu were invited to think about the past, present and future. The second was the role of conspiracy theories – especially antisemitism – in radicalisation 'waves', which were found to be uniform neither in content nor degree across contexts. The third was the relationship between radical thinking and radical action, in particular the move to violence, where the studies found no simple or consistent relationship; one does not have to be present for the other to occur. Finally, the case studies explored the relationship between radical milieus, violent political groups and the broader social and political climate and found that the radical milieu might act both as an accelerant and as a potential inhibitor to radical action (see also Busher, Holbrook and Macklin 2019).

Trajectories through Radical(ising) Milieus

The focus on trajectories of radicalisation and non-radicalisation in this volume means that most contributions draw primarily on the ethnographic strand of work in the DARE project. This element of the research sought to elicit emic understandings of 'radicalisation' by asking how young people in radical(ising) milieus themselves understand this phenomenon, and the discourse surrounding it, as well as the role such discourse itself potentially plays in radicalisation trajectories. It aimed to unpick why some young people become engaged in violent extremist ideologies while others, in similar structural locations, take non-radicalisation trajectories. Understanding how sustained inequalities and perceived injustice impact these outcomes was central to this. The ethnographic studies also sought to tease out the role of social relationships (in-person or virtual) in facilitating radicalisation of ideas and behaviour and how extra-ideological factors – emotional experiences, sense of identity and 'coolness' of radical milieus – shape radicalisation trajectories. At the heart of these ethnographic studies was the aim to capture young people's trajectories as they unfolded – with all their stops and starts,

forward and backward movements, motivational logics and inconsisten-
cies – rather than elicit the individual's retrospective narration of their
trajectory using a life-history or biographical interview approach. Thus,
in devising the case studies of young people's trajectories, researchers
sought appropriate 'Islamist' and 'extreme-right' milieus as the focus of
study. By studying young people's engagement with radicalisation messages in situ (in their everyday milieus) and over a sustained period of
time, the aim was to capture the complexity and situational nature of the
paths young people take. This approach was premised on the theoretical
understanding of radicalisation as relational, interactional and situational
set out above.

Ethnographic studies were conducted in ten 'Islamist' and nine 'extreme-right' milieus across twelve countries (see Appendix for an overview of the cases and national locations). For the purposes of selecting
case studies, the notion of milieu was operationalised broadly – as the
people, physical and social conditions, events, networks and communications that shape a person's subjectivity and life trajectory – to allow
flexibility. The selected milieu was not required to be territorially fixed
and it was anticipated that in most cases it would not be. However, to
constitute a milieu, there should be an evident connection (human, material, communicative, ideological) between individuals interviewed and
observations conducted. An appropriate milieu for selection should also
be a space of encounter with radical or extreme messages (via the presence in the milieu of recruiters, high receptivity to radical messages and
so on). However, anticipating the high degree of dissonance between
how movements and ideologies are described exogenously and endogenously, it was not a requirement that participants in milieus themselves
thought of the milieu – or themselves – as 'extreme-right' or 'Islamist'.
Indeed, from an ethical as well as methodological standpoint, it was important that we approached young people without pre-defining them as
'radical' or, conversely, 'normal' but as milieu actors, all of whom were of
potential interest, since our concern was with the social interactions, attitudes and behaviours that are shaped and play out within these milieus.
Thus, the boundaries of the milieu were drawn to include those at the
margins, who 'sympathize or share some elements of opinions or style;
who mingle socially with activists; and who drift in or out of the scene'
(Bjørgo 2009: 30). This was particularly important given the high degree
of stigmatisation and surveillance that milieu actors already experience.
There was also no requirement that the selected milieu be 'typical' of
the country or that multiple milieus be included in order to cover the
range of different forms that radicalisation takes. Rather, the selected
milieu should constitute a pertinent case in the country context and be

sufficiently similar to other milieus in other country locations to allow the transnational synthesis of cases.

Empirical research for the case studies mainly took place from April 2018 to April 2019, although, in some cases, field research extended longer. All researchers completed ethical clearance procedures ahead of commencing fieldwork either through their own institutional ethical review committees or via a formally constituted procedure for ethical re- view via a sub-committee within the consortium management structure.[11] All participants in the studies were recruited on the principle and practice of informed consent and relations with respondents were conducted in strict adherence to the ethical guidelines adopted for the project.[12] In most cases the identity of research participants was protected by assign- ing a pseudonym (often chosen by the individual themselves) but where even this was felt to present a potential risk, numbers were assigned. The sub-committee on ethics operated throughout the project, providing a point of reference for all researchers to raise questions and issues arising in the course of fieldwork, analysis and writing up of findings.

The case studies conducted were all 'ethnographic' in that they em- ployed a research method involving 'direct and sustained contact with human agents, within the context of their daily lives (and cultures); watch- ing what happens; listening to what is said; asking questions...' (O'Reilly 2005: 2). This minimal definition of an ethnographic approach meant all case studies were fieldwork-based – a total of 534 field diary entries based on observation were recorded across the nineteen case studies – while retaining sufficient flexibility to ensure the appropriateness of the meth- odology for the range of milieus in which researchers were working. The relative weight between observation and interview material, for example, varies significantly between case studies. Each case employed a combi- nation of fieldwork techniques including: semi or unstructured person- to-person audio recorded or online interviews with milieu actors; the creation of a detailed field diary to record observations, reflections and questions for further inquiry; and written records of informal conversa- tions with individuals or groups. Events attended included religious ser- vices and related social events, organisation meetings, demonstrations, protests, leisure events including football matches, informal get-togethers, discussion groups and criminal trials. A wealth of visual and online mate- rials (streamed chat shows, videos and other materials created by respon- dents) as well as text documents (information booklets, flyers for events, mission statements, stickers, pamphlets etc.) were also collected.

As part of the ethnographic fieldwork, across all nineteen cases just under four hundred interviews with 369 young people were conducted. These interviews used a common skeleton interview schedule, which was designed to be used as a baseline for interviews for both the 'extreme-right' and 'Islamist' case studies. It consisted of twelve blocks of questions including, in each block: a series of opening questions pertinent to the theme of the block; suggested prompts; and follow up questions. While each of the themes underpinning these blocks of questions were intended to be addressed in each case study, partners were encouraged to adapt and add to the 'prompts' and 'follow up questions' elements of the skeleton interview schedule in order to reflect their country or case context. As part of the implementation of cases, partners translated, amended and extended the skeleton interview schedule. The interview schedule was long and often a second interview was conducted with respondents to ensure key issues were covered. The interviews were conducted as informally and organically as possible – moving between themes and questions as they occurred naturally in the conversation rather than asking questions in the order presented in the interview schedule – and a one-page graphic representation of the themes and their purpose was produced for interviewers to use as an unobtrusive aide memoire. Individuals were interviewed in dozens of venues, from home, leisure and sports clubs, indoor public spaces such as cafes, shopping centres and bars, outdoor public spaces such as parks and squares through to prisons and court buildings. For each interviewee (or other key respondent), researchers also completed a socio-demographic data sheet collecting standardised data on age, gender, education, employment, household, ethnicity and religion. These profiles of the respondent sets were used in the case study reports, but were not intended to 'profile' individuals or milieus or to try to gain a representative sample from the milieu. Researchers were guided only to stay as close as possible to the target age range for the study and to try to capture the experiences of women as well as men. In many cases, interviews with 'experts' or milieu members outside the target age range of the project were also conducted. These individuals were often crucial to gaining access to the selected milieus or to provide a more holistic view of the milieu, and the interviews were used to inform analysis and interpretation. In relation to gender, on average across all milieus, around three-quarters (77%) of the respondents were male and just under a quarter (23%) were women. This gender imbalance was discussed on an ongoing basis during the course of fieldwork and, in most cases, the imbalance reflects the composition of the milieus studied. However, in three 'Islamist' case studies (in Russia, France and Belgium) and one 'extreme-right' case study (in France), the milieus were exclusively, or almost exclusively, male. This was due to the high proportion of respondents being accessed in prison settings in the French and Belgian cases and due to the strong gender norms in the

Russian case, which made it difficult to access female respondents. The absence of women in these four cases also lowers the overall proportion of women across all cases.[13]

The data collected from the ethnographic study of the selected milieus were analysed in a two-stage process. First, the data were analysed holistically by the field researchers as individual case studies to produce case study reports[14] and then a cross-case analysis was conducted employing a meta-ethnographic synthesis method (see Dechesne, this volume; Pilkington and Vestel, this volume). This two-stage approach was adopted to ensure the meaningful analysis of individual case studies in context, following the epistemological premise underpinning Burawoy's (1998: 13) extended case method that 'context is not noise disguising reality but reality itself'. While seeking to understand (non)radicalisation beyond the single case study, the DARE project also started from the premise that these locations are not limitations on, but central to, the knowledge produced through social research. Details of the data analysis method used at each stage can be found in Pilkington and Vestel 2020 and Pilkington and Vestel 2021 and it is briefly outlined below.

At the individual case study level, data analysis was conducted using a 'multi-grounded theory' (Goldkuhl and Cronholm 2010) approach, which works on the principle not that new theory is induced from data analysis but that theory is essential to interpretation and knowledge production and can result in the revision or refining of theory. In practical terms, this meant that researchers employed standard inductive coding followed by a process of theoretical matching and validation against both data and existing theoretical frameworks at the interpretative level. Coding was conducted by all teams using NVivo 12 computer-assisted qualitative data analysis software. At this first stage, all qualitative data sources (for example, semi-structured interview transcripts, field diaries, images, social media communications) from each milieu studied were coded in native language by partners as separate, individual NVivo 'projects'. These data were coded, in the first instance, to a maximum of two hierarchical levels: inductively generated codes (in native language[15]); and 'parent' codes (in English) imported from an agreed 'skeleton coding tree'. The development of the 'skeleton coding tree' from initial, pilot coding as well as from the interview schedule and initial research questions, meant that it was possible to group most inductively generated codes under appropriate pre-determined parent codes. However, where inductive codes did not fit – for example because this activity or experience was specific to the case – new parent codes were created for that case only. Equally, if no data fitted a pre-designed parent code, this was left unpopulated and researchers reflected on the absence of such data in their reports.

Extensive guidelines on coding, designed to standardise coding practice (length of text coded, multiple-coding, types of codes generated and so on) as far as possible across cases, were provided across the research team. Following coding to two hierarchical levels and the production of documents required for cross-case analysis, researchers continued to analyse their data sets, drawing on theoretical frameworks as appropriate to their particular case to generate third-level nodes or 'themes' and interpret their data and prepare the case study report.

The second stage of analysis consisted of conducting cross-national synthesis analyses for the nine 'extreme-right' milieus and the ten 'Islamist' milieus. These transnational multi-case analyses were conducted separately but using the same methodological approach based on the meta-ethnographic synthesis approach (Noblit and Hare 1988; Britten et al. 2002) but adapted to allow for the synthesis of transnational qualitative empirical data rather than published studies (Pilkington 2018). This constitutes an alternative to comparative approaches which pre-determine the parameters for comparison and often translate into a common language only 'indicative' interviews or interview summaries, which tend to lose the 'outliers' or refutational cases, the inclusion of which is crucial to the principles of qualitative research. It combines context-sensitive coding of data in original language (as set out above) with the production of detailed primary data summaries ('node memos'[16]) and respondent profiles ('respondent memos'[17]) in English. These, alongside the single case study reports, were used as the objects of synthesis. In this way, the synthesis approach facilitates the construction of a 'bigger picture' from profoundly contextually embedded data and allows for not only commonalities but also differences to be elucidated and for the retention of a significant amount of contextuality. The details of the five stages of the synthesis process, and how the approach used here differs from classic meta-ethnographic synthesis, are set out elsewhere (see Pilkington 2018; Pilkington and Vestel 2021) and are not detailed here. However, it is important to note that, following an initial scoping of the data, the following five questions were used to guide the syntheses:

- How do milieu actors understand 'radicalism', 'extremism' and 'terrorism'?
- How and where are radical(ising) messages encountered in the milieus studied?
- How do milieu actors understand (in)equality and its role in radicalisation?
- How do milieu actors recount their trajectories towards and away from extremism?

- What do milieu actors want to change in society and how do they envisage achieving that change?

These questions were used in the synthesis of both 'extreme-right' and 'Islamist' cases (see Dechesne, this volume; and Pilkington and Vestel, this volume).

Limitations of the DARE Project

There are, of course, many limitations to the DARE study. First, while the specific research design and method employed has allowed us to uncover some of the complex non-linear, situational and affective dimensions of radicalisation pathways, the milieu approach that facilitates this also has its drawbacks. The inclusion of milieu actors who had not crossed the threshold into violent extremism provides the basis for our reflections on trajectories of non-radicalisation but may limit comparison with other studies where 'radicalisation' was studied based on the trajectories of those who had crossed that line. There is also an inevitable element of self-selection in terms of access to radical milieus and to individuals and groups who were willing to engage in such a research study. Secondly, these same access factors mean that the milieus studied, as well as the local and national contexts in which they are situated, are extremely diverse and not open to simple comparison. Thirdly, the ethnographic approach is focused on eliciting actors' own understandings of the world, their experiences of it and journeys through it, which we see as vital to our understanding of radicalisation. Readers should be aware that this means some extracts from interviews and diaries used in this volume contain discriminatory and offensive material. Contributors have not reproduced this gratuitously, however, and have sought to interrogate, triangulate – through observation – and critically interpret these accounts. It is important to note here also that the 'close-up' nature of the ethnographic approach brings with it ethical responsibilities that, in some cases, outweigh the goal of interpretation. This means that, when interpreting data, some potentially important explanatory factors are not outlined in publications because their explication might reveal details (of movement affiliation, personal traits or relationships, key incidents in moving individuals towards or away from radicalisation) that could lead to the identities of individuals or groups being exposed (to others in the movement as well as outsiders) in a way that could cause harm to research participants.

In relation to the meta-ethnographic synthesis of milieu studies, it is also important to note a number of limitations. Although all cases synthesised in this study were drawn from a common research project (supported by cross-project guidelines and protocols), differences between data remained. This was partially a result of the inductive rather than deductive process of selecting cases, which meant that the cases reflected a broad range of milieus (see Dechesne, this volume; Pilkington and Vestel, this volume) experiencing different proximities to radical(ising) messages and being more or less internally homogenous. The nine 'extreme-right' milieus studied, for example, might be considered to fall into two broad clusters of cases (see Figure A.1): those where the milieu consists of activists in nationalist, radical or extreme-right or 'new right' movements (France, Malta, Norway, Netherlands, UK); and those where the milieu is focused around a non-political interest (e.g. football, shooting, religion) but there are ideological connections between the milieu and nationalist, radical or extreme-right movements and ideologies (Germany, Greece, Poland, Russia). However, it should not be assumed that those active in ideologically-oriented movements are necessarily more radical in attitude or behaviour. Placing the milieus on a 'political compass' according to views within the milieu relating to (i) level of support for democratic or non-democratic forms of governance or non-democratic ways to achieve change (a 'pro-democracy-anti-democracy' spectrum) and (ii) degree of identification with, and prioritisation of the needs of, a nationally or ethnically defined in-group and expression of hostility towards out-groups or minority groups (an 'inclusive-exclusive' spectrum), suggests the most anti-democratic and most exclusionary positions are found in the Greek milieu, with the Polish, Russian, French and part of the Maltese milieu also showing more anti-democratic and exclusionary attitudes than the other milieus (see Pilkington and Vestel 2021: 17–19). The ten 'Islamist' milieus also varied significantly, not least in that they included studies in countries of both Muslim majority (Turkey, Tunisia) and non-Muslim majority (Belgium, France, Germany, Greece, the Netherlands, Norway, Russia, UK) composition. These studies might be very loosely grouped into two clusters (see Figure A.2): those conducted in urban districts or neighbourhoods associated with Islamist activism, migrants from Muslim majority countries and, often, social deprivation (Belgium, Germany, the Netherlands, Norway, Tunisia, UK); and those focusing on particular sites or channels (family and informal networks, non-official prayer houses, civil society organisations, prisons) of potential 'Islamist' radicalisation (France, Greece, Russia, Turkey). The degree of proximity to violent extremism also varies significantly across these milieus; the closest proximity is found in the milieus studied in Belgium and France (where research was conducted in prisons) and in Tunisia and Turkey (where recruitment to jihadist organisations in the districts studied was high). In other milieus, research participants were resident in neighbourhoods or engaged in groups or networks associated with such recruitment but not taking up these offers themselves.

The cases also reflect a certain unevenness inherent in any multi-sited ethnography. While some studies were deeply ethnographic, including extensive field diaries, visual data and 20–30 semi-structured interviews, others – especially in countries with small 'extreme-right' or 'Islamist' scenes – generated fewer interviewees. Others secured substantive interview material but the case afforded less opportunity for ethnographic observation; in three cases, where all or many interviews were conducted in prison, for example, observation opportunities within prison were limited and interviewees were almost all men. We should also note that, notwithstanding the synthesis approach, which was designed to capture as much context and particularity as possible, only a fraction of the data collected across the milieu studies could be included. In the initial selection of questions to guide the synthesis, we focused on questions that allowed inclusion of the maximum number of studies. This meant a number of important issues, especially in terms of personal and affective dimensions of radicalisation – the role of stress, anxiety, trauma, adverse childhood experience, for example – are under-represented due to non-availability of such personal data across all cases or all individuals in cases.

Finally, while the project had an integrated research design – with each of the strands of research briefly outlined above intended to inform and enhance understanding of other strands – in practice, given the time-limited nature of the project, these strands were conducted in parallel and findings from one strand were fed into the design or revised design of other strands less consistently than we would have liked. Moreover, given the focus of this volume on trajectories of radicalisation and non-radicalisation, the specific findings related to other aspects of the research, especially online radicalisation, interactional radicalisation and preventing and countering radicalisation, are not fully represented.

Contributions to the Book

The volume is structured in three parts, moving from the more general to the more micro level of analysis. In Part I, a cross-European perspective on trajectories of radicalisation is presented drawing on the meta-ethnographic synthesis of ten cases of 'Islamist' radical(ising) milieus (Dechesne, Chapter 1) and nine cases of 'extreme-right' radical(ising) milieus (Pilkington and Vestel, Chapter 2). Both chapters identify the milieu approach as central to understanding how young people's trajectories of radicalisation and non-radicalisation are shaped through processes of encounter with, and responses to, radical(ising) messages. Dechesne argues that this approach avoids the tendency of security-focused perspectives to amplify the role of identified factors in problematic forms of radicalisation by failing to consider their contribution also to cases of non-radicalisation. Based on findings from the ethnographic study of milieus with a high prevalence of 'Islamist' extremist messaging (including prisons, mosques and relatively deprived areas with a known presence of 'Islamist' extremist recruiters) in ten countries (Belgium, France, Germany, Greece, the Netherlands, Norway, Russia, Tunisia, Turkey and the UK), Dechesne identifies participation/non-participation in society, a conflict/cooperation mind-set and engagement/non-engagement in violence as key components of radicalisation *and* resistance to radicalisation. In Chapter 2, Pilkington and Vestel draw on the synthesis of research findings from the study of 'extreme-right' milieus in nine countries (France, Germany, Greece, Malta, Poland, Norway, Russia, the Netherlands and the UK) to explore how young people's trajectories of radicalisation, including partial, stalled or non-radicalisation, are shaped in concrete social contexts. They identify social structures, within which young people are embedded, and the extremist ideas and behaviours diffused within the milieus they inhabit, as key factors in shaping trajectories as reflected in a range of ideologically and experientially articulated (political and personal) grievances. However, trajectory outcomes are found to be strongly mediated also by situational and affective factors, which can encourage young people to advance along, but also halt and draw back from, radicalisation pathways. Through tracing individual trajectories, the radical milieu appears as a site of encounter and engagement with radicalising forces, messages and agents, which can facilitate the movement towards extremism, but also constrain radicalisation and pull young people back from extremism. Thus, Pilkington and Vestel concur with Dechesne that the same factors, or dimensions of, radicalisation can simultaneously be a source of radicalisation and non-radicalisation.

Part II explores a range of sites and channels of radicalisation and non-radicalisation. In Chapter 3, Franc, Poli and Pavlović provide a review of the evidence base to date on whether, and if so in what contexts, inequality drives radicalisation. Drawing on a systematic review/meta-ethnographic synthesis methodology, they consider the findings of over two hundred empirical studies for what they tell us about the relationship between inequality and radicalisation in relation to 'Islamist' and 'extreme-right' radicalisation. They find some evidence for the existence of either a direct or indirect relationship between inequality and radicalisation but also studies that find no such relationship or a bi-directional relationship (inequality facilitates radicalisation but radicalisation also plays a role in producing inequality). The inconsistency of findings reflects the multi-dimensionality of inequality and the authors emphasise, in particular, the importance of distinguishing between objective and subjective dimensions and the salience in existing studies of subjective (perceived) inequality and of socio-political rather than economic inequality in facilitating radicalisation. The conditionality of findings also reflects differences in what outcome variable (indicating 'radicalisation') is taken across different strands of radicalisation and different country contexts (the definitional problem discussed earlier in this introductory chapter). The authors conclude that the link between inequality and radicalisation is context dependent, if not case-by-case dependent. In Chapter 4, Sakellariou considers the question of the relationship between religion and political violence, specifically how this relationship has been presented in relation to Islam in contemporary political and public discourse in Greece. Drawing on the ethnographic study in the Athens region of an extreme-right milieu, he shows how Greek Orthodox anti-Muslim groupings work together with anti-immigrant, extreme-right nationalist groups, such as supporters of Golden Dawn, to shape increasingly anti-Muslim public discourse, epitomised in the extended fight against the construction of the first official mosque in Athens. Drawing on a parallel ethnographic study with participants in a Muslim milieu, centred on non-official prayer houses in Athens, the potential for the targeted stigmatisation of Muslims as well as physical attacks on individuals and sites of worship to facilitate a process of reciprocal radicalisation is demonstrated. The responses, and strategies, developed by these milieu actors from within to prevent such escalation are explored and the implications of this for understanding the relationship between religion and violence considered. In Chapter 5, Poliakov considers family, friendship and kinship networks as channels of radicalisation, non-radicalisation and deradicalisation. Based on in-depth interviews with young men from the North Caucasian republics of the Russian Federation, now living in Moscow and Saint Petersburg, he argues that these networks function as an enabling infrastructure for mutual emotional support, the development of a common identity and the reframing of views. The family, he suggests, is pivotal to two distinct patterns of radicalisation among this second urban generation of young people. On the one hand, intergenerational conflict, and emotional disengagement, within the parental family, reinforced by discrimination and horizontal inequalities encountered in Russian cities, can facilitate pathways of radicalisation. On the other hand, the establishment of relationships of affinity and trust with other family members (especially siblings) or within leisure or sports-based peer groups may open young people to radical worldviews or steer them down paths of non-radicalisation and deradicalisation.

In Part III, the focus turns to exploring the situational and interactional dynamics of radicalisation. In Chapter 6, Pilkington draws on ethnographic research with young activists in 'extreme-right' movements in the UK to explore the significance of micro-situational interactions for explaining trajectories into and away from (political) violence. Drawing on ethnographic and interview data, the chapter identifies a disjuncture between research participants' almost universal rejection of the legitimacy of violence in pursuit of political causes and the engagement by some of them in violence. Focusing on four individual cases – three of whom were involved in violence, one who was not – the chapter explores the significance, as well as limitations, of micro-situational interactions for understanding where, when and what violence occurs. The author concludes that violence is neither the apex of radicalisation pathways, nor wholly situationally explained, but a socio-cultural practice imbued with a range of meanings for individuals and embraced or rejected in response to situational and interactional dynamics shaped by chains of previous encounters outside of political activism. In Chapter 7, Conti challenges the vision of prison as a 'terroristogenic' site that has become embedded in public as well as academic discourse. By drawing on ethnographic research in a French prison, with prisoners convicted of terrorism-related offences and those convicted of other offences, he is able to explore the complex interactions within the prison environment that lead some young prisoners to turn to radical Islam while others do not. A key factor in this is the inequality that permeates the daily life of Muslim prisoners, leading to a widely shared sense of injustice, which exacerbates existing crises of identity and sense of social anomie. Against this background, Conti considers the offer radical Islam provides to those whose links to society are already fragile, to make a complete break with that world and be resocialised into a new affective community of the neo-*Ummah*. Tracing individual journeys in which radical Islamism is adopted, it is shown to offer the basis of a new, valorised identity, a means to seek justice for a persecuted and humiliated Muslim community and a feeling of, at last, not being the 'losers' but the 'chosen ones'. Alongside such trajectories, he identifies cases where individuals resist the offer of these radicalising messages and are able to mobilise resources – family, spiritual, social connections – to re-establish roots and connections that protect them against radicalising messages. He concludes that the differences between these outcomes are often no more than 'tiny threads' maintaining affective and social connectedness. In Chapter 8, Kerst draws on the findings of his research with young members of marksmen's clubs in Germany to explore how milieu members respond to radical(ising) messages, and their messengers, which they encounter in everyday situations. These marksmen's clubs are traditionally politically conservative and have attracted right-wing or extreme-right actors seeking to influence, and appropriate, certain aspects of the club milieu. He finds a wide spectrum of responses, ranging from outright rejection – of the message, its messenger or both – to their uncritical acceptance or trivialisation leading to a potential normalisation of the views expressed. By considering how these responses are shaped by the context and interactional dynamics of their encounter, he explores some of the factors that encourage and maintain resilience to radicalisation at both the individual and milieu level.

The concluding chapter elaborates a number of themes that emerge across the very different case studies drawn on through the volume and critically reflects on their implications for the theoretical models and debates that shape contemporary radicalisation research. It proposes that radicalisation is best understood as a relational concept reflecting a social phenomenon that is the product of social interactions rather than social profiles or psychological dispositions. It draws on findings from contributions to the volume to suggest that such interactions – with family, friends, movement leaders, influential figures, institutional actors – may facilitate but also constrain radicalisation. It argues that, if we are to avoid overdetermining our understanding of this process by the exclusive study of its relatively rare endpoint in violent extremism, it is vital that we study not only radicalisation but partial radicalisation, stalled radicalisation and non-radicalisation. Further, while recognising the particular contribution of radicalisation studies in understanding how, rather than why, people engage with radical ideas and behaviour, it is argued that the 'why' question must not be ignored. Indeed, understanding the concerns that drive people to activism in radical milieus may help explain why so few journeys through them end in violent extremism. Finally, it calls for the study of radicalisation journeys that do not end in violent extremism for what they tell us about the protective factors, resilient qualities and individual agency that combine to establish the 'red lines' that milieu members choose not to cross. This situated knowledge of actors in radical(ising) milieus, it suggests, may inform work to strengthen resistance to violent and anti-democratic responses to individual and collective grievances.

Acknowledgements

The research drawn on in this chapter is part of the Dialogue about Radicalisation and Equality (DARE) project, which received funding from the

European Union's Horizon 2020 research and innovation programme under Grant Agreement No. 725349. It reflects only the views of the author; the European Commission and Research Executive Agency are not responsible for any information it contains.

Hilary Pilkington is Professor of Sociology at the University of Manchester and Fellow of the Academy of Social Sciences. She has conducted ethnographic research on youth and youth subculture, youth political participation, activism and extremism and published also on ethnographic research methods and meta-ethnographic synthesis. She was coordinator of the H2020 DARE (Dialogue about Radicalisation and Equality) project (University of Manchester, 2017–21). She is a member of the Academic-Practitioner Countering Extremism Network of the Commission for Countering Extremism and served as independent Commissioner on the GMCA Preventing Violent Extremism and Promoting Social Cohesion Commission.

NOTES

1. The terms 'emic' and 'etic', emanating from linguistic anthropology, are used here in line with their adoption in the social sciences to distinguish between concepts and categories rooted in actors' self-understanding and 'insider accounts' ('emic') and those devised and deployed by external, scientific or policy/practice communities ('etic') (Whitaker 2017; Sieckelinck et al. 2019: 677).
2. The Ahmed and Lynch rapid appraisal considered articles published in three academic terrorism studies journals (2001–18) while the Franc and Pavlović systematic review, conducted as part of the DARE project, considered a wider range of publications (2001–17) based on quantitative empirical studies on the relationship between inequality and radicalisation. The parallel meta-ethnographic synthesis of published qualitative empirical studies conducted as part of the DARE project found a higher proportion of studies (25%) to be focused on the 'extreme-right' (see Franc, Poli and Pavlović, this volume).
3. While the incidence rate between 2019 and 2021 is clearly heavily impacted by COVID, comparative figures from 2017–19 suggest that right-wing extremism accounted for just 2.6% of terrorist attacks reported by EU member states (Europol 2020: 11).
4. It should be noted that Cragin (2014: 347) emphasises the importance of differentiating between factors of 'resistance to' and 'desistance from' violent extremism.
5. Pre-emption implies that the risks of radicalisation are knowable and can be intercepted or averted by taking precautionary action. In radicalisation policy and practice this approach underpins resilience-based policies that seek to

teach individuals to live with uncertainty and develop skills that allow them to adapt and respond to risks and harms that are likely to occur (Hardy 2015: 80).

6. Resilience is used to describe the capacity to absorb the impact of, and recover from, shock, trauma or disturbance (Hardy 2015: 79).

7. For further details of the project and the findings of the project in a series of reports, Research Briefings and Policy Briefs, see https://sites.manchester.ac.uk/dare/.

8. For the country-level reports, as well as an introduction to these studies setting out the methodology employed, see https://sites.manchester.ac.uk/dare/home/research-reports/online-radicalisation/.

9. For the country-level reports on case studies of interactional radicalisation, see https://sites.manchester.ac.uk/dare/home/research-reports/interactional-radicalisation/.

10. See https://documents.manchester.ac.uk/display.aspx?DocID=58627.

11. The project received ethical approval from the EU prior to the conclusion of the Grant Agreement No. 725349 (2017). Each Consortium partner subsequently secured ethical approval through its own institutional ethics board for the research in which it participated or through the DARE Ethics Sub-Committee. As Coordinator, the project was submitted to the University of Manchester Research Ethics Committee 4 and received approval Ref: 2017–1737–3255 (14 June 2017) with subsequent amendments and reapprovals (25 April 2018 and 11 June 2020). The procedures and standards of this Committee were used to inform the DARE Ethics Sub-Committee.

12. Detailed guidelines on methods for data collection and analysis, ethical and security protocols including procedures for transcription, pseudonymisation, preparation, storage and sharing of various forms of data (textual, visual, audio etc.) were provided for all researchers in a dedicated project Data Handbook. This Data Handbook also included the ethical guidelines, protocols on researcher safety and research instruments such as the shared interview schedule and the skeleton coding tree. Some of these are outlined in Pilkington and Vestel 2020.

13. In three cases – the studies of 'extreme-right' milieus in Germany and Malta and of the 'Islamist' milieu in Turkey – the respondent set was roughly evenly split between young men and young women even though the milieu studied was predominantly male.

14. The individual case study reports on 'Islamist milieus' can be found at https://sites.manchester.ac.uk/dare/home/research-reports/islamist-radical-milieu-studies/. The case study reports on 'extreme-right' milieus can be found at https://sites.manchester.ac.uk/dare/home/research-reports/extreme-right-radical-milieu-studies/.

15. This inductive coding was conducted in the languages of the interviews being coded but 'node' names were subsequently translated into English to facilitate cross-national analysis.

16. 'Node memos' are thematic memos including detailed descriptions of the range and content, as well as illustrative quotes, for each node.
17. 'Respondent memos' were generated in English for each individual respondent, providing a quick reference point for the main socio-demographic characteristics of the respondent and other contextual information of relevance to the interpretation of the data.

REFERENCES

Abbas, Madeline-Sophie. 2019. 'Producing "Internal Suspect Bodies": Divisive Effects of UK Counter-Terrorism Measures on Muslim Communities in Leeds and Bradford', *British Journal of Sociology* 70(1): 261–82.

Ahmed, Yasmine, and Orla Lynch. 2021. 'Terrorism Studies and the Far Right: The State of Play', *Studies in Conflict & Terrorism*. Published online first at https://www.tandfonline.com/doi/full/10.1080/1057610X.2021.1956063.

Barzegar, Abbas, Shawn Powers and Nagham El Karhili. 2016. *Civic Approaches to Confronting Violent Extremism: Sector Recommendations and Best Practices*. British Council, Georgia State University and ISD.

Beck, Colin J. 2015. *Radicals, Revolutionaries and Terrorists*. Cambridge: Polity Press.

Berger, John M. 2016. 'Making CVE Work: A Focused Approach Based on Process Disruption', *The International Centre for Counter-Terrorism – The Hague* 7(5), http://dx.doi.org/10.19165/2016.1.05.

Bjørgo, Tore. 2009. 'Processes of Disengagement from Violent Groups of the Extreme Right', in Tore Bjørgo and John Horgan (eds), *Leaving Terrorism Behind: Individual and Collective Disengagement*. London: Routledge, pp. 30–48.

Bjørgo, Tore, and Jacob A. Ravndal. 2019. *Extreme-Right Violence and Terrorism: Concepts, Patterns, and Responses*. The Hague: The International Centre for Counter-Terrorism.

Borum, Randy. 2011a. 'Radicalization into Violent Extremism I: A Review of Social Science Theories', *Journal of Strategic Security* 4(4): 7–36.

———. 2011b 'Radicalization into Violent Extremism II: A Review of Conceptual Models and Empirical Research', *Journal of Strategic Security* 4(4): 37–62.

———. 2011c. 'Rethinking Radicalization', *Journal of Strategic Security* 4(4): 1–6.

Bouhana, Noémie. 2019. *The Moral Ecology of Extremism: A Systemic Perspective*. London: Commission for Countering Extremism. Retrieved 22 December 2021 from https://www.gov.uk/government/publications/the-moral-ecology-of-extremism-a-systemic-perspective.

Britten, Nicky, et al. 2002. 'Using Meta Ethnography to Synthesise Qualitative Research: A Worked Example', *Journal of Health Services Research & Policy* 7(4): 209–15.

Burawoy, Michael. 1998. 'The Extended Case Method', *Sociological Theory* 16(1): 4–33.

Busher, Joel, Donald Holbrook and Graham Macklin. 2019. 'The Internal Brakes on Violent Escalation: A Typology', *Behavioral Sciences of Terrorism and Political Aggression* 11(1): 3–25.

Campbell, Colin. 1972. 'The Cult, the Cultic Milieu and Secularisation', in *A Sociological Yearbook of Religion in Britain* 5. London: SCM Press, pp. 119–36.

———. 2012. 'The Cultic Milieu Revisited', Lecture at University of Leipzig. Retrieved 10 August 2022 from https://www.researchgate.net/publication/280947007_The_Cultic_Milieu_Revisited?channel=doi&linkId=55ce1c0508ae502646a80c42&showFulltext=true.

Choudhury, Tufyal, and Helen Fenwick. 2011. *The Impact of Counter-Terrorism Measures on Muslim Communities*. Equality and Human Rights Commission Research Report 72. Retrieved 22 February 2022 from https://www.equalityhumanrights.com/en/publication-download/research-report-72-impact-counter-terrorism-measures-muslim-community.

Christmann, Kris. 2012. *Preventing Religious Radicalisation and Violent Extremism: A Systematic Review of the Research Evidence*. Youth Justice Board for England and Wales.

Costanza, William A. 2015. 'Adjusting Our Gaze: An Alternative Approach to Understanding Youth Radicalization', *Journal of Strategic Security* 8(1): 1–15.

Council of Europe. 2018. *Reference Framework of Competences for Democratic Culture – Volume 3. Guidance for Implementation*. Strasbourg: Council of Europe. Retrieved 22 February 2022 from https://rm.coe.int/prems-008518-gbr-2508-reference-framework-of-competences-vol-3-8575-co/16807bc66e.

Cragin, Kim. 2014. 'Resisting Violent Extremism: A Conceptual Model for Non-Radicalization', *Terrorism and Political Violence* 26: 337–53.

Cragin, Kim, et al. 2015. 'What Factors Cause Youth to Reject Violent Extremism? Results of an Exploratory Analysis in the West Bank', Rand Corporation. Retrieved 5 January 2022 from https://www.rand.org/pubs/research_reports/RR1118.html.

Crenshaw, Martha. 2007. 'Thoughts on Relating Terrorism to Historical Contexts', in Martha Crenshaw (ed.), *Terrorism in Context*. University Park, PA: The Pennsylvania State University Press, pp. 3–24.

Dalgaard-Nielsen, Anja. 2010. 'Violent Radicalization in Europe: What We Know and What We Do Not Know', *Studies in Conflict & Terrorism* 33(9): 797–814.

Dawson, Lorne L. 2017. 'Sketch of a Social Ecology Model for Explaining Homegrown Terrorist Radicalisation', *The International Centre for Counter-Terrorism – The Hague* 8(1): 1–15. Retrieved 22 December 2021 from https://icct.nl/publication/sketch-of-a-social-ecology-model-for-explaining-homegrown-terrorist-radicalisation/.

Della Porta, Donatella. 2018. 'Radicalization: A Relational Perspective', *Annual Review of Political Science* 21: 461–74.

Europol. 2020. *European Union Terrorism Situation and Trend Report* (TE-SAT), European Union Agency for Law Enforcement Cooperation. Retrieved 12 August 2022 from https://www.europol.europa.eu/activities-services/main-reports/european-union-terrorism-situation-and-trend-report-te-sat-2020.

———. 2022. *European Union Terrorism Situation and Trend Report* (TE-SAT), European Union Agency for Law Enforcement Cooperation. Retrieved 12 August 2022 from https://www.europol.europa.eu/cms/sites/default/files/documents/Tesat_Report_2022_0.pdf

Ezekiel, Raphael S. 2002. 'An Ethnographer Looks at Neo-Nazi and Klan Groups: The Racist Mind Revisited', *American Behavioral Scientist* 46: 51–71.

Franc, Renata, and Tomislav Pavlović. 2021. 'Inequality and Radicalisation: Systematic Review of Quantitative Studies', *Terrorism and Political Violence*. Published online first at https://doi.org/10.1080/09546553.2021.1974845.

Gill, Paul. 2007. 'A Multi-Dimensional Approach to Suicide Bombing', *International Journal of Conflict and Violence* 1(2): 142–59.

Goldkuhl, Göran, and Stefan Cronholm. 2010. 'Adding Theoretical Grounding to Grounded Theory: Toward Multi-Grounded Theory', *International Journal of Qualitative Methods* 9(2): 187–205.

Gøtzsche-Astrup, Oluf. 2018. 'The Time for Causal Designs: Review and Evaluation of Empirical Support for Mechanisms of Political Radicalisation', *Aggression and Violent Behavior* 39: 90–99.

Grossman, Michele. 2021. 'Resilience to Violent Extremism and Terrorism: A Multisystemic Analysis', in Michael Ungar (ed.), *Multisystemic Resilience: Adaptation and Transformation in Contexts of Change*. New York: Oxford University Press, pp. 293–317.

Grossman, Michele, et al. 2016. *Stocktake Research Project: A Systematic Literature and Selected Program Review on Social Cohesion, Community Resilience and Violent Extremism 2011–2015*. Community Resilience Unit, Department of Premier and Cabinet, State of Victoria.

Hardy, Kieran. 2015. 'Resilience in UK Counterterrorism', *Theoretical Criminology* 19(1): 77–94.

Hickman, Mary J., et al. 2012. 'Social Cohesion and the Notion of "Suspect Communities": A Study of the Experiences and Impacts of Being "Suspect" for Irish Communities and Muslim Communities in Britain', *Critical Studies on Terrorism* 5(1): 89–106.

Horgan, John. 2008. 'From Profiles to Pathways and Roots to Routes: Perspectives from Psychology and Radicalization into Terrorism', *The Annals of the Academy of the Political and Social Sciences* 618: 80–94.

———. 2012. 'Discussion Point: The End of Radicalization?' National Consortium for the Study of Terrorism and Responses to Terrorism (START). Retrieved 21 February 2022 from http://www.start.umd.edu/news/discussion-pointend-Radicalization.

———. 2017. 'Psychology of Terrorism: Introduction', *American Psychologist* 72(3): 199–204.

Kaplan, Jeffrey S., and Heléne Lööw. 2002. 'Introduction', in Jeffrey S. Kaplan and Heléne Lööw (eds), *The Cultic Milieu: Oppositional Subcultures in an Age of Globalization*. Walnut Creek, CA: AltaMira Press, pp. 1–11.

Kapoor, Nisha. 2018. *Deport, Deprive, Extradite: 21st Century State Extremism*. London: Verso.

Kewley, Stephanie. 2017. 'Strength Based Approaches and Protective Factors from a Criminological Perspective', *Aggression and Violent Behaviour* 32: 11–18.

Koehler, Daniel. 2016. 'Right-Wing Extremism and Terrorism in Europe: Current Developments and Issues for the Future', *PRISM* 6(2): 85–104.

Kruglanski, Arie W., et al. 2017. 'To the Fringe and Back: Violent Extremism and the Psychology of Deviance', *American Psychologist* 72(3): 217–30.

Kühle, Lene, and Lasse Lindekilde. 2012. 'Radicalisation and the Limits of Tolerance: A Danish Case-Study', *Journal of Ethnic and Migration Studies* 38(10): 1607–23.

Kundnani, Arun. 2012. 'Radicalisation: The Journey of a Concept', *Race and Class* 54(2): 3–25.

———. 2014. *The Muslims Are Coming! Islamophobia, Extremism, and the Domestic War on Terror*. London: Verso.

Lee, Benjamin, and Kim Knott. 2022. 'Fascist Aspirants: *Fascist Forge* and Ideological Learning in the Extreme-Right Online Milieu', *Behavioral Sciences of Terrorism and Political Aggression* 14(3): 216–40.

Lindekilde, Lasse, Stefan Malthaner and Francis O'Connor. 2019. 'Peripheral and Embedded: Relational Patterns of Lone-Actor Terrorist Radicalization', *Dynamics of Asymmetric Conflict* 12(1): 20–41.

Linden, Annette, and Bert Klandermans. 2007. 'Revolutionaries, Wanderers, Converts, and Compliants: Life Histories of Extreme Right Activists', *Journal of Contemporary Ethnography* 36(2): 184–201.

Malthaner, Stefan. 2017. 'Radicalization: The Evolution of an Analytical Paradigm', *European Journal of Sociology* 58(3): 369–401.

Malthaner, Stefan, and Peter Waldmann. 2014. 'The Radical Milieu: Conceptualizing the Supportive Social Environment of Terrorist Groups', *Studies in Conflict and Terrorism* 37(12): 979–98.

McCauley, Clark, and Sophia Moskalenko. 2008. 'Mechanisms of Political Radicalization: Pathways Toward Terrorism', *Terrorism and Political Violence* 20(3): 415–33.

———. 2017. 'Understanding Political Radicalization: The Two-Pyramids Model', *American Psychologist* 72(3): 205–16.

McGhee, Derek. 2008. *The End of Multiculturalism? Terrorism, Integration and Human Rights*. Maidenhead: Open University Press.

Moghaddam, Fathali M. 2005. 'The Staircase to Terrorism. A Psychological Exploration', *American Psychologist* 60(2): 161–69.

Moskalenko, Sophie, and Clark McCauley. 2009. 'Measuring Political Mobilization: The Distinction between Activism and Radicalism', *Terrorism and Political Violence* 21(2): 239–60.

Neumann, Peter. 2013. 'The Trouble with Radicalization', *International Affairs* 89(4): 873–93.

Noblit, George W., and R. Dwight Hare. 1988. *Meta-Ethnography: Synthesizing Qualitative Studies*. Newbury Park: Sage.

O'Reilly, Karen. 2005. *Ethnographic Methods*. London: Routledge.

Pavlović, Tomislav, Ingrid Storm and Renata Franc. 2021. Report on Findings of New Survey Data. DARE Research Report. [Unpublished report].

Pilkington, Hilary. 2017. 'Radicalisation Research Should Focus on Everyday Lives', *Research Europe* 9: 7. Retrieved 31 December 2021 from https://www.researchresearch.com/news/article/?articleId=1366511.

———. 2018. 'Employing Meta-Ethnography in the Analysis of Qualitative Data Sets on Youth Activism: A New Tool for Transnational Research Projects?', *Qualitative Research* 18(1): 108–30.

———. 2022. 'Why Should We Care What Extremists Think? The Contribution of Emic Perspectives to Understanding the "Right-Wing Extremist" Mind-Set', *Journal of Contemporary Ethnography* 51(3): 318–46.

Pilkington, Hilary, and Viggo Vestel. 2020. *Young People's Trajectories through Anti-Islam(ist) and Extreme Right Milieus: Introduction*. DARE Project Report. Retrieved 28 August 2022 from https://documents.manchester.ac.uk/display.aspx?DocID=58693.

———. 2021. *Young People's Trajectories through Anti-Islam(ist) and Extreme Right Milieus: Cross-National Synthesis Report*. DARE Research Report. Retrieved 28 August 2022 from https://documents.manchester.ac.uk/display.aspx?DocID=58676.

Poli, Alexandra, and Onur Arun. 2019. *Report on the Meta-Ethnographic Synthesis of Qualitative Studies on Inequality and Youth Radicalisation*. DARE Research Report. Retrieved 28 August 2022 from https://documents.manchester.ac.uk/display.aspx?DocID=58616.

Ragazzi, Francesco. 2016. 'Suspect Community or Suspect Category? The Impact of Counter-Terrorism as "Policed Multiculturalism"', *Journal of Ethnic and Migration Studies* 42(5): 724–41.

Ravn, Stiene, Rik Coolaset and Tom Sauer. 2019. 'Rethinking Radicalisation: Addressing the Lack of a Contextual Perspective in the Dominant Narratives on Radicalisation', in Noel Clycq et al. (eds), *Radicalisation: A Marginal Phenomenon or a Mirror to Society?* Leuven: Leuven University Press, pp. 21–46.

Ravndal, Jacob A. 2016. 'Right-wing Terrorism and Violence in Western Europe: Introducing the RTV Dataset', *Perspectives on Terrorism* 10(3): 2–15.

Rosand, Eric. 2018. 'Multi-Disciplinary and Multi-Agency Approaches to Preventing & Countering Violent Extremism: An Emerging P/CVE Success Story?', in *Global Terrorism Index 2018: Measuring the Impact of Terrorism*. Sydney: Institute for Economics and Peace, pp. 72–75.

Sageman, Marc. 2004. *Understanding Terror Networks*. Philadelphia: University of Pennsylvania Press.

———. 2014. 'Low Return on Investment', *Terrorism and Political Violence* 26(4): 614–20.

Schmid, Alex P. 2013. 'Radicalisation, De-Radicalisation, Counter-Radicalisation: A Conceptual Discussion and Literature Review', ICCT Research Paper. The Hague: International Centre for Counter-Terrorism.

———. 2014. 'Violent and Non-Violent Extremism: Two Sides of the Same Coin?' ICCT Research Paper. The Hague: International Centre for Counter-Terrorism.

Schuurman, Bart. 2020. 'Non-Involvement in Terrorist Violence', *Perspectives on Terrorism* 14(6): 14–26.

Sedgwick, Mark. 2010. 'The Concept of Radicalisation as a Source of Confusion', *Terrorism and Political Violence* 22(4): 479–94.

Sieckelinck, Stijn, and Amy-Jane Gielen. 2017. *RAN Issue Paper: Protective and Promotive Factors Building Resilience against Violent Radicalisation*. Amsterdam: RAN Centre of Excellence. Retrieved 22 February 2022 from https://ec.europa.eu/home-affairs/sites/homeaffairs/files/what-we-do/networks/rad icalisation_awareness_network/ran-papers/docs/ran_paper_protective_ factors_042018_en.pdf.

Sieckelinck, Stijn, et al. 2019. 'Transitional Journeys into and out of Extremism: A Biographical Approach', *Studies in Conflict & Terrorism* 42(7): 662–82.

Stephens, William, and Stijn Sieckelinck. 2021. 'Resiliences to Radicalization: Four Key Perspectives', *International Journal of Law, Crime and Justice* 66: 1–14. Published online first at https://doi.org/10.1016/j.ijlcj.2021.100486.

Storm, Ingrid, Tomislav Pavlović and Renata Franc. 2020. *Report on the Relationship between Inequality and Youth Radicalisation from Existing European Survey Datasets*. DARE Research Report. Retrieved 28 August 2022 from https://documents.manchester.ac.uk/display.aspx?DocID=58618.

Whitaker, Emilie M. 2017. 'Emic and Etic Analysis', in Bryan S. Turner (ed.), *The Wiley-Blackwell Encyclopedia of Social Theory*, 1–2. Hoboken, NJ: John Wiley & Sons. Retrieved 21 March 2021 from https://onlinelibrary.wiley.com/doi/10.1002/9781118430873.est0640.

Wiktorowicz, Quintan. 2005. *Radical Islam Rising: Muslim Extremism in the West*. Oxford: Rowman & Littlefield.

Wilkinson, Matthew, et al. 2021. 'Prison as a Site of Intense Religious Change: The Example of Conversion to Islam', *Religions* 12(3): 162.

Youngblood, Mason. 2020. 'Extremist Ideology as a Complex Contagion: The Spread of Far-Right Radicalization in the United States between 2005 and 2017', *Humanities and Social Sciences Communications* 7(49). Retrieved 11 August 2022 from https://www.nature.com/articles/s41599-020-00546-3.

PART I

※ ※ ※

Cross-European Perspectives on Trajectories of (Non)Radicalisation

CHAPTER 1

Non-Radicalisation under a Magnifying Glass

A Cross-European 'Milieu Perspective' on Resistance to Islamist Radical Messaging

Mark Dechesne

Introduction

Radicalisation can be described as a complex dynamic process involving a collection of tendencies including (socio-)psychological distancing from society, adoption of a 'radical' alternative viewpoint considered by others to be incompatible with societal norms and values and increasing willingness to use violent means to bring this radical viewpoint to the attention of relevant representatives in society.

For the past two decades, Europe and North America have witnessed a surge in interest in so-called Islamist radicalisation following the September 11 attacks of 2001. In the interests of national security, the attacks prompted a significant shift towards a more prevention-focused approach, which included, among other measures, a thorough consideration of the process that had led the perpetrators to commit their horrendous acts and the factors that were involved in this process. In line with this shift in focus, policy analysts, think tanks and academics stepped up their efforts to analyse the process through which individuals make the transition from 'normal' young citizens, and, in the case of the 9/11 perpetrators, of considerable wealth and education levels, to self-perceived holy warriors willing to kill themselves in the service of a higher socio-political cause. A great many models have since been developed describing this process, the potential steps involved and the trigger factors that make violent extremism appear as a way to advance one's cause.

However, as policy makers and practitioners considered the practical implications of these models, some anomalies have come to the fore. Perhaps the 'elephant in the room' has been the fact that the vast majority of people for whom surveillance and intervention programmes might be designed, were not radicalised, would be unlikely to become radicalised and might actually radicalise as a result of exposure to such programmes (Kundnani 2012; Ragazzi 2017). Emblematic in this context is the critical reception of the UK Prevent programme, the preventative arm of the Counter Terrorism strategy implemented through social institutions to address grievances and misperception among at-risk youth. The implementation, involving a variety of community workers, teachers and so on, has been criticised for promoting a sense of stigmatisation and polarisation rather than redressing radicalisation (Stanley, Guru and Gupta 2018; Abbas 2019). Thus, our understanding of radicalisation and violent extremism, and our ability to act on this understanding, may be considered currently incomplete and ineffective.

As implicit in the brief overview of the evolution of our understanding of radicalisation above, this incompleteness and ineffectiveness may be attributed in part to a design problem. Specifically, the security angle that has driven the interest in radicalisation has been based on a thorough analysis of perpetrators but has failed to take into account that a significant proportion of the population, indeed the vast majority, has no affinity with radicalisation. Moreover, the process-tracing method that starts from acts of terrorism in order to identify risk factors of radicalisation in earlier life stages of the perpetrators has failed to take into account the pathways of those who, at one point or another, had taken a different direction despite identical 'early-warning' indicators (Sarma 2017). This design problem can be described as a case of 'base-rate neglect' (Yang and Wu 2020), that is, a neglect of the phenomenon of non-radicalisation. This has been recognised in recent scholarly work, which has noted that we should not only aim to understand radicalisation, but also to understand non-radicalisation (Cragin 2014; Schuurman 2020). A stronger version of this argument might be that we can only understand radicalisation to the extent that we can understand it in relation to non-radicalisation and vice versa.

However, developing an understanding of non-radicalisation comes with considerable challenges. This chapter seeks to contribute to the emerging interest in non-radicalisation by further reflecting on the complexities of studying trajectories through radical milieus that do not lead to violent extremism. After a discussion of the challenges this brings, the chapter seeks to provide some, preliminary, answers as to how we overcome them by outlining the 'milieu approach' adopted in this study (see also the Introduction to this volume) and the insights it has generated for understanding the phenomenon of radicalisation. Specifically, in this chapter, these insights are drawn from extensive ethnographic work and in-depth interviews conducted in what we call 'Islamist extremist milieus' across Europe and some neighbouring countries.

The Challenges of Studying a 'Non'

Why is it challenging to study non-radicalisation? The main difficulty is that a thorough understanding of a phenomenon is based on empirical research, but non-radicalisation, similarly to other 'non-phenomena', does not exist and we cannot empirically investigate phenomena that are not empirical. Hence, in order to study it, a non-phenomenon needs to be described based on its relation to a phenomenon that does exist and a model that specifies the relevant dimensions on the basis of which the phenomenon and non-phenomenon can be related and compared. In the context of radicalisation and non-radicalisation, we need to spec- ify the relevant dimensions based on which non-radicalisation might be contrasted with radicalisation, in order to arrive at an account of the factors that contribute to either non-radicalisation or radicalisation. To complicate matters, there are no objective standards for relevant dimensions.

In the case of radicalisation, one focus has been on the dimension of violence, that is, the understanding of the difference between those who engage in violence and those who do not engage in violence (McCau- ley and Moskalenko 2017). As several models of radicalisation prescribe, however, active support for a violent group without active engagement in violence can still be considered indicative of radicalisation (Moghaddam 2005; Storer cited in Shainin 2006). One may then turn to the difference between those who are sympathetic towards a violent extremist organisa- tion and those who are not; although the heterogeneity of the latter group is of such magnitude that it (i.e. the 'non-group') loses its usefulness as a comparison group. For example, when studying Islamist violent extrem- ism in Europe, identifying the most appropriate 'non-radical' compari- son group becomes highly subjective due to the significant heterogeneity among the vast group of those who are not Islamist violent extremists, since this group constitutes the vast majority of citizens in Europe. The choice of comparison group, moreover, will shape our subsequent under- standing of what constitutes 'non-radicalisation'.

In one of the very few attempts to formulate a model of non-radicali- sation, Kim Cragin (2014) determines a set of factors that reduce the ap- peal of, or likelihood of membership in, violent extremist organisations of

various ideological currents, including jihadists, but also Maoists, Marx-
ists and separatist groups. She states that, in her model, 'the term non-
radicalization is used synonymously with the phrase resistance to violent
extremism. It does not consider individuals who have never been exposed
to, or considered, radical ideologies or violence' (Cragin 2014: 342) and
focuses specifically on organised forms of radicalisation, as opposed to
lone-wolves and self-radicalised individuals. Cragin modestly describes
her model as a first step, based on an analysis of newspaper articles,
reports and academic papers describing cases of non-radicalisation. The
model identifies instrumental, social and moral factors that are considered to reduce the number of recruits to an organisation and increase
the number of members who leave the organisation. Potential recruits
are assumed to refrain from joining for four main reasons: (1) joining
would come with too high personal costs (as a result of repression, leaving behind one's social life or moving to another place); (2) the organisation is assumed to be ineffectual in achieving its, and the recruit's, aims;
(3) there are no social ties to connect the potential recruit to the organisation; and (4) the organisation's deeds are too morally repugnant to
affiliate with. Members are considered as likely to leave the organisation
for a similar set of instrumental, social and moral factors, described as:
(1) perceived costs (repression, family obligations, mistreatment and loss
of inducements); (2) perceived organisational ineffectiveness (feelings of
burnout and disillusionment); (3) loss of social ties connecting the individual to the organisation; and (4) empathy for others.

Cragin's model brings to mind linkages to the literature on collective
social action, that is, action by a collective to raise awareness and redress
collectively felt grievances. The concepts used in the model can, for instance, be considered the inverse of factors identified by Van Zomeren,
Postmes and Spears (2008) in their influential social identity model of
collective action. This integrative 'SIMCA' model posits social identification, perceived efficacy and perceived injustices as the key drivers of
mobilisation of a collective to engage in action for a group-related cause.
Comparing the SIMCA model of collective action with Cragin's model of
non-radicalisation, we can see considerable similarities between 'social
identification' of the former and 'social ties' of the latter, and between
'perceived efficacy' of the former and 'perceived ineffectiveness of the
group and personal cost' of the latter. Perhaps 'injustices' of the former
and 'moral repugnance and empathy with others' are slightly different in
connotation, but they may also be considered inversely related; once one
empathises with others, one is likely to be considerably less concerned
with the injustices committed to oneself or one's group. Moreover, the
perception of being unjustly treated can be considered a moral justifica-

tion for the use of vengeful violence, indeed as an opposite to the notion of 'moral repugnance'.

To a certain extent, the similarities between Cragin's model and the SIMCA model can be considered a corroboration of Cragin's model. Terrorism is in many, and particularly in its most disruptive, expressions a form of collective action (e.g. della Porta and Diani 2015) and thus factors opposite to those predictive of collective action are likely to be predictive of non-engagement in terrorism. However, collective action implicates a far broader repertoire of action to advance a collective cause than the use of or threat to use violence. To understand non-radicalisation as opposed to collective inertia, we need to adopt a more fine-grained and differentiated perspective alongside addressing the heterogeneity problem discussed earlier.

The Potential of a Milieu Approach

A central claim of this chapter is that the milieu approach may contribute to the inclusion of this more fine-grained and differentiated perspective on radicalisation in the analysis of non-radicalisation and help to contextualise some of the heterogeneity that prevents a thorough study of non-radicalisation.

Essential to the milieu approach is the focus on a contextualised understanding of radicalisation and non-radicalisation. These phenomena are viewed as best understood when we zoom in on the lives and the experienced context (i.e. life space) of the people who are confronted with radical messages. The milieu approach seeks to identify the complex and dynamic interactions and processes involved in the appeal or rejection of these messages. Within the milieu approach, people who are exposed to radicalising messages are not considered passive victims of these messages but active agents with their own views and understandings of their lifeworld and with their own role in shaping their (social) environment. Those exposed to radical messaging should be recognised as active agents who have their own understanding of the world in which they live and who actively contribute to the shaping of their world on the basis of this understanding. In this sense, the milieu approach recognises the importance of emic (circumstances as perceived by the subject) as opposed to etic (circumstances as perceived by outside observers) factors in the emergence of radicalism and rejection of radicalism.

Focusing on the dynamic, situational, social and interactional qualities of radicalisation enables a more fine-grained understanding of the various expressions of radicalisation as they occur in very similar conditions, enabling the analysis of meaningful variance (i.e. differences in expression of radicalisation/non-radicalisation) while reducing unwanted heterogeneity (i.e. reducing variability in conditions under which radicalisation and non-radicalisation are observed). Moreover, by assuming dynamism, hence variation over time, we may also be able to develop a better understanding of the various stages of radicalisation, alongside stages of non-radicalisation. In addition, we can relate in situ dynamics to parallel dynamics occurring at macro (societal), meso (social) and micro (individual) levels. Finally, if we are to give serious attention to agency, then it is essential to focus on the lived experience of the people involved, taking into account the meanings that subjects themselves assign to particular experiences, message content and events (e.g. what is morally repulsive, and what is not, in the eye of the beholder). This, as discussed later, has important implications when considering policies and practices to address radicalisation.

Islamist Non-Radicalisation in Europe from a Milieu Perspective

A critical requirement for the successful application of the milieu approach are sufficient time and research effort to secure a profound in situ understanding of radicalisation and non-radicalisation processes, based on extensive observation and in-depth interviews with those directly exposed to radical messages. This was possible in this case due to the initial research design of the Dialogue about Radicalisation and Equality (DARE) project, which provided for time and space to generate a sufficiently rich data set to afford inferences about the nature and origin of 'Islamist non-radicalisation' in Europe (Dechesne 2021). The DARE project enabled the ethnographic study of milieus in ten countries across Europe and its neighbouring territories. Although the sites of ethnographic study varied across the countries, the research was designed with a shared emphasis on places where young Muslims meet (physically and online) and encounter radical messages (again, physically or online) that trigger a response (see the Appendix to this volume for an overview of the milieus). In some of these milieus, the dominant response was non-radicalisation whereas in others the response was radicalisation.

In France, for instance, the ethnographers studied young prisoners many of whom had been convicted for terrorism-related offences (Conti 2020). In Turkey, the focus was on civil society organisations with increasing Islamist influences; organisations which were studied at a time that many of their members had had a more or less extended period of involvement in the Syrian civil war, just across the border (Kurt 2020). In many countries, the research focused on specific areas in major cities, known for their high incidence of radicalisation (or at least their portrayal as such) alongside poor social and economic circumstances. In Belgium, the research focus was on young people with direct exposure to radicalising messages in the 'poor crescent' area of Brussels (including Molenbeek) (Benaïssa 2021). In the Netherlands (Dechesne and Van der Valk 2021), Germany (Nanni 2021) and the UK (Hussain 2021), the focus was on particular areas in large cities with a high presence of first- or second-generation immigrants from Muslim majority countries, often poor social and economic circumstances and a known presence of Islamist influences. In Tunisia, the focus was also on areas known for their poor socio-economic conditions and the rapid rise of Islamist influences in recent years (Memni 2021). In Russia, second-generation immigrants to northern Russian cities from the North Caucasus region were studied (Poliakov and Epanova 2021). The fieldwork in Norway and Greece also touched upon the often difficult social and economic circumstances of urban Muslim youth, but here the focus was more specifically on networks and their meeting places. The Greek ethnographic work zoomed in on young Muslims attending non-official Islamic prayer houses in Athens (Sakellariou 2021). The Norwegian research studied young Muslims who had been involved in two Norwegian Islamist social media platforms (Vestel and Ali 2021). The studies of the various locations have yielded a data set of approximately two hundred in-depth interviews with young people, numerous other interviews with experts and family members and additional ethnographic material.

One of the common conclusions of the varied milieu studies is that non-radicalisation and radicalisation come in various shapes and sizes. Radicalisation may be found in the tendency to turn away from society and stop participating in it and to adopt an alternative lifestyle. But that is quite different from adopting a new identity and actively engaging in a relationship of conflict with society and the state in particular. Moreover, even if one adopts this conflict mind-set vis-à-vis society, this does not necessarily imply that one will engage in violence to advance one's cause. Indeed, many of the existing models of radicalisation take note of various stages or 'steps' in the radicalisation process, which do take into account these distinctions. Sprinzak's (1991) Linkage theory of political delegitimisation, for instance, highlights the importance of distinguishing between a crisis of confidence (an initial loss of confidence in state leadership), a conflict of legitimacy (a loss of confidence in the state) and a crisis of legitimacy (a hatred towards anything and anyone affiliated with the state). More directly related to Islamist radicalisation, in his analysis of Salafist radicalism in Europe, Wiktorowicz (2004) emphasises the

importance of distinguishing between apolitical Salafists, political Salafists and jihadi Salafists (with only the latter group considering violence
as a way to advance their cause). We should highlight that, unlike 'staircase models', we have not observed a 'conveyor belt' of radicalisation
whereby an individual gradually moves from one phase to another, with
violence as an inevitable outcome of the process.

In outlining below the insights afforded by the milieu approach
adopted in DARE, a distinction is made between those insights that resulted from a comparison between those who did show indications of
radicalisation and those who did not show these indications, on the one
hand, and the investigation of those who chose a path of radicalisation
(in some form) and eventually turned away from radicalism, on the other.
For different expressions of radicalisation – turning away from society,
adopting a conflict frame and engaging in violence – we were able to
identify several critical factors that distinguished between those respondents who might be considered 'non-radicalised' and those who might be
considered 'radicalised'.

Turning Away from Society

Across the fieldwork sites, we found that the feeling of loss of control
was a common factor among those who, at some point, turned away from
society while those who did not radicalise in response to exposure to
radical(ising) messages often displayed the mental control, or social or
religious resources to interpret and compartmentalise such messaging
such that it did not impact on their life as a whole. This is consistent with,
for instance, psychological theorising by Hobfoll (2012) regarding the
importance of cognitive, social and material resources in the ways people
cope with stress in life and perspectives in crisis management on social
capital as a critical factor in resilience to natural or man-made disasters.
A difference between 'non-radicals' and 'radicals' lies in the ability of the
former to leverage cognitive, social and religious resources to cope with
stress in life. The latter, lacking these resources, will seek these resources
outside of society and sometimes find them in radicalism.

If we are to believe some of our 'non-radical' respondents, non-radicalisation is, to a certain extent, a matter of mental control. For instance,
a respondent in Germany believed those who joined ISIS lacked such
mental control, describing 'these radical Islamists' as 'destroyed individuals even before they go there'. In some cases, these individuals, the
respondent continued, had suffered a 'difficult childhood', but their defining characteristic was that 'they're broken junkies. All of them. Broken junkies, fucked-up junkies or whatever, who had no stability in their

lives'. In Russia, we found a similar perspective, shared by Said,[1] who stated, 'I think when it concerns religious and Islamic people, extremist Muslims, I think such people are having a brain failure .... That's the only way I can understand it'.

In this context, it seems of pertinence that radicalisation is also very much a youth phenomenon, being primarily observed among adolescents and young adults. As noted by the classic theorist of development, Erikson (1968: 17), this age group is particularly faced with challenges related to identity formation and ego development. Dealing with these critical and strenuous challenges potentially leads to what Erikson labelled a 'loss of ego identity', that is, in his words, an impairment in 'central control over themselves for which, in the psychoanalytic scheme, only the "inner agency" of the ego could be held responsible'. Consistent with this statement, we found many of our respondents turned away from society and towards an exploration of religion in response to an identity crisis.

Yet, the experience of identity crisis or a general incapacity for self-control were not the critical factors distinguishing radicals from non-radicals. To understand this distinction, we also need to take the receptiveness and support of the social environment into account. To continue using Hobfoll's terminology, the social environment can be a critical resource to deal with stressful life-events and the absence of social bearings brings the magnitude of existential challenges to the fore. One of the Dutch respondents, for example, told us about his experiences after converting to Islam:

> I felt disappointed to see that I was not accepted. You often hear about people losing touch with old friends but my friends distanced themselves from me. We always went to Germany with a group of friends. After I had converted I said, I want to go, but no pork and no alcohol. Then, the group turned against me. They said, 'We are going to Germany to be away from those Muslims around us'. They knew my history, they came to visit me while I was in foster care. It was hard for me that they did not support me. Even when I got married, they thought it was strange. ... Now I still have the same problems, but I did not know how to deal with them then, I had no one to ask for advice. We felt alone. We started to feel out of place, and we stopped studying and working.

The absence of a supportive social network was a common thread through the stories of these respondents and concerned not only the absence of friends. We also often encountered accounts of the strained relationships that many of the more radical respondents had with their parents. In line with what Khosrokhavar (2021: 233) has termed the 'headless patriarchal family', we found several expressions of this lack of social support by one's parents. This social syndrome may be expressed in the absence of parents (as alluded to by the Dutch respondent cited above), or as observed by Nanni (2021) in her German field study, in the sense that parents are lacking in their provision of moral guidance. It may also be expressed in a family situation where a child only has an affective relationship with the mother, but not with the father. Across the fieldwork sites, it was observed that the absence of a father, as a result of his death, criminal conviction or inability to relate to his wife and children, constituted a risk factor for radicalisation. In contrast, a supportive family environment constituted, in many cases, a factor contributing to the rejection of radical messaging.

Conflictual relationships among the more radicalised segments of our respondent set were also found in other domains of social life. For instance, some respondents reported a lack of social connection at school or work. In his fieldwork in France, Conti (2020) interviewed Adrian, an immigrant with, initially, no knowledge of French who went on to develop an excellent command of the language and an interest in studying linguistics, but who was sent to a technical college against his wishes and eventually dropped out of education. In relation to school, a fairly common theme in the narratives of the more radical respondents was the experience of rejection when applying for an internship. This was the case for Adrian as well as for the following Dutch respondent, who characterised his radicalisation trajectory as being a result of:

> Coincidence, meeting someone, it is not only that you have lost someone or you want to deepen your knowledge, it is also coincidence, circumstances. No internship, a lot of time on your hands, you meet someone when you are vulnerable; if I had found an internship I would have been busy and it would have been different.

The workplace was another social environment where many of the respondents found little support. The experience of discrimination and lack of acceptance of Muslims was quite commonly reported. The wearing of the headscarf was considered problematic, as a Greek respondent Eleftheria, for instance, told the researcher: 'No matter how much you study, a girl wearing a headscarf finds it difficult to be hired by anyone. They might put you in the laundry, they might take you on somewhere to clean, so you will not be front of house'. Norwegian respondent Omar recounted another story about the lack of social support that resonates for many young Muslims throughout Europe. Omar studied journalism, but dropped out, and found a job at a restaurant chain (which involved grilling pork meat). He recalled that one night he was approached by senior staff:

> Then one of them says, 'Don't you feel well? ... I feel sorry for you'. I say, 'Why?' He says that the US had just bombed the Taliban and so on, so many people have died. And I think, 'Huh, why is he telling me this? What's that got to do with me?' So, then the head chef comes up, smiling a kind of icky smile. 'What's up, our little jihadist?' They made a laughing stock of me ... And suddenly I got the shift list. He had put me on all the night shifts – the least wanted and the most unpopular shifts.

On the basis of these experiences, at home, at school or at work, young Muslims turn away from society and find their own identification. The 'neighbourhood' was often mentioned as a basis for social connection and identity. In France, respondent Paul described the value of neighbourhood identification:

> Because they're confusing people, they're lumping terrorists and Muslims together, they're lumping Muslims, thieves and black people together ... then they wonder why you don't like the police, why you don't like anybody, then they wonder why you don't like all that. ... in our neighbourhoods, nobody comes to piss us off, we are quiet, we don't piss anybody off, we are among ourselves, we know each other. ... We are in our little village, we have everything we need in our village. In the neighbourhood there is everything we need – food, the bakery, everything. Why should we leave our quarter? To do what?

In this quote, the neighbourhood is described as a provider of connection and social support in a positive way. The ethnographic research in Belgium and the UK also identified several cases of individuals having had profound encounters with radical messaging and also concluded that neighbourhood connection constitutes a safe haven and a factor in non-radicalisation. In Germany, Salih notes the importance of friends in non-radicalisation pathways:

> Even if inequality, even if there is inequality here, that is not so relevant. If I don't get into a club, what do I lose? And I think my friends are like that, I was against it from the beginning, so. For me it was far away and terrible how one can do something like that. If a guy like that would come to me and try to persuade me somehow, there would be no possibility from the beginning, because I take something like that with a smile and reject it [clicks] I wouldn't do something like that. But what is it now, what really stops me from doing that? [Gasps] My friends, I'd say.

Respondents in many of the fieldwork sites have noted that, in principle, Islamic faith can serve to bridge the sense of being different and being involved in society. In the Netherlands, a respondent emphasises that being a Muslim means taking on a role of responsibility in society:

> When you look at a true Muslim, he is very scared. Not scared, but
> afraid of himself, in the sense that, when he works, he wants to do
> a good job, because he gets paid for it. He views that as something
> very serious. He works long hours, because he really does not want
> to earn money that is forbidden money to us, when you say you work
> but actually, you don't. Actually, it is something very beautiful. He
> gives it the full 100%, because it is his cost. That is actually, what a
> real Muslim is. He would not lie and cheat to make his money.

A significant group of respondents in many of the fieldwork sites emphasised that their religiosity guides them and keeps them from social deviance. They emphasise that Islam is a religion of tolerance and moderation
(although many Muslims also reject the externally imposed distinction
between moderate and extremist Islam), and point to religious scriptures
to underscore that Islam itself denounces radicalism and extremism. Of
particular prominence in the respondents' accounts is the story of the
Kharijites, a religious sect of the early times of Islam known for their
uncompromising stances and their compulsive following of rules. Many
of the respondents consider this sect an example of how religion should
not be practised.

This means that correct religious education is important for non-radicalisation, as one Dutch respondent explained. He emphasised that religious lessons help young people to become resilient and explained that
many of the young people in his surroundings who went to Syria and
joined ISIS lacked the commitment to take religious classes. He also believed religious teaching helped in distinguishing between truth and false-
hood and in taking a stance towards injustice in the world: 'God is going
to ask, "What have you done in a positive way?" He does not ask you to
take up arms but rather to deal with matters that affect you personally'.

The lack of opportunities for a thorough religious education emerged
from the stories of the respondents as a significant factor in their radicalisation trajectories. The Islamic religious world (at least in Western
Europe) is characterised by fragmentation and internal division. Islamic
institutions are often linked to specific ethnic groups, and this makes it
difficult for young people (also) growing up in a Western European context to relate to the religious teachings and practices of these institutions,
not least because they have no command of the language. In this context,
the internet and religious 'bricolage' (self-invention) become the primary
foundation for religious identity development, culminating in an understanding of Islam that is quite far removed from the understandings of
those with a profound religious educational background.

Needless to say, the ethnographic data generated in this study are tre-
mendously rich, and any general statement on the nature of radicalisa-

tion and non-radicalisation fails to do justice to the many special cases observed and analytical insights developed by the case study researchers. However, we might tentatively conclude that self-control capabilities, social connection and thorough religious education on Islam are three critical factors in retaining young Muslims' participation in European societies, that is, our first component of 'non-radicalisation'. Low self-control, living in social disorder and rejection, and the absence of authoritative religious teaching, are all contributing factors to alienation and a move away from society.

Adopting a Conflict or Cooperative Frame

Alienation from society is, in itself, not an indication of (violent) radicalisation; turning your back on society is. The second essential component of radicalisation proposed here is thus the adoption of a conflict frame when confronted with social differences; in contrast, the adoption of a cooperative frame signals non-radicalisation. Before pursuing this argument, it should be stated that, in a democratic society, this second essential component of radicalisation is not necessarily problematic but creates the conditions under which a third essential part of radicalisation – the use of violence – is contemplated.

The conflict frame is central to the discussion of Islamist radicalisation, especially in relation to the issue of *al-walā' wa-l-barā'*, a prescription of loyalty and love for the sake of Allah, but also renunciation, implying avoidance, disdain and hostility towards anything other than a purist interpretation of Islam (as discussed in Wagemakers 2012). In many of the interviews conducted in the course of this study, we found indications that the adoption of a conflict frame is an essential, constitutive part of the radicalisation process. The 'radical' not only experiences others within society as being different but that this engenders a competition over righteousness and legitimacy. This is experienced as a conflict over social dominance but against a stronger opponent (Obaidi et al. 2018). Despite feeling morally superior, the radical feels unjustly treated and 'wronged' by an authority they consider illegitimate. Non-radicalisation, then, consists, at least in part, in avoiding relational conflict over social dominance.

Indications of the presence of a conflict frame were reported in a number of fieldwork sites. In France, for instance, Conti (2020) records Romain remarking that, 'It's actually a war that's been going on for centuries. Between right and wrong. Between true and false ... We're all part of this war. Even you, you're part of it [we laugh] ... There's no neutral, you're either against or for'. When the interviewer asked whether there would be a winner and loser in this war, Romain replies, 'Of course. We're the winners. Here and in the afterlife, we will be the winners'. In the Netherlands, we also found indications of this frame that pits the 'us' and the 'them' against each other, emphasising the conflictual nature of intergroup relations. One of the respondents told us:

> I no longer saw the other as an equal. I saw the unbelievers as the beasts, as the enemies of Islam. They kill Muslims elsewhere. They kill Muslims in our Islamic countries. They dehumanise those other people, so that they no longer see them as human beings. That's how I started to see the unbelievers too. Not as humans anymore.

With the firm embrace of this Manichean worldview, which pits the right against the wrong and the pure against the impure, there also emerges a desire to convert others to one's own side. The same Dutch respondent shared:

> When I radicalised, I started to tell my sisters to wear headscarves. At home, I started to instruct my mother about Islamic customs, because I thought I had the truth. I thought I had really found the path of Islam and that now, yes, I was going to teach my own family. I was a brat. Wet behind the ears, and then I wanted to lecture my own mother, yes, on how Islam should actually be.

This tendency to claim to be right, while others are considered wrong, was also mentioned by a number of respondents in other countries in the study (see, e.g., Conti 2020).

In considering the factors involved in the development of conflict frames, it is worth noting the emphasis placed on cultural context – in which males feel socially compelled to assert themselves and express their dominance over others – in understanding the radicalisation journeys in the Russian milieu studied (Poliakov and Epanova 2021; see also Poliakov, this volume). Whether understood as indicative of a 'toxic masculinity culture' (Poliakov and Epanova 2021) or 'honour culture' (Hatch 1989; Nisbett and Cohen 1996), what is identified is a culture characterised by a strong separation of male and female social life, with high value placed on female chastity alongside pressure on males to defend the honour of the family and the tribe. Here, growing up as a male means asserting oneself as a valiant defender of the honour of the family (female members in particular) or tribe as a whole. For males, it also means engaging in a struggle with any (potential) threat to family honour. The reflection of the Dutch adolescent noted above on how he, when still 'wet behind the ears', had started, nonetheless, to lecture his mother also fits this idea of toxic masculinity or honour culture.

It would be overly simplistic, however, to conclude from the foregoing observations that radicalisation is only to be analysed in terms of individual, cultural and religious characteristics. In general, we should be wary of falling into the trap of 'correspondence bias', as psychologists Gilbert and Malone (1995) call it, that is, the tendency to draw inferences about a person's (or in our discussion, a culture's or religion's) unique and enduring dispositions from behaviours. In the current discussion, the adoption of a conflict frame is not simply a matter of personal dispositions, or even cultural or religious dispositions, that exist and can be studied in isolation from the relationship with individuals and groups outside one's community. In understanding the dynamics of the adoption or rejection of a conflict frame, or more broadly of radicalisation or non-radicalisation, it is crucial to take relationships into account (Malthaner 2017; della Porta 2018)

Across the fieldwork sites, there were reports of grievance regarding the way Muslims are treated and especially the way in which counter-terrorism and counter-radicalisation contribute to further rift and relational conflict. In the Netherlands, it is notable how often the term 'cat-and-mouse game' is used by respondents to describe the relationship between themselves and security agencies. However, the label 'game' appears to be applied euphemistically; a strong sense of persecution, deemed to warrant a response, is evident. Sakellariou (2021: 28), for instance, recounts how after Evgenia left the Orthodox church and converted to Islam, relatives and family members had started to refer to her as 'Turkosporos' (of Turkish origin, a particularly insulting remark in Greece) and a jihadist. Based on her personal experience, she told the researcher, she understood why Muslims joined extremist groups and expressed her belief that followers of Islam are being persecuted and that the West is responsible for both the immigrant waves coming into Europe and violent reactions by Muslims.

While it is impossible to do justice here to the multitude of examples of ways in which responses towards Muslims contribute to a conflictual relationship, the views of Osman from Norway are indicative (see Vestel and Ali 2021). Osman highlights the role of politicians in creating an atmosphere of conflict:

> The thing is that they place so much focus, indirectly, on Islamic elements ... I feel that it's a problem because people can't be themselves. People are slowly but surely attacking Islam. Because they're not talking about prohibiting the kippa, they're not talking about forbidding the turban. Usually it's about hijabs in the police, hijabs for children. And again, it's the media playing on that and the politicians fall into the trap. I feel that this is negative too because it will lead to

people saying: 'You know what? We don't want to have you here in this country'.

Reports of security surveillance and counter-terrorism operations that have contributed to distrust, and the adoption of a conflict mind-set, can be found in reports from the UK to Turkey, from Norway to Tunisia, indeed in all reports. Summarising the experience of many across Europe, Benaïssa (2021: 17) notes the reflections of a Belgian psychologist working in the area of Molenbeek on the profound impact of the 'targeting and the global labelling of this district' on its population, an impact he describes as 'traumatic'.

Taken as a whole, these responses towards Muslims in societies throughout Europe contribute to a sense of 'us' versus 'them' and the idea that us and them are involved in a fight until the bitter end. For many, the words of George Bush in September 2001 that 'you are with us or with the terrorists' still resonate and have contributed to distrust in Western democracy. Many of the respondents are caught in a spiral of fear whereby the treatment of Muslims with suspicion by outspoken politicians, the media, security agencies and the general public means that Muslims feel threatened and suspicious of institutional actors, from whom they expect unjust treatment. Moreover, as described by Pilkington and Vestel (2021), 'anti-Islamist' actors use their own narratives and imaginary to convince themselves, and attempt to convince others, of the existential threat that comes with Islamic presence in Europe. Islamists, meanwhile, have their own narratives that they are the ones who are being persecuted, not just in Europe but around the world, and are at risk of extinction. Moreover, materials including videos that evidence this are circulated, as Belgian respondent Primo describes:

> And so when I see these videos, I am shocked … They arrived in a mosque, because Bashar Al Assad's soldiers were helped by the Iranians … this video on YouTube is called 'more than fifty-one dead children in a mosque', the first image I see, a *padre*, a father, *meskin* [poor guy], he takes a girl and says 'O country of Arabs! Is this little girl old enough to die?' And you see the girl, her teeth, her jaw completely ripped off, and a little boy who had his whole top part removed and you see his brain exposed … *Wallah*, the kid was four years old.

In this way, radicalisation consists in part of being absorbed into a culture of fear (Dechesne 2015; see also Hobfoll 2018) where particular anxiety-provoking events contribute to a state of fear of the other and heightened vigilance of threats coming from the other. This survival mechanism promotes an excessive focus on such threats while being oblivious to anything other than the threatening situation and the threatening others. Especially in the case of two parties being caught up in this spiral of fear, the risk of perpetuation and escalation of conflict is significant.

Non-radicalisation, it follows, consists partly of staying out of this spiral of fear and conflict. The above-mentioned factors of self-control, social connection and embedding and religious knowledge are likely to contribute to the ability to do so. There are, however, additional indicators involved in non-radicalisation. For one, in some cases there is an honour culture that promotes conflict, but in other cases there have also been indications of a culture of cooperation that diminishes conflict. In the UK, for instance, respondent Abu Abdullah mentioned the positive role that a mosque had played in coping with the devastating fire at Grenfell Tower:

> I mean after Grenfell, it's helped change people's perceptions – some people's perceptions. It's all about that contact. A mosque needs to have that contact and the contact comes through the people. So, the Prophet's biggest form of like call to Islam and stuff like that, was that one to one, that physical contact sort of thing. It's not by killing and stuff like that. So, the Prophet established that. And as Muslims, they say about two, three million Muslims live in the UK. If, for example, every Muslim spoke to every person that he met, within a month you would reach all seventy million people that live in the UK on a conversational basis. But, a lot of people give a bad perception of Islam, or a bad image. First impressions count man. A lot of Muslims are not holding up what Islam teaches them.

The perceived importance of establishing positive contact was also documented in other conversations, for instance in the Netherlands where one respondent told us about his way out of hatred, when a serious illness led to his hospitalisation and his treatment caused him to almost faint due to the pain. At that moment, a female surgeon had comforted him and he recounts how:

> I felt the tears running down my cheeks. It was the first moment that I realised what that ideology meant, and that I could kill her and her colleagues too. Because they are unbelievers. See what happened in Paris, see what happened in Nice. The people who were murdered there ... among them, there may actually have been the surgeon who could have saved you some day, or the trainer who would have trained your children, or the community policeman who would have been there to help you and to bring you to the hospital and to try to keep you on the right track. That's what I realised for the first time, at that moment.

The same respondent subsequently wrote to the mayor of his hometown and, after a receptive response, the respondent became involved in ef-

forts to raise awareness of the impact of jihadism, which reached thousands of young people.

In these stories of non-radicalisation, we find opposite tendencies to
those identified in the stories of radicalisation insofar as they pertain to
the factors involved in adopting a conflict frame. In particular, where
a culture of honour contributes to the adoption of a conflict frame, a
culture of cooperation (as for instance in the case of the community
activities of the mosque following the Grenfell Tower fire) contributes to
non-radicalisation. Secondly, where repression is thought to contribute
to, and exacerbate, conflict framing, an inclusive response (for instance
by a mayor) can contribute to non-radicalisation. Thirdly, where a culture of fear contributes to further escalation of conflict, a sense of trust
(as for instance suddenly found in the relationship between surgeon and
patient) contributes to non-radicalisation.

Non-Violence versus Violence

The discussion above of the social and psychological aspects that contribute to the adoption or rejection of an extremist mind-set should not
imply that such a mind-set necessarily leads to actual engagement in
violence. For this aspect of radicalisation or non-radicalisation, that is,
the actual engagement in violence or disengagement from it, to manifest,
several situational factors need to be taken into account.

The proximity of an actual major conflict area is a very important factor in this. The ethnographic report on Turkey addresses involvement in
violence in a much more direct way than, for instance, the Norwegian
report where, for many, the idea of a global struggle does not translate
into actual violent engagement. In many European countries, the outflow
of young Muslims to the conflict areas of the Middle East has been a trag-
edy for all involved, and the numbers have been significant. However, it
is very important to continue to reiterate that only a minute fraction of
young Muslims have affinity with the jihadist cause. The situation is very
different in Southern Turkey at the time of the war in Syria. Involvement
in conflict zones makes one more likely to engage in violence because of
necessity and the availability of weapons.

Across the fieldwork sites, we found a parallel situation (although of
much less omnipresence) for those involved in criminal milieus. Many
of the respondents had been involved in criminal activities and through
these activities had developed weapons skills. To illustrate, Benaïssa
(2021: 24), who conducted field research in Belgium, describes the story
of Primo:

His early socialisation into violence, delinquency and then robbery, and finally into the prison world, and later his confrontation with the traumatic experience of death, that of his childhood friends but also that of his little brother, can be cited among the deep causes of his entry into extremist political violence. Not to mention the fact that robberies and hold-ups project him into a world where the initiation to the handling of weapons becomes an obligatory passage, as attested to by the exchange I have with him about the entry into prison of one of his childhood friends who, with other acolytes, had robbed the town police station to recover uniforms, computers and, for one of them, a handgun.

In Russia, the ethnographers mention the story of Omar who says that, in Dagestan, 'it's cool to be bad among young people, fuelling crime gangs and a cult against the police'. According to Omar, there is a clear connection with Islamist radicalism, as 'the same bad guys', as he calls them, find 'in' or, more accurately, 'around' Islam a similar way of mobilising against the police and 'for war'. But engaging in violence out of self-interest or out of jihadist involvement are not the same. The violence perpetrated for a jihadist cause has a moral quality that criminal engagement lacks. For instance, the Belgian respondent Primo (quoted above) shares that:

> I stole all the time, I only worked a little, otherwise I stole all the time, I wasted it on the *haram* [illicit] – discos, casino, trips. I said to myself that this is not life, I found myself many times saying to myself, 'Imagine dying in this condition...'. And then you end up being convinced and you say to yourself that those who are against jihad, who are Muslims, because there are many of them, we hear them speak on television and so on, they don't have as many arguments as those who are for jihad and who have arguments, they have hadiths, the Qur'an and so on.

In this sense, the actual use of violence for the Islamist cause is to a certain extent a matter of the necessity to use violence (in war zones) or having experience with the use of weapons (in criminal milieus) but also the moral justification for the use of violence. The arguments provided by the jihadists, that there is a global struggle between the right and the wrong, and that Muslims worldwide are under threat, propels many young people towards the conviction that it is justified to pick up arms, even though the fighting itself may not be particularly appealing to the higher side of human endeavour. This is explained by the following Dutch respondent:

> It is war. But, we can't play it holy. America doesn't either. Performing executions. For example, the Kurds in Iraq, the court in Iraq,

where the young people are now being convicted for what they have committed in Syria, they are all being murdered. Hung. Yes, that's bad too. We cannot say this is less bad and this is more bad. Do you understand? Both are bad.

At the same time there are respondents, falling into the category of 'non-radicals', who are quite vocal in disconnecting their religion from violence. As Greek respondent Pavlos summarises it:

From all these [i.e. the teachings of Islam] it is easy for someone to see Islam's position on terrorism. Terrorism is a form of hostility during which innocent people are targeted in order to frighten the population. As a consequence, Islam's position on terrorism is related to the Islamic position on hostile acts. It is clear from the above that, even during war time, it is not permissible for Muslims to target civilians. ... Murdering innocent people is a crime, even during war. Whoever intentionally murders innocent people is a criminal and should be punished for his crime. Terrorism is absolutely forbidden in Islam.

Considering the difference between those who engage in violence and those who do not, we find a difference, first, in access, or lack thereof, to conflict zones or criminal networks, providing experience with the use of weapons. Secondly, we identify a difference in the moral justification for the use of violence. Violence tends to be considered justified when it is carried out in defence of a cherished value or identity. Very rarely do people condone violence that is used to attack without a prior provocation.

Conclusion

On the basis of the study of the ten Islamist milieus reported on here, we have been able to identify a number of factors that allow us to differentiate between the lifeworlds of those moving into violent extremism and those resisting it. Table 1.1 provides an overview of the analysed elements of radicalisation and the factors that we have identified as contributing to non-radicalisation or radicalisation.

In our analysis, we have encountered variables that have been identified previously in Cragin's (2014) model. Like Cragin, we see social access, moral repugnance and considerations of costs and benefits as playing a role in radicalisation. However, whereas Cragin envisages radicalisation and non-radicalisation as a singular, planned behaviour (indeed, her model seems to fit well with Azjen's (1991) theory of planned behaviour), our, albeit preliminary, 'milieu' analysis stresses rather the

Table 1.1. Overview of factors contributing to non-radicalisation or radicalisation.

Elements of Radicalisation	Non-radicalisation	Radicalisation
Societal participation versus non-participation	Self-control	Lack of control
	Social connection	Isolation
	Religious education	Religious 'bricolage'
Cooperation versus conflict	Culture of cooperation	Honour culture
	Inclusive society	Repression
	Sense of trust	Culture of fear
Non-violence versus violence	Societal stability	Presence violence/ crime
	No access to radical networks	Access to radical networks
	No justification for violence	Moral justification for violence

dynamic and interactive nature that creates a quite different perspective on radicalisation.

In closing, two points warrant reiteration. First, the hallmark characteristic of the milieu approach is its focus on localised dynamism. Non-radicalisation and radicalisation, from this perspective, are inherently relational phenomena that are assumed to emerge from social interactions that take place on multiple levels (see also della Porta 2018). As such, the milieu perspective avoids a correspondence bias (discussed above) that seems inherent to many of the current 'security' perspectives on radicalisation and non-radicalisation. Secondly, as alluded to in the introduction, avoiding this correspondence bias is especially important when implementing programmes to prevent and counter violent extremism. Rather than suggesting that radicalisation is a problem that is owned by 'them', the present approach comes with the potential of a shift to a more positive approach, highlighting the potential of any milieu to create an environment and find answers to challenges in a constructive and sustainable way.

Acknowledgements

The research drawn on in this chapter is part of the Dialogue about Radicalisation and Equality (DARE) project, which received funding from the European Union's Horizon 2020 research and innovation programme under Grant Agreement No. 725349. It reflects only the views of the author; the European Commission and Research Executive Agency are not responsible for any information it contains.

Mark Dechesne is Associate Professor at the Dual PhD Centre of Leiden University – Faculty of Governance and Global Affairs. Trained as an experimental social psychologist, he has always had an interest in the psychological and societal impact of 'terror' experiences. In the DARE project, Mark Dechesne was the coordinator of the Dutch national team and the project lead for the study of Islamist radicalisation.

NOTE

1.   Where names are attached to respondent statements, these employ pseudonyms to preserve anonymity.

REFERENCES

Abbas, Tahir. 2019. 'Implementing "Prevent" in Countering Violent Extremism in the UK: A Left-Realist Critique', *Critical Social Policy* 39(3): 396–412.

Ajzen, Icek. 1991. 'The Theory of Planned Behavior', *Organizational Behavior and Human Decision Processes* 50(2): 179–211.

Benaïssa, Chaïb. 2021. *Radicalisation from the 'Poor Crescent' Area*. DARE Research Report. Retrieved 28 August 2022 from https://documents.manchester.ac.uk/display.aspx?DocID=58681.

Conti, Bartolomeo. 2020. *Trajectories of (Non)Radicalisation in a Prison Milieu*. DARE Research Report. Retrieved 28 August 2022 from https://documents.manchester.ac.uk/display.aspx?DocID=58683.

Cragin, Kim. 2014. 'Resisting Violent Extremism: A Conceptual Model for Non-Radicalization', *Terrorism and Political Violence* 26(2): 337–53.

Dechesne, Mark. 2015. 'Radicalization and Mass Violence from a Beckerian Perspective: Conceptual and Empirical Considerations', *Journal for Deradicalization* 3(2): 149–77.

———. 2021. *Young People's Trajectories through Radical Islamist Milieus: Cross-National Synthesis Report*. DARE Research Report. Retrieved 28 August 2022 from https://documents.manchester.ac.uk/display.aspx?DocID=58677.

Dechesne, Mark, and Ineke Van der Valk. 2021. *Islamist Radicalisation in the Netherlands*. DARE Research Report. Retrieved 28 August 2022 from https://documents.manchester.ac.uk/display.aspx?DocID=58688.

della Porta, Donatella. 2018. 'Radicalization: A Relational Perspective', *Annual Review of Political Science* 21(1): 461–74.

della Porta, Donatella, and Mario Diani (eds). 2015. *The Oxford Handbook of Social Movements*. Oxford: Oxford University Press.

Erikson, Erik. 1968. *Identity, Youth and Crisis*. New York: Norton.

Gilbert, Daniel, and Patrick Malone. 1995. 'The Correspondence Bias', *Psychological Bulletin* 117(1): 21–38.

Hatch, Elvin. 1989. 'Theories of Social Honor', *American Anthropologist* 91(2): 341–53.

Hobfoll, Stevan. 2012. 'Conservation of Resources and Disaster in Cultural Context: The Caravans and Passageways for Resources', *Psychiatry* 75(3): 227–32.

———. 2018. *Tribalism: The Evolutionary Origins of Fear Politics*. Cham: Palgrave Macmillan.

Hussain, Ajmal. 2021. *'Muslim Street'* DARE Research Report. Retrieved 28 August 2022 from https://documents.manchester.ac.uk/display.aspx?DocID=58692.

Khosrokhavar, Farhad. 2021. *Jihadism in Europe: European Youth and the New Caliphate*. New York, NY: Oxford University Press.

Kundnani, Arun. 2012. 'Radicalisation: The Journey of a Concept', *Race & Class* 54(2): 3–25.

Kurt, Mehmet. 2020. *When the Salt Stinks: The Syrian War, Kurdish Question and Borderline Radicalisation in Turkey*. DARE Research Report. Retrieved 28 August 2022 from https://documents.manchester.ac.uk/display.aspx?DocID=58691.

Malthaner, Stefan. 2017. 'Radicalization: The Evolution of an Analytical Paradigm', *European Journal of Sociology* 58(3): 369–401.

McCauley, Clark, and Sophia Moskalenko. 2017. 'Understanding Political Radicalization: The Two-Pyramids Model', *American Psychologist* 72(3): 205–16.

Memni, Chokri. 2021. *Young People's Trajectories through Radical Islamist Milieus: Tunis (Tadhamon), Bizerte, Menzel-Bourguiba*. DARE Research Report [Unpublished report].

Moghaddam, Fathali. 2005. 'The Staircase to Terrorism', *American Psychologist* 60(2): 161–69.

Nanni, Sara. 2021. *Neustadt and Beyond*. DARE Research Report. Retrieved 28 August 2022 from https://documents.manchester.ac.uk/display.aspx?DocID=58684.

Nisbett, Richard, and Dov Cohen. 1996. *Culture of Honor: The Psychology of Violence in the South*. Boulder, CO: Westview Press.

Obaidi, M., et al. 2018. 'The Mistreatment of My People: Victimization by Proxy and Behavioral Intentions to Commit Violence among Muslims in Denmark', *Political Psychology* 39(3): 577–93.

Pilkington, Hilary, and Viggo Vestel. 2021. *Young People's Trajectories through Anti-Islam(ist) and Extreme Right Milieus: Cross-National Synthesis Report.* DARE Research Report. Retrieved 28 August 2022 from https://documents.manchester.ac.uk/display.aspx?DocID=58676.

Poliakov, Sviatoslav, and Yulia Epanova. 2021. *Urban Second Generation Muslims from the North Caucasus in St Petersburg and Moscow, Russia.* DARE Research Report. Retrieved 28 August 2022 from https://documents.manchester.ac.uk/display.aspx?DocID=58690.

Ragazzi, Francesco. 2017. 'Countering Terrorism and Radicalisation: Securitising Social Policy?', *Critical Social Policy* 37(2): 163–79.

Sakellariou, Alexandros. 2021. *Young Muslims in Unofficial Prayer Places of Athens.* DARE Research Report. Retrieved 28 August 2022 from https://documents.manchester.ac.uk/display.aspx?DocID=58686.

Sarma, Kiran. 2017. 'Risk Assessment and the Prevention of Radicalization from Nonviolence into Terrorism', *American Psychologist* 72(3): 278–88.

Schuurman, Bart. 2020. 'Non-Involvement in Terrorist Violence: Understanding the Most Common Outcome of Radicalization Processes', *Perspectives on Terrorism* 14(6): 14–26.

Shainin, J. 2006. 'The Ziggurat of Zealotry', *New York Times*, 10 December. Retrieved 25 March 2022 from https://www.nytimes.com/2006/12/10/magazine/10section4.t-11.html.

Sprinzak, Ehud. 1991. 'The Process of Delegitimation: Towards a Linkage Theory of Political Terrorism', *Terrorism and Political Violence* 3(1): 50–68.

Stanley, Tony, Surinder Guru and Anna Gupta. 2018. 'Working with PREVENT: Social Work Options for Cases of "Radicalisation Risk"', *Practice: Social Work in Action* 30(2): 131–46.

van Zomeren, Martijn, Tom Postmes and Russel Spears. 2008. 'Toward an Integrative Social Identity Model of Collective Action', *Psychological Bulletin* 134(4): 504–35.

Vestel, Viggo, and Qasim Ali. 2021. *Globalisation, Identity and Islam: The Case of Radical Muslim Youths in Norway.* DARE Research Report. Retrieved 28 August 2022 from https://documents.manchester.ac.uk/display.aspx?DocID=58689.

Wagemakers, Joas. 2012. 'The Enduring Legacy of the Second Saudi State: Quietist and Radical Wahhabi Contestations of Al-walā' wa-l-barā'', *International Journal of Middle East Studies* (1): 93–110.

Wiktorowicz, Quintan. 2004. *Islamic Activism: A Social Movement Theory Approach.* Bloomington: Indiana University Press.

Yang, Yun-Yen, and Shih-Wei Wu. 2020. 'Base Rate Neglect and Neural Computations for Subjective Weight in Decision under Uncertainty', *Proceedings of the National Academy of Sciences* 117(29): 16908–19.

CHAPTER 2

Situating Trajectories of 'Extreme-Right' (Non)Radicalisation
The Role of the Radical Milieu

Hilary Pilkington and Viggo Vestel

Introduction

In light of the critical approach to the concept of radicalisation outlined in the Introduction to this volume, in this chapter we employ the notion of trajectories through 'extreme-right' milieus to explore the complexity, diversity and evolving nature of young people's engagement with radical(ising) forces, messages and agents. The milieu approach firmly roots individual trajectories in their social context by envisaging milieus (and the social networks and communication channels they host) as 'micromobilization-settings' (Malthaner 2017a: 376). This is not to suggest that wider structural factors are not important; the role of grievances that arise from social structural factors, and are instrumentalised by extremist movements and influencers, are central to shaping young people's ideas and actions. However, we find no direct and consistent relationship between structural condition and violent extremism response (see Franc, Poli and Pavlović, this volume) but a dynamic process in which a range of individual, movement and institutional interactions are critical in shaping outcomes. In this sense, 'structure becomes a structure of relations' (Alimi, Bosi and Demetriou 2012: 8). Thus, in line with recent 'ecological' approaches (see Dawson 2017: 3; Bouhana 2019), we understand turns to extremism as the result of the intersection of people and context whose study, therefore, must integrate the role of social structural factors, the search for ontological security or 'significance' that such conditions evoke and the role of extremist narratives to which people are exposed (Dawson 2017: 3).

While recognising the importance of social and spatial environments of radical milieus in themselves (Malthaner and Waldmann 2014; Malthaner 2017a: 389), our primary concern is with *individual trajectories* through those milieus. Our focus on young people means we are not able to capture the whole 'career' (see Fillieule 2010: 11) of activists in radical milieus, but through ethnographic research that follows individuals moving in radical(ising) milieus over an extended period of time, we can provide insight, in particular, into two factors shaping those trajectories. This relates, first, to the reflexive capacity and agency of young people in shaping their own pathways. This agency is observable in how they understand the world around them, how they interpret their experiences in it, the decisions they take about becoming active in voicing or acting upon grievances they hold and their choices at critical moments about the directions their pathways take. Secondly, the approach taken captures how participation in radical milieus sits within the broader, largely 'normal', lives of young research participants who simultaneously engage in multiple groups, which may intersect through 'communication interlocks' (Fine and Kleinman 1979: 10) or which may collide, leading to conflict with, or exclusion from, former circles or relationships. These factors – agency (often expressed as the will to 'do something') and social connectedness – we argue, are crucial factors in bringing young people into radical milieus but also in shaping their trajectory through them towards outcomes of partial, stalled or non-radicalisation.

Context and Agency in (Non)Radicalisation Trajectories: Theoretical Starting Points

The theoretical framework employed to illuminate the findings from this empirical study starts from the premise that radicalisation is a process that is non-linear, complex and situational. It builds on four main interventions in the literature to date: the turn to the study of 'routes' (trajectories) rather than 'roots' of radicalisation; the importance of situating those trajectories in context (milieus) and the interactions that take place therein; the recognition that outcomes of these journeys can be non-radicalisation as well as radicalisation; and the suggestion that these outcomes are shaped by the choices young people make (agency) and carry a strongly affective dimension.

In efforts to understand the relative importance of, and relationship between, societal, group and individual drivers of extremism, John Horgan's (2008) call to move away from a search for 'profiles' of terrorists (focusing on 'root' causes) to pathways (or 'routes') to violent extremism has been pivotal. It allows a switch of focus to the study of the process of radicalisation itself (the 'how?'), to individual journeys (rather than patterns in socio-demographic or psychological variables shared by individuals) and to the meaning, for the individual, of engagement with that process (ibid.: 92). Notwithstanding the significance of Horgan's intervention, the retention of focus on case histories of terrorists has led to the characterisation of radicalisation pathways as the progression of individuals through 'incrementally experienced stages' (ibid.). While Horgan sees disengagement also as a potential phase in this pathway, his model does not capture the more fluid and multi-directional movements to and from milieus identified in our studies where individuals participate in radical milieus but, in most cases, have not crossed the threshold into violent extremism. Nor does it capture the potential for others, including organisations and movements, within that milieu to act not only to socialise individuals towards violent extremism, but also constrain their radicalisation or encourage a movement away from extremism.

While following Horgan's call to focus on pathways not profiles, therefore, this study traces trajectories not to violent extremism but *through radical(ising) milieus*. Here we draw in particular on the work of Malthaner (2017a, 2017b) and Malthaner and Waldmann (2014) in understanding a radical milieu as an evolving relational and emotional field of activity through which collective identities and solidarities are constructed (Malthaner and Waldmann 2014: 983). These radical milieus, and the networks that constitute them, link individual trajectories to social context by acting as 'micromobilization-settings' (Malthaner 2017a: 376). They can be religious, ethnic or political (or a combination of these) and form the supportive and sustaining social 'environments' in which 'grievance' narratives and 'stigmatised' knowledge are disseminated and from within which those engaged in violent activity can gain affirmation for their actions (Malthaner 2017a: 389).

However, radical milieus are not simply 'hotbeds' of radicalisation but social environments in which individuals can also criticise, challenge or confront the messages encountered there (Malthaner and Waldmann 2014: 994). This understanding of the milieu, as not only inciting and escalating violence but potentially inhibiting and constraining it, underpins the design of the study we draw on here, which is interested in individuals' trajectories through milieus, their encounters with radical(ising) forces, agents and messages and how they respond to them. This means that we anticipate, and seek to understand, a range of outcomes of these journeys. Understanding why individuals do not become involved in political violence is reflected in the work of Cragin (2014), who sets out a conceptual model of non-radicalisation and tests it through an empirical study (on the West Bank of Palestine) designed to explain why some people remain non-radicalised in such violence-laden contexts (Cragin et al. 2015). More recently, Schuurman (2020: 16) has pointed also to the need to investigate what might explain non-involvement in terrorist violence by disaggregating multiple possible outcomes of radicalisation rather than drawing conclusions about what propels people towards terrorism by studying the pathways of only those who end up committing terrorist acts. Cragin (2014: 342) identifies various factors whose presence or absence may encourage or discourage individuals from joining violent extremist causes and conceptualises non-radicalisation as 'resistance to violent extremism'. In contrast, our study is concerned with the process of encounter and response of young people to radical(ising) forces, agents and messages in the milieus in which they engage and aims to capture some of the complexity of (non)radicalisation trajectories and work towards conceptualising the role of situation, interaction, affect and agency in shaping those pathways.

Recent developments in situational and interactional approaches to understanding radicalisation have brought significant new insight to the field and are explored in more detail in the chapters by Pilkington and Kerst in this volume. In this chapter, we use the narratives of actors in nine radical milieus, rather, to provide an overview of what drives trajectories towards extremism, drawing attention to the importance of the affective dimension of ostensibly ideological drivers (grievances) towards extremism. We also seek to redress the tendency in the study of 'extreme-right' activism and radicalisation literature to adopt a largely instrumental view of agency, which envisages radicalisation as something 'done to' an individual (Pilkington 2016: 3, 8; McDonald 2018: 10).[1] In so doing, we recognise the risk of over-privileging the actor's interpretation of their own pathway, by giving too much weight, for example, to a life-changing moment, which an individual may deploy to narrate their journey but may be no more significant than structural factors that often go unarticulated. We are also cautious about taking at face value assertions of actors that 'I've always made my own choices' (Sieckelinck et al. 2019: 669). Rather, we use an ethnographic method to approach radicalisation as an embodied communicative practice (McDonald 2018: 189–90) that takes different forms, produces different kinds of affect and does not exist discretely in ideologically, or communicatively, exclusive groups but is diffused through 'communication interlocks' (Fine and Kleinman 1979: 10). By this we mean that ostensibly discrete milieus – of the 'radicalised' and 'non-radicalised' – may be connected through shared communicative practices (xenophobic and racist talk, 'standing up for oneself' through fighting and violence), developed while growing up in the same neighbourhood, attending the same schools or sharing social spaces (Pilkington 2014: 24–26), and are not exclusive or exclusively ideological. Individuals often participate in several groups simultaneously and maintain acquaintance relationships outside their main communication group requiring conformity to different norms in different situations (Fillieule 2010: 4). This would lead us to expect not only trajectories of both radicalisation and partial, stalled and non-radicalisation to co-exist within any radical milieu but also for individual pathways to combine radical and non-radical elements.

Method and Milieus

In this chapter, we draw on the synthesis of research findings from the study of 'extreme-right' milieus in nine countries – France, Germany, Greece, Malta, Poland, Norway, Russia, the Netherlands and the UK.

Introducing the Milieus

Our conceptual understanding of 'milieu' was outlined in the previous section and was operationalised for the selection of cases by understanding it as the people, the physical and the social conditions and events and networks and communications in which someone acts or lives and which shape that person's subjectivity, choices and trajectory through life. An eligible milieu was thus not necessarily territorially fixed or even physically manifest; it was anticipated that milieus would likely have both online and offline forms. However, to constitute a milieu, there should be an evident connection (human, material, communicative, ideological) between individuals interviewed and observations conducted. An appropriate milieu for selection should also be a space of encounter with radical or extreme messages (via the presence in the milieu of recruiters, high receptivity to radical messages and so on) and these should be of an 'extreme-right' or 'anti-Islamist' character.

What is meant by these terms requires some contextualisation in the academic literature on what constitutes 'right-wing extremism'. In a review of the literature, Mudde (2000: 11) identifies twenty-six different definitions of the phenomenon including fifty-eight characteristics, of which only five were mentioned by at least half the authors. Among attempts to bring taxonomic clarification and systematisation to the field, Mudde (2007: 25) distinguishes between 'populist radical right' parties and movements that are nominally democratic (although oppose some fundamental values of liberal democracy) whilst upholding a core ideology combining nativism, authoritarianism and populism and movements of the 'extreme right', which are inherently anti-democratic (ibid.: 31). Carter's (2018) 'minimal' definition of 'right-wing extremism' also positions it as an ideology that encompasses authoritarianism, anti-democracy and exclusionary and/or holistic nationalism. Bjørgo and Ravndal (2019: 3) maintain a distinction between 'radical' and 'extreme' right actors whilst seeing both the radical right and the extreme right as sub-sets of the broader 'far right'. They distinguish between three types of 'nationalism' – cultural (primarily anti-Muslim and concerned with so-called Islamisation of western societies), ethnic (often expressing itself through anti-immigration attitudes and critiques of multiculturalism) and racial (expressed through white supremacism, antisemitism and 'white genocide') – and view radical right movements as embracing cultural and ethnic nationalism while extreme-right movements deploy ideologies of racial and ethnic nationalism (ibid.). Thus, it seems there is agreement within academic discourse that both right-wing radicals and right-wing extremists are characterised by ideologies incorporating some form of exclusionary nationalism and intolerance (especially, although not exclusively, in relation to ethnicity, race and religion), but that right-wing extremism differs from right-wing radicalism in its opposition to democracy and legitimation of violence as well as a higher degree of cognitive 'closedness' demonstrated in characteristics such as in-group preference, dogmatism and intolerance of ambiguity (on the latter, see Schmid 2013: 9–10).

Based on these categorisations, the milieus studied in the DARE project generally fall within the 'radical'- as opposed to the 'extreme'-right camp due to the support for democratic governance among the majority of those participating in the study. However, mapping these broad characteristics onto the current ideological spectrum and organisational actors across Europe is not straightforward. Movements, still more the looser milieus that are the object of the current study, are characterised by significant internal differentiation; individuals may belong to a range of movements (or none) and subscribe to a wide range of views, often consciously assembling their own distinct way of seeing the world, critical of established positions both inside and outside the milieu. Moreover, these etic descriptors are rarely used by actors themselves, more often being consciously rejected.

At the stage of selection of milieus for study, therefore, explicit differentiation between 'radical' and 'extreme' right was not deployed. Rather, the umbrella term 'extreme right' was understood broadly as a political ideology characterised by opposition to democracy, racial, ethnic or cul-

MALTA:
Supporters of extreme-right ideas and movements embracing nostalgic representations of the Maltese nation.

FRANCE:
Corsican nationalist movements, inspired by the French 'new right'.

GERMANY: Participants in Marksmen's clubs associated with mainstreaming authoritarian populist, right-wing and racist attitudes.

NORWAY:
Activists in a range of radical anti-Islamist & nationalist movements (including identitarians, neo-Nazis and 'national conservatives').

Activists in nationalist/ radical/ extreme right or 'new right' movements

Non-political interest groups with strong ideological connection to nationalist, radical/extreme-right movements and ideologies

GREECE:
Islamophobic/anti-Muslim attitudes among youth associated with the Greek Orthodox Church.

NETHERLANDS:
Those identifying with the 'new right' (including alt-right, alt-light and identitarian movements).

UK:
Activists in a broad range of movements routinely referred to as 'extreme right' or 'far right'.

RUSSIA: Young (neo) Cossacks in St Petersburg.

POLAND: Radical football fans linked to nationalist ideological expression and violence.

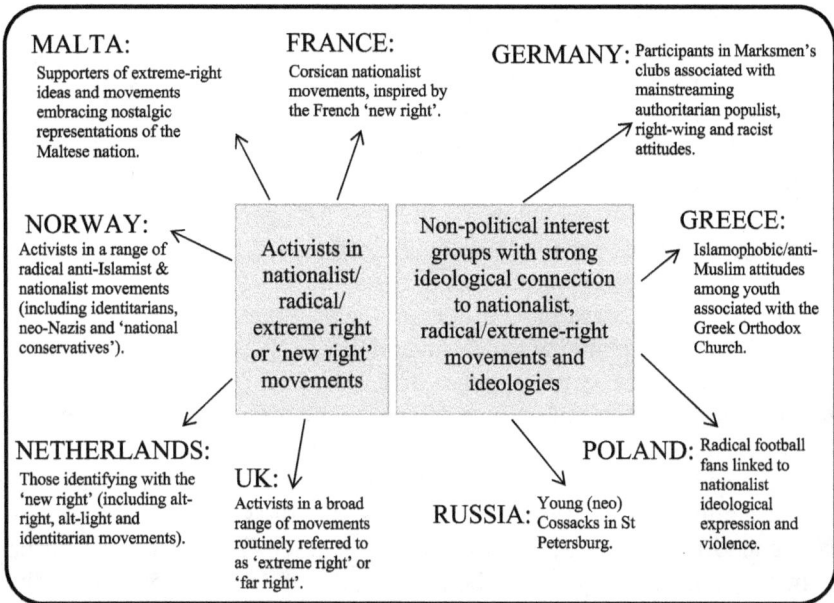

Figure 2.1. Overview of 'extreme-right' milieus studied. Created by Hilary Pilkington.

tural racism and/or antisemitism while 'anti-Islamism' was understood as active opposition to what its proponents refer to as 'radical Islam' or the 'Islamification' of western societies but that often includes a general antipathy towards Islam or all Muslims and is thus often characterised by Islamophobia or cultural racism. Anticipating the high degree of dissonance between how movements and ideologies are described exogenously and endogenously, it was not a requirement that participants in selected milieus thought of the milieu as 'extreme-right' or Islamophobic; if the milieu, movements or participants in them were considered as such in public discourse, then it was considered a potential site of study.

While no formal criterion for 'clustering' of cases was employed, a constant process of discussion of cases being considered for selection ensured that all cases had some point of connection with other cases. Two clusters of cases emerged: those where the milieu consists of activists in nationalist, radical or extreme-right or 'new right' movements (France, Malta, Norway, Netherlands, UK); and those where the milieu is focused around a non-political interest (e.g. football, shooting or religion) but there are strong ideological connections between this milieu and nationalist, radical or extreme-right movements and ideologies (Germany, Greece, Poland, Russia) (see Figure 2.1).

Post-hoc analysis of views and behaviours confirmed the anticipated heterogeneity within and across milieus. Some milieus, for example, include actors who hold strong antisemitic views as well as those with pro-Israeli views, while others include those with pro-authoritarian or anti-democratic views and political strategies alongside those who consistently oppose violence or other non-democratic forms of achieving one's aims. This diversity is explored within each milieu in the country-level reports (see Appendix for details). Below, we identify five ideological frameworks referenced across the milieus and in accordance with which, or against which, individuals articulate their personal positions.

The first is associated with classic national socialist, neo-Nazi or fascist organisations represented in our milieus by the Nordic Resistance Movement in Norway, National Action in the UK, Golden Dawn in Greece, the National-Radical Camp (Obóz Narodowo-Radykalny or ONR) in Poland and Imperium Europa in Malta. Such movements are the most likely to espouse antisemitism. While such groups and ideas are encountered and referenced frequently across the milieus studied, most research participants in our study rejected their ideologies. Second, movements that uphold racist or white supremacist ideologies are also referenced and mainly rejected by milieu actors participating in this study. However, this is true where racism is understood as biological racism (believing someone is inferior because of their 'race'); anti-migrant and anti-Muslim sentiments are often excluded from the category of 'racist' by research participants and understood and justified on other grounds (such as cultural 'incompatibility'). Individuals within milieus may also see 'race' as a 'natural' differentiating factor and express the belief that people prefer to live with others who are racially similar rather than different to them. The most frequent reference to 'race' relates to the belief that white people are subject to racism (being discriminated against because they are white) or made to feel guilty for being so. The third type of ideological framework is identitarianism, also referred to as ethnopluralism. This ideological framework also underpins, or grew out of, what is often simply called the 'new right' (in France or the Netherlands) and underpins (although often unconsciously) more routine criticisms of globalisation or multiculturalism. Identitarian ideology is rooted in the ideas of French new right thinkers such as Alain de Benoist, which support distinct and strong identities in the face of what is seen as 'the unprecedented menace of homogenisation' wrongly imposed by the West through religious crusades, colonialism, economic and social development models and moral principles rooted in human rights (de Benoist and Champetier 2012: 28–32). To counterpose multiculturalism, European new right theory proposes ethnopluralism, which promotes the recognition of the rights and equality of all ethnic groups but also their difference and thus the desirability of their separate territorial existence. Where identitarianism itself is not supported – because it is not known or because it is viewed as too extreme – milieu actors often nevertheless reject multiculturalism – as an ideology 'forced on' people by elites who benefit from the globalising project – and support monocultures. These views are thus often linked to the rejection of liberal hegemonic elites seen to be imposing multiculturalism for their own ideological reasons and facilitating the 'Great Replacement' of the native, white European population with non-European immigrant populations. Participants in a number of milieus were members of, or had contacts with, the Generation Identity movement (see Zúquete 2018), which is a key proponent of this ideology. Although sharing much in common with identitarianism, alt-right – referring to individuals, platforms and alternative media promoting a wide range of white nationalist views but most closely associated with Richard Spencer's Alternative Right online blog and a number of widely shared memes such as Pepe the frog – is considered here as a fourth ideological framework. Its central tenet is that 'white identity' is threatened by multiculturalism and left-wing political correctness, egalitarianism and universalism. In some of the countries studied here, such as the Netherlands, there is a strong sense of a national alt-right movement distinct from (if largely imitating) American alt-right discourse. However, in other countries, alt-right is used largely to refer to American milieus and influencers. While 'white' identity is not referenced so explicitly in European identitarianism as in alt-right discourse, 'European identity' is assumed to be white European identity. Finally, milieu members mobilise a range of anti-Muslim, anti-Islam and anti-migrant ideological frameworks, which are mostly articulated as 'defensive', that is, designed to protect 'own' (European or national) culture from the threat of Islamic culture or Muslim immigrants. In some milieus studied here (e.g. the Greek, Russian and Polish milieus), Christianity or Christian identity of the country or region is a key reference point because the milieu is closely aligned with religious institutions or feels it is defending a 'national' faith (Catholicism in Poland and Malta, Orthodoxy in Greece and Russia). However, in other cases, Christianity is used more loosely as a signifier of European identity/civilisation in relation to 'Eastern' or 'Muslim' others. In other milieus (e.g. Germany, the Netherlands, the UK, France and Norway), hostility towards Islam is mainly framed as rejection of a backward, misogynistic and expansionist force that threatens European or national culture. Sometimes conspiracies of an Islamic takeover facilitated by political leaders (along the lines of the Great Replacement) are expounded. Sometimes anti-immigration and anti-Muslim views are intertwined, either because

Muslims are seen as making up most incoming refugees or migrants or because of the association of Muslim incomers with terrorism. In other cases, an end to all immigration is called for on grounds that the flows are too large to allow 'integration' and/or based on grievances over the perceived privileged treatment afforded to those arriving in the country over existing inhabitants.

By focusing the study broadly, on milieus in which young people encountered 'extreme-right' or 'anti-Islam(ist)' messages rather than individuals convicted of terrorism or hate-crime offences, we were able to select milieus with high relevance to the national or regional context and to maximise the potential for ethnographic access. However, this decision had consequences for both generalisation within the country and comparison across cases. Selected milieus were internally heterogeneous and not necessarily 'typical' of the wider national scene, especially in countries with large populations (such as the Russian Federation) or with wide-ranging and regionally differentiated extreme-right scenes (such as Germany and France). While national representativeness of the milieu studied was not an objective of the study – only national relevance – we did seek to study milieus that were sufficiently similar to one another to allow the transnational analysis of cases. The choice of a synthesis, rather than comparative, method for transnational analysis was made also in expectation that there would be significant variation between milieus and to allow differences to be accounted for, rather than excluded.

Full details of each case, including an overview of the socio-demographic characteristics of respondents and discussion of the research process (access, ethical issues, researcher positionality) can be found in the individual case study reports (see Appendix for details), while an overview of the differences between milieus with regard to degree of 'radicalism' (cognitive and behavioural) can be found in Pilkington and Vestel 2021: 17–19.

Data and Data Analysis

The data used for the transnational synthesis emanate from the nine case studies conducted by the national teams of DARE project researchers and include a total of 188 interviews with 184 research participants. The research participants were active members of the milieus selected and are referred to using pseudonyms or respondent number[2] and country code (see Table 2.1).

Most research participants were aged between eighteen and thirty years, although a small number of interviews were conducted with important milieu members outside this age range.[3] Interviews with a range of community members and professionals engaged in countering extremism

Table 2.1. Data set on 'extreme-right' milieus by case study.

	Country code	No. of interviewees	Audio/video* interviews	Field diary entries	Other materials
France	FR	17	17	32	Several hundred Facebook posts
Germany	DE	23	23	15	Approx. 50 documents (flyers, leaflets, press statements, advertisements), 230 still images (photos) and 77 short videos from fieldwork
Greece	GR	21	17	15	24 photos
Malta	MT	15	15	6	YouTube videos and forums linked to extreme-right figures. Anti-immigrant Facebook group pages
Netherlands	NL	20	24	9	Text documents
Norway	NO	13	23	4	A large number of YouTube videos created by or related to milieu actors
Poland	PL	26	17	15	Printed newsletters, photos and (limited edition) books for fans
Russia	RU	22	22	2	57 photos and 8 videos shot during fieldwork
UK	UK	21	30	61	Approx. 300 photos and short videos from fieldwork, 9 documents (flyers, manifestos, leaflets received during fieldwork
Total		184	188	159	

Note: * Five interviews were video recorded (all in the UK case), all others were audio recorded.

and promoting social cohesion were conducted in most cases also but are not included in the formal data set for analysis. The number of interviewees per case varied from thirteen to twenty-six and the number of interviews conducted ranged from fifteen to thirty. Ethnographic observation was undertaken in all case studies although the number of observations varied depending on the nature of the milieu and access to milieu events.

The data from these nine cases were analysed using an approach that adapts the classic meta-ethnographic synthesis method (see Noblit and Hare 1988; Britten et al. 2002) to allow for the synthesis of transnational qualitative empirical data (rather than published studies) (Pilkington 2018). This method, and the five research questions explored, are outlined in the Introduction to the volume (see also Pilkington and Vestel 2021). Of those, the question addressed in this chapter is: How do milieu actors recount their trajectories towards and away from extremism? As is evident from the framing of this question, we are conscious that the data we capture represent the understandings among research participants of the forces, agents and messages that propel them (and others in their milieu) along trajectories towards, and away from, extremism. In analysing the data, we therefore draw on wider findings from existing literature to critically interpret these narratives but also discern what new insight they bring to our understanding of trajectories of radicalisation, including partial, stalled or non-radicalisation.

Trajectories Towards and Away from Extremism

The synthesis of findings from the milieus studied illustrates the complex interweaving of grievances and affective and situational factors that shape individual pathways of milieu actors. McCauley and Moskalenko (2008: 417–19) distinguish between *political* and *personal* grievances in radicalisation pathways; in the case of the latter, a personal experience of victimisation moves an individual to radical action, while in the former this is a response to political trends or events. However, in practice the two are deeply intertwined (see Figure 2.2). Political grievances – here represented by three themes from the data, 'influx of difference', 'societal crisis of identity' and 'relational inequality' – motivate actors and frame what they 'stand against' and what they seek to change through their action. However, they are not purely ideological but profoundly emotionally inflected and often recounted through personal experiences of feeling angry or humiliated, being treated unfairly or inappropriately (Berger 2018: 127–31) or exposure to societal changes which appear to threaten values, ways of life and the state of 'what is'.

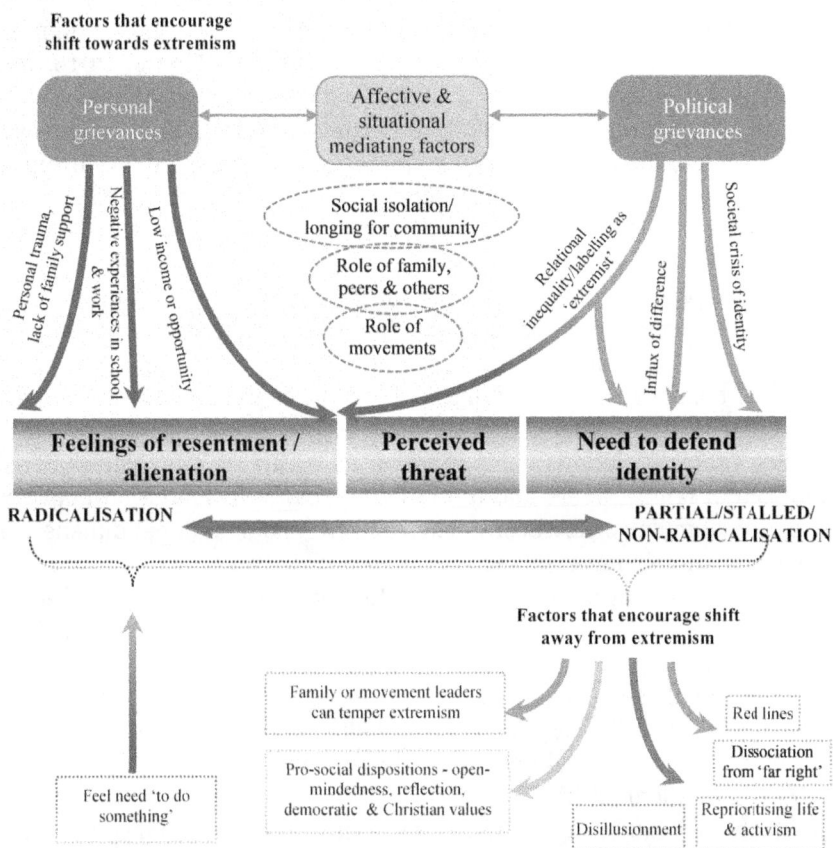

Figure 2.2. Factors encouraging shifts towards and away from extremism. Created by Hilary Pilkington.

Personal grievances – captured in Figure 2.2 as personal trauma, lack of family support, negative experiences in work or school and low income or lack of opportunity – on the other hand, are unlikely to motivate to radical action unless the personal is framed and interpreted as representative of a group grievance (McCauley and Moskalenko 2008: 419). This is in line with Honneth's (1995: 163–64) argument that collective resistance can emerge only if subjects are able to articulate the feelings of disrespect endured personally within an intersubjective framework of interpretation that captures the experience of an entire group. Thus, while for some research participants, particular events or experiences may radically shift their perspectives or motivate them to action – akin to the trajectories of 'converts' identified by Linden and Klandermans (2007) – for most, external events or personal experiences release a deeper, simmering anger or pre-existing resentment or grievance (Pilkington 2016: 76). Similarly, those who take radical action – such as joining an illegal rally or march – may well be deterred from further action if met with sanctions or repression; those who act out of personal grievance are less likely to view the costs as too high and to continue or even escalate their action (McCauley and Moskalenko 2008: 425).

The process by which personal grievances become political grievances and political grievances take on profoundly personal meaning is shaped by a range of situational or affective factors such as feelings of isolation, dislocation and frustration which, for some, contribute to a sense of collective existential insecurity and the perception of the need for radical action. These are discussed below in relation to three such factors – social isolation (and longing for community), role of movements and role of family, peers and others – in bringing research participants into radical milieus. However, these affective and situational dimensions of participation in radical milieus, it is argued, may also work to constrain engagement; family members, friends and movement leaders or influencers may temper extremism or steer individuals away from more extreme movements.

Alongside these mediating factors, research participants also talk about experiences of life developments which halt their movement or cause them to pull back from radical positions. They recount these shifts as a result of disappointment or disillusionment but also as conscious acts of agency in which they establish their own 'red lines' – thresholds they would not cross – or reprioritise the role of political activism in their lives.

Whilst emphasising the interwoven natures of these three dimensions of young people's (non)radicalisation pathways, below we present the empirical findings of the study in three sections, which consider: salient political grievances; affective and situational factors; and factors encouraging young people away from extremism. The role of personal grievances is discussed in all three sections and highlighted in two vignettes capturing the individual trajectories of Arne and Alice (see Vignette 1 and 2).

Political Grievances: Difference, Identity and Relational Inequality

The influx of difference – in beliefs, values, attitudes, culture, gender relations and ways of being – which research participants associate with the arrival and presence of immigrants and refugees, and perceive as threatening to existing culture, economies or even core civilisational values of the West, is found across almost all milieus. For respondents in France, Greece, the Netherlands, Norway and the UK, resentment and alienation is exacerbated by the belief that governments and elites support unrestrained immigration and conceal the benefits they reap from it.

> I therefore blame the government and the European Union. That is why many people hate it so much, because they have not intervened all this time and have not said, 'Okay, we are going to stop this immigration flow and we are going to sort our own people first'. ... People here also have rights. People live here and they don't want so many foreigners here. (21, NL)

This fuels a narrative in which 'they' (elites) are viewed as ignoring the experiences and difficulties faced by 'us' (Ulf, NO).

Such resentments have been mobilised by movements and parties across Europe from new mass political parties like the Alternative für Deutschland (AfD) in Germany, through pan-European youth movements such as Generation Identity to openly neo-Nazi formations such as Golden Dawn in Greece or the Nordic Resistance Movement (NRM) in Norway. For example, Gunnar (NO), who had stepped back from activism after a neo-Nazi group he had been associated with was disbanded, re-engaged in 2015 when he became aware of Generation Identity and its message that immigration in Europe would lead to so-called cultural replacement and relegation of the native population to minority status. Generation Identity's ethnopluralist claims about the uniqueness and territorial rootedness of cultures (de Benoist and Champetier 2012; Sellner 2018; Camus 2019: 76–78) is reflected in Bobby's (FR) views also: 'We're clearly being replaced, we're disappearing little by little through migration, through interbreeding'. Bobby's aim is to achieve a Corsica, France and Europe 'without Arabs' and 'without Islam' whilst arguing, likewise, that 'the Whites have nothing to do in Africa either ... each population has its own land...'. Others, like Dan (UK), talk about demographic change, including their fear that 'we are becoming a minority in our own country' whilst rejecting theories of the Great Replacement that attribute this to a plan to replace White European populations.

Muslim communities and Islam are singled out by research participants as being particularly hostile and culturally threatening. This is often referred to as a process of the 'Islamisation of Europe' (Mikaël, FR) through the (territorial) imposition of Islam in non-Islamic countries or the (cultural) transfer of values, traditions and practices related to Islam through their increasing accommodation. Respondents point to the rising proportion of the population in cities across Europe who are Muslim, which they understand as constituting a gradual 'colonisation':

> We have to understand that a lot of the Muslim population are colo-
> nising; they're not integrating with the rest of us ... they are pushing
> people out of their homes. ... Phoning the police every time they hear
> music, because it's against their culture ... so the police come and
> tell them that they're causing offence – they need to turn their music
> off. ... I believe that that is to try and push that neighbour out of that
> house, in order to have a Muslim family move in. (Cara, UK)

Islamist-inspired terror attacks also feature in respondents' narratives
as a source of grievance inflected with fear. Arina (RU) and Marlene (DE)
connect their feelings of being 'terrified' to use the metro or go out at
night with the 'flow of people' arriving in their cities and reported terrorist attacks. Billy (UK) believes such fear drives people to seek out anti-
Islam(ist) groups, suggesting: 'A lot of people went to Generation [Iden-
tity] because of the actual Manchester arena bombings'. For Paul (UK),
the example of the 7/7 bombers is indicative of an intrinsic problem with,
and the power of, Islam:

> The 7/7 bombers were all British-born Muslims who we were told
> would have integrated. And you're not gonna buy these people off,
> like they're white people. ... Because they have something deeper,
> which is what politicians don't understand. The depth of their faith
> and their belief system is greater, deeper and stronger than young
> white lads'.

In this way, Islam is exceptionalised, that is, it is seen as not just another
element in a twenty-first-century societal mix but uniquely incompatible
with other faiths and cultures.

For many milieu actors, the influx of difference is indicative of a deeper
societal crisis of identity. Moghaddam and Love (2012: 249) suggest extremism can be understood as a (dysfunctional) defence mechanism adopted 'when the in-group is facing an uncertain future, and there is a
real possibility of serious in-group decline and even extinction'. While
Moghaddam and Love (ibid.) are writing about collective existential uncertainty and Islamic fundamentalism, a similar perception of existential
crisis is apparent among the 'extreme-right' milieus studied here. This is
encapsulated in Christopher's (FR) stark statement that France as a country and identity 'is dead' but also in Anita's (NO) more nuanced sense
that, in a time of flux, people 'have a stronger need to find a way back to
our own identity, to who we are, to be able to hold on to something...'.
The sense that this identity is slipping away is found also among Dutch,
British, French and German respondents as they describe feeling displaced and alienated in city spaces that, to them, no longer resemble
their home country:

When you see it, you think, 'Is this really the Netherlands?' For example, [names street], a beautiful street with old houses, but almost every shop is Arabic – kebab shops, shops with Arabic fashion such as
headscarves and Arabic texts … People who just don't speak Dutch.
Then I think, 'Where are the Dutch? Where have I ended up?' (14,
NL)

Greek and Russian respondents – whose milieus were closely tied to
Greek and Russian Orthodox churches respectively – see the underlying
societal crisis as having strongly moral and spiritual roots. Alexey (RU)
views the world as characterised by 'an ideological, spiritual degener-
acy', while Father Gabriel (GR) asserts that Greek society is 'in a state
of decay' that can only be addressed by a return to spirituality. Even in
less religious milieus, there is a sense that religion provides an important
counterforce to 'progressive ideas' by maintaining traditional values and
ideas – something 'to hold on to' as Anita (NO) puts it above – as crisis
threatens to engulf society.

For some milieu actors, it is this 'uncertain' future – imagined as end-
ing in the 'replacement' or 'extinction' of white Europeans – that leads
people to become 'more extreme' (14, NL) and feel the need to physically
defend 'their' country or 'their' people. This is expressed most consistently in the UK, Dutch, French, Norwegian, Greek and Russian milieus
through a narrative of the imminent threat of destructive civil conflict.
For Sauveur (FR), civil conflict is the only way to achieve 'change': 'Until
there's a war, a real civil war, until the French move to get them out of the
country, things won't change. It will get worse and worse. You think the
Arabs should be moved out of the country … I think the French should
take up arms and get them out'. Dan (UK) refers to the possibility of civil
war several times, emphasising that some people are actively preparing
for it: 'I don't mean like preparing for it like the militias and all that. But
they're saying, "Look. Demo-ing is not the way to go now. You know,
there's a civil war coming here. We need to prepare"'. However, militias
are exactly what Thomas (GR) is organising when he describes how his
paramilitary organisation had taken direct action in a local town hosting
a refugee camp: 'They took down the ISIS flag and then they wrote on the
wall the slogan "THIS IS GREECE. ISLAM WILL NOT PREVAIL. VICTORY
OR DEATH"' (Field diary, GR). Even research participants who expressed
fear of civil war and sought non-violent resolutions to the perceived crisis –
such as Dan and Mikey (UK) and Per and Gunnar (NO) – worried that civil
conflict was now inevitable.

In contrast, grievances of a socio-economic nature are less salient.
Personal grievances about material circumstances are articulated relatively infrequently with greatest dissatisfaction expressed by actors in the

Greek and Polish milieus, where there is a high level of pessimism about future employment and income; 'there is no prospect, we feel it and we know it' (Melpo, GR). However, in other country contexts, experiences of poor housing or neighbourhoods and unemployment can feature in individuals' development of hostility towards others who are perceived as, unjustly, having more; such perceived horizontal inequality in relation to immigrant families is discussed in Arne's trajectory below (see Vignette 1). In other cases, relational inequality is experienced as vertical inequality, expressed as the injustice that 'people like us' live in poverty while 'they' ('the elites') are 'living in complete luxury' (DT, UK).

While milieu actors often accept inequality as rooted in naturalised difference and view the fight for equality as the misguided folly of 'social justice warriors', in some instances perceived and experienced inequalities are articulated by research participants as injustices. These relate primarily to the unfair treatment of milieu actors due to their political views and activism and is often expressed in relation to the perceived indiscriminate labelling of right-wing activists as 'extremist' by institutions – the state, the media, the police – with the power to do so. In some cases, personal experiences are recounted of being sacked or refused employment when their political positions or activities become known. Will (UK), for example, explains how he was first suspended and then asked to resign after his movement affiliation became publicised; when he refused, he was fired. Trying to get a new job in his line of work became impossible, since, he said, 'part of your application is an adverse media check. You type my name into Google, it's, "Fascist, fascist, fascist, fascist"' (Will, UK).

Such experiences are seen as indicative of a wider socio-political inequality whereby the views of those on the Right are rejected out of hand because they run counter to 'accepted' opinion. This sense of being *silenced* often forms as a personal grievance early in research participants' political development. Tonya (UK) had been reprimanded in college about an essay she had written, which was deemed to express 'radical' views on Islam and, during work experience, felt 'beaten into submission, like, "Your opinion is not accepted here. Do not say a damn thing." So I didn't'. Peter (DE) also notes that many people 'don't want to speak out' because they fear the consequences of being immediately tarred with the 'Nazi' brush. Jason's (UK) political awareness and activism had also started from a moment when he had objected to his teacher comparing Tommy Robinson to Hitler: 'That day's the day I just lost it. I stood up and started saying my views. ... And so many people had told me privately that they agreed, but were too scared to speak out...' (Jason, UK). The narrative of being 'silenced' was found most frequently in the UK milieu

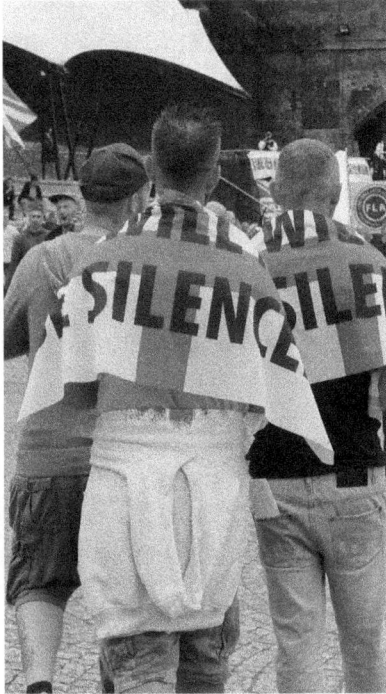

Figure 2.3. 'We will not be silenced' flags at Democratic Football Lads Alliance demonstration, 2018. © Hilary Pilkington.

(see also Pilkington 2016: 203–21) and publicly demonstrated at milieu events attended (see Figure 2.3).

Research participants note that what they experience as attempts to delegitimise, and silence, political views may in fact propel people towards more radical views or movements. As Craig (UK) elaborates, 'if a political voice and a political analysis is not allowed, because it's deemed to be too extreme or whatever, where do those people go and what do they do if they're not allowed a political voice?' An answer is provided by Norwegian respondents who recount routes into 'extreme-right' milieus as often being through participation in gaming communities or 4chan (Espen, NO), a reminder that Norwegian terrorist Anders Breivik also developed his ideas drawing on transnational right-wing channels on the Internet (Borchgrevink 2012; Bangstad 2014; Sætre 2013). However, the space afforded by social media was also experienced as being under threat through the imposition of temporary and permanent bans from platforms. For Dan (UK), this ran the risk of pushing people down a radicalisation pathway since 'social media and marches do help people get their anger out'. It is to this role of emotions and collective activism (see also Beck 2015: 36; McCauley and Moskalenko 2017: 214; Jasper 2018) in shaping radicalisation and non-radicalisation outcomes of milieu actors' journeys that we turn next.

Affective and Situational Factors: Social Ties, the Longing for Community and the Role of Movements

Pre-existing social ties have been identified consistently as a key factor in initiating participation in radical movements while socialisation within movements is viewed as central to radicalisation into violent extremism (see, *inter alia*, Linden and Klandermans 2007: 185; Christmann 2012: 27; Malthaner 2017a: 376–77). In this study, however, we identified the *absence* of social ties – a sense of social isolation and longing for community – as a factor also pulling individuals towards 'extreme-right' movements. Moreover, pre-existing social ties (family, friends) as well as influential figures encountered within movements were found to play a more ambiguous role – not only bringing research participants into radical milieus but, in some cases, constraining engagement or steering individuals away from more extreme movements or actions.

Family – mostly parents or siblings but sometimes grandparents and uncles – were mentioned as influencing research participants' trajectories both towards and away from extremism. Several respondents in France, Germany, Poland and the UK said that their parents held values sympathetic to extreme-right views. Brandon (FR) says the fact that his mother (who had been left-wing in her own youth) was also 'seduced' by the Front National 'reinforced my choice' while Mona and Lena (DE) described how their parents had instilled in them that they should not bring home, or marry, a Muslim. Dan and Robbie (UK) had both been introduced to the milieu by their fathers, who were already active there, while Peter (DE) and Sandra (PL) had been brought into radical milieus by siblings. Peter's elder brother belonged to a neo-Nazi group, which had led him to 'develop opinions in that direction', and Sandra followed her elder brothers into football-related fighting. However, respondents in Germany, Norway, the Netherlands, France and the UK also mentioned having had left-wing family members who influenced their upbringing and trajectories. Redford (FR) credits his grandfather's and parents' leftist ideologies for holding him back from adopting more extreme right-wing views, while Brandon (FR) feels that he resisted the everyday cultural racism that was rife in his school because his parents had brought him up to be 'open-minded' and never 'consciously, ideologically, racist'.

It is important to recognise young people's agency in these relationships too. We encountered a number of cases of generational role reversal in which respondents influenced their parents or older family members. Paul's (UK) parents followed him into the extreme-right party in which he was active and Anita (NO) initially inspired her father to become active, alongside her, in Stop Islamisation of Norway (SIAN). However, the relationship between activist parents and their activist children was also one of mutual care and respect; experience was shared by parents who wanted to keep their children safe and vice versa. Thus, Robbie and Dan (UK) talk about how their fathers had played important roles in steering them away from engaging in violent action, whilst Robbie and Tonya monitor their dads' use of social media because they worry that they have become too involved or shared too much online. Young people are thus not 'victims' of parental socialisation but may also shape the political contours of their immediate environment.

Friends act as influencers both towards and away from extremism. Three participants in the French case, who had been friends from childhood, formed a Corsican nationalist movement together, while Jonathan (MT) had become involved with the Imperium Europa party after making a new friend at university who was a member. However, once he had read more, and been at university longer, Jonathan realised those initial friends were 'not the ones I would have chosen' and he started to 'make my own choices'. This confirms other narratives from the data set that qualify the relationship between friendship and radicalisation. Dan (UK) said friends from the English Defence League (EDL) were now moving in the direction of Generation Identity but he would not follow them because he felt the movement was too extreme. As a teenager, Robbie (UK) had consciously decided that he did not want to follow his, older, friends into the EDL: 'They were going on these marches, and they told me what they'd seen, what they'd heard, what they'd said. And . . . even at thirteen, I thought, "That's not the right way to go about it"'. These examples illustrate how friends moving in a more radical direction are not necessarily followed. Rather, such encounters may act as moments of reflection when research participants draw their own lines in terms of what they believe or how they want to act.

Acknowledging young people's agency in their radicalisation journeys, rather than focusing on their vulnerability to radicalisers or radicalising messages, is not to suggest that the particular social-emotional (Sieckelinck et al. 2019) and cognitive (Costanza 2015) developmental challenges faced by young people do not play a role. Qualitative studies of young activists in extremist movements have found families rarely appear as stable, strong and protective environments but often as sites of trauma and resilience (Pilkington 2016: 80–83; Sieckelinck et al. 2019: 668). In our study, where individuals lacked supportive or bonding relationships with family and/or peers, this was often reflected in low self-esteem, a sense of social isolation and a longing for community or belonging. In such cases, activist groups could provide a positive sense of 'family' or 'community' that helped to build their self-esteem and self-worth. Arne's (NO) trajectory exemplifies the intersection of complex social problems, feelings of social isolation and longing for 'the unity, the community' that activism offered (see Vignette 1), but this is also present in the trajectories narrated by others. One Dutch respondent associated 'real' family with those in the milieu rather than blood family (18, NL). Jason (UK), who was still living at home and studying at college, also felt unsupported by his parents in dealing with mental health issues and had received an intervention from social services. Jason's political activist community appears in his narrative as the family he craved during what he describes as a 'terrible' childhood:

> It's like a family to me. It's like my chairman, she's like that really wild, stubborn member of the family, I'd say. And then you've got another ... youth member there, he's like the brother type of guy ... showing you all these funny things on his phone – memes, all that stuff. You have family like that, and then you got [names colleague in the organisation] is like that really proud parent ... 'This is Jason', and all that, 'look what he's done'.

Although his activism had helped build self-confidence and self-esteem, Jason still suffers from mental health problems and, like Arne, describes himself as 'very lonely at the moment' (Field diary, 16 March 2020).

Arne's story (see Vignette 1) not only exemplifies how personal grievance (lack of familial support, material insecurity and loneliness) is translated into political grievance in the context of perceived relational inequality ('foreigners who get ... help with this and that' while he is told 'no, no, no'), but also illustrates the affective dimension of how research participants encounter and respond to radical messages. Arne's social isolation makes the community and brotherhood offered by the NRM attractive, but their willingness to engage in political violence is a moral 'red line' that he cannot cross: 'I wanted to become part of them', he says, but could not because he had 'too much love for other people' to engage in violence. Similar situations in which they encountered those they considered 'too extreme' were recounted by Billy, Dan and Lee (UK); all three had experienced recruitment attempts by more extreme movements but had resisted pressure to join. For others, resistance was expressed by not applauding speeches that were 'derogatory of Muslims' (Robbie, UK) or not carrying a placard carrying a message they did not approve (Jason, UK).

VIGNETTE 1. Arne's Trajectory

Arne is twenty-six, unemployed and living on disability benefit. His childhood felt shaped by his parents' divorce. He had few friends growing up, felt excluded, developed mental health problems and dropped out of school. He retains contact with his mother but feels she is not interested in him. His anti-immigrant views developed after the family moved from a prosperous and 'Norwegian' area of one city to another city where there was an asylum centre in the neighbourhood. This magnified Arne's sense of exclusion, especially as he struggled to survive financially while perceiving that asylum seekers received more state support:

> It started quite slowly when I got those disability benefits. I had very little income and when you're in town and encounter many different cultures and become perhaps a little aggressive because others have a better car and so on, you feel envious. Then I went into some right-wing extreme milieus, read about foreigners who get a free driver's licence, help with this and that, money here and there. Then I go on the dole and try to get a bit of furniture. And you get 'no, no, no' from them.

He was living in social housing where he was the only resident with a purely Norwegian background. The area suffered from drugs and crime problems and he felt unsafe. The combination of these issues, and a sense of profound loneliness, led him into petty crime (for which he served two years in prison) and what he describes as 'right-wing extreme milieus'. Despite being unsure about the politics of the movement, and not endorsing the use of violence, the NRM offered the community he longed for:

> What is tempting with the NRM is the unity, the community, being in a group where everyone knows everyone, and where everyone feels a deep hatred for people outside the Nordic race and that it is that race that is right. That unity feels very exciting. But when it comes to violence? I see that as meaningless. Like I have said many times, I want them [immigrants] out of Norway but I don't want to kill them.

Arne's story is strongly shaped by personal grievance but, especially at moments where he is strongly attracted to the NRM, they are expressed as political grievances. He articulates the NRM position that anyone who is not a true Norwegian – who does not descend from at least three Norwegian-born generations – has no place in Norwegian society. The country should be 'cleansed' of such immigrants and the culture they bring with them. At this point, Arne identified as a Nazi, expressed antisemitic conspiracy narratives and an 'understanding' of, although not support for,

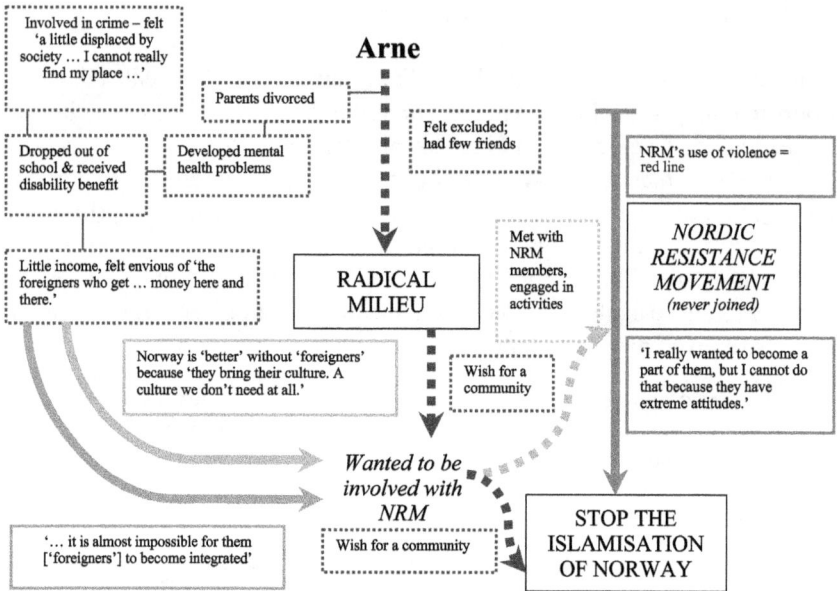

Figure 2.4. Arne's trajectory. Created by Hilary Pilkington.

the actions of Anders Breivik. He moved closer to acceptance into the NRM and participated in their stickering campaigns.

However, Arne's own reflection on his dislike of violence as well as his disapproval of the NRM's anti-LGBT stance (he describes himself as bi-sexual) halts his trajectory towards violent extremism. He abandons the idea of joining the organisation because they wanted 'to make people use violence' and he starts to associate himself with SIAN. While those around him, including the police and his own father, suggest he resembles Breivik and might be capable of committing similar terrorist atrocities, he reflects: 'I have too much love for other people to be able to do such a thing'.

◆

Some milieu actors saw themselves as consciously steering others, espe-cially younger members, away from 'extremist' elements in the milieu. Espen (NO) talks about a group of youngsters on social media channels, whom he tries to 'keep … on the straight and narrow', that is, away from the extremist Nordic Resistance Movement and the glorification of right-wing terrorist acts and actors. Paul (UK), similarly, describes how his efforts to persuade young activists to stay away from National Action had helped prevent extremism. A Dutch respondent recounted how milieu actors with whom he had previously spent a lot of time had attacked a mosque but, he argued, labelling them 'Nazis' and excluding them from movements would just increase the likelihood of radical action (3, NL). This view is found in the UK milieu too, where some movements considered 'extremist' in public discourse were felt to be trying hard 'to keep a lid on things' (Craig, UK). Of course, where the line is drawn regarding what is tolerable, and can be addressed by channelling anger and grievances, and when individuals need to be ejected from the movement or even reported to the authorities, is – like extremism itself – relative. This is exemplified by the case of Paul (UK), who saw himself as stopping younger actors becoming extremist but was described by others in the milieu as promoting precisely the kind of extremism that they were trying to prevent people moving towards.

Shifts away from Extremism

Disillusionment, Priorities and Marking Red Lines

High expectations of the emotional dimensions of the new community bring potential disillusionment when political goals, friendship or a sense of belonging and purpose are left unfulfilled (Bjørgo 2011: 284). In our study, when the support or purpose sought was not forthcoming, it resulted in feelings of disappointment, disillusionment and sometimes hurt or betrayal. This was most clearly articulated by respondents who had made the decision to move away from activism. At the time of interview, Lee (UK) had recently been released from prison where he had experienced a growing sense that he had wrongly prioritised activism over family in the past. This was reinforced when others in the movement failed to assist his girlfriend and children financially whilst he was in prison even though he himself had established a hardship fund for this purpose and helped others convicted before him.

VIGNETTE 2. Alice's Trajectory

Alice, a 28-year-old graduate with a secure socio-economic background and supportive family, began her activism in movements on the Left. She became disillusioned when she felt her contribution was not valued and left Black Lives Matter because 'everyone was bickering with each other, and I got called something because I was white and that pissed me off'. Listening to podcasts, especially by conspiracy theorist Alex Jones, she felt increasingly 'wound up'

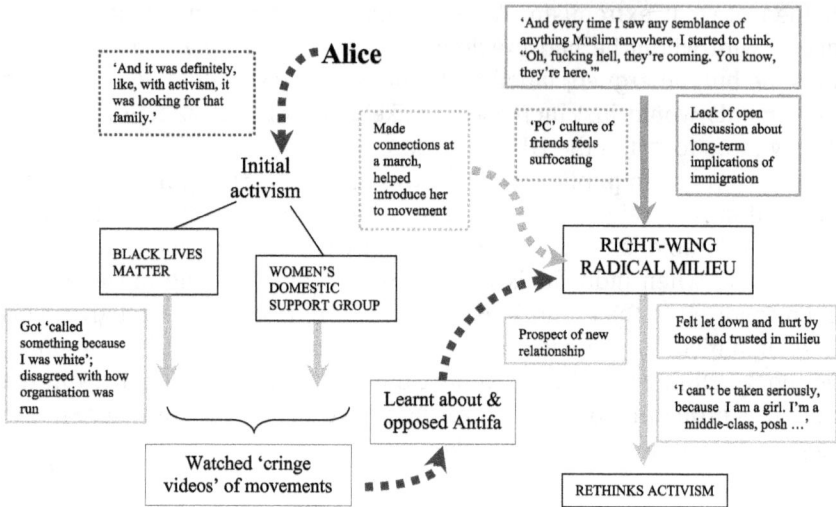

Figure 2.5. Alice's trajectory. Created by Hilary Pilkington.

but also displaced. The 'culture shock' she felt when she first moved to the city now seemed threatening; '…every single time I saw a hijab, I started getting really annoyed'. She criticises the lack of open discussion about the long-term implications of immigration and, although she is not sure she believes alt-right theory about 'a plan' to outbreed white people, she thinks, 'if the population is going to change to such an extent that we're no longer a majority white … country … well I don't know if I want that, to be honest'.

Alice's period of deep engagement in the milieu is recounted as situational; a chance meeting led her, rapidly, into the inner circle around a prominent 'extreme-right' milieu figure. She felt part of a grand cause and, comparing the process to that of being an 'ISIS bride', she made the decision to 'pack up and leave' her old life and move into a house with others working for the movement. However, after a dispute with the milieu figure, Alice was sacked and suffered a torrent of online abuse including accusations that she was an infiltrator. Without income or a place to live, she moved back in with her parents. She was shunned by her former circle but the revelation that she had only ever been partially accepted was most hurtful. At first she saw this as a deep personal betrayal but later as a wider problem in the movement, in which there was little space for someone with her gender and class background: 'I do feel like I'm on the right side, but … in a way, I can't be taken seriously, because yeah, I am a girl. I'm a middle-class, posh…'.

Although communication was re-established a year later, Alice remained damaged by her earlier treatment in the milieu. Her disappointment was less with the causes the movement promoted than feeling let down and hurt by those she had trusted. Whilst connections had been reforged, she is no longer deeply engaged and plans to write a book about her experience. She also links this reprioritisation of activism in her life to the prospect of a new relationship. Having met somebody in whom she was interested, she started to anticipate the shame she would feel if they had seen her previous partic-ipation in live-streamed shows in which she had been effectively 'nodding along' to antisemitic remarks. She sees the future as one in which she keeps her political, work and private life separate from one another: 'I think it's better to think of it as the job. ... And then you come back and you're wor-ried about like tea and what we're doing tonight and shall we go and see this film. And I think it's nice to keep it separate'.

◆

Female respondents expressed criticism of milieus in which they were left feeling they did not 'fit'. Tina (NO) concludes that the Alliance party, to which she had been affiliated, is 'macho at root' after her own ap-proach to gender and sexual freedom clashed with their highly conser-vative views on gender. This was a key factor in Tina's decision to leave; she states: 'It is really impossible to be a female in that movement'. This disillusionment is illustrated in Alice's (UK) trajectory (see Vignette 2) in which a personal grievance, when she feels her experience and contribu-tion are dismissed by left-oriented groups in which she is initially active, feeds her curiosity about the Right, whose messages appear to confirm a broader dislocation she feels after moving (from a rural area) to a ma-jor city. She narrates her movement into the heart of the 'extreme-right' milieu as strongly situational, but embraces what she sees as a 'noble cause' until betrayed by those around her who, she concludes, never re-ally accepted her.

As Alice seeks to re-balance her life, she notes the importance of inti-mate and family relationships, but also social life and future prospects in general, in individual decisions to step away from extremism. Paolo (UK) also points to the change in priorities among his football-related milieu when they become involved in serious relationships:

> I know a lot of lads who've got kids and that now, and they're not the same. I mean, I know lads that would have put you through a phone box two years ago, now, need to ask the missus' permission to come to the pub. Completely different.

Paolo thought he was heading in that direction himself when he be-came engaged to his girlfriend and they were expecting a baby. He took a step back from the football milieu to focus on taking responsibility for his family – as he put it, 'I settled myself down. And I didn't want to risk losing that'. However, after he and his partner lost the baby and subsequently separated, he was 'straight back' to the milieu.

Lee's disillusionment with his movement when they failed to support his girlfriend and family during his imprisonment was noted above and reinforced a growing sense that he had wrongly prioritised activism over family. The decisive moment came when, just before his release, social workers warned him that if he returned to activism after release, he risked losing access to his own and his partner's children, and he remembers, 'Straight away that gripped me, the switch went, and I thought, "That's it. I can't do it anymore. I can't, I can't run the risk of my kids and [names girlfriend]'s kids being taken away"' (Lee, UK). Samuel (MT) had also been compelled to rethink his direction after getting to know a colleague of immigrant background better:

> I had never spoken to a black person before in my life. So it was, you know, because it was a collegial relationship, I didn't have much choice in the matter, and then I remember this person offered me to go and have drinks with him, and I said OK. … And you know, after repeatedly working together and having drinks, I started to realise that this person is like everybody else … And then obviously I started to feel this internal conflict within me, I was like 'What the fuck am I doing man? What is this crap?' … Life's too short, for hating, and all this stuff, and this guy, changed my mind.

Samuel's realisation is reflected in other journeys in moments when individuals become aware that to continue would mean crossing a line ideologically or in terms of personal morality that made them uncomfortable. These red lines vary significantly, as they are drawn relative to the individual and the milieu they inhabit. However, the way they are narrated by research participants illustrates how recognising what they find *too extreme* can clarify those lines and propel them away from extremism. This was evident in Alice's anticipated shame at being seen 'nodding along' to antisemitic statements of others while, within the Dutch milieu, a research participant (2, NL) recalls encounters on Facebook with an individual sympathising with Breivik, which they found 'disgusting'. Being compared to Breivik by his schoolmates was also a wake-up call for Espen from the Norwegian milieu. Initially drawn to the Norwegian Defence League (NDL) at the age of just thirteen, Espen had begun to feel disappointed with the movement: 'It was a typical echo chamber. And I liked to discuss things. So I did not get much out of it after a while'. The terrorist acts committed by Breivik on 22 July 2011 brought things to a head as he found himself confronted by comparisons of his own ideologi-cal attitudes with those of Breivik: 'The 22 July thing inflamed everything. I thought about what it could mean for my future. And my whole social life. I did not want to lose that because of me being in the NDL...' (Espen, NO). Dan (UK) describes making a last-minute decision not to attend an event organised by a regional Infidels group because he was worried by something he had seen online which he felt was a 'bit too racist, like they were a bit white pride'. Similarly, SIAN member Anita (NO) draws her own 'limit' with reference to the Nordic Resistance Movement's ambition to create a 'white Scandinavia': 'They [NRM] are concerned with race and they want to have a white Scandinavia and that is something that I am not concerned with at all ... I feel that crosses a limit'.

Conclusion

The study of radicalisation directs almost exclusive attention to the least likely outcome of engagement with radical ideas – their pursuit through violent extremism. By studying young people's activism in a wide range of 'extreme-right' milieus, we make visible, and open to analysis, more frequent trajectories in which young people encounter and engage with radical(ising) forces, messages and agents but do not cross the threshold into violent extremism. By focusing on the radical milieu, we are able to root individual trajectories in their social context, including the social networks and communication channels they host, the interactions that take place and the affect that is generated there.

In this chapter, we have provided a brief sketch of the detailed and complex trajectories identified across very different milieus, themselves internally heterogeneous, in nine European countries. The themes ex-tracted from the synthesis of the data reflect milieu actors' own narratives of what propels people towards and away from more radical positions. These include a range of political grievances, of which the most salient relate to the perceived threat to self and own group emanating from ra-cialised 'others' ('immigrants', 'Muslims') and those who are perceived to promote their interests (liberal elites, self-serving politicians, global networks of conspirators and so on). Such grievances are forged out of the interaction between individual experiences (of economic and social dislocation, population movement, urban change) and political messages encountered which, once shared with others and endorsed through the narratives of authoritative figures, come to be understood as the experi-ence of the group (see Honneth 1995: 163). They are articulated, first and foremost, in the context of the experience of the influx of difference and the perception of such difference as representing a threat – sometimes a security threat but more often a threat to existing values, attitudes, beliefs, ways of living and cultural practices. For many milieu actors this threat is interpreted as indicative of a profound societal crisis reflected in visions of the future that are almost universally pessimistic, sometimes apocalyptic, as they imagine the physical 'replacement' of white European populations through immigration and demographic change and the subsequent loss of unique national and regional identities.

This sense of crisis, we find, is underpinned by feelings of uncertainty at individual and group levels and is augmented through mediating affective factors such as feelings of isolation, dislocation and frustration into a sense of collective existential insecurity and impending violent conflict (expressed in the expectation of an imminent civil war). These environmental conditions of 'normative threat' are demonstrated by Stenner (2005: 80–81) to be a crucial factor in activating individual predispositions to authoritarianism resulting in the heightened expression of intolerance. Thus, while political grievances tend to dominate milieu actors' narratives of trajectories, they far from determine a path towards violent extremism. Personal grievances such as negative experiences in school or employment, low income as well as adverse childhood experiences, personal trauma and mental health issues (related or unrelated to these experiences) play an important role in how young people narrate their journeys. Moreover, we identify a number of vital – affective and situational – factors including the role of family and peers, as well as situations of isolation, social and health problems, loneliness and desire for community, that play a crucial part in understanding how our research participants came to be where they were.

However, it is important not to see the milieu as static (Malthaner 2017a: 393) or as somehow disconnected from the other communication circles in which young people are simultaneously engaged. By employing the notion of 'trajectories', we signal the dynamic nature of young people's engagements within the milieu and their movement towards more radical positions but also away from them in response to their encounters there as well as their wider changing life circumstances and cognitive and emotional development. Exploring themes around the role of movements, family and peer influences and a longing for community, we find that these factors are important not only in bringing research participants into radical milieus but also in constraining their engagement or encouraging them to establish their own 'red lines' in terms of how much, and what forms of, engagement they have. Families may provide a form of socialisation into 'extreme-right' activism, but even where siblings acknowledge the same 'incentive' for participation ensuing from close relatives' positions in such movements, their paths may take very different courses (Pilkington 2016: 78). Finding a welcoming community and gaining in self-esteem through activism may sustain participation in radical milieus. However, it can also facilitate the development of skills, self-belief and identity that reduces ontological insecurity and allows participants to see ways to pursue the change they desire without recourse to violent action. Moreover, the disappointment with the emotional support or solidarity anticipated may be crucial in decisions to disengage or reprioritise activism within wider lives.

It is essential to recognise that as young people move through these milieus they make choices, and that these choices are informed not only by interactions within the radical milieu but by the multiple environments in which they engage in their everyday lives. This social connectedness may be the source of their original desire to politically engage – a feeling of wanting to 'make a difference' – but also what pulls them back from crossing the threshold into violent extremism. Understanding radicalisation as practices of embodied communication that generate different kinds of affect (McDonald 2018) allows us to see the meaning that is attached to activism, to the bonds forged with other milieu actors and the causes to which these are tied. These practices are not confined to one group of 'predisposed' individuals but infused in narratives resident in the social structures in which young people are embedded (Costanza 2015) and diffused in radical milieus, through interactions both within the milieu and with external forces and discourses beyond, through the 'communicative interlocks' that connect milieu actors with everyday worlds.

Acknowledgements

The research drawn on in this chapter is part of the Dialogue about Radicalisation and Equality (DARE) project, which received funding from the European Union's Horizon 2020 research and innovation programme under Grant Agreement No 725349. This article reflects only the views of the authors; the European Commission and Research Executive Agency are not responsible for any information it contains.

The nine case studies of 'extreme-right' milieus drawn on in this analysis were conducted by members of the DARE project. These case studies are published as individual reports, details of which can be found in the Appendix to this volume. This synthesis of findings could not have been written without the commitment to research and the analytic insight of all the researchers and authors involved in these case studies and we are deeply indebted to them. We thank Rosie Mutton also for her contribution to the development of Figures 2.2, 2.4 and 2.5. We want to thank, especially, all the research participants who agreed to take part in the individual case studies for their time, but also for their willingness to put their trust in the researchers and the research process.

Hilary Pilkington is Professor of Sociology at the University of Manchester and Fellow of the Academy of Social Sciences. She has conducted ethnographic research on youth and youth subculture, youth political participation, activism and extremism and published also on ethnographic research methods and meta-ethnographic synthesis. She was coordinator of the H2020 DARE (Dialogue about Radicalisation and Equality) project (University of Manchester, 2017–21). She is a member of the Academic-Practitioner Countering Extremism Network of the Commission for Countering Extremism and served as independent Commissioner on the GMCA Preventing Violent Extremism and Promoting Social Cohesion Commission.

Viggo Vestel is a social anthropologist and senior researcher at Oslo Metropolitan University. He has published books, reports and articles in various anthologies and in journals including: *Young – Nordic Journal of Youth Research*; *Journal of Muslims in Europe*; *Social Movement Studies*; and *Ethos – Journal for the Society for Psychological Anthropology*. He has done extensive research on multicultural youth milieus in Norway, with a special focus on popular culture, hybridisation and the development of social relations. In recent years, he has focused on political mobilisation and political radicalisation both among the radical right and among radical Muslims.

....
NOTES

1. Attention to individual agency in shaping pathways of right-wing extremist activism emerges primarily in empirical studies, especially those which draw on life history or ethnographic approaches (see Ezekiel 1995; Blee 2002; Linden and Klandermans 2007; Simi and Futrell 2015; Pilkington 2016).
2. The procedures and practices implemented to ensure the ethical collection and storage of research material are detailed in each report as well as in the Introduction to case study reports (see Pilkington and Vestel 2020). In most cases the identity of research participants was protected by assigning a pseudonym, but where even this was felt to present a potential risk, numbers were assigned.
3. Research participants cited here who are aged over forty are: Christopher (FR); Father Gabriel and Thomas (GR); and Craig (UK).

REFERENCES

Alimi, Eitan Y., Lorenzo Bosi and Chares Demetriou. 2012. 'Relational Dynamics and Processes of Radicalization: A Comparative Framework', *Mobilization* 17(1): 7–26.

Bangstad, Sindre. 2014. *Anders Breivik and the Rise of Islamophobia*. London: Zed Books.

Beck, Colin J. 2015. *Radicals, Revolutionaries and Terrorists*. Cambridge: Polity Press.

Berger, John M. 2018. *Extremism*. Cambridge, MA: MIT Press.

Bjørgo, Tore. 2011. 'Dreams and Disillusionment: Engagement in and Disengagement from Militant Extremist Groups', *Crime, Law and Social Change* 55(4): 227–85.

Bjørgo, Tore, and Jacob A. Ravndal. 2019. *Extreme-Right Violence and Terrorism: Concepts, Patterns, and Responses*. The Hague: The International Centre for Counter-Terrorism.

Blee, Kathleen M. 2002. *Inside Organized Racism: Women in the Hate Movement*. Berkeley: University of California Press.

Borchgrevink, Aage Storm. 2012. *En Norsk Tragedie* [A Norwegian Tragedy]. Trondheim: Gyldendal.

Bouhana, Noémie. 2019. *The Moral Ecology of Extremism: A Systemic Perspective*. London: Commission for Countering Extremism. Retrieved 22 December 2021 from https://www.gov.uk/government/publications/the-moral-ecology-of-extremism-a-systemic-perspective.

Britten, Nicky, et al. 2002. 'Using Meta Ethnography to Synthesise Qualitative Research: A Worked Example', *Journal of Health Services Research & Policy* 7(4): 209–15.

Camus, Jean-Yves. 2019. 'Alain de Benoist and the New Right', in Mark Sedgwick (ed.), *Key Thinkers of the Radical Right: Behind the New Threat to Liberal Democracy*. New York: Oxford University Press, pp. 73–90.

Carter, Elisabeth. 2018. 'Right-Wing Extremism/Radicalism: Reconstructing a Concept', *Journal of Political Ideologies* 23(2): 157–82.

Christmann, Kris. 2012. *Preventing Religious Radicalisation and Violent Extremism: A Systematic Review of the Research Evidence*. Youth Justice Board for England and Wales. Retrieved 24 January 2022 from https://assets.publishing.service.gov.uk/government/uploads/system/uploads/attachment_data/file/396030/preventing-violent-extremism-systematic-review.pdf.

Costanza, William A. 2015. 'Adjusting Our Gaze: An Alternative Approach to Understanding Youth Radicalization', *Journal of Strategic Security* 8(1): 1–15.

Cragin, Kim. 2014. 'Resisting Violent Extremism: A Conceptual Model for Non-Radicalization', *Terrorism and Political Violence* 26: 337–53.

Cragin, Kim, et al. 2015. *What Factors Cause Youth to Reject Violent Extremism? Results of an Exploratory Analysis in the West Bank*. Rand Corporation. Retrieved 22 December 2021 from https://www.rand.org/content/dam/rand/pubs/research_reports/RR1100/RR1118/RAND_RR1118.pdf.

Dawson, Lorne L. 2017. 'Sketch of a Social Ecology Model for Explaining Homegrown Terrorist Radicalisation', *The International Centre for Counter-Terrorism – The Hague* 8(1): 1–15. Retrieved 22 December 2021 from https://icct.nl/publication/sketch-of-a-social-ecology-model-for-explaining-homegrown-terrorist-radicalisation/.

de Benoist, Alain, and Charles Champetier. 2012. *Manifesto for a European Renaissance*. London: Arktos.

Ezekiel, Raphael S. 1995. *The Racist Mind: Portraits of American Neo-Nazis and Klansmen*. New York: Penguin Books.

Fillieule, Olivier. 2010. 'Some Elements of an Interactionist Approach to Political Disengagement', *Social Movement Studies* 9(1): 1–15.

Fine, Gary Alan, and Sherryl Kleinman. 1979. 'Rethinking Subculture: An Interactionist Analysis', *American Journal of Sociology* 85(1): 1–20. Retrieved 22 December 2021 from http://www.jstor.org/stable/2778065.

Honneth, Axel. 1995. *The Struggle for Recognition: The Moral Grammar of Social Conflicts*. Cambridge, MA: MIT Press.

Horgan, John. 2008. 'From Profiles to Pathways and Roots to Routes: Perspectives from Psychology and Radicalization into Terrorism', *The Annals of the Academy of the Political and Social Sciences* 618: 80–94.

Jasper, James M. 2018. *The Emotions of Protest*. Chicago: University of Chicago Press.

Linden, Annette, and Bert Klandermans. 2007. 'Revolutionaries, Wanderers, Converts, and Compliants: Life Histories of Extreme Right Activists', *Journal of Contemporary Ethnography* 36(2): 184–201.

Malthaner, Stefan. 2017a. 'Radicalization: The Evolution of an Analytical Paradigm', *European Journal of Sociology* 58(3): 369–401.

———. 2017b. 'Processes of Political Violence and the Dynamics of Situational Interaction', *International Journal of Conflict and Violence* 11: 1–10.

Malthaner, Stefan, and Peter Waldmann. 2014. 'The Radical Milieu: Conceptualising the Supportive Social Environment of Terrorist Groups', *Studies in Conflict and Terrorism* 37(12): 979–98.

McCauley, Clark, and Sophia Moskalenko. 2008. 'Mechanisms of Political Radicalization: Pathways toward Terrorism', *Terrorism and Political Violence* 20(3): 415–33.

———. 2017. 'Understanding Political Radicalization: The Two-Pyramids Model', *American Psychologist* 72(3): 205–16.

McDonald, Kevin. 2018. *Radicalization*. Cambridge: Polity.

Moghaddam, Fathali M., and Karen Love. 2012. 'Collective Uncertainty and Extremism: A Further Discussion on the Collective Roots of Subjective Experience', in Michael A. Hogg and Danielle L. Blaylock (eds), *Extremism and the Psychology of Uncertainty*. Oxford: Wiley-Blackwell, pp. 246–62.

Mudde, Cas. 2000. *The Ideology of the Extreme Right*. Manchester: Manchester University Press.

———. 2007. *Populist Radical Right Parties in Europe*. Cambridge: Cambridge University Press.

Noblit, George W., and R. Dwight Hare. 1988. *Meta-Ethnography: Synthesizing Qualitative Studies*. Newbury Park, CA: Sage.

Pilkington, Hilary. 2014. '"If You Want to Live, You Better Know How to Fight": Fighting Masculinity on the Russian Punk Scene', in Matthew Worley (ed.), *Fight Back: Punk, Politics and Resistance*. Manchester: Manchester University Press, pp. 13–33.

———. 2016. *Loud and Proud: Passion and Politics in the English Defence League*. Manchester: Manchester University Press.

———. 2018. 'Employing Meta-ethnography in the Analysis of Qualitative Data Sets on Youth Activism: A New Tool for Transnational Research Projects?', *Qualitative Research* 18(1): 108–30.

Pilkington, Hilary, and Viggo Vestel. 2020. *Young People's Trajectories through Anti-Islam(ist) and Extreme Right Milieus: Introduction*. DARE Research Report. Retrieved 28 August 2022 from https://documents.manchester.ac.uk/display.aspx?DocID=58693.

———. 2021. *Young People's Trajectories through Anti-Islam(ist) and Extreme Right Milieus: Cross-national Synthesis Report*. DARE Research Report. Retrieved 28 August 2022 from https://documents.manchester.ac.uk/display.aspx?DocID=58676.

Sætre, Simen. 2013. *Fjordman. Portrett av en Antiislamist* [Fjordman: Portrait of an Anti-Islamist]. Trondheim: Cappelen Damm.

Schmid, Alex P. 2013. 'Radicalisation, De-Radicalisation, Counter-Radicalisation: A Conceptual Discussion and Literature Review', ICCT Research Paper. The Hague: International Centre for Counter-Terrorism.

Schuurman, Bart. 2020. 'Non-Involvement in Terrorist Violence', *Perspectives on Terrorism* 14(6): 14–26.

Sellner, Martin. 2018. *Identitær. Et Uppbrotts Historia* [Identitarian: The Story of an Awakening]. Søderhamn: Debattforlaget.

Simi, Pete, and Robert Futrell. 2015. *American Swastika: Inside the White Power Movement's Hidden Spaces of Hate*. Lanham, MD: Rowman & Littlefield.

Sieckelinck, Stijn, et al. 2019. 'Transitional Journeys into and out of Extremism. A Biographical Approach', *Studies in Conflict & Terrorism* 42(7): 662–82.

Stenner, Karen. 2005. *The Authoritarian Dynamic*. Cambridge: Cambridge University Press.

Zúquete, José P. 2018. *The Identitarians: The Movement against Globalism and Islam in Europe*. Notre Dame: University of Notre Dame Press.

PART II

❁ ❁ ❁

Sites and Sources of (Non)Radicalisation

CHAPTER 3

What Is the Connection between Inequalities and Radicalisation?
Reviewing the Evidence Base

Renata Franc, Alexandra Poli and Tomislav Pavlović

Introduction

There is a widespread presumption – found in public opinion (Bentley, Lekalake and Buchanan-Clarke 2016; Coolsaet 2017) as well as among policy and practice experts in the field of countering violent extremism – that inequality is a key driver of radicalisation. The evidence from empirical studies, however, suggests that the relationship between inequality and radicalisation is not so straightforward. A number of published synthesis studies in the field of radicalisation and terrorism have been unable to draw definitive conclusions about the role of inequality or have come to different conclusions (e.g. Campana and Lapointe 2012; Meierrieks 2014; Desmarais et al. 2017; Lösel et al. 2018). In relation to radicalisation, for instance, Munton et al. (2011: 13) identified perceived inequality (grievances, frustration with limited socio-economic opportunities) as a consistent motivating factor for Al Qaeda-influenced violent extremism. On the other hand, Christmann (2012: 26) concludes that relative deprivation and failed integration are likely to be 'only, at best, a background or distal factor (the cause of the causes) in any process of radicalisation, and then not a necessary one'.

Scoping existing synthesis studies revealed that systematic reviews to date included quantitative studies alone and that these syntheses of quantitative findings often conflated results across outcomes of radicalisation (i.e. radicalised opinions *and* radicalised behaviours) (see McCauley and

Moskalenko 2017) or across ideologies. In some cases, the reviews also covered only some dimensions of inequality. In designing the syntheses on which this contribution is based, therefore, we sought to undertake the first meta-ethnographic synthesis (MES) of qualitative studies on the inequality-radicalisation relationship, alongside a systematic review (SR) of quantitative findings. This parallel study, we proposed, would allow us to acknowledge the distinct strengths and limitations of both approaches and integrate our findings to produce a deeper and more complex understanding of the inequality-radicalisation relationship. This integration was facilitated by using a similar and complex conceptualisation of radicalisation and inequality for each of the syntheses. Radicalisation was understood as a relational process shaped by context and ideological orientation. Inequality was understood as: manifested at both individual and social levels; existing objectively and subjectively; and taking economic and social-political forms.

Method

The inclusion/exclusion criteria, search strategy and limitations of the two syntheses conducted are outlined below. Further details of the procedures (and results) can be found in Franc and Pavlović (2018, 2021) and Poli and Arun (2019, 2021).

Inclusion and Exclusion Criteria

Studies included in the reviews had to be empirical (quantitative, qualitative or mixed-method) and relevant to both inequality and radicalisation. We limited the search to publications (journal articles, books, book chapters or reports) in English that were published between 1 January 2001 and 31 December 2017 and focused on terrorism or Islamist and/or extreme-right radicalisation. The starting date reflects the year in which the concept of 'radicalisation' began to appear more often in the literature (Neumann and Kleinmann 2013). We included studies regardless of whether they employed primary or secondary data, their research design and approaches to data collection, analytical procedures or geographical context of the data analysed. No limitations regarding age, gender, ethnicity or nationality were imposed. Finally, relevant populations of the studies published included terrorist or radicalised groups, states or other aggregate units (in the case of quantitative terrorism studies) alongside individuals.

Search Strategy

The search strategy was founded on the central concepts (inequality and radicalisation) as understood and interpreted within the DARE project (DARE 2016; see also Franc and Pavlović 2018; Poli and Arun 2019). A search was conducted of seven databases (Web of Science Core Collection – excluding Chemical Indexes; SCOPUS; Current Contents® – Social & Behavioral Sciences; SocINDEX – full texts; PsychINFO; EconLit – EBSCO; and MEDLINE®), with the additional hand-search of two journals (*Journal for Deradicalization* and *Perspectives on Terrorism*) and a grey literature search. The initial search identified 5,511 manuscripts. After several rounds of screening and eligibility checks, cross-referencing and expert advice,[1] our final data set consisted of 141 publications based on quantitative and mixed studies and ninety-four publications based on qualitative and mixed studies.

Of the 141 publications presenting quantitative findings, forty-two were based on surveys among non-radicalised individuals, fifteen on biographical evidence from radicalised individuals and eighty-four on analyses of terrorism data. Within the SR, we differentiated between: (1) level of investigation: individual (indicators such as income, education level, (un)employment etc.) or societal (indicators such as national GDP or poverty rate); (2) type and ideological base of radicalisation (cognitive or behavioural, Islamist or extreme-right, international or domestic terrorism); (3) type of inequality: economic or socio-political, and its objective/measurable or subjective/perceived basis.

Of the ninety-four publications presenting qualitative findings, seventy focused on Islamist radicalisation, and twenty-four focused on extreme-right, racist or anti-Islamic radicalisation. The MES generated interpretive explanations of the relationship between inequality and radicalisation derived from synthesising the findings of multiple empirical studies. The assessed studies varied in terms of geographic location and in the profiles of interviewees included.

Main Limitations

Both reviews were limited by the search criteria, which failed to reach all available databases as well as texts in languages other than English. Furthermore, we did not discriminate between studies with respect to quality, given that all texts identified were already cited and are used in forming policies. Therefore, in deciding between maximising the breadth of the evidence base or restricting inclusion in order to ensure the highest quality of studies, we opted for the former, whilst acknowledging that excluding studies with a less rigorous methodological approach might have led to more consistent findings.

Results

In view of the different methodologies used in the frame of the MES and the SR, we have chosen to present the results in a successive manner. This highlights the range of approaches and concepts and the specific emphases that emerge from each type of synthesis. In the Conclusion, we combine the findings to provide general insights and a more complex understanding of the relationships between inequalities and radicalisation.

Configurations of the Relationship between Inequality, Injustice and Radicalisation: The Meta-Ethnographic Synthesis

In the MES, three main interpretations of the relationship between inequality and radicalisation were identified: direct, indirect and 'contested'. Those studies identifying a direct relationship suggested that structural inequality (such as belonging to a disadvantaged group, class, district, country), but also perceived inequality, are directly connected to the process of radicalisation. Where an indirect relationship was posited, the studies identified a series of other factors, drivers or variables that mediate the link between inequality and radicalisation. In those cases where indirect links only are established, the authors point to the absence of consistent inequality-radicalisation relationships and the complex nature of the relationship. Finally, a third interpretation emerges from refutational studies, which suggest a lack of relationship between inequality and radicalisation. In all cases, attention should be paid to the direction of the relationship since inequality may be understood as a root cause of radicalisation but also as a consequence of it.

Decentring Ideology: Inequality and Social Injustice as the Bedrock of Radicalisation

Two main lines of argument posit a direct relationship between inequality and radicalisation. In the first case, this pertains to structural inequality while, in the second, to subjective inequality (perceived injustice).

A number of studies suggested that poor socio-economic conditions – rather than ideology or religion – lie at the root of radicalisation into violent extremism associated with Islam (Christensen 2015; Ahmed 2016). Such 'conditions' included high unemployment (or under-employment), permanent dependence on state welfare, an inadequate public health care system, a poor school system and poor social mobility due to an intractable class system (Boukhars and Amar 2011; Shetret, Schwartz and Cotter 2013; Coolsaet 2017). In some texts, a direct relationship between inequality and radicalisation is suggested through the depiction of radicalised individuals' backgrounds, even though this does not result in a sustained argument by the author about the relationship between inequality and radicalisation (Hegghammer 2010; Aasgaard 2017; Azam and Fatima 2017). Radicalisation into extreme-right movements is also associated by some authors with social problems – understood as a real situation or a feeling of being excluded – rather than ideology alone (Christensen 2015; Busher 2016; Pilkington 2016). Thus, although individuals themselves rarely connect their material circumstances with their trajectory into extreme-right activism (Pilkington 2016: 85), those circumstances – of being out of work, in low-income jobs or earning a living through precarious and semi-legal activities – remain an important context for understanding life decisions.

The relationship between inequality (coming from a lower or lower middle-class socio-economic background, poverty or deprivation) and radicalisation is a common feature of radicalised people in the different studies. However, the nature of qualitative research – with its relatively small samples and often inductively driven research questions – means that direct relationships between structurally rooted socio-economic conditions (at individual or societal level) and radicalisation are difficult to test, model or generalise.

Another important illustration of the direct link between radicalisation and inequality refers more explicitly to the subjectivity of radicalised individuals. Here the relationship between perceived injustice and radicalisation differs, depending on whether the study deals with extreme-right or Islamist radicalisation.

In relation to the extreme right, while social inequality experienced by activists is not objectively proven, studies show that activists perceive themselves to be unjustly treated while preferential treatment is given to 'others'. In such cases, perceived inequality gives rise to grievance, which fuels radicalisation (on the nature and role of 'grievance', see Pilkington and Vestel, this volume). The feeling of having received 'unjust treatment' by authorities is one of the main frames of thought identified among supporters and activists in different countries (De Koster and Houtman 2008; Klandermans and Mayer 2009; Rhodes 2011; Pilkington 2016). Activism provides a mechanism for resisting this perceived second-class status (Bartlett, Birdwell and Littler 2011: 174) through a discursive reordering of privilege and prejudice in which 'we' are seen as the discriminated and those in power are exposed as a liberal elite of 'do-gooders' who have little understanding of the everyday worlds of ordinary people (Pilkington 2016: 228).

In the case of numerous studies on Islamist extremism, the relationship between inequality and radicalisation is inverted. Terrorist events, and the perception of Muslims as perpetrators of them, act as a source of social vulnerability for Muslim populations, leading to, or embedding, discrimination and inequality. Indeed, one of the strongest associations encountered in the body of texts studied is that terrorism and counter-terrorism are a particular burden for (non-radicalised) Muslim populations in the West, leading to – among other things – an increase in social vulnerability. Terrorist events are shown to have a major and direct impact on Muslims' experience in Western countries and consequently on their economic status and sense of injustice. The numerous studies which develop this perspective emphasise, in different ways, and from different perspectives and experiences, the social burden of terrorism and counter-terrorism for Muslims. They draw attention to the acute social vulnerability of Muslims in many societies since 9/11 and, in some cases, following the implementation of counter-terrorism policies. In the wake of this argument, the MES revealed a discrete line of argument that identified a vicious circle in which social inequality and radicalisation are co-produced through processes of stigmatisation and exclusion. A shared interpretation among a number of studies is that the process of stigmatisation of Muslims impacts negatively on their sense of belonging to their country of residence and may engender forms of radicalisation. In other words, the sense of exclusion of Muslims from citizenship in Western societies – as a result of stigmatisation and discrimination following terrorist acts and targeting of Muslim communities through counter-terrorism policies – strengthens adherence to Islam and susceptibility to radicalisation. This vicious circle may develop in relation not only to terrorism but to religious extremism more widely (Abbas and Siddique 2012; Ahmed 2016; Coolsaet 2017). However, this causal chain is far from systematically repeated and, as noted in the discussion above, a number of studies point to outcomes other than radicalisation, especially resistance and resilience of people facing calls to radicalisation (Hussain and Bagguley 2013) or agency and creative responses to the challenges faced (Abbas and Siddique 2012; Bonino 2015).

While a less developed line of argument arising from the literature, some studies of the extreme right also point to the vicious circle between stigmatisation, social exclusion and radicalisation. Blee's (2002: 9)

study of women activists in a range of extreme-right and white supremacist movements in the United States documents evidence that socio-
economic disadvantage was a consequence rather than the cause of radicalisation in some cases. This finding is also identified in Pilkington's
(2016) study of English Defence League (EDL) activists. Similarly, Van
der Valk and Wagenaar (2010: 28–29) noted that even though former
extreme-right radicals in the Netherlands generally continued to work in
the same sector, they experienced problems at work after moving away
from the extreme right 'because their right-wing extremist activities
somehow became known through an internet publication, for example,
or because of publicity after arrest' (ibid.). A sense of injustice due to
discriminatory treatment by employers on grounds of their political views
has been found across extreme-right milieus in more recent studies too
(see Pilkington and Vestel, this volume). It is notable that studies of radicalisation tend to call for the decentring of the debate away from ideology
and/or religion when discussing Islam and Muslims, while, when focused on the extreme right, they call for greater attention to the views of
extreme-right supporters or activists.

Indirect Relationships between Inequality and Radicalisation

A clear line of argument emerging from the MES is that a relationship
between inequality and radicalisation exists but is mediated by interven-
ing factors or variables. This is underpinned by the general position that
radicalisation is caused by a complex and individually specific set of factors. For instance, the importance of understanding the socio-economic
situation of an individual or a group in combination with individual life
experiences is noted by Botha (2015) in a study of four radical organisations in Kenya and Uganda. This author argues that it is a combination
of factors that explains radicalisation trajectories and this combination
will differ from person to person. For Botha, socio-economic trends may
be important in encouraging radicalisation, especially where there are
'economic disparities within identifiable ethnic, religious and geographic
groups' (ibid.: 12). In this line of argument, it is notable that all authors
emphasise that it is subjectively experienced inequality that is at play
here and that radicalisation is the outcome of the accumulation of drivers.
However, a number of key concepts capturing mediating factors can be
discerned and are found in studies of both Islamist and extreme-right
radicalisation.

Some authors, for example, understand poverty, marginalisation and
social exclusion as potentially facilitating the radicalisation process but
see other factors, such as social ties, as more significant in radicalisation

trajectories (Sageman 2004: 121–30; Ahmad 2014, 2016). Hegghammer (2010: 236) also finds in-group loyalty to be more important than ideological factors in the recruitment of Saudi jihadists. Of those recruited between 1996 and 2001, he argues, many were linked by kinship or friendship to other militants (ibid.: 130), while later (post-2001) recruits often emerged from jihadi social networks to which former fighters in Afghanistan turned after feeling betrayed by the state and society (often experiencing arrest and interrogation) after return from Afghanistan (ibid.: 190).

Studies of extreme-right radicalisation also point to the centrality of social ties in recruitment. Blee's (2002: 28) study of female participants in a range of white supremacist, neo-Nazi and skinhead groups in the United States demonstrated that women get involved through personal contacts and become racist as a consequence of associating with members of racist groups rather than joining racist groups because they are racist (that is, for ideological reasons) or for structural reasons.

There is also significant evidence that space or, more accurately, milieu mediates socio-economic inequality in driving extreme-right radicalisation. Miller-Idriss (2009: 100–101), for example, identifies the milieu of young working-class people to be a crucial factor in determining trajectories into support for the extreme right, with particular districts in Berlin being 'renowned for the highly visible right-wing extremist youth who live and hang out among the housing complexes in the neighbourhood'.

Another driving factor in the relationship between inequality and radicalisation for both Islamist and right-wing extremism is gender (Aslam 2014; Speckhard 2017). For example, in the Pakistan context, Aslam (2014: 148) suggests that 'poverty jeopardises masculine honour at a subjective level' and may lead individuals to seek to regain their position in the gender order through 'acts of violence that are culturally perceived as normative performances of the masculine'.

Jensen et al. (2016: 68) suggest inequality in material terms is never the sole driver of radicalisation but is always accompanied by other factors such as a personal or community crisis, psychological vulnerability and so on. Cragin et al. (2015: 5) also posit the feeling of 'despair' as an important affective dimension of material circumstance or disadvantage that potentially contributes to radicalisation; while despair among members of Hamas and Fatah does not lead to radicalisation on its own, it can reinforce revolutionary tendencies in as much as it causes individuals to subjugate their identity to that of the group. We might understand conversion to jihadist Islam in prison as similarly indicating the role of personal crisis in guiding individuals towards a radicalisation pathway (Sporton, Valentine and Bang Nielsen 2006: 215; see also Conti, this volume).

Studies of young people supporting extreme-right views or active in extreme-right movements confirm the consistent importance of personal trauma. Gabriel's (2014: 36) study of twenty-six young people expressing racist attitudes and behavioural dispositions in Switzerland led to the conclusion that 'social marginality' is less influential than 'deprivation or disintegration as a result of domestic violence and parental conflicts' in leading to such outcomes. This study also identified a strong 'culture of non-attention' among families, which has an effect on the biographies of right-wing actors (see also Pilkington, this volume). Among racist Russian skinheads, a sense of parental abandonment was also expressed by respondents, who felt that 'parents have given up caring' about their children (Pilkington, Omel'chenko and Garifzianova 2010: 49). This cultural disposition was aggravated by early mortality, especially of men in the region, leading to many young people experiencing the loss of fathers at a young age (ibid.: 50). Of Kimmel's (2014: 71) sample of former neo-Nazi skinheads in Scandinavia, 'all but one' had experienced bullying in school, while a number of respondents in Pilkington's (2016: 69) study of EDL activists also recounted experiences of bullying. In the latter study, many trajectories into the movement included childhood trauma, and it was rare to find family contexts described as stable, strong or protective (ibid.: 80).

Finally, the failure of mainstream political parties (Garland and Treadwell 2010, 2012; Rhodes 2010, 2011) or the lack of power-sharing institutions (Bunte and Vinson 2016) to address inequality and the resentment associated with low economic positions may transform poverty, marginalisation or deprivation into push factors of radicalisation. Ford and Goodwin (2014: 243, 249–50) characterise support for UKIP (United Kingdom Independence Party) as 'heavily concentrated among older, blue-collar workers with little education and few skills', which, they say, are groups who have been left behind by the economic and social transformation of Britain and who have lost faith in the ability of traditional politics to solve their everyday problems. However, it is important to recognise that the inequality experienced is not only socio-economic; it is also socio-political. The formal political realm is experienced as one of 'silencing' of the voices of the 'white working class', policed, according to Pilkington's (2016: 204–14) respondents, by the application of the 'racism label' with the aim of teaching those with, what are judged to be, unacceptable views to 'keep their mouth shut'. Among respondents in Pilkington's (ibid.: 210) study, there is an active disavowal of the formal political sphere. The 'political class', respondents believe (and regardless of party affiliation), are 'just do-gooders' who 'act like ... everything's for the people when nothing is' (ibid.: 175). This potentially fuels radicalisation trajectories in that those who feel silenced reject formal politics as the 'politics of talk' in favour of a 'not-politics of action' (ibid.: 210; Pilkington, Omel'chenko and Garifzianova 2010: 102). Similar recognition of the silencing of the expression of national pride is identified by Miller-Idriss (2009) as crucial to the rise of popular support for the right wing among working-class youth.

A Contested Relationship between Inequality and Radicalisation

In the analysed studies, a third line of argument refutes the idea that either objective, material inequality or subjective socio-economic grievances lead to violent extremism. Although none of the authors included in our corpus denies the (potential) role played by socio-economic inequality in the radicalisation process, all suggest that less centrality should be given to it and propose different readings of the interplay between religion, ideology, poverty and radicalisation. In explaining radicalisation, a significant proportion of the analysed texts discuss a number of alternative drivers including: a quest for adventure or attraction to the 'buzz' of violence; the search for status and meaning; ideology (including racism, Islamophobia and jihadist religio-politics); religious duty; feelings of belonging, companionship and loyalty; family or peer socialisation; subcultural 'cool' or trend; and social environment or milieu. The range of issues and factors considered in the analysed studies should alert us to the importance of not artificially opposing different positions and of understanding radicalisation in a holistic way.

That radicalisation is not solely characteristic of the socio-economically disadvantaged is, of course, old news; this was, in fact, the conventional wisdom especially through the 1980s and 1990s. Basra, Neumann and Brunner (2016: 13), for example, note that Egyptian sociologist Saad Eddin Ibrahim established in the early 1980s that a high proportion of imprisoned Egyptian Islamists were engineers and doctors from well-to-do families. Hegghammer's (2010: 242) study of three waves of Saudi jihadists (drawing on a total of 539 biographies) also shows that Al Qaeda recruits were generally better educated than the national male average and 'were neither losers nor disgruntled graduates nor ideologically driven rich kids' (ibid.: 130). Sageman (2004: 75) also challenges the notion that poverty engenders terrorism by pointing to evidence that three-quarters of the global Salafist *mujahedin* were upper or middle class. Sageman also found his sample to be well educated (40% were college-educated), socio-economically aspirational, globally connected and multilingual (ibid.: 77).

Research on more recently radicalised individuals points in the same direction, as shown in the studies conducted by the Centre for Prevention of Radicalisation Leading to Violence (CPRLV 2015, 2016), which highlight the diversity of profiles of young radicalised women in Quebec in terms of education, life history, psychological antecedents, family history and environments as well as level of social integration. In the same vein, Dawson, Amarasingam and Bain (2016: 38) find little reference to material deprivation in the previous lives of foreign fighters, concluding that 'pull factors' such as ideology, narrative, ideas and religiosity are relatively more important in journeys to radicalisation than material factors.

Studies of the extreme right also find 'no evidence that "right-wing actors" come from "socially disadvantaged groups"' (Gabriel 2014: 44). Gabriel finds that young people with extreme-right trajectories come from 'all social strata, though mainly from lower middle-class families' and do not suffer from social exclusion or social deprivation. Blee's (2002: 8) study of female extreme-right activists in the United States also challenges the 'common stereotypes about racist women as uneducated, marginal members of society raised in terrible families and lured into racist groups by boyfriends and husbands'. On the contrary, she argues, most were not poor, were educated and had good jobs (ibid.: 9).

Finally, the shared interpretation of authors adopting a critical line of argument is that socio-economic factors may be present but not determining in radicalisation. Hegghammer (2010: 133) suggests that it is very difficult to pinpoint socio-economic factors with a strong predictive value for individual Saudi recruitment to Al Qaeda. Speckhard (2017: 13) also recognises that particular forms of inequalities, such as high unemployment and material benefits, play a significant role in pathways to radicalisation among Kosovan women travelling to Syria to join ISIS, but argues that such inequalities alone do not provide sufficient explanation.

With regard to right-wing extremism, Gabriel (2014: 45) concludes that 'macro-sociological explanations of right-wing extremism alone are too narrow' and that 'even if we accept that socio-structural conditions have considerable influence, a large measure of autonomy remains'. Pilkington (2016: 154) also suggests that part of the problem lies in a limited understanding of inequality, which is manifest not only in individual social and economic profiles or backgrounds but also in community fragmentation, loss of meaning and the fracturing of individuals' sense of self which can lead to resignation, shame and fear but also resentment and resistance.

Inequality-Radicalisation/Terrorism Relationship from a Quantitative Perspective

In our SR of quantitative studies, we sought to establish whether or not there was an association between inequality and radicalisation and, if so, how, when and where it was present and how it might be explained.

Whether such associations can be established or not, our findings suggest, depends on a number of factors including: whether we are interested in the relationship between inequality and radicalisation at an individual level, or inequality and terrorism at a social level; concrete type, dimensions and indicators of inequality used (economic or social-political, objective or more subjective inequality); context (socio-political, demographic, geographical, whether countries have majority Muslim populations, USA, Western Europe); or point in the radicalisation process (cognitive or behavioural radicalisation). Below, we summarise the main findings of the reviewed studies in relation to these key factors.

Is Economic Inequality Related to Radicalisation and Terrorism?

Within the thirty-six analysed studies relevant for understanding the role of objective economic inequality at an individual level, objective economic inequality is frequently operationalised as educational level, personal income or poverty and, less often, as job status or social class. Findings did not support any firm conclusion regarding a relationship between such objective economic inequality indicators and a cognitive Islamist radicalisation in the context of Muslim majority countries. For example, regarding education, in some studies, more support for radicalised attitudes (e.g. support for suicide bombing or confidence in bin Laden) was characteristic for the less-educated (e.g. Fair, Hamza and Heller 2017). In other studies or countries, this was found to be more likely among the more educated (e.g. Cherney and Povey 2013). In some cases, even in the same study, education was differently related to different radicalised beliefs (e.g. Muluk, Sumaktoyo and Ruth 2013). Thus, the relationship between individual education, income, poverty and Islamic radicalisation in Muslim majority countries probably depends on a combination of individual characteristics (e.g. a combination of higher education and poverty) or on some contextual characteristics (e.g. concrete country or poverty or violence in a district). In contrast, in the case of the fifteen analysed studies focusing on behavioural radicalisation, studies analysing the characteristics of terrorists generally indicate that participation in an Islamist terrorist group is more likely for more educated individuals (e.g. Berrebi 2007; Fair 2014). However, this relationship may depend on other individual factors, such as the role of the individual in the terrorist group, their direct participation in violence (or not) and type of violence (Perliger, Koehler-Derrick and Pedahzur 2016), as well as contextual characteristics such as poverty at an individual and district level (e.g. Kavanagh 2011; Saeed and Syed 2018). In the context of Western European countries, notwithstanding all the obstacles and limitations of studies of radicalised individuals, data generally suggest that Islamist radicalisation is more likely among the less educated and persons from a lower economic status (e.g. Bakker 2006; Bakker and de Bont 2016; Ljujic, van Prooijen and Weerman 2017; PROTON 2017; Reynolds and Hafez 2017).

In the case of the eighty-four analysed terrorism studies, when investigating the inequality-terrorism relationship at the societal level, economic inequality was studied using indicators related to poverty, income inequality and the country's economic development (e.g. GDP p.c., HDI, unemployment rates). The findings suggest that the relationship between indicators such as poverty and income inequality and terrorism are inconsistent, with two exceptions: higher poverty was consistently related to a higher incidence of transnational terrorism; and higher interregional inequality seems to be related to a higher incidence of domestic terrorism. The findings regarding national economic development were similar. With regard to domestic and transnational terrorism, there is an inconsistent tendency for higher GDP p.c. to be associated with higher incidence of attacks. However, more advanced studies indicate that countries with a low and those with a high GDP p.c. tend to have a lower incidence of terrorism than countries with an average GDP p.c. Regarding unemployment rates, results generally confirm the importance of inequality since the probability of general terrorism attacks is higher for countries with higher unemployment rates. Findings regarding other economic development indicators were inconsistent. Moreover, the robustness of all these conclusions may be questionable due to the scarcity of empirical findings.

Subjective economic inequality (e.g. income dissatisfaction, perceived individual poverty or unemployment worry, economic status) is less frequently investigated as a determinant of Islamist cognitive radicalisation than objective economic inequality. Generally, in the context of Muslim majority countries, perceived economic inequality is not related to cognitive Islamist radicalisation, although the results are not completely consistent (e.g. Ciftci, O'Donnell and Tanner 2017; Fair, Hamza and Heller 2017). Moreover, one experimental study (in the context of Pakistan) demonstrates that perceived individual poverty lowers the likelihood of cognitive Islamist radicalisation, especially in combination with the perception of a high level of violence in the country (Fair et al. 2018). In the context of Western European countries, those – rare – studies including subjective economic inequality provided inconsistent results (Deckard and Jacobson 2015; Berger 2016).

Is Socio-Political Inequality Related to Radicalisation and Terrorism?

At an individual level, the twenty-six detected findings on the relationship between cognitive radicalisation and perceived socio-political inequality (e.g. personal or group deprivation, unfair treatment, discrimination) are generally more consistent than is the case for economic inequality. Namely, regardless of the ideological base of radicalisation and context, individuals perceiving themselves or their group as more deprived and in an unjust position were more likely to exhibit more radicalised responses in conducted surveys. Such a positive relationship between perceived socio-political inequality and Islamist cognitive radicalisation is suggested by studies in the context of Muslim majority countries (e.g. Fischer et al. 2008; Tausch et al. 2011; Muluk, Sumaktoyo and Ruth 2013) and in the European context (e.g. Tausch et al. 2011; Doosje, Loseman and Van Den Bos 2013; Schils and Pauwels 2016). The few studies of extreme-right radicalisation in the Western European context also point to a positive relationship between perceived social inequality and cognitive radicalisation (Doosje et al. 2012; Pauwels and De Waele 2014; Pauwels and Heylen 2017). However, these studies are mainly based on multi-item reliable measures of radicalisation and inequality and frequently use more advanced statistical analyses, which may explain why more consistent results were obtained.

In the case of analysed terrorism studies, socio-political inequality was investigated through indicators such as democracy (most often, i.e., fifty-two findings detected among the eighty-four analysed studies), respect for physical integrity rights (thirty findings detected) or gender equality (eight findings detected). Although it seems that a higher level of democracy is related to a higher incidence of terrorist attacks, studies also indicate a higher incidence of terrorism in countries with a medium level of democracy. In the case of repression, as well as respect for physical integrity rights, a small number of studies indicate that a higher incidence of general or domestic terrorism is more characteristic for countries with a higher level of repression and lower respect for physical integrity rights. Findings regarding respect for civil rights and liberties are inconsistent, while results give a modest indication of a higher level of gender equality being related to lower terrorism incidence at the general and transnational level, but not at the domestic level. Altogether, it seems that suppression of rights (civil rights and liberties, physical integrity rights, women's rights) is related to higher terrorism rates.

Where, When and How is Inequality Related to Radicalisation?

Only a few of the analysed quantitative studies explored whether the inequality-radicalisation relationship depends on some additional individual or contextual factors. Results of some studies indicate the possible importance of the combined effect (interaction) of two specific inequality indicators (e.g. poverty/income and education) (Chiozza 2009; Kavanagh 2011; Saeed and Syed 2018). Other studies suggested the importance of different contextual factors such as level of urbanisation or level of violence (Mousseau 2011; Fair et al. 2018). Mousseau (2011) demonstrates that poverty is accompanied by higher support for Islamist terrorism only in urban areas, while findings from Pakistan indicate that the presence of violence caused by militant organisations in combination with individual-level poverty reduces support for violent groups (Blair et al. 2013; Fair et al. 2018). These findings could also explain the previously mentioned interactive relationship between poverty and level of urbanisation (Mousseau 2011) since violence may be more concentrated in urban areas.

Some studies of macro-level determinants of terrorism demonstrate that the relationship between economic development and terrorism may also depend on additional markers of inequality or other contextual factors. For instance, Ghatak and Gold (2017) demonstrated that only in countries with a high GDP p.c. did the rate of an excluded population relate to the rising number of terrorist attacks, while no relationship between an excluded population and terrorism was found in countries with a low GDP p.c. There have been some indications also that the relationship between GDP and terrorism depends on the type of government – democracy or autocracy (Piazza 2013; Nemeth, Mauslein and Stapley 2014) – or may have a different direction of association (positive or negative) in low- compared to high-income groups of countries (Enders and Hoover 2012). Democracy also appears to interact with heterogeneity costs.[2] In immature democracies, higher heterogeneity costs were related to higher rates of terrorism, while this relationship was much less consistent in autocracies and completely developed democracies (Ghatak 2016b). Moreover, Brockhoff, Krieger and Meierrieks (2015) found that a more democratic government was related to a higher incidence of domestic terrorism in less developed countries but a lower incidence of domestic attacks in more developed countries. Further, Ghatak (2016a) revealed that in weak democracies, the predicted number of terrorist attacks sharply grew as the percentage of excluded population increased, which was not found in other regimes. Similarly, Choi and Piazza (2016a) specified the relevance of both political rights and political discrimination in predicting terrorism.

Regarding the question of *how* inequality is related to radicalisation, only a small number of analysed studies provide relevant findings which could explain the relationship between some of the inequality measures and radicalisation. For now, it seems that a positive relationship between perceived social inequality and Islamist or extreme-right radicalisation could be explained by a different social-psychological process related to ideological attitudes (like fundamentalist religiosity in the case of Islamist radicalisation or authoritarianism in the case of extreme-right radicalisation), intergroup attitudes and emotions (like perceived group threat) or an aspect of social identity (like in-group superiority) (Tausch et al. 2011; Doosje et al. 2012; Doosje, Loseman and Van Den Bos 2013; Schils and Pauwels 2016).

At the macro level, rare studies suggest that increasing socio-political inequality (worsening of physical integrity or human rights) can increase suicide terrorism or lead to popular grievances, which help fuel terrorist campaigns (Choi and Piazza 2016b; Piazza 2016).

Conclusions

The syntheses of findings from quantitative and qualitative research studies generated important insights into the relationship between inequality and radicalisation that either confirm or supplement each other.

The important insight based on analyses of qualitative studies is the identification of a bi-directional relationship between inequality and radicalisation. On the one hand, as is often presumed, inequality produces radicalisation. On the other hand, however, radicalisation also plays a role in producing inequality (or injustice/discrimination). Poverty, marginalisation, deprivation, low economic backgrounds and/or discrimination and perceived injustice at the societal and/or personal level are understood as contributing in varying degrees to radicalisation or as resulting from radicalisation.

A second insight concerns the tension between objective and subjective dimensions of inequality – both of which may lead individuals to follow a radicalisation pathway. The synthesis of qualitative studies suggests that the subjective meanings of inequality – that is, the perception of being disadvantageously positioned in relations of power, regardless of whether this is associated with an objective situation or not – supersede the objective variables of inequality in triggering a path towards radicalisation. Likewise, the SR of quantitative studies suggests that perceived socio-political inequality could be more important than economic inequality in understanding the drivers of radicalisation and terrorism. On a general level, these findings are in accordance with the most recent systematic review findings (Wolfowicz et al. 2020; Jahnke, Abad Borger and Beelmann 2022). Wolfowicz et al. (2020), for example, have shown that variables we considered as relevant for objective economic inequality (e.g. being unemployed or welfare recipient) are in the group of risk factors with the smallest effects on radical attitudes and intentions. At the same time, indicators relevant for perceived socio-political inequality (e.g. perceived injustice, relative deprivation) were confirmed as factors with slightly more substantial impact on radical attitudes and intentions. Similarly, recent meta-analysis of predictors of political violence outcomes among young people revealed group relative deprivation as one of the factors consistently linked to political violence outcomes (Jahnke, Abad Borger and Beelmann 2022).

Since subjective inequality and perceived injustice are confirmed as potential motivators of political or collective action in general in the social science literature, future studies could further clarify the potential importance of perceived injustice in the context of differentiation of radicalisation from other forms of political and collective action. Considering that socio-political inequality could be more important than economic inequality, policymakers should invest additional efforts to prevent the potential for existing policies and measures, aimed at increasing safety and lowering the risk of radicalisation and terrorism, to backfire by increasing perceived injustice and discrimination among relevant populations. Moreover, both syntheses revealed that a relationship between subjective inequality and radicalisation exists and is probably complex.

From the qualitative perspective, the demonstrated difference in the importance of subjective and objective inequality raises the question of whether, and how, objective economic inequality interacts with a sense of injustice in the production of radicalisation pathways. It also warns against the tendency to reify the link between social inequality, religion and radicalisation. The intertwining of social exclusion, religion and radicalisation could undermine the treatment of important social issues for affected populations (such as discrimination, racism, inequality) and risk reducing any social issues concerning Muslim populations to the problem of radicalisation. The weight attached to subjective experiences of injustice in the qualitative studies also points to the fact that radicalisation is more similar to a process than a state. Each experience of injustice is reflected, interpreted and potentially mobilised via a multiplicity of other factors, including socio-economic situation, personal background, family ties and national context. In the case of the qualitative studies, the mosaic of composite findings that emerges underlines a set of contrasts that tends to bring into tension different perspectives regarding the causes of radicalisation.

From the quantitative perspective, the complexity of the relationship between inequality and radicalisation or terrorism is demonstrated by findings that the inequality-radicalisation relationship could be conditional on some other individual or contextual (macro) factor. Moreover, more sophisticated survey studies indicate that the relationship between perceived inequality and radicalisation could be explained by a different socio-psychological process related to ideological attitudes, intergroup attitudes and emotions and aspects of social identity. At the same time, some of the terrorism studies indicated that testing the non-linear relations between inequality on the societal level and terrorism might offer a more useful way forward than studying linear relationships.

This leads naturally to general insights from both the SR and MES, namely that the link between inequality and radicalisation is context dependent, if not case-by-case dependent. The importance of context identified in the SR is extended by the findings of the MES that suggest that inequality (poverty, marginalisation, disenfranchisement etc.) at the level of individual experience not only fails to consistently explain radicalisation, but that feelings of victimisation and injustice that steer people down a radicalisation path may be formed not at the level of experience at all, but be part of a subjective reality forged 'in the realm of imaginary' of individuals and groups (Khosrokhavar 2018).

In interpreting insights and conclusions of both reviews, it should be noted that they represent 'informed' assumptions rather than firm causal conclusions. Namely, the type of evidence we investigated (primarily descriptive or correlational studies) prevents any firm causal conclusions. Thus, for enhancing understanding of the inequality-radicalisation relationship, the challenges for future studies are to get as close as possible to the subjectivities of actors (in the case of a qualitative approach) and to explore the inequality-radicalisation relationship using experimental and longitudinal research designs (in the case of a quantitative approach). Integration of findings of experimental or longitudinal research designs with insights from in-depth interviews could serve as a basis for valid causal conclusions by comparing, for instance, the general evolution of conceptions of social justice in different types of society with the individual approach of feelings of injustice. These orientations could constitute a starting point for the development of models of radicalisation and deradicalisation which highlight the nexus between political and social inequality beyond the prism of relative frustration.

Acknowledgements

The research leading to this publication has received funding from the European Union's Horizon 2020 Research and Innovation Programme, under Grant Agreement No. 725349. The views and conclusions contained in this chapter are those of the authors. The Agency and the Commission are not responsible for any use that may be made of the information it contains.

Tomislav Pavlović's work on DARE has been supported by a Croatian Science Foundation within Young Researchers' Career Development Project – Training of Doctoral Students (DOK-01-2018) financed by the European Union from the European Social Fund (ESF).

Renata Franc has a PhD in Psychology and is senior scientific adviser and team leader at the Institute of Social Sciences Ivo Pilar in Zagreb, Croatia and full professor of Social and Political Psychology (University of Zagreb). Her research interests include youth, social and political attitudes and values, political and social participation, intergroup relations, and quality of life. She has particular expertise in research methodology, the quantitative approach and survey research along with experience of qualitative research methods.

Alexandra Poli has a PhD in Sociology and is CNRS Researcher at the Centre d'Etudes des Mouvements Sociaux (EHESS, Paris). Her research interests focus on racism, antisemitism, discrimination, Islam, migration and radicalisation. These themes serve as entry points for the study of the interactions between the social, institutional and political production of otherness and contemporary conceptions of social justice, at different scales of analysis: global, national, local, collective and individual.

Tomislav Pavlović is a PhD student and research assistant at the Institute of Social Sciences Ivo Pilar in Zagreb, Croatia. His PhD study is focused on the development of predictive models of radicalisation. He has specialist qualifications in research methodology and quantitative data analysis.

············

NOTES

1. For a complete description of the search flow, see Figure 1 in Franc and Pavlović 2018, 2021.
2. Heterogeneity costs represent deprivation of a minority group from public goods due to ideological or physical differences from the majority group ('the ruling elite'), and were operationalised by combining the heterogeneity index of a country and economic discrimination (Ghatak 2016b).

REFERENCES

Aasgaard, Andrea. 2017. 'Scandinavia's Daughters in the Syrian Civil War: What Can We Learn from Their Family Members' Lived Experiences?' *Journal for Deradicalization* 13: 243–75.

Abbas, Tahir, and Assma Siddique. 2012. 'Perceptions of the Processes of Radicalisation and De-radicalisation among British South Asian Muslims in a Post-Industrial City', *Social Identities: Journal for the Study of Race, Nation and Culture* 18(1): 119–34.

Ahmad, Akhlaq. 2014. 'The Role of Social Networks in the Recruitment of Youth in an Islamist Organization in Pakistan', *Sociological Spectrum* 34(6): 469–88.

———. 2016. 'The Ties That Bind and Blind: Embeddedness and Radicalisation of Youth in One Islamist Organisation in Pakistan', *Journal of Development Studies* 52(1): 5–21.

Ahmed, Shamila. 2016. 'Citizenship, Belonging and Attachment in the "War on Terror"', *Critical Criminology* 24(1): 111–25.

Aslam, Maleeha. 2014. 'Islamism and Masculinity: Case Study Pakistan', *Historical Social Research* 39(3): 135–49.

Azam, Zubair, and Syeda Bareeha Fatima. 2017. 'Mishal: A Case Study of a Deradicalisation and Emancipation Program in SWAT Valley, Pakistan', *Journal for Deradicalization* 11: 1–29.

Bakker, Edwin. 2006. 'Jihadi Terrorists in Europe, Their Characteristics and the Circumstances in Which They Joined the Jihad: An Exploratory Study', Netherlands Institute of International Relations.

Bakker, Edwin, and Roel de Bont. 2016. 'Belgian and Dutch Jihadist Foreign Fighters (2012–2015): Characteristics, Motivations, and Roles in the War in Syria and Iraq', *Small Wars & Insurgencies* 27(5): 837–57.

Bartlett, Jamie, Jonathan Birdwell and Mark Littler. 2011. *The New Face of Digital Populism*. London: Demos Press.

Basra, Rajan, Peter R. Neumann, and Claudia Brunner. 2016. 'Criminal Pasts, Terrorist Futures: European Jihadists and the New Crime-Terror Nexus,' ICSR. Retrieved 21 February 2022 from https://icsr.info/wp-content/uploads/2016/10/ICSR-Report-Criminal-Pasts-Terrorist-Futures-European-Jihadists-and-the-New-Crime-Terror-Nexus.pdf.

Bentley, Thomas, Rorisang Lekalake and Stephen Buchanan-Clarke. 2016. 'Threat of Violent Extremism from a "Grassroots" Perspective: Evidence from North Africa', *Afrobarometer Dispatch N°.100*. Retrieved 5 November 2021 from http://afrobarometer.org/sites/default/files/publications/Dispatches/ab-r6-dispatchno100-violent-extremism-nth-africa-en.pdf.

Berger, Lars. 2016. 'Local, National and Global Islam: Religious Guidance and European Muslim Public Opinion on Political Radicalism and Social Conservatism', *West European Politics* 39(2): 205–28.

Berrebi, Claude. 2007. 'Evidence about the Link between Education, Poverty and Terrorism among Palestinians', *Peace Economics, Peace Science, & Public Policy* 13(1): 1–36.

Blair, Graeme, et al. 2013. 'Poverty and Support for Militant Politics: Evidence from Pakistan', *American Journal of Political Science* 57(1): 30–48.

Blee, Kathleen M. 2002. *Inside Organized Racism: Women in the Hate Movement*. Berkeley: University of California Press.

Bonino, Stefano. 2015. 'Visible Muslimness in Scotland: Between Discrimination and Integration', *Patterns of Prejudice* 49(4): 367–91.

Botha, Anneli. 2015. 'Radicalisation to Terrorism in Kenya and Uganda: A Political Socialisation Perspective', *Perspectives on Terrorism* 9(5): 2–14.

Boukhars, Anouar, and Ali O. Amar. 2011. 'Trouble in the Western Sahara', *Journal of the Middle East and Africa* 2(2): 220–34.

Brockhoff, Sarah, Tim Krieger and Daniel Meierrieks. 2015. 'Great Expectations and Hard Times: The (Nontrivial) Impact of Education on Domestic Terrorism', *Journal of Conflict Resolution* 59(7): 1186–215.

Bunte, Jonas B., and Laura Thaut Vinson. 2016. 'Local Power-Sharing Institutions and Interreligious Violence in Nigeria', *Journal of Peace Research* 53(1): 49–65.

Busher, Joel. 2016. *The Making of Anti-Muslim Protest: Grassroots Activism in the English Defence League*. London: Routledge.

Campana, Aurélie, and Luc Lapointe. 2012. 'The Structural "Root" Causes of Non-Suicide Terrorism: A Systematic Scoping Review', *Terrorism and Political Violence* 24(1): 79–104.

Cherney, Adrian, and Jenny Povey. 2013. 'Exploring Support for Terrorism among Muslims', *Perspectives on Terrorism* 7(3): 5–16.

Chiozza, Giacomo. 2009. *How to Win Hearts and Minds? The Political Sociology of Popular Support for Suicide Bombing*. Working Paper, Vanderbilt University. Retrieved 28 March 2022 from https://www.exeter.ac.uk/media/university ofexeter/elecdem/pdfs/giacomochiozzatraining/How_to_Win_Hearts_and_ Minds.pdf.

Choi, Seung-Whan, and James A. Piazza. 2016a. 'Ethnic Groups, Political Exclusion and Domestic Terrorism', *Defence and Peace Economics* 27(1): 37–63.

———. 2016b. 'Internally Displaced Populations and Suicide Terrorism', *Journal of Conflict Resolution* 60(6): 1008–40.

Christensen, Tina Wilchen. 2015. 'How Extremist Experiences become Valuable Knowledge in EXIT Programmes', *Journal for Deradicalization* 3: 92–134.

Christmann, Kris. 2012. 'Preventing Religious Radicalisation and Violent Extremism: A Systematic Review of the Research Evidence', Youth Justice Board for England and Wales. Retrieved 5 November 2021 from https://pure.hud.ac.uk/ en/publications/preventing-religious-radicalisation-and-violent-extremism- a-syste.

Ciftci, Sabri, Becky J. O'Donnell and Allison A. Tanner. 2017. 'Who Favors Al-Qaeda? Anti-Americanism, Religious Outlooks, and Favorable Attitudes toward Terrorist Organizations', *Political Research Quarterly* 70(3): 480–94.

Coolsaet, Rik. 2017. 'Molenbeek and Violent Radicalisation: A Social Mapping', EIP European Institute of Peace. Retrieved 5 November 2021 from https:// view.publitas.com/eip/eip-molenbeek-report-16-06/page/14-15.

CPRLV. 2015. 'Radicalisation Leading to Violence in Quebec Schools: Issues and Perspectives', Centre for the Prevention of Radicalisation Leading to Violence. Retrieved 21 February 2022 from https://info-radical.org/wp-content/uploads/2016/10/rapport-cprlv.pdf.

———. 2016. 'Women and Violent Radicalisation'. Retrieved 28 March 2022 from https://www.csf.gouv.qc.ca/wp-content/uploads/radicalisation_recherche_anglais.pdf.

Cragin, Kim, et al. 2015. 'What Factors Cause Youth to Reject Violent Extremism? Results of an Exploratory Analysis in the West Bank', RAND Corporation. Retrieved 21 February 2022 from https://www.rand.org/pubs/research_reports/RR1118.html.

DARE. 2016. 'Description of Action'. Unpublished document.

Dawson, Lorne L., Aamarnath Amarasingam and Alexandra Bain. 2016. *Talking to Foreign Fighters: Socio-Economic Push versus Existential Pull Factors*. TSAS Working Paper Series, No 14–16. Retrieved 21 February 2022 from https://www.globalgovernancewatch.org/library/doclib/20160831_TalkingtoForeignFighters.pdf.

Deckard, Natalie Delia, and David Jacobson. 2015. 'The Prosperous Hardliner: Affluence, Fundamentalism, and Radicalization in Western European Muslim Communities', *Social Compass* 62(3): 412–33.

De Koster, Willem, and Dick Houtman. 2008. '"Stormfront Is Like a Second Home to Me": On Virtual Community Formation by Right-Wing Extremists', *Information, Communication & Society* 11(8): 1155–76.

Desmarais, Sarah L., et al. 2017. 'The State of Scientific Knowledge Regarding Factors Associated with Terrorism', *Journal of Threat Assessment and Management* 4(4): 180–209.

Doosje, Bertjan, et al. 2012. '"My In-Group is Superior!": Susceptibility for Radical Right-Wing Attitudes and Behaviors in Dutch Youth', *Negotiation and Conflict Management Research* 5(3): 253–68.

Doosje, Bertjan, Annemarie Loseman and Kees Van Den Bos. 2013. 'Determinants of Radicalisation of Islamic Youth in the Netherlands: Personal Uncertainty, Perceived Injustice, and Perceived Group Threat', *Journal of Social Issues* 69(3): 586–604.

Enders, Walter, and Garry A. Hoover. 2012. 'The Nonlinear Relationship between Terrorism and Poverty', *American Economic Review* 102(3): 267–72.

Fair, Christine C. 2014. 'Insights from a Database of Lashkar-e-Taiba and Hizbul-Mujahideen Militants', *Journal of Strategic Studies* 37(2): 259–90.

Fair, Christine C., Ali Hamza and Rebecca Heller. 2017. 'Who Supports Suicide Terrorism in Bangladesh? What the Data Say', *Politics and Religion* 10(3): 622–61.

Fair, Christine C., et al. 2018. 'Relative Poverty, Perceived Violence, and Support for Militant Politics: Evidence from Pakistan', *Political Science Research and Methods* 6(1): 57–81.

Fischer, Ronald, et al. 2008. 'Support for Resistance among Iraqi Students: An Exploratory Study', *Basic and Applied Social Psychology* 30(2): 167–75.

Ford, Robert, and Matthew J. Goodwin. 2014. *Revolt on the Right: Explaining Support for the Radical Right in Britain*. London: Routledge.

Franc, Renata, and Tomislav Pavlović. 2018. *Systematic Review of Quantitative Studies on Inequality and Radicalisation*. DARE Research Report. Retrieved 28 August 2022 from https://documents.manchester.ac.uk/display .aspx?DocID=58619.

———. 2021. 'Inequality and Radicalisation: Systematic Review of Quantitative Studies', *Terrorism and Political Violence*. https://doi.org/10.1080/09546553 .2021.1974845.

Gabriel, Thomas. 2014. 'Parenting and Right-Wing Extremism: An Analysis of the Biographical Genesis of Racism among Young People', in Cas Mudde (ed.), *Youth and the Extreme Right*. New York: IDEBATE Press, pp. 36–47.

Garland, Jon, and James Treadwell. 2010. '"No Surrender to the Taliban": Football Hooliganism, Islamophobia and the Rise of the English Defence League', *Papers from the British Criminology Conference* 10: 19–35. Retrieved 28 March 2022 from https://www.researchgate.net/publication/48185074_'No_surren der_to_the_Taliban'_Football_hooliganism_Islamophobia_and_the_rise_of_ the_English_Defence_League.

———. 2012. 'The New Politics of Hate? An Assessment of the Appeal of the English Defence League amongst Disadvantaged White Working-Class Communities in England', *Journal of Hate Studies* 10(1): 123–41.

Ghatak, Sambuddha. 2016a. 'Challenging the State: Effect of Minority Discrimination, Economic Globalization, and Political Openness on Domestic Terrorism', *International Interactions* 42(1): 56–80.

———. 2016b. 'Willingness and Opportunity: A Study of Domestic Terrorism in Post-Cold War South Asia', *Terrorism and Political Violence* 28(2): 274–96.

Ghatak, Sambuddha, and Aaron Gold. 2017. 'Development, Discrimination, and Domestic Terrorism: Looking beyond a Linear Relationship', *Conflict Management & Peace Science* 34(6): 618–39.

Hegghammer, Thomas. 2010. *Jihad in Saudi Arabia: Violence and Pan-Islamism since 1979*. Cambridge: Cambridge University Press.

Hussain, Yasmin, and Paul Bagguley. 2013. 'Funny Looks: British Pakistanis' Experiences after 7 July 2005', *Ethnic and Racial Studies* 36(1): 28–46.

Jahnke, Sara, Katharina Abad Borger and Andreas Beelmann. 2022. 'Predictors of Political Violence Outcomes among Young People: A Systematic Review and Meta-Analysis', *Political Psychology* 43(1): 111–29.

Jensen, Michael, et al. 2016. *Final Report: Empirical Assessment of Domestic Radicalisation (EADR) Report to the National Institute of Justice, Office of Justice Programs, U.S. Department of Justice*. START. Retrieved 21 February 2022 from https://www.start.umd.edu/pubs/START_NIJ_EmpiricalAssessmentof DomesticRadicalizationFinalReport_Dec2016_0.pdf.

Kavanagh, Jennifer. 2011. 'Selection, Availability, and Opportunity: The Conditional Effect of Poverty on Terrorist Group Participation', *Journal of Conflict Resolution* 55(1): 106–32.

Kimmel, Michael. 2014. 'Racism as Adolescent Male Rite of Passage: Ex-Nazis in Scandinavia', in Cas Mudde (ed.), *Youth and the Extreme Right*. New York: IDEBATE Press, pp. 65–82.

Klandermans, Bert, and Nonna Mayer. 2009. *Extreme Right Activists in Europe: Through the Magnifying Glass*. London: Routledge.

Khosrokhavar, Farhad. 2018. *Le nouveau jihad en Occident* [The New Jihad in the West]. Paris: Robert Laffont.

Ljujic, Vanja, Jan Willem van Prooijen and Frank Weerman. 2017. 'Beyond the Crime-Terror Nexus: Socio-Economic Status, Violent Crimes and Terrorism', *Journal of Criminological Research, Policy and Practice* 3(3): 158–72.

Lösel, Friedrich, et al. 2018. 'Protective Factors against Extremism and Violent Radicalisation: A Systematic Review of Research', *International Journal of Developmental Science* 12: 89–102.

McCauley, Clark, and Sophia Moskalenko. 2017. 'Understanding Political Radicalization: The Two-Pyramids Model', *American Psychologist* 72(3): 69–85.

Meierrieks, Daniel. 2014. 'Economic Determinants of Terrorism', in Raul Caruso and Andrea Locatelli (eds), *Understanding Terrorism: A Socio-Economic Perspective*. Emerald Group Publishing Limited, pp. 25–49.

Miller-Idriss, Cynthia. 2009. *Blood and Culture: Youth, Right-Wing Extremism and National Belonging in Contemporary Germany*. Durham, NC: Duke University Press.

Mousseau, Michael. 2011. 'Urban Poverty and Support for Islamist Terror: Survey Results of Muslims in Fourteen Countries', *Journal of Peace Research* 48(1): 35–47.

Muluk, Hamdi, Nathanael G. Sumaktoyo and Dhyah M. Ruth. 2013. 'Jihad as Justification: National Survey Evidence of Belief in Violent Jihad as a Mediating Factor for Sacred Violence among Muslims in Indonesia', *Asian Journal of Social Psychology* 16(2): 101–11.

Munton, Tony, et al. 2011. 'Understanding Vulnerability and Resilience in Individuals to the Influence of Al Qa'ida Violent Extremism: A Rapid Evidence Assessment to Inform Policy and Practice in Preventing Violent Extremism'. Report prepared for the Office for Security and Counter-Terrorism, UK Home Office. Occasional Paper 98.

Nemeth, Stephen C., Jacob A. Mauslein and Craig Stapley. 2014. 'The Primacy of the Local: Identifying Terrorist Hot Spots Using Geographic Information Systems', *Journal of Politics* 76(2): 304–17.

Neumann, Peter, and Scott Kleinmann. 2013. 'How Rigorous Is Radicalisation Research?', *Democracy and Security* 9(4): 360–82.

Pauwels, Lieven, and Marteen De Waele. 2014. 'Youth Involvement in Politically Motivated Violence: Why Do Social Integration, Perceived Legitimacy, and

Perceived Discrimination Matter?', *International Journal of Conflict and Violence* 8(1): 135–53.

Pauwels, Lieven, and Ben Heylen. 2017. 'Perceived Group Threat, Perceived Injustice, and Self-Reported Right-Wing Violence: An Integrative Approach to the Explanation Right-Wing Violence', *Journal of Interpersonal Violence* 35(21–22): 4276–302.

Perliger, Arie, Gabriel Koehler-Derrick and Ami Pedahzur. 2016. 'The Gap between Participation and Violence: Why We Need to Disaggregate Terrorist "Profiles"', *International Studies Quarterly* 60(2): 220–29.

Piazza, James A. 2013. 'The Cost of Living and Terror: Does Consumer Price Volatility Fuel Terrorism?', *Southern Economic Journal* 79(4): 812–31.

———. 2016. 'Oil and Terrorism: An Investigation of Mediators', *Public Choice* 169(3–4): 251–68.

Pilkington, Hilary. 2016. *Loud and Proud: Passion and Politics in the English Defence League*. Manchester: Manchester University Press.

Pilkington, Hilary, Elena Omel'chenko and Al'bina Garifzianova. 2010. *Russia's Skinheads: Exploring and Rethinking Subcultural Lives*. London: Routledge.

Poli, Alexandra, and Onur Arun. 2019. *Report on the Meta-Ethnographic Synthesis of Qualitative Studies on Inequality and Youth Radicalisation*. Retrieved 28 August 2022 from https://documents.manchester.ac.uk/display.aspx?DocID=58616.

———. 2021. 'Exploring the Connection between Inequalities and Radicalisation: A Focus through a Meta-Ethnographic Synthesis of Qualitative Studies', in Rebecca Lemos Igreja and Camilo Negri (eds), *Desigualdades Globais e Justiça Social: Interfaces Teóricas, Acesso à Justiça e Democracia* [Global Inequalities and Social Justice: Theoretical Interfaces, Access to Justice and Democracy]. Brasilia: FLACSO, Coleção Estudos Globais, pp. 394–437.

PROTON. 2017. 'T2.7: Socio-Economic Background of Terrorism Suspects in Europe', in *D2.1: Report on Factors Related to Terrorism*. Retrieved 26 January 2022 from https://www.projectproton.eu/wpcontent/uploads/2018/01/D2.1-Report-on-fact-related-to-terrorism.pdf.

Reynolds, Sean C., and Mohammed M. Hafez. 2017. 'Social Network Analysis of German Foreign Fighters in Syria and Iraq', *Terrorism and Political Violence* 31(4): 1–26.

Rhodes, James. 2010. 'White Backlash, "Unfairness" and Justifications of British National Party (BNP) Support', *Ethnicities* 10(1): 77–99.

———. 2011. '"It's Not Just Them, it is Whites as Well": Whiteness, Class and BNP Support', *Sociology* 45(1): 102–17.

Saeed, Luqman, and Shahib Haider Syed. 2018. 'Insights into Selected Features of Pakistan's Most Wanted Terrorists', *Terrorism and Political Violence* 30(1): 47–73.

Sageman, Marc. 2004. *Understanding Terror Networks*. Philadelphia: University of Pennsylvania Press.

Schils, Nele, and Lieven Pauwels. 2016. 'Political Violence and the Mediating Role of Violent Extremist Propensities', *Journal of Strategic Security* 9(2): 70–91.

Shetret, Liat, Matthew Schwartz and Danielle Cotter. 2013. *Mapping Perceptions of Violent Extremism: Pilot Study of Community Attitudes in Kenya and Somaliland*. Center on Global Counterterrorism Cooperation. Retrieved 21 February 2022 from https://www.globalcenter.org/wp-content/uploads/2013/02/Jan2013_MPVE_PliotStuday.pdf.

Speckhard, Anne. 2017. *Drivers of Radicalisation and Violent Extremism in Kosovo: Women's Roles in Supporting, Preventing & Fighting Violent Extremism*. ICSVE Research Reports. Retrieved 28 March 2022 from https://www.icsve.org/drivers-of-radicalization-and-violent-extremism-in-kosovo-womens-roles-in-supporting-preventing-fighting-violent-extremism/.

Sporton, Deborah, Gill Valentine and Katrine Bang Nielsen. 2006. 'Post Conflict Identities: Affiliations and Practices of Somali Asylum Seeker Children', *Children's Geographies* 4(2): 203–17.

Tausch, Nicole, et al. 2011. 'Explaining Radical Group Behavior: Developing Emotion and Efficacy Routes to Normative and Nonnormative Collective Action', *Journal of Personality and Social Psychology* 101(1): 129–48.

Van der Valk, Ineke, and Willem Wagenaar. 2010. *The Extreme Right: Entry and Exit*. Racism and Extremism Monitor Report. Anne Frank House/Leiden University. Amsterdam: Amsterdam University Press. Retrieved 15 January 2018 from https://annefrank.global.ssl.fastly.net/media/imagevault/IbWeY80VYsdcdUDSGrh7.pdf.

Wolfowicz, Michael, et al. 2020. 'A Field-Wide Systematic Review and Meta-Analysis of Putative Risk and Protective Factors for Radicalization Outcomes', *Journal of Quantitative Criminology* 36(3): 407–47.

CHAPTER 4

Islam and Violence in Greek Society
The Stigmatisation of Muslims, the Extreme Right and Resistance to Reciprocal Radicalisation

Alexandros Sakellariou

Introduction

The debate on the place and role of violence in religion is as old as religions themselves and distinguishes between two core dimensions of the relationship. The internal dimension concerns the role of violence, physical and symbolic, perpetrated inside the religious field in order to secure and strengthen religious faith (Girard 1991, 2017; Roux 1998), while the external dimension relates to the deployment of violence towards wider society either as a defence mechanism or as a tool for expansion (Lewis 2017; Hagège 2018).

While there is a long tradition of the study of political Islam, Islamism and Salafism (see, for example, Kepel 1992, 2000; Roy 1994; Basbous 2003), it has only been in the course of the last twenty years, that is, after the events of 9/11, that the relationship between Islam, violence and terrorism has become a dominant theme in academic research (Mamdani 2004; Roy 2006; Khosrokhavar 2009; Blanc and Roy 2021) and the public sphere. Following this landmark act of terrorism, a huge volume of publications have sought to understand why some, especially young, Muslims come to embrace violence; violence targeted not only at Western but also Muslim societies. After the expansion of Daesh, the so-called Islamic State (IS), in 2014–15 and the attacks perpetrated in Europe, this issue rose still higher up the agenda of social science research (Kepel 2015; Neumann 2016; Roy 2017). The primacy of the concern over how the West should defend itself against such attacks, moreover, meant that a security and terrorist studies approach came to dominate the field of study (Neumann and Kleinmann 2013: 361). At the same time, over these two decades, Islam has been portrayed – mainly in politics and the media – as a monolithic, fundamentalist and violent religion that is incompatible with European and Western civilisations and societies (Karim 2000). Such stereotypical and negative images and discourses of Islam in the West were already present (Said 1981; Arjana 2015), but, in the aftermath of 9/11, they dominated the public sphere and gradually became mainstream (Kallis 2013). At the same time, violent attacks against Muslims, their homes and places of worship have been on the rise in most Western societies, contributing to the reproduction of what is referred to as Islamophobia and anti-Muslim hatred (Esposito and Kalin 2011; Zempi and Awan 2019). It is in these anti-Muslim debates (and actions) that the extreme right has played a central role in inciting a panic about Islam (Morgan and Poynting 2012), mainly through the population replacement conspiracy theory.

When it comes to the Islamic presence in the West, the role of mosques is critical and has been subject to considerable analysis (Cesari 2005; Alievi 2009; Maussen 2009; Astor 2011). The mosque is central to Islam's urban visibility and is the centre of Muslim communal life. It is not only a space for prayer but also a community centre, where pre-existing networks of solidarity come together and where various rituals that mark Islamic family life – marriage, circumcision and death – take place (Cesari 2005: 1017–18). However, mosques have been at the centre of the debates about radicalisation and violence also. Mosques, official and non-official, in the West have been targeted regularly by extreme-right political groups, the media, state authorities and wider society as places where radicalisation and violence are propagated. Although in many cases radical views and messages have indeed been diffused in and through mosques, contributing to violent radicalisation, the perception that all or the majority of mosques constitute a fertile ground for radicalisation is usually an external one, fuelled by the wider stigmatisation of Islam and Muslim communities as inherently violent and dangerous.

The purpose of this chapter is twofold. First, it presents and discusses etic[1] perspectives on Islam and violence and how they have shaped negative perceptions of mosques in Greek society. Drawing on findings from fieldwork conducted in an extreme-right milieu characterised by anti-Islam views and attitudes, moreover, the intersection, and potential mutual reinforcement, of etic (media, public, policy) perspectives with those manifest within the extreme-right milieu are demonstrated. Although not in direct contact and communication, the extreme-right milieu is partly

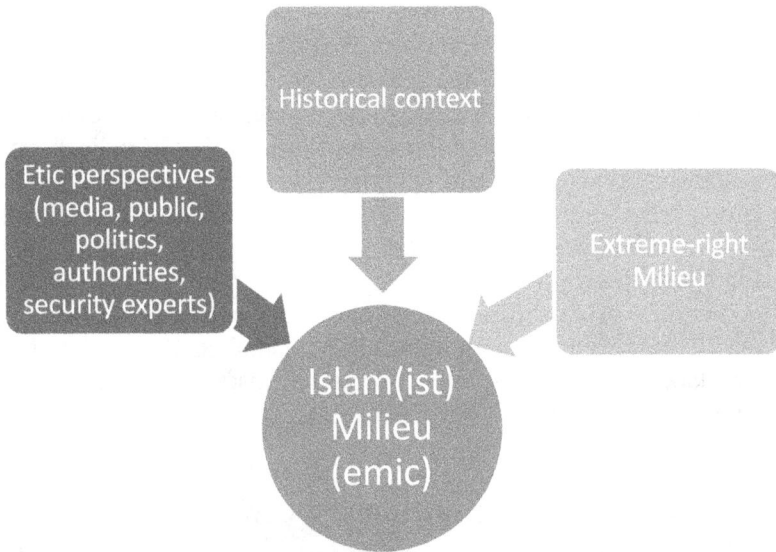

Figure 4.1. The Islam(ist) milieu between history, etic perspectives and the extreme-right milieu. Created by Alexandros Sakellariou.

self-defined by the presence of the Islam(ist)[2] milieu. Tropes that link Islam and violence and portray mosques as a threat play a significant role in identity formation on the individual and the collective level within the milieu. Second, the chapter draws on fieldwork with Muslim communities to examine emic perspectives, specifically the responses from the Islam(ist) milieu studied, to these external perceptions and attitudes, and the role they play in the radicalisation or non-radicalisation process. The relationships between the two milieus, although it should be noted that neither milieu is homogeneous, and with wider society are depicted in Figure 4.1.

The empirical material drawn on in this chapter emanates from the DARE project (see Introduction, this volume) and is based on the ethnographic study of two very different milieus in the Athens region: an Islam(ist) milieu associated with non-official mosques (Sakellariou 2021b); and an extreme-right milieu (Lagos et al. 2021). Both studies involved participant observation and semi-structured interviews and the analysis of related materials (e.g. videos, audios, leaflets, online texts) collected as part of the field research. While the focus of this contribution is on the non-official mosque milieu, insights from the extreme-right milieu help understand and explain the responses of young Muslims.

This contribution starts by setting the perceptions of Islam and Muslims in historical and contemporary societal context, delineating discourses found in politics, media, security and public domains. It focuses on the representation of the relationship between Islam and violence, the portrayal of Muslims as a threat and of mosques as sites of radicalisation. It then considers the role of the extreme right in these debates and perceptions, paying attention to the intersection of tropes from within this milieu and wider public/policy/academic debates. The chapter, finally, considers how this discourse impacts on Muslim respondents, including their experience of stigmatisation and physical attack and their responses to them. It explores understandings within this milieu of the relationship between Islam and violence and the role of mosques in facilitating, or preventing, radicalisation.

Islam and Muslims in Context

In Greece, debates on Islam are deeply rooted in, and strongly intertwined with, the experience of the Ottoman occupation (1453–1821) and the revolution against it in 1821, which are crucial for the construction of the collective national identity. Subsequent conflicts between Greece and Turkey, such as the Greek-Turkish war of 1897, the 'Asia Minor Catastrophe' of 1922 and the Turkish invasion of Cyprus in 1974, have further bolstered the national(ist) narrative against Turkey and Islam (Katsikas 2021), both of which remain perceived by the majority of the Greek population as fundamentally hostile forces. Thus, contemporary perceptions of Islam and Muslims must be examined in relation to the broader historical legacies of the creation of the Greek nation-state after centuries of Ottoman rule. This state-building process had a clearly religious dimension and shaped a deeply rooted dichotomous discourse, which pits the national Christian Orthodox 'self' against the religious 'other', particularly the Muslim 'other' (Sakellariou 2015: 45).

Negative perceptions of Islam have risen alongside the rise in the number of Muslim immigrants and refugees in Greek society. This increase dates back to the 2000s but became more visible in 2015 with the so-called 'refugee crisis' related to the Syrian civil war.[3] It is important to distinguish here between what is referred to as 'Old' and 'New' Islam in Greece. The former label is ascribed to the Muslim minority of Thrace, located in the northeastern part of Greece, consisting of about 120,000 Muslims living alongside the Greek Christian majority (Tsitselikis 1999; Ktistakis 2006; Katsikas 2012). Thrace's Muslim community, along with the Greeks of Constantinople in Turkey, were protected by the 1923 Treaty of Lausanne, which exempted them from the mandatory population exchanges between Greece and Turkey. Despite this protection, Muslims of Thrace have faced integration obstacles, discrimination and social exclusion due to their religion, but also their ethnic background, which is mostly Turkish.[4] This group is distinct from the recently arrived Muslim immigrants and refugees – who come from a variety of ethnic backgrounds and profess a range of religious dogmas – referred to as 'New' Islam (Tsitselikis 2012). It is this latter group that has been the object of concerns about the security threat posed in relation to radicalisation and Islamist extremism.[5]

In relation to this threat, it is important to note that, while extremist violence by terrorist organisations proclaiming a leftist ideology and by extreme-right groups, like Golden Dawn, is well documented (Psarras 2012; Sakellariou 2020), Greece has not witnessed any organised Islamist violence. Although from the 1970s until the 1990s a series of Islamist-inspired terrorist attacks occurred in Greece, these were sporadic and mainly related to international issues such as Israel's invasion of Lebanon or the Palestinian issue (Bossi 1996: 143–44). They were not targeted at Greek society directly and lacked any religious dimension. Thus, notwithstanding these attacks, there was no ostensible anti-Muslim hatred or stereotypes against Islam and Muslims in Greek politics or society until the 2000s, and sympathy and support for Palestinians continued to be expressed.

One final historical aspect to take into account concerns the ongoing historical, legal and political issues surrounding the debate over the construction of a mosque in Athens, which was finally inaugurated in 2020 (for illuminating studies of this debate, see Triandafyllidou and Gropas 2009; Anagnostou and Gropas 2010; Antoniou 2010). Although official mosques exist on the islands of Rhodes and Kos as well as in Thrace (the home of the longest-standing Muslim community, whose members are Greek citizens, as discussed above), the lack of an official mosque in Athens has been one of the burning issues for Muslims for many years (Verousi and Allen 2021). The history of the construction of a mosque in Athens began in the late 1970s, although such discussion is documented as far back as the end of the nineteenth century (Tsitselikis 2004: 281–90). The absence of a mosque in Athens, alongside the lack of an Islamic cemetery, is viewed by Muslims as illustrative of the religious inequality they face. In the absence of an official and state-recognised mosque, Muslims in Greece have found their own locations (former storehouses, derelict houses and factories and open public spaces) to practise their religious duties (Sakellariou 2011).

Politics: The Dominance of the Extreme Right

Although 9/11 marked a watershed moment in the rise of anti-Muslim sentiments and violence in most Western countries (Hilal 2022; Zine 2022), in Greece it was only after the terrorist attacks in Madrid (2004) and London (2005), and the parallel rise of the extreme right in Greek society, that Islamophobic discourses and violent attacks against Muslims and their places (mosques and homes) started to take place. The key theme in political and public debate during the 2000s was the construction of an official mosque in Athens, the only European capital without one (until 2020). The debate was initiated in relation to the 2004 Olympic Games, when domestic and international actors began to exert pressure on the Greek government to build a mosque. In 2000, a new law was passed (Law 2833, Government Gazette A150) providing for the construction of a mosque in Athens as well as an Islamic Centre. The mosque was to be built far from the city centre, close to the new airport. This law was never implemented, and six years later, new legislation was initiated (Law 3512, Government Gazette A264). It was this law that, after almost fifteen years, was finally implemented and the mosque started to function in 2020.

During the parliamentary discussion about the 2000 law, all the political parties unanimously acknowledged the need for the construction of a mosque, notwithstanding the issues it raised. Even in 2006, despite the preceding attacks in the US, Madrid and London, the majority of MPs agreed once more on the necessity of constructing a mosque on the grounds of respect for human rights and religious freedom. Although issues of cultural identity and homogeneity, terrorism and security, all related to the mosque, were first raised during that period, at this point, extreme voices were marginal. However, the construction of the mosque in Athens and the presence of a large number of Muslims in Greek society subsequently started to play a central role in the public debates stigmatising Muslims for their perceived criminal and terrorist activity. This was evident in the parliamentary discussion of the legislation noted above. In 2000, an independent MP from the conservative party, and later the leader of the extreme right-wing LAOS party,[6] asked a parliamentary question about the existence of illegal mosques (prayer houses) in Athens, arguing that these places were used as centres of proselytisation and propagation and sought to disrupt the ethno-religious homogeneity of the Greek nation.[7] In the discussions from 2006 onwards, such views multiplied and even a socialist MP argued that preventing the new mosque falling under the control of fundamentalist and extremist groupings would be very difficult.[8]

The rising threat presented by possible infiltration of the new mosque by Al-Qaeda and other extremist organisations featured prominently in the arguments of the extreme right against the establishment of the mosque.[9] A general fear of criminality around the new mosque was used as a further argument against its construction:

> Look what is happening around Europe! We are not suggesting that these people should not pray somewhere. However, it is impossible to build a huge mosque with Muftis and minarets . . . and create a ghetto, a place where no one would speak Greek! And you know it, because you have experience from abroad, you have seen the dead ends they [Western societies] face in places where big Muslim mosques have been constructed. We could find alternative places – not such huge premises that could become an attraction for [danger- ous] people in times when fundamentalism is on the rise.[10]

One of the major issues raised about the construction of the mosque related directly to the protection and preservation of national identity. Even in 2000, when the majority of MPs agreed on the need to build the mosque, some marginal voices opposed the selected site. The conser- vative party MP (later the LAOS party leader) mentioned above strongly objected, arguing that that there is no reason to 'advertise the mosque' by building it near the airport. Similar views were expressed by other conservative MPs, arguing that such a decision would give the impres- sion to visitors to the country that Greece was an Islamic country.[11] These debates might be compared to those around the Swiss minarets and the associated reactions and mobilisations that led to the 2009 referendum (Mazzoleni 2016: 52–56).

Since these two laws were passed (in 2000 and 2006), four populist and/or extreme right-wing parties entered parliament: the Popular Or- thodox Rally (LAOS) in 2007, Golden Dawn in 2012, Independent Greeks (ANEL) in 2012 and Hellenic Solution in 2019. The fragmentation of the political system, especially after the economic crisis of 2010, gave space to new political parties or empowered already existing but marginal ones, for whom the 'problem' of immigrants in general, and Muslims in particu- lar, was at the top of their agenda. Exploiting the economic crisis to evoke fear about Islam and Muslims, especially in relation to refugee and immi- grant flows from the Muslim world, these parties have managed to gain influence in the wider public sphere, especially regarding debates on Is- lam and on the construction of the mosque in Athens. Consequently, from 2010 onwards, Greece entered a phase of open anti-Muslim hatred and violence against Muslims and their prayer houses in Athens. After the electoral breakthrough of Golden Dawn (2010–12), a political party with a national-socialist ideology, this discourse intensified and Islamisation became portrayed as the principal threat to national identity (Sakellariou 2017). Golden Dawn's MPs claimed that 'Greece will become Islamised and Greeks will listen to the *muezzin* from minarets and thus experience a new Ottoman rule' and pledged to fight against the Islamisation of Greece.[12] As argued elsewhere, populist and extreme-right parties regularly present themselves as the protectors of Christianity and Christian values (Marzouki, McDonnell and Roy 2016), and this is mirrored in the case of Golden Dawn in Greece (Sakellariou 2021a: 19–20). MPs from the party Independent Greeks argued that it was impossible to achieve the social inclusion of Muslims in Greek society,[13] while MPs from the right-wing party New Democracy claimed Muslims opposed the Western way of life.[14] Thus, in the extreme right-wing political discourse, Islam and Muslims appear as a threat to Greek national identity and Greek-Orthodox values while the construction of an official mosque in Athens and the existence and functioning of non-official prayer houses are portrayed as places of violence and religious fundamentalism and, as such, a threat to the country's security.

In this way, Islam has become a core theme in what has been called the politics of fear (Furedi 2006). Furedi argues that the term 'fear' is used, or rather over-used, not to indicate a reaction to a specific danger, but as a broader cultural metaphor to interpret and make sense of a range of experiences through a narrative of fear. The culture of fear increases the role of instability and exacerbates distinctions between the friendly 'us' and hostile 'others', which may be exploited for political gain as well as to construct a kind of national and religious homogeneity. The major purpose of these discourses of fear is to promote a sense of disorder and a belief that 'things are out of control', implying that someone needs to take back control. In this way, fear is 'being exploited by numerous claims-makers, including politicians, who promote their own propaganda about national and international politics' (Altheide 2003: 10); the extreme right in Greece has been doing this systematically in relation to Islam and Muslims.

The Media: Reproducing Panic about Islam

It was during the 2010s that, despite the lack of evidence on Islamist extremist violence, the stigmatisation of Islam and Muslims in Greece started to be fuelled by information emanating from the police and the secret service through the media. Several press articles and headlines claimed that fanatics or jihadists had been present, and in some cases had preached, in the non-official mosques of Athens. One example was the headline of a populist right-wing newspaper *To Proto Thema* (The

First Issue), on 13 August 2015, which read: 'Government's great crime: Hundreds of thousands of illegal immigrants arrive [in Greece] without control. Who knows how many jihadists came to Greece?'. Of course, no evidence was provided in the article, nor any figures regarding the number of jihadists that might have crossed the border. Another example was the front page of the newspaper *Eleftheria tou Typou* (Freedom of Press) on 28 August 2017. The front page showed the inside of a mosque (not from Greece) and, next to it, an image of people wearing masks and holding rifles. The title read: 'Mosques of hatred in Attica. The police has put under its microscope three (of the eighty monitored) places of the Muslim cult (*sic*) where extreme speeches were given'. In a third example, the moderate right-wing newspaper *I Kathimerini* (The Daily) published an article on 9 September 2017 with the title 'Imams of hate', based on an alleged 'highly confidential' police report about Islamist extremist activities in Greece and, in particular, in Muslim prayer houses. The article described how one of these non-official mosques had close relations with the Muslim Brotherhood – 'an organisation of political Islam, which has as its slogan *"jihad* is our path"'. The article also noted that 'the anti-terrorist service is highly interested in a cultural centre and improvised mosque which operates near Piraeus, because according to police information the person responsible for the place seems to be involved in cases of illegal transfer of people from North Africa to the regions of the Caliphate [i.e. ISIS]'. It is not unusual for the media to reproduce information emanating from the security services or the police, but in these cases it was reproduced without any additional concrete evidence to support the argument for the presence of extremists in Greek society.

The media have played a central role in the reproduction of moral panics in the modern age by repeatedly warning of the possible dangers of moral laxity. Such panic plays, and capitalises, on the fears of the majority (Cohen 1972; Thompson 1998; Goode and Ben-Yehuda 2009). As this panic increasingly shifts towards 'aberrant' behaviours of Muslims, a kind of 'religious panic' has been generated in which 'Muslims in the West have emerged as the new "folk devils" of both popular and media imagination' (Zempi and Chakraborti 2014: 24). This is evident in the Greek case where a significant number of mainstream media outlets elaborate and reproduce this kind of panic about Islam and Muslims.

Security Experts and State Authorities:
Securitising Islam and Muslims

Alongside the media, there is a second source of information about the activities of Islamist extremists in Greek society, particularly regarding the non-official prayer houses. This source consists of self-proclaimed security specialists who try to present a more substantiated argument about the threats from such activism in the form of reports, which are mainly published abroad, as well as websites dedicated to the monitoring of radical Islam (e.g. RIMSE-Radical Islam Monitor in Southeast Europe).[15] The evidence included in these reports and online texts is mainly from anonymous police/secret service sources through the implementation of informal, in some cases off the record, discussions or interviews, but also from the media. There thus appears to be a network of police sources, media and security specialists, which circulates more or less the same information.

After the rise of ISIS, the main question asked by these security specialists was when Greece would become a target of a future terrorist attack. The country's geographical location, for example, in relation to the immigration issue, is considered to create a significant threat for Greece (Symeonides 2017), and there is a pragmatic expectation that radical Islamist groups could participate in low-risk assignments and operations (e.g. recruitment, funding and propaganda) that would not be detected easily by the Greek authorities. The Greek context facilitates such operations, it is argued, for a number of reasons: geographical proximity to countries that export extremism; illegal immigration and porous borders; social unrest; a growing Muslim community; indigenous terrorist networks; and corruption in the private and public sectors. According to this analysis, the networks based in Greece to date have performed mainly non-violent activities, but provide support for other groups located in other European cities (Kostakos 2010: 3–5).

Such reports commonly argue that, although no verified Islamist terrorist attack has been organised and executed in Greece, in recent years there is evidence of increased, mainly background, logistical, recruitment and accommodating activities, which have created a hub of uncontrollable, 'loose' individuals who act and operate freely (Giannoulis 2011: 22). This makes the trafficking of people from Asia and the Middle East through Greece easier and facilitates recruitment of Islamist radicals for operations beyond the borders of Greece (ibid.). It is suggested also that signs of Wahhabism and radicalism in Greece have been detected and that the country is likely to face difficult challenges in the years ahead (Kostakos 2007). Some authors (Papageorgiou and Samouris 2012: 377) have urged the authorities to be cautious and control those Islamic groups and associations in Greece whose goal is to implement the Sharia law in Greek society or practise *dawah* as a way to attract converts. They also note that 'the arrival in Greece of people with extreme extremist (*sic*) (jihadist) action creates the risk of the transfusion of Salafist jihadism among the communities of Muslim immigrants' (ibid.: 384).

It is important to emphasise, however, that while the authorities and police have initiated some programmes to tackle Islamist extremism, they have never stated openly or officially that Islamist extremist groups have been active in Greek society, being very cautious with the information they reveal and their characterisations. However, as stated in a pocket guide (KEMEA 2016: 28–29) published for public servants in the field (including security services and police officers on the mainland and along the borders), 'Greece, due to its geographical location, is at the epicentre of the issue of "foreign fighters", because their main movements and activities take place either in or through countries neighbouring Greece', implying mainly Turkey, but also the MENA region. Furthermore, security services and the police have started to surveil Muslim activities and non-official mosques, including paying visits to keep an eye out for radical ideologies. As discussed below, this kind of surveillance has been received very negatively by Muslim communities as it stigmatises them as potential threats to the country and as terrorists.

Public Perceptions of Islam and Muslims

This raises the question of how Islam and Muslims are perceived in wider society and how public opinion stands towards the construction of a mosque in Athens. It was at the end of the 2000s that anti-Muslim attitudes started to become more open and diffused not only in the political sphere but in wider society as well. This was illustrated by a 2010 opinion poll (Public Issue Survey 2010) on Greeks' views about Islam and Muslims, which confirmed the negative perceptions: 51% of the respondents believed that Islam engenders violence much more easily than other religions; 53% considered that relations between Islam and the West are bad or quite bad; 67% answered that there is probably a clash between Islam and Christianity currently; and 55% foresaw a clash between Christianity and Islam in the future. When it came to the context of Greece, 27% believed that the country is threatened by Islam and more were against the construction of a mosque in Athens (46%) than in favour of it (41%). A few years earlier, in 2006, 52% had been in favour of the construction and 34% against, and in 2009, 56% were in favour and 29% against – a significant shift within only four years.

Such views were also illustrated in more recent opinion polls. In one of these (Dianeosis 2015), 40.8% of the interviewees said that they would be disturbed by the establishment of a mosque in Athens ('yes'/'probably yes') as opposed to 58.6% who responded 'no'/'probably no'. When people were asked if they would be disturbed by the construction of a mosque in the area in which they live, 45.1% replied 'yes'/'probably yes',

while 54.4% answered 'no'/'probably no' (Dianeosis 2016a). Finally, according to another survey regarding the refugee crisis (January 2016),
the words 'Islam', 'Muslim' and *jihad* appeared to have negative con-
notations and a terrorist attack in Greece was considered as possible according to 39% of the participants (Dianeosis 2016b). Two comparative
surveys conducted by the Pew Institute in 2014 and 2016 also showed
high levels of negative attitudes among the Greek population. In 2014,
Greece had the second-highest level of unfavourable views towards Muslims (53%) of seven EU countries studied. In a subsequent survey, in
2016, focused on attitudes towards immigrants and refugees, Greece was
ranked fourth (of ten EU countries) in terms of negative views towards
Muslims, with almost two-thirds (65%) holding such views.[16]

These data suggest that the politics of fear, reproduced mainly but not
exclusively by the extreme right, and the panic about Islam disseminated
by the media facilitated by security experts and the ever-present historical past have managed to shape negative perceptions about Islam and
Muslims in the minds of the population at large.

The Extreme-Right Milieu: Islam as Threat

The primary role in the reproduction of anti-Muslim hatred and Islamophobic discourses on the political and societal levels is played by the
extreme right, spearheaded by Golden Dawn (Sakellariou 2015, 2019).
Golden Dawn was the primary organiser of large demonstrations against
the construction of the mosque in Athens and has openly opposed its
construction either through the party's websites or through its newspaper under the slogan 'No, to an Islamic mosque, either in Athens, or in
any other place'. In October 2018, together with a committee of locals,
the party organised a rally objecting to the location of the mosque in the
Votanikos district of Athens. The call for the rally on the party's website
declared that 'our region can't afford further degradation; we don't want
to become a centre of illegal immigration; we can't afford more unemployment and criminality; our region should not be Islamised' (Sakellariou 2020: 16–17). Similar demonstrations continued to be organised
right up until the mosque's official opening, while slogans against Islam,
Muslims and the construction of the mosque were graffitied at the site
selected for its construction. In this sense, space, in its various formulations, might be examined not only as a locus of religious activity but also
as a tool used by religious and political groups to engage in society, to
exert authority and power and to reinforce or subvert a dominant order,
regime or discourse. Thus, space is an important analytical tool that can

help reveal the inherently complex interrelationships between religious and political groups and parties, the state and wider society through the disclosure of new ontological conditions of difference (Kong and Woods 2016: 163; Hussain 2022).

The study of the extreme-right milieu revealed that it included a number of Christian Orthodox, anti-Muslim groupings, which have a common ethno-religious identity and perceived enemies and who cooperate with one another in order to confront them. Two of the groups in the milieu – the Military Union and the Greek-Orthodox Group – have common members and, along with other Greek-Orthodox associations, had co-organised a public event against globalisation, religious ecumenism and the 'New World Order', which was also attended by representatives of extreme-right organisations and parties. Apart from being personal friends, the two leading figures of these groups joined forces in the 2016 four-month protest occupation of the Athens mosque construction site and participated in the protest organised by Golden Dawn in 2018 noted above (Lagos et al. 2021: 57).

For the milieu participants, the mosque was considered alien to Greek-Orthodox culture and a dangerous development that could pave the way towards Greece's Islamisation. Even those informants who, in the context of respect for religious freedom, recognised the right of Muslims to freely practise their religion, disagreed with the financing of the Athens mosque from the Greek state budget, interpreting this as an injustice done to Orthodoxy, whose temples and churches the Greek state does not fund. In fact, this is an unfounded grievance, since the Greek state regularly funds construction and restoration work on Greek-Orthodox churches and monasteries as well as, among other things, the digitalisation of their archives. Participants also expressed discontent and frustration that a mosque in Athens would evoke the country's Ottoman past, blurring and eroding the image of an alleged homogeneous Greek-Orthodox society, while at the same time increasing the risks of Islamic extremism not only in Greece but in Europe as well (Lagos et al. 2021: 44).

Mediated by the historical and long-lasting rivalry and enmity between Greece and Turkey (Sakellariou 2017: 519–20; Katsikas 2021), the perception and interpretation of Islam and Muslims reproduces nationalist generalisations and stereotypes that generate prejudice, fear and hostility towards them. According to the milieu participants, Islam is completely alien to the Christian European and Greek-Orthodox cultures and values. Muslims are seen as hostile to Europe, Greece and Orthodoxy and as unable to achieve any degree of integration in Christian European societies. One of the informants (Vangelis 1) framed the above through the reproduction of common stereotypes, that is, that Islam and Muslims are 'incompatible with European culture' because 'Islam is a religion that teaches about disciplining women through beating' and women are treated as inferior to men and have no rights. The stereotypical perception of Islam as a backward religion that degrades and abuses women and accepts sexual relations with minors, which is incompatible with the Christian European culture, is interwoven with anti-immigrant stereotypes that stigmatise immigrants as potential rapists (Pilkington 2016: 132–35). The combination of Islamophobic prejudice that views Islam as 'a religion of hate' whose followers 'accept incestuous relationships, rape and paedophilia' (Thomas) and fears of immigrant criminality such as the generalisation that 'in every robbery, in every crime, in every rape, a foreigner is involved' (Kosmas) defines the cultural framework within which Muslim immigrants are perceived as both dangerous and incompatible with Greek-Orthodox culture (Lagos et al. 2021: 41). This kind of discourse not only incorporates conspiracy theories about the Islamisation of the West via migration and Islamic extremism, but also justifies Islamophobic discourses and anti-Muslim radicalism and extremism as inevitable or even necessary.

This incompatibility and threat emerge from the discourse of even the most moderate of the respondents when they reject multiculturalism and consider the integration of Muslims in Christian societies as practically impossible. The fear of Greece's Islamisation, through the mixing of incompatible peoples, religions and cultures, indicates the operation of a racialising mechanism in the production of Muslim 'otherness', revealing Islamophobia as a contemporary form of racism (Hafez 2014; Kirtsoglou and Tsimouris 2018; Kaya and Tecmen 2019). These, relatively less radicalised respondents pointed out the Islam-Christianity/West 'historical rivalry' manifest in a generalised image of Muslims as 'not forgetting the Crusades' whilst also underlining what they called 'the West's responsibility' for Islamist extremism, referring to the geopolitical intervention of Western powers in the Middle East and other Muslim countries; this responsibility is similarly attributed to the West by some of the participants in the Islam(ist) milieu (Sakellariou 2021b: 29–30). Those with stronger anti-Muslim attitudes in the milieu – though few denied the 'West's responsibility' for contemporary Islamist extremism – tended to emphasise their view of Islam as a religion in which fanaticism and violence are endogenous, that is, included in and propagated by Imams in mosques and through its core teachings (Lagos et al. 2021: 33).

The stronger the anti-Muslim sentiment among the milieu participants, the more they stressed fanaticism as a core characteristic of Islam. For the more radicalised respondents, Islamist extremism stems from the Qur'an and Sharia, while Islamophobia and anti-Muslim attitudes and activism are responses towards the perceived threat of the Islamisation of Greece, and Europe, and the failure of the mainstream political parties to address such threats. The belief expressed by these milieu actors that they are at war with an 'absolute evil' (Thomas) and a 'satanic religion' (Father Gabriel) underpins the connection between Orthodox zeal – captured in the slogan 'Orthodoxy or Death' – and anti-immigrant, extreme-right nationalism and authoritarianism articulated by the Greek-Orthodox paramilitaries and neo-Nazi supporters of Golden Dawn also active in the milieu (Lagos et al. 2021: 49).

In addition to their active shaping of public discourse during the 2010s, extremist groups have regularly attacked mosques and prayer houses as well as immigrants and refugees. These have taken the form of (occasional) arson attacks, graffitiing the walls or throwing pigs' heads, and have taken place in prayer houses and mosques around Greece, for example on the island of Crete and in Komotini in Northern Greece, where the native Muslim minority lives, as well as in Athens (Sakellariou 2020: 19–21).

The dominant stance within the milieu is that of disapproval towards extremist messages and views. The strong correlation between extremism and violence and the perception of extremists as uneducated and marginalised fanatics generates aversion to, and rejection of, extremist messages by the non-radicalised part of the milieu. Extremist attitudes and behaviours are perceived as 'zeal without awareness' and 'mob force' without real effectiveness, even in the case of causes that are recognised as just and legitimate (Lagos et al. 2021: 31, 34). Moderation, as well as Christian and humanitarian values, are promoted and mobilised by these respondents. For these participants, Orthodox ideals and teachings help control passions and violent instincts and are essential both for individual and social betterment.

In the radical discourse of some informants, however, violence – physical and symbolic – is omnipresent, celebrated, planned and necessitated by the dire 'situation of the country that requires us to be tough' (Thomas) (Lagos et al. 2021: 61). These respondents accuse those with moderate attitudes of 'cowardice' and 'passivity' and talk about their own experience of violent confrontation with opponents holding extremist ideologies, mainly Islamists (Lagos et al. 2021: 34–35). The leader of the paramilitary Military Union, for example, described the operation of his group to bring down an ISIS flag that reportedly had been raised in a refugee camp. He repeatedly referred to the threat that Muslim extremists, who are supposedly entering the country in disguise as immigrants/refugees, are seen to represent, although research has shown the absence of any radical milieu among refugees (Eleftheriadou 2020). Along with other Greek-Orthodox

anti-Muslim radicals among the respondents, he stressed the need to prepare and organise in order to confront them, should they decide to revolt
and attack the locals. His Military Union, comprising former commando
soldiers with extreme-right ties, trains and prepares for the armed suppression of such an anticipated revolt (Lagos et al. 2021: 35).

In general, immigration, mostly referring to Muslims, is seen as involving and posing serious national, social and cultural risks. These cover a
wide range of dangers and threats from criminality, terrorism, degradation and decline of neighbourhoods to fears of alteration of the Greek-
Orthodox national, religious and cultural identity of the country through
Islamisation. It is not surprising, then, that the vast majority of the milieu favours strict limitations to immigration as well as the deportation
of large numbers of immigrants, particularly of Muslims, while they are
suspicious, reluctant or even totally negative towards the construction
and operation of the Athens mosque. This threat of cultural difference
through what has been described as the 'influx of difference' (i.e. the
arrival of large numbers of Muslim immigrants and refugees) (see Pilkington and Vestel, this volume) is found in other extreme-right milieus
across Europe and has rendered Muslim immigrants the main 'other' after 9/11 (Marzouki and McDonnell 2016: 5).

Religion plays a central role in the radicalisation of some of those within
the extreme-right milieu. It is not the Orthodox religion itself that drives
radicalisation, however, but the perception of Islam as an inherently violent religion and a direct threat to Orthodox religion and culture. In this
way, Islam – as in the case of the construction of the Athens mosque –
becomes a symbol of threat. This appears to confirm Juergensmeyer's
(2017: 18) argument that violent extremism is driven by the sense and
fear of a loss of identity and control in the modern world. At the same
time, many milieu participants emphasise Orthodox teachings as a way
to underline their opposition to violence and extremism. Thus, whilst for
some, religion appears to offer a path to radicalisation, in other cases, religion stalls the radicalisation process and guides individuals away from
embracing violence.

The Islam(ist) Milieu:
Islam as Bulwark against Radicalisation

As evident from the discussion above, Muslims in Greece have become
explicitly and routinely stigmatised and perceived as a threat to Greek
society and culture. Islam is widely considered an inherently violent religion, and mosques, official and non-official, to be sites of the promotion

of violence, terrorism and radicalisation. It is also clear that the extreme-right milieu has taken up this etic discourse, fuelling and reinforcing negative perceptions of Islam, Muslims and mosques. At the same time, Muslims have often felt the exercise of acts of violence against them in the places they live and pray. This raises the question of how young Muslims respond to this stigmatisation, how they react to acts of violence and whether this might encourage radicalisation in their milieu.[17]

Despite many cases of violence perpetrated against Muslims, the evidence from the study of this milieu indicates that significant effort has been expended in order not to respond to such attacks. Such attitudes prevailed even in conditions of close territorial proximity to Golden Dawn, as in the case of one informal mosque located just a short walking distance from Golden Dawn's offices in Athens city centre. Although the interviewee stated that no problems had arisen, he added:

> Now, on how are we going to react, I generally believe in the same calm way as towards all other provocation and disturbances that we have faced till now here and there; calmly and without actually responding to them. Okay, at this moment for good or bad what we Muslims do is that we can't do anything. We have only what the law offers us. There is no other way, this is the right thing to do and this is how things should be done. And if something happens and we can't deal with that, then we should all get up and leave the country. . . . We will never use any other means [of reaction]. If we get to the point of no return, to which we are slowly moving, if we can't stand it anymore, we will get up and leave . . . (Vangelis 2)

Dialogue between Muslim communities and wider Greek society was another crucial dimension of dealing with the extreme right. As another interviewee explained, the Muslim community did not avoid spaces where they might encounter Golden Dawn, but sought to avoid clashes with them and react through dialogue and communication:

> we didn't stay quiet; we didn't stop, or be afraid of . . . but we tried to control our own people too. This was not an easy task, because many of us, from many communities were angry, their 'blood was boiling' . . . meaning that they might also have attacked [Golden Dawn] with whatever means, using anything they could. Imagine that. . . . This is what we tried to control, through dialogue, using other tricks. . . . We did that so as not to give any excuse from our side, because it would be us who paid for this afterwards . . . not them [the extremists]. Unfortunately, everyone would say, 'Look, immigrants did that'. (Vassilis)

Vassilis acknowledges here that the actions of Golden Dawn caused an angry reaction among many in the community, which might have resulted in a process of cumulative extremism (Eatwell 2006; Busher and Macklin 2015; Knott, Lee and Copeland 2018) or reciprocal radicalisation. The latter is described by Pratt (2019: 50) as 'the phenomenon of a perception of a religious "other" as being an inherent threat whereby, in response, an extreme action is undertaken that, relative to the religion or cultural norms of those responding, is abnormal'. However, despite the targeting, with hate speech and violent attacks, of Muslims in Greece by many extremist groups and the grievances they have expressed over their lack of rights, violent reactions on the part of Muslims have not materialised. On the contrary, it seems that Muslims and their official organisations have sought to absorb any grievances or negative feelings caused by the perpetration of violence and racist speech.

International events – which build on existing grievances and perceived injustices – could also play a crucial role in the radicalisation process. For example, following the attack on two mosques in Christchurch, New Zealand which left forty-nine Muslims dead and fifty wounded, one of the milieu participants made a specific reference to the attack in his message after the Friday prayers. However, he employed a peaceful and reconciliatory tone, emphasising that such acts are outside of the logic of Islam, an implicit call against any retaliation.

> I end today's talk with a reference to something . . . all of us as believers woke up shocked by what happened with those gun shootings in the two mosques [New Zealand], an incident which left many dead Muslims in a prayer house. All of us pray that God will forgive those who died and we need to stress that Islam, Islam's values, have nothing to do with these kinds of acts, and that Islam despises these kinds of behaviours. (Nikos)

The above excerpt could be considered as another effort to avoid any violent reactions on the part of Muslims and thus works towards the prevention of reciprocal radicalisation.

Surveillance from the authorities was another key issue for Muslim respondents, who felt there was an institutional discrimination and racism, especially on the part of the security services, who sought to control their places of prayer:

> After all, we started [the mosque] . . . and the day we had the presentation, which was Friday . . . they came, they broke down the door with the Counter-Terrorism agency . . . There was a panic here and of course I realised that this was the plan of the secret service. It was a clear . . . a plan to scare us, to let us know 'we are here'. (Dimitris)

This relationship with the secret service was described as long-standing and typical for such informal mosques, and in some cases started in the 1980s. However, this kind of relationship is interpreted as direct discrimination because no other religion is required to have contact with, or permission from, the police or the secret service in order to open a religious venue. This kind of behaviour from state authorities, as implied by Dimitris, could even be counterproductive and encourage radicalisation.

> In order to get the paperwork for the mosque you must have links to the secret service. If you do not have a good relationship and you do not have a specific goal, you will not be allowed to do it. That is to say, instead of going through the Ministry of Education, we go through the Ministry of Citizen Protection. That is wrong from the beginning. A young person may take this in a different way. This is inequality and it is one of the major forms of inequality – that a Muslim should be under surveillance by the Ministry of Citizen Protection. That means, automatically, you are dangerous, right? This is one of the first forms of inequality that I have experienced very strongly and badly. . . . Okay, partly I understand the stress that exists but on the other hand you can't digest, I personally can't accept the notion that you belong to a ministry that has to do with the country's defence. As if I'm a threat. . . . But you know, and this is how it is born, that is, it is one of the causes of radicalisation. When someone perceives you as a threat to the defence of his country from the beginning, then the other [Muslim] starts to live and behave that way [as a potential threat]. This kind of [state] behaviour, implying that the country is in danger [from Muslims] could lead some [Muslims] to feel ok with this [and become radicalised]. (Dimitris)

Grievances about human rights and religious freedom, such as the construction of an official mosque in Athens, racism, Islamophobia, the role of the state authorities and international issues, such as the transfer of the US embassy to Jerusalem or the situation in Palestine, were mentioned by the majority of the participants. Thus, this milieu seems to reflect the findings of others that the two most common grievances among young Muslims are not being able to enjoy all the rights and opportunities to which they are entitled and feeling constrained by various forces, including family, society as a whole and political power (Abbas and Hamid 2019: 6). The Greek milieu also appears to confirm that sociopolitical inequalities are a crucial factor in radicalisation (see Franc, Poli and Pavlović, this volume).

The fieldwork revealed that some participants had personally encountered extremist and radical messages through their established relationships (friends, brothers, online communication). In all the cases mentioned, the participants managed to deal with the messages and none of them was involved in, or established, any relation with radicals online or offline. One respondent recounted one such incident when he was in the Netherlands: 'I was threatened by Muslims, younger ones. . . in the Netherlands. Online, of course, curses, threats, etc. Not for any serious reason, but because I wanted to organise a group of Muslims, Christians and Jews for charitable purposes, and, let's say, some young ones didn't like that and thought they should warn me' (Kyriakos).

The common response to such incidents was either to step back from their plans or to leave the online sphere (such as a Facebook group) in order to avoid any conflicts, as in the following example:

> I left because I just expressed my opinion. And unfortunately . . . one principle of Islam that at the moment is not implemented among all Arabs is the acceptance of other opinions. . . . If you disagree, you shouldn't quarrel, that means that disagreement shouldn't lead to quarrel; [nowadays] there is no respect for a different opinion. (Nikos)

Stepping back and being silent was not the only option. An interesting finding emerging from the interviews was that, in some cases, those who considered others to have expressed radical or pro-violence views had responded by reporting this to the authorities.

> If I knew someone who held views similar to ISIS and Al Qaeda, an Imam or an ordinary Muslim, I would have mentioned this to the counter-terrorism authorities, as I already did once. I saw someone, it doesn't matter from which country, a migrant, clearly writing various things [on social media] . . . he was trying to convince people that a particular [Islamic] organisation was right. I reported this to the police, I sent an email saying that this person in his Facebook account says that . . . etc. and you should look into this. . . . I did what I thought was the right thing. (Pavlos)

Indeed, as noted above and stressed by a number of interviewees, many Muslims, especially those running prayer houses, had to keep close relations with the police and the secret service, and, if any extreme element appeared, the police would have known. This casts doubt on the media reports discussed earlier claiming informal mosques are centres of extremism and radicalisation; such reports are probably exaggerated and have the effect, primarily, of reproducing fear about Islam.

The role of religion in the rise of violence has been a key theme of public debate. While some have suggested that religion is the key to understanding violence and terrorism, however, other scholars have argued that religion is not a major factor in violent radicalisation (Sonn 2016: 105–13; Cavanaugh 2017; Juergensmeyer 2017; Nanninga 2017). Studies of former terrorists have also confirmed that religion has played a minimal role in their recruitment (Botha and Abdile 2014). According to Roy (2017: 76, 159), those who radicalise do not embrace violence after re-

flection on sacred texts; they have neither the necessary religious education nor interest. They are radicalised not because they misinterpret the
sacred texts or because they are manipulated, but because they choose
this path. Radicalisation has many, complex, origins but is, fundamentally, a personal, and political, choice (ibid.: 164).

Contrary to the perception constructed by the media, extreme-right
politicians, vigilante groups and state authorities, young Muslims have
consistently argued that in Islam, and in the non-official mosques, they
have found a religious path and gateway to a life of non-violence. All of
the participants denied that the atrocities committed in the name of Islam have anything to do with Islam's true message, which is only peace.
According to one respondent, extremism is 'anything that doesn't cope,
anything that is out . . . of Islam, for me anything that is not Islamic, how
much out of Islam it is. Eh, okay, there are variations to that, but . . . if it
is out of the path, out of the spirit, the values and the principles of Islam,
more or less, it is out' (Nikos).

Common to all the explanations offered by the milieu participants as
to why young Muslims engage in violent extremism is a lack of religious
knowledge and religious education, that is, a lack of awareness of the
true substance of Islam (see also Dechesne, this volume). Religion, thus,
is seen as playing a crucial role in radicalisation, through its absence
or, more often, its distortion. At the same time, evidence from the fieldwork shows that religion can also act as a protective factor against radicalisation by functioning as a barrier. This was explicitly articulated in
the interview with one female respondent who argued that religion can
become a factor for challenging extremism: 'Because what every religion says about loving one another, for example, the same is said in the
Qur'an' (Maria). Emphasising the dimensions of peace and love in Islam,
she argued that true knowledge of Islam is crucial in order to protect
Islam, and its teachings, from distortion but also to help those young people who have embraced violence to find a path towards deradicalisation.
This group of informants was not suggesting the need for more religion,
however, but rather for the importance of tolerance and co-existence,
achieved through a more open and looser interpretation of Islam. In this
way, they appear to confirm Beck's (2010) argument that a solution to
religious violence would be to *combine* truth with peace rather than to
replace one with the other. Other participants, however, while also stress-
ing the need to live in peace and present the true meaning of Islam to
other Muslims and the public, argued that this necessitated a stricter
version of Islam (usually Salafism).

The above analysis suggests that religion plays a key role both in radicalisation and non-radicalisation. Indeed, as Wilkinson et al. (2021: 22)

demonstrate in their study of conversion to Islam in prison, switching to, or intensification of belief in, Islam, in some cases, leads to the development of an 'Us' versus 'Them' Islamist worldview, while in other cases it encourages more positive attitudes among prisoners to rehabilitation (engagement with work, education and the avoidance of crime). Extremism is thus not a product of religious belief, nor is it confined to any one religion; jihadism is a movement based on a specific version of Islam and only one way of interpreting the religion (Khosrokhavar 2009: 2). However, the fact that religion is not a proximate cause of extremism is not a reason to avoid studying how religion informs extremism. The desire for simple explanations keeps many of these incorrect assumptions about the connection between Islam and extremism alive. However, in order to understand why people become extremists and how to combat extremist violence, it is necessary to move beyond the clichés (Berger 2018: 85–87). Here, we suggest, the holistic case study approach (Selengut 2003), which examines all the dimensions and context of each case in which the relationship between a specific religion and violence is studied, is the most appropriate.

Conclusions

This chapter has explored the etic discourse on Islam and violence in Greek society as well as the responses by young Muslims to the negative perceptions of, and violence towards, Muslims that this discourse has generated. It has shown, first, that contemporary Greek society is characterised by an anti-Muslim/anti-Islam social and political environment. Stereotypical images about Islam and Muslims are repeatedly reproduced, including by the mainstream media, and are reflected in the findings of a number of opinion polls measuring Greek people's attitudes towards Islam, Muslims, immigrants and the construction of a mosque in Athens. Secondly, we have shown that the extreme right plays a leading role in shaping this stigmatising discourse through its systematic promotion of openly anti-Muslim attitudes. Through empirical research with one such extreme-right milieu in Greece, we have identified distinct segments of radicalised and non-radicalised actors within the milieu alongside the important role of religion across the milieu. This is expressed, by the radicalised, as the need to protect the Orthodox religion from the alleged threat of Islam, implying a clash of civilisations, while the non-radicalised milieu members suggest Orthodox teachings and values can be used to prevent violence and extremism. We find, thirdly, that members of the Islam(ist) milieu consistently avoid violent responses to the extreme right or to other etic stigmatisation. Here, again, religion appears as a barrier against radicalisation and violent extremism. While religion can play a significant role in the embracement of violence (Selengut 2003), it would be inaccurate to claim that religion has a single, unchanging and inherently violent essence (Armstrong 2014). This study of both extreme-right and Islam(ist) milieus, and the struggle over the building of the Athens mosque, thus appear to suggest that the non-response by the latter milieu to stigmatisation and violence by the former has avoided a spiral of reciprocal radicalisation. Moreover, in both milieus, religion was far from always 'the problem'; rather, as Juergensmeyer (2004: 3, 6–9) suggests, 'religion can offer images of a peaceful resolution, justifications for tolerating differences, and a respect for the dignity of all life'.

Acknowledgements

The research drawn on in this chapter is part of the Dialogue about Radicalisation and Equality (DARE) project, which received funding from the European Union's Horizon 2020 research and innovation programme under Grant Agreement No. 725349. It reflects only the views of the author; the European Commission and Research Executive Agency are not responsible for any information it contains.

Alexandros Sakellariou is an adjunct lecturer in Sociology at the Hellenic Open University and has extensive experience as a researcher in large-scale European research projects. He studied Philosophy, Pedagogics and Psychology at the Faculty of Philosophy of Athens and continued his studies at post-graduate level at Panteion University of Social and Political Sciences of Athens, studying Sociology and Social Psychology. In 2008 he defended his PhD at Panteion University, Department of Sociology, in the field of Sociology of Religion. He has taught a course on 'Forms of contemporary religious violence' at Panteion University (Department of Sociology) and completed post-doctoral research on 'Forms of atheism in contemporary Greek society'.

NOTES

1. For a discussion of 'etic' and 'emic' perspectives and their role in the DARE project overall, see the Introduction to this volume.
2. As discussed in the Introduction to this volume, milieus were considered appropriate for selection for the study if they were widely considered to be

'Islamist' in etic discourse. This was the case here, especially in the context of the influence of the anti-Islam extreme-right milieu on etic debates. However, our research findings, as well as the distinctions drawn in the wider literature on Islam between 'mainstream Islam', 'Islamism' and 'Islamist extremism' (Wilkinson 2019), led us to conclude that the milieu studied belonged primarily to mainstream Islam, whilst including some Islamist (e.g. activist Islam, contingent Muslim/non-Muslim separation) and non-violent Islamist extremism elements (e.g. absolute Muslim/non-Muslim separation). For this reason, we refer to it as 'Islam(ist)' rather than 'Islamist'.

3. In 2015 alone, more than 800,000 refugees crossed the border with Turkey into Greece.
4. On the social exclusion of Muslims in Thrace, see http://www.mar.umd.edu/chronology.asp?groupId=35001 (retrieved 23 March 2022).
5. Prior to this, during the 1990s, most debates and conflicts around Islam in Greece were related to the minority of Thrace, which was marginalised and discriminated against.
6. Laikos Orthodoxos Synagermos (Popular Orthodox Rally) was an extreme-right political party, which played a crucial role in anti-Muslim hatred and Islamophobia.
7. Parliamentary Minutes, Plenary Session 25 October 2000: 1503.
8. Parliamentary Minutes, Plenary Session 7 November 2006: 903.
9. Parliamentary Minutes, Plenary Session 10 December 2010: 2389–90.
10. Parliamentary Minutes, Plenary Session 19 November 2010: 1415.
11. Parliamentary Minutes, Plenary Session 12 June 2000: 22, 27, 29.
12. Parliamentary Minutes, Plenary Session 27 April 2015: 49; Parliamentary Minutes, Plenary Session 8 May 2015: 264.
13. Parliamentary Minutes, Plenary Session 12 May 2015: 176.
14. Parliamentary Minutes, Plenary Session 24 June 2015: 71.
15. For more on RIMSE, see https://www.rimse.gr (retrieved 23 March 2022).
16. For these opinion polls, see https://www.pewresearch.org/global/2014/05/12/chapter-4-views-of-roma-muslims-jews/ and https://www.pewresearch.org/global/2016/07/11/negative-views-of-minorities-refugees-common-in-eu/ (retrieved 23 March 2022).
17. For more details about the milieu and the findings from the ethnographic study, see Sakellariou 2021b.

REFERENCES

Abbas, Tahir, and Sadek Hamid (eds). 2019. *Political Muslims: Understanding Youth in a Global Context.* New York: Syracuse University Press.

Alievi, Stefano. 2009. *Conflicts over Mosques in Europe.* London: Network of European Foundations.

Altheide, David L. 2003. 'Mass Media, Crime and the Discourse of Fear', *The Hedgehog Review* 5(3): 9–25.

Anagnostou, Dia, and Ruby Gropas. 2010. 'Domesticating Islam and Muslim Immigrants: Political and Church Responses to Constructing a Central Mosque in Athens', in Victor Roudometof and Vasilios N. Makrides (eds), *Orthodox Christianity in 21st Century Greece: The Role of Religion in Culture, Ethnicity and Politics*. Surrey: Ashgate, pp. 89–109.

Antoniou, Dimitris. 2010. 'The Mosque That Was Not There: Ethnographic Elaborations on Orthodox Conceptions of Sacrifice', in Victor Roudometof and Vasilios N. Makrides (eds), *Orthodox Christianity in 21st Century Greece: The Role of Religion in Culture, Ethnicity and Politics*. Surrey: Ashgate, pp. 155–74.

Arjana, Sophia R. 2015. *Muslims in the Western Imagination*. New York: Oxford University Press.

Armstrong, Karen. 2014. *Fields of Blood: Religion and the History of Violence*. New York: Knopf.

Astor, Avraham Y. 2011. 'Mobilizing against Mosques: The Origins of Opposition to Islamic Centers of Worship in Spain', PhD thesis. Michigan: University of Michigan.

Basbous, Antoine. 2003. *Islamismos: Mia Apotihimeni Epanastasi?* [Islamism: A Failed Revolution?]. Athens: Papadimas.

Beck, Ulrich. 2010. *A God of One's Own: Religion's Capacity for Peace and Potential for Violence*. Cambridge: Polity.

Berger, John M. 2018. *Extremism*. Cambridge, MA: The MIT Press.

Blanc, Théo, and Olivier Roy (eds). 2021. *Salafism: Challenged by Radicalization? Violence, Politics, and the Advent of Post-Salafism*. San Domenico di Fiesole: European University Institute.

Bossi, Mary. 1996. *Ellada kai Tromokratia: Ethnikes kai Diethneis Diastaseis* [Greece and Terrorism: National and International Dimensions]. Athens: Ant. N. Sakkoulas.

Botha, Anneli, and Mahdi Abdile. 2014. *Getting Behind the Profiles of Boko Haram Members and Factors Contributing to Radicalisation Versus Working Towards Peace*. The International Dialogue Centre (KAICIID). Retrieved 23 March 2022 from https://www.kaiciid.org/publications-resources/getting-behind-profiles-boko-haram-members-summary.

Busher, Joel, and Graham Macklin. 2015. 'Interpreting "Cumulative Extremism": Six Proposals for Enhancing Conceptual Clarity', *Terrorism and Political Violence* 27(5): 884–905.

Cavanaugh, William T. 2017. 'Religion, Violence, Nonsense, and Power', in James R. Lewis (ed.), *The Cambridge Companion to Religion and Terrorism*. New York: Cambridge University Press, pp. 23–31.

Cesari, Jocelyn. 2005. 'Mosque Conflicts in European Cities: Introduction', *Journal of Ethnic and Migration Studies* 31(6): 1015–24.

Cohen, Stanley. 1972. *Folk Devils and Moral Panics*. Great Britain: McGibbon and Kee Ltd.

Dianeosis. 2015. 'Ti Pistevoun oi Ellines' ['What Greeks Believe']. Retrieved 23 March 2022 from https://www.dianeosis.org/2016/02/apopsi_twn_ellinwn_ gia_toys_metanastes_/.

———. 2016a. 'Oi Ellines kai to Metanasteftiko Provilma' ['The Greeks and the Refugee Problem']. Retrieved 23 March 2022 from http://www.dianeosis.org/ wp-content/uploads/2016/02/immigration_04.pdf.

———. 2016b. 'Ti Pistevoun oi Ellines' ['What Greeks Believe']. Retrieved 23 March 2022 from http://www.dianeosis.org/wp-content/uploads/2016/02/ ti_pistevoun_oi_ellines_spreads_C.pdf.

Eatwell, Roger. 2006. 'Community Cohesion and Cumulative Extremism in Contemporary Britain', *The Political Quarterly* 77(2): 204–16.

Eleftheriadou, Marina. 2020. 'Fight after Flight? An Exploration of the Radicalization Potential among Refugees in Greece', *Small Wars & Insurgencies* 31(1): 34–60.

Esposito, John, and Ibrahim Kalin (eds). 2011. *Islamophobia: The Challenge of Pluralism in the 21st Century*. New York: Oxford University Press.

Furedi, Frank. 2006. *Culture of Fear Revisited*. London: Continuum.

Giannoulis, Alexis. 2011. *Islamic Radicalisation Processes in Greece: The Islamic Radicalization Index (IRI)*. International Institute for Counterterrorism (ICT), IDC Herzliya. Retrieved 28 March 2022 from https://www.ict.org.il/ictFiles/0/ IRI%20-%20Greece.pdf.

Girard, René. 1991. *I Via kai to Iero* [Violence and the Sacred]. Athens: Exandas.

———. 2017. *Via kai Thriskeia* [Violence and Religion]. Athens: Nissos.

Goode, Erich, and Nachman Ben-Yehuda. 2009. *Moral Panics: The Social Construction of Deviance*. Singapore: Wiley-Blackwell.

Hafez, Farid. 2014. 'Shifting Borders: Islamophobia as Common Ground for Building Pan-European Right-Wing Unity', *Patterns of Prejudice* 48(5): 479–99.

Hagège, Claude. 2018. *Thriskeies, Logos kai Via* [Religions, Discourse and Violence]. Athens: Exandas.

Hilal, Maha. 2022. *Innocent until Proven Muslim: Islamophobia, the War on Terror, and the Muslim Experience since 9/11*. Minneapolis: Broadleaf Books.

Hussain, Ajmal. 2022. 'Street Salafism: Contingency and Urbanity as Religious Creed', *Society & Space*. Retrieved 23 March 2022 from https://journals.sage pub.com/doi/full/10.1177/02637758211069989.

Juergensmeyer, Mark. 2004. 'Is Religion the Problem?', *UC Santa Barbara: Global and International Studies*. Retrieved 23 March 2022 from https://escholar ship.org/uc/item/4n92c45q.

———. 2017. 'Does Religion Cause Terrorism?', in James R. Lewis (ed.), *The Cambridge Companion to Religion and Terrorism*. New York: Cambridge University Press, pp. 11–22.

Kallis, Aristotle. 2013. 'Breaking Taboos and "Mainstreaming the Extreme": The Debates on Restricting Islamic Symbols in Contemporary Europe', in Ruth Wodak, Majid KhosraviNik and Brigitte Mral (eds), *Right-Wing Populism in Europe: Politics and Discourse*. London: Bloomsbury, pp. 55–71.

Karim, Karim H. 2000. *The Islamic Peril: Media and Global Violence*. Montreal: Black Rose Books.

Katsikas, Stefanos. 2012. 'The Muslim Minority in Greek Historiography', *European History Quarterly* 42(3): 444–67.

———. 2021. *Islam and Nationalism in Modern Greece, 1821–1940*. New York: Oxford University Press.

Kaya Ayhan, and Ayşe Tecmen. 2019. 'Europe versus Islam? Right-Wing Populist Discourse and the Construction of a Civilizational Identity', *The Review of Faith & International Affairs* 17(1): 49–64.

KEMEA. 2016. *Odigos gia Epaggelmaties Protis Grammis: Draseis kata tis Rizospastikopoiisis kai tou Extremismou* [A Guide for Frontline Professionals. Actions against Radicalisation and Extremism]. Athens: Hellenic Police Headquarters/Centre for Security Studies.

Kepel, Gilles. 1992. *I Ekdikisi tou Theou* [The Revenge of God]. Athens: Livanis.

———. 2000. *Tzihad: Ieros Polemos* [Jihad: Holy War]. Athens: Kastaniotis.

———. 2015. *Terreur dans l'Hexagone: Genèse du Djihad Français* [Terror in the *Hexagon*: The Genesis of French Jihad]. Paris: Éditions Gallimard.

Khosrokhavar, Farhad. 2009. *Inside Jihadism: Understanding Jihadi Movements Worldwide*. Boulder, CO: Paradigm Publishers.

Kirtsoglou, Elisabeth, and George Tsimouris. 2018. 'Migration, Crisis, Liberalism: The Cultural and Racial Politics of Islamophobia and "Radical Alterity" in Modern Greece', *Ethnic and Racial Studies* 41(10): 1874–92.

Knott, Kim, Ben Lee and Simon Copeland. 2018. *Reciprocal Radicalisation*. London: Centre for Research and Evidence on Security Threats.

Kong, Lilly, and Orlando Woods (eds). 2016. *Religion and Space: Competition, Conflict and Violence in the Contemporary World*. London: Bloomsbury.

Kostakos, Panagiotis. 2007. 'The Threat of Islamic Radicalism to Greece', *Terrorism Monitor* 5(15). Retrieved 23 March 2022 from https://jamestown.org/program/the-threat-of-islamic-radicalism-to-greece/.

———. 2010. 'Islamist Terrorism in Europe: Could Greece Be Next?' *Terrorism Monitor* 37(4): 3–5.

Ktistakis, Gannis. 2006. *O Ieros Nomos tou Islam kai oi Mousoulmanoi Ellines Polites* [The Sacred Law of Islam and the Greek Muslim Citizens]. Athens-Thessaloniki: Sakkoulas.

Lagos, Evangelos, et al. 2021. *Young Orthodox Greeks with Islamophobic/Anti-Muslim Views and Attitudes*. DARE Project Report. Retrieved 28 August 2022 from https://documents.manchester.ac.uk/display.aspx?DocID=58696.

Lewis, James R. (ed.). 2017. *The Cambridge Companion to Religion and Terrorism*. New York: Cambridge University Press.

Mamdani, Mahmood. 2004. *Good Muslim, Bad Muslim: America, the Cold War and the Roots of Terrorism*. New York: Pantheon.

Marzouki, Nadia, and Duncan McDonnell. 2016. 'Populism and Religion', in Nadia Marzouki, David McDonnell and Olivier Roy (eds), *Saving the People: How Populists Hijack Religion*. London: C. Hurst & Co, pp. 1–11.

Marzouki, Nadia, Duncan McDonnell and Olivier Roy (eds). 2016. *Saving the People: How Populists Hijack Religion*. London: C. Hurst & Co.

Maussen, Marcel. 2009. 'Constructing Mosques: The Governance of Islam in France and the Netherlands', PhD thesis. Amsterdam: Amsterdam School for Social Science Research.

Mazzoleni, Oscar. 2016. 'Populism and Islam in Switzerland: The Role of the Swiss People's Party', in Nadia Marzouki, David McDonnell and Olivier Roy (eds), *Saving the People: How Populists Hijack Religion*. London: C. Hurst & Co, pp. 47–60.

Morgan, George, and Scott Poynting (eds). 2012. *Global Islamophobia: Muslims and Moral Panic in the West*. Surrey: Ashgate.

Nanninga, Pieter. 2017. 'The Role of Religion in Al-Qaeda's Violence', in James R. Lewis (ed.), *The Cambridge Companion to Religion and Terrorism*. New York: Cambridge University Press, pp. 158–71.

Neumann, Peter. 2016. *Oi Neoi Tzihadistes: To Islamiko Kratos, I Evropi kai to Epomeno Kima Tromokratias* [The New Jihadists: Islamic State, Europe and the Next Wave of Terrorism]. Athens: Diametros.

Neumann, Peter, and Scott Kleinmann. 2013. 'How Rigorous is Radicalization Research?', *Democracy and Security* 9(4): 360–82.

Papageorgiou, Fotis, and Antonis Samouris. 2012. *Islamismos kai Islamophobia: Pera apo tin Prokatalipsi* [Islamism and Islamophobia: Beyond Prejudice]. Athens: Taxideftis.

Pilkington, Hilary. 2016. *'Loud and Proud': Passion and Politics in the English Defence League*. Manchester: Manchester University Press.

Pratt, Douglas G. 2019. 'Reacting to Islam: Islamophobia as a Form of Extremism', in John L. Esposito and Derya Iner (eds), *Islamophobia and Radicalization: Breeding Intolerance and Violence*. Cham: Palgrave Macmillan, pp. 35–53.

Psarras, Dimitris. 2012. *I Mavri Vivlos tis Xrissis Avgis* [The Black Book of Golden Dawn]. Athens: Polis.

Public Issue Survey. 2010. 'Oi Ellines kai to Islam: Ti Gnorizei kai ti Pistevei I Koini Gnomi' ['The Greeks and Islam: What Public Opinion Knows and Believes']. Retrieved 23 March 2022 from https://www.publicissue.gr/islam-2009/.

Roux, Jean-Paul. 1998. *To Ema: Mythoi, Symvola kai Pragmatikotita* [Blood: Myths, Symbols and Reality]. Athens: Livanis.

Roy, Olivier. 1994. *The Failure of Political Islam*. Cambridge, MA: Harvard University Press.

———. 2006. *To Pagosmiopoiimeno Islam* [Globalised Islam]. Athens: Scripta.

———. 2017. *Tzihad kai Thanatos* [Jihad and Death]. Athens: Polis.

Said, Edward. 1981. *Covering Islam*. London: Routledge.

Sakellariou, Alexandros. 2011. 'The Invisible Islamic Community of Athens and the Question of the Invisible Islamic Mosque', *Journal of Shi'a Islamic Studies* 4(1): 71–89.

———. 2015. 'Anti-Islamic Public Discourse in Contemporary Greece: The Reproduction of Religious Panic', in Arolda Elbasani and Olivier Roy (eds), *The*

Revival of Islam in the Balkans: From Identity to Religiosity. Basingstoke: Palgrave Macmillan, pp. 42–61.

———. 2017. 'Fear of Islam in Greece: Migration, Terrorism, and "Ghosts" from the Past', *Nationalities Papers* 45(4): 511–23.

———. 2019. 'Islamophobia in Greece: The Muslim "Threat" and the Panic about Islam', in Irene Zempi and Imran Awan (eds), *The Routledge International Handbook of Islamophobia*. Oxon: Routledge, pp. 198–211.

———. 2020. *Radical Milieus in Historical Context: Greece*. DARE Project Report. Retrieved 28 August 2022 from https://documents.manchester.ac.uk/display.aspx?DocID=58706.

———. 2021a. *Historical Case Studies of Interactive Radicalisation: Greece*. DARE Project Report. Retrieved 28 August 2022 from https://documents.manchester.ac.uk/display.aspx?DocID=58624.

———. 2021b. *Young Muslims in Unofficial Prayer Places of Athens*. DARE Project Report. Retrieved 28 August 2022 from https://documents.manchester.ac.uk/display.aspx?DocID=58686.

Selengut, Charles. 2003. *Sacred Fury: Understanding Religious Violence*. Lanham, MD: Altamira Press.

Sonn, Tamara. 2016. *Is Islam an Enemy of the West?* Cambridge: Polity Press.

Symeonides, Tassos. 2017. 'Islamic Terrorism: Could Greece Be Next?' Research Institute for European and American Studies. Retrieved 23 March 2022 from https://www.rieas.gr/images/editorial/bluebook17.pdf.

Thompson, Kenneth. 1998. *Moral Panics*. London: Routledge.

Triandafyllidou, Anna, and Ruby Gropas. 2009. 'Constructing Difference: The Mosque Debates in Greece', *Journal of Ethnic and Migration Studies* 35(6): 957–75.

Tsitselikis, Konstantinos. 1999. 'I Thesi tou Moufti stin Elliniki Ennomi Taxi' ['The Place of the Mufti in the Greek Legal System'], in Dimitris Christopoulos (ed.), *Nomika Zitimata Thriskeftikis Eterotitas* [Legal Issues of Religious Diversity]. Athens: Kritiki, pp. 271–329.

———. 2004. 'I Thriskeftiki Eleftheria ton Metanaston: I Periptosi ton Mousoulmanon' ['Religious Freedom of Immigrants: The Case of Muslims'], in Miltos Pavlou and Dimitris Christopoulos (eds), *I Ellada tis Metanastefsis* [Greece of Immigration]. Athens: Kritiki, pp. 267–302.

———. 2012. *Old and New Islam in Greece: From Historical Minorities to Immigrant Newcomers*. Leiden: Brill.

Verousi, Christina, and Chris Allen. 2021. 'Problematising the Official Athens Mosque: Between Mere Place of Worship and 21st Century "Trojan Horse"', *Religions* 12(7): 485. Retrieved 23 March 2022 from https://doi.org/10.3390/rel12070485.

Wilkinson, Matthew L.N. 2019. *The Genealogy of Terror: How to Distinguish between Islam, Islamist and Islamist Extremism*. London: Routledge.

Wilkinson, Matthew, et al. 2021. 'Prison as a Site of Intense Religious Change: The Example of Conversion to Islam', *Religions* 12: 162. Retrieved 23 March 2022 from https://doi.org/10.3390/rel12030162.

Zempi, Irene, and Neil Chakraborti. 2014. *Islamophobia, Victimisation and the Veil*. Basingstoke: Palgrave Macmillan.

Zempi, Irene, and Imran Awan (eds). 2019. *The Routledge International Handbook of Islamophobia*. Oxon: Routledge.

Zine, Jasmin. 2022. *Under Siege: Islamophobia and the 9/11 Generation*. McGill-Queen's University Press.

CHAPTER 5

Family, Relatives and Friendship as Channels of (Non)Radicalisation in the Narratives of the Second Urban Generation of North Caucasian Youth

Sviatoslav Poliakov

Introduction

There is consensus in the academic literature that social connections play a key role in radicalisation, facilitating the transmission of ideological views and involvement in violent actions through mutual emotional support, the development of a common identity and encouragement to adopt new views (Sageman 2004; Bakker 2007; Asal, Fair and Shellman 2008; McCauley and Moskalenko 2010; Hafez and Mullins 2015). As Sageman (2004: 135) states, social connections 'are more important and relevant to the transformation of potential candidates into global mujahedin than postulated external factors, such as a common hatred for an outside group. ... As in all intimate relationships, this glue, in-group love, is found within the group. It may be more accurate to blame global Salafi terrorist activity on in-group love than out-group hate'. Scott Atran (2011: 49) comes to a similar conclusion, noting that 'predictors for involvement in suicide attacks are, again, small-world aspects of social networks and local group dynamics rather than large-scale social, economic, and political indicators, such as education level and economic status'.

In this chapter, based on data gathered as part of the DARE (Dialogue on Radicalisation and Equality) project, I examine the role played by family, kinship and friendship ties in the radicalisation, non-radicalisation and deradicalisation of male youth from the most Islamicised region of

the Russian Federation, the North Caucasus. More specifically, the focus of research interest is on the second urban generation of youth from
the North Caucasus, the children and younger brothers of migrants who
moved from the villages of the North Caucasus republics to large cities
outside their home region. This group, research evidence suggests, is
particularly sensitive to politicised versions of Islam, including its radical
forms (Yarlykapov 2010; 'Prichiny radikalizatsii...' 2016).

The Historical and Social Context of
Islamist Radicalisation in the North Caucasus

The North Caucasus is a historical and cultural region in the south of the
Russian Federation which includes seven republics – Adygeia , Chechnia,
Dagestan, Ingushetia, Kabardino-Balkaria, Karachai-Cherkessia and North
Ossetia. The Islamisation of the North Caucasus began with the Arab con-
quests in the seventh and eighth centuries, but Islam was first established
on the territory (except for North Ossetia) in the sixteenth century. At the
same time, in Dagestan, Chechnia and Ingushetia, the Shafi'i school of
law and religion (*madhhab*) was established, while the Hanafi school was
set up in Karachai-Cherkessia and Kabardino-Balkaria (Yarlykapov 2006).
There were also Shi'a communities in Derbent and some villages of southern Dagestan bordering Azerbaijan (ibid.). Sufi brotherhoods (*tariqas*)
became widespread in Dagestan, Chechnia and Ingushetia, the most
influential of which were Naqshbandiyah and Qadiriyya (Matsuzato and
Ibragimov 2006). In the post-Soviet period, the North Caucasian republics
went through a rapid re-Islamisation process in which religion filled the
ideological vacuum left by the collapse of communism and became a central vector of regional identity (Drambyan 2009; Kisriev 2009).

The North Caucasus has a long history of religious radicalism in which
aspirations to build a theocratic Sharia state were combined with ideas of
political independence from Russia. In the nineteenth century, the region
became the stage for the Caucasian War, waged by mountain communities against the Russian Empire under the banner of *ghazavat*, a holy war
against infidels (Zelkina 2002; Kurbanov 2004). In the 1930s–40s, these
highlanders resisted the Soviet system, which imposed the collectivisation
of agriculture, repressed political and religious elites and fought against
the religion and traditional ways of the North Caucasian peoples. At the
end of World War II, several North Caucasian ethnic groups (Chechens,
Ingush, Karachais and Balkars) were deported to Central Asia and Siberia
(Polyan 2001). The collective trauma of deportation played an important
role in the escalation of the Chechen conflict of the 1990s–2000s.

The recent history of Islamist radicalisation in the North Caucasus has three stages, which differ in terms of the set of actors, ideological orientation, methods and geographical coverage involved. The first stage covers the period from 1991 to 1996. Attempts by Chechen separatists to secede from Russia led to a bloody confrontation with Russian armed forces, the so-called First Chechen War (1994–96). At that stage, the separatists' guiding ideology was ethnic nationalism. The role of the Islamic factor was secondary. It helped to consolidate the Chechen resistance and to attract financial and human resources from Muslim countries. At the same time, radical Islamic groups did not declare themselves as an independent force and were formally subordinated to the secular leadership of the self-proclaimed Ichkeria. The second phase consists of the Second Chechen War (1999–2008), the prologue to which was the invasion of Dagestan by Chechen fighters led by Shamil Basayev to assist the self-proclaimed Wahhabi enclaves in four villages in Tsumadinsky district. By the end of the Second Chechen War, the conflict had spread throughout the entire North Caucasus. Having been defeated in confrontations with the federal army and the militia, the militants turned to a form of subversive and terrorist war, waged under the slogan of building an independent Sharia state that embraced all the North Caucasian republics (Dobaev 2009; Markedonov 2010). At that time, Islamist groups (such as Caucasus Emirate, Jamia Sharia, Jamia of Kabardino-Balkaria) were institutionalised and organised according to a network principle, consisting of local cells formed along ethnic and territorial lines (Yarlykapov 2010; Polyakov 2015).

The current stage is characterised by a significant decline in the activity of radical groups in the North Caucasus. This is due, first, to the organisational defeat of many jihadist networks and the elimination of their leaders. The second reason is the departure of a significant number of radicalised young people to Syria and Iraq to participate in *jihad* on the side of ISIS and other Islamist groups (Youngman 2016). However, according to researchers, this lull is temporary, as the systemic factors associated with radicalisation persist, namely, the low quality of governance, corruption and privatisation of life chances by local elites and uncontrolled activities of security forces leading to extensive human rights violations (Ratelle and Souleimanov 2017; Benedek 2018).

The dynamics of small groups must also be taken into account. The North Caucasus is a region where kinship and community relations are highly valued. Relatives and fellow villagers of jihadists may not themselves share radical views. However, they provide a supportive milieu of the radical underground; they feed, treat and shelter combatants and serve as a reserve of human resource (Tekushev 2012). In the republics of the North Caucasus, there is a fairly wide stratum of people who have lost relatives and friends in so-called counter-terrorist operations – both by the underground and by law enforcement agencies – and have reason to want revenge. In some highland areas, the institution of blood feud persists (Ratelle and Souleimanov 2017; Albogachieva and Babich 2010), sanctioning such behaviour. All these factors could become drivers of new waves of radicalisation.

Methods and Sample

The focus of this chapter is young men with a North Caucasian regional background currently living in two Russian megacities – Saint Petersburg and Moscow. In this case study, they come mainly from Dagestan, the largest and most Islamised republic in the North Caucasus, which is also a forerunner in urbanisation processes and the main arena of confrontation between regional and federal authorities and jihadists. Respondents of other nationalities (Chechens, Ingush, Azerbaijanis) were recruited as part of networks organised by those originally from Dagestan.

I refer to this respondent set as the 'second urban generation' to indicate that they are second-generation city dwellers – the sons of migrants from the countryside. Thus, their family stories combine two migratory tracks: from the countryside to urban centres; and from the North Caucasus to other regions of the Russian Federation. Concerning religion, the second urban generation is the first generation born after the beginning of the post-Soviet re-Islamisation of the North Caucasus (Bobrovnikov 2007; Kisriev 2009). Unlike their parents and older relatives, who are more likely to be adherents of traditional Sufi Islam or so-called cultural Muslims, the second urban generation is more likely to opt for fundamentalist versions of Islam (Yarlykapov 2010; 'Prichiny radikalizatsii...' 2016). Their religious views are characterised by a high degree of protest politicisation (ibid.). Those from this social milieu reportedly predominate among young people who have gone to fight in Syria on the side of the Islamic State (prohibited in Russia) (ibid.).

The collection of empirical data lasted for a period of eleven months, from September 2018 to July 2019, and includes seventeen in-depth semi-structured interviews with men between the ages of twenty-four and thirty. All respondents profess Islam and refer to themselves as practising believers, but they self-identify with a range of Islamic traditions including Salafi, Sufi, Shi'a and 'just Muslim'. Ten respondents were born and lived in the North Caucasus republics before they migrated, six were born outside the region, of whom two were born in the city of their current residence. Eight respondents reside with their parents and/or siblings, five live alone or with friends, and the rest already have their own families with whom they reside. Among those who have migrated, three main migration tracks can be identified: (a) migration for higher education; (b) moving together with, or following, a migrating parent family; and (c) migration in search of work. Some family mobility trajectories include multiple moves from one Russian city to another with periodic returns to the North Caucasus. Most often, this is due to the itinerant nature of the parents' employment or business.

Two researchers, Sviatoslav Poliakov and Rasul Abdulkhalikov, conducted the interviews. Drawing on the published literature on radicalisation in Russia relating to milieus potentially receptive to radical ideas, recruitment of participants took place via two main channels and using a number of criteria relating to migration experience and religious participation. The first was an institutional channel – North Caucasian compatriots' associations in Saint Petersburg. The second channel was the social media platform VKontakte, where we recruited individuals fitting our criteria by setting a geo-filter (Saint Petersburg) and the filter 'religious beliefs' (Muslim) to select our informants. We then searched for people who participated in several religious groups and invited them to take part in the research. Additional participants were recruited using the snowball method.

The ethnicity and religiosity of the researchers were consequential in terms of positionality. Rasul is a representative of one of the ethnic groups of Dagestan and a Muslim. He did not experience difficulties while working with informants as they perceived him as 'one of them'. Sviatoslav (an ethnic Russian and Orthodox Christian) faced certain barriers. When recruiting via social media, he was always asked about his nationality and religion, and often this question turned out to be a filter, after which many potential participants stopped communicating. However, his positionality as Orthodox turned out to be advantageous in that many informants found engaging in dialogue with someone who was religious, but of a different faith, less problematic than with someone of no religion or of an atheist conviction.

Family and City

The crucial social context for thinking about the role of social networks in the radicalisation of the second urban generation is the complex transformation of North Caucasian society, the main drivers of which are two interrelated processes. The first is the unfinished process of late urbanisation, in which rural residents move to cities and are thus drawn into the orbit of the urban lifestyle (Starodubrovskaya et al. 2011). The second is the intensive migration of North Caucasian residents to other Russian regions (Mkrtchyan 2019). This urbanisation is associated with the breakdown of the extended traditional family and the emancipation of the individual from the authority of family and community that is characteristic of traditional society. The speed of such social change is not uniform across the different republics and localities of the North Caucasus. In relatively sparsely urbanised republics such as Chechnia and Ingushetia, where the population lives compactly in clans, the structures of extended family and traditional society continue to play an important role in people's everyday lives (Starodubrovskaya 2019). In neighbouring Dagestan, where urbanisation processes are most intense, there is a more diversified picture of family patterns, indicating a deeper erosion of the traditional family (ibid.). At the same time, the North Caucasian city is unable to 'digest' sustainable migration from the countryside, which is not of an individual but of a family and territorial-neighbourly nature, largely contributing to the preservation of rural society institutions in urban conditions (Starodubrovskaya et al. 2011; Starodubrovskaya and Kazenin 2014).

As our case study shows, the older generation, even outside the North Caucasus, tries to reproduce the matrix of the traditional North Caucasian family, demanding obedience, discipline and unconditional recognition of paternal authority from the younger members of the family. It is also evident that, even at later stages of life, the family tries to maintain control over its younger members. The second urban generation is under pressure from their elders to choose educational trajectories, professional careers and even marriage partners of which they approve:

> Why did I choose to study to be a customs officer? Well, this is also a question … Most likely, it wasn't me who chose it, it was my father. As in most cases, when you are seventeen years old, you graduate from school, you do not particularly know which education path to choose, you are simply told, and you obey. (Hamzat)

> Yes, my parents are Avars too. They are from the same village. We got married traditionally, that is, my parents introduced us and we got married quickly. Everything went traditionally. It's the most standard way in Dagestan. (Khabib)

However, migration, especially outside the North Caucasus, erodes the resource and ideological foundations of parental authority. Parents cannot rely on either the resources of the extended family or the support of the neighbourhood, which is often indifferent or hostile towards ethnic 'outsiders'. In urban contexts, control becomes rather superficial, focusing on external attributes of their sons' social well-being such as academic performance and/or success in sports:

> The only thing my father wanted was for me to become a world champion in Ultimate Fighting. He told me to go to fights, judo. Told me to devote myself completely to my studies or sports. Anyway, when I got two Bs and the rest As, he'd say, 'Go into sports. You're no good at anything'. (Magomet Ali)

'Traditional' families outside the North Caucasus can only count on limited 'credit' of obedience, which is granted less as a result of the recognition of parental authority than out of conformism or pragmatic unwillingness to lose access to family resources. At the same time, parents are unable to handle even the simplest manifestations of nonconformity on the part of their children. For example, some respondents recalled that if they fought with their peers or did poorly at school as children, their parents would conclude that they could not provide the 'right' upbringing and send them off to live with relatives in a Dagestani village for a period of time.

In some cases, migration outside the North Caucasus allowed research participants to distance themselves not only from family and community but also from the institutions of control associated with parental religion. Sufi brotherhoods – *tariqas*, membership of which is inherited within the clan and multigenerational family – are widespread in Dagestan. The *tariqas* carry a significant mobilisation resource and influence, not only religious but also in economic and political life (Matsuzato and Ibragimov 2006). For instance, members of *tariqas* are well represented in government and law enforcement agencies. As shown in the interviews, in the North Caucasus context, this power resource is actively used to put pressure on 'deluded' members of the brotherhood to bring them back into line. For example, Salekh, who headed up a small Salafist group (*jamaat*) in Moscow, recounted how, whilst in Dagestan, he had been regularly subjected to pressure from relatives who accused him of apostasy and tried to force him to return to 'traditional' Islam.

> Respondent: All my relatives, and my cousin, are all *tariqa* followers, they work in the state structures, so they put pressure on me.
> Interviewer: Did they pressure you physically?
> Respondent: No, it didn't get to that, I just left, thank God. (Salekh)

In the big city, young people with a North Caucasian background engage in identification processes of 'self-discovery', an integral part of which is a critical reflection on the legitimacy of both parental authority and the social order. Children, often more educated than their parents, have to find their values and meanings in a culturally heterogeneous urban environment and develop their ways and methods of adaptation. In this context, the role of horizontal urban communities is increasing and beginning to overtake kinship hierarchies (Starodubrovskaya 2016).

Given the high level of Islamisation among young people from the North Caucasus, it is not surprising that religion often becomes the primary language through which they articulate and defend their meanings and values. As researchers have noted (Yarlykapov 2010; Starodubrovskaya 2015, 2016), the popularity of confrontational versions of Islam among urban North Caucasian youth is, not least, due to the fact that it offers young people an ideological basis for challenging generational hierarchies. Islamic fundamentalism, which, unlike traditional *tariqa* Islam, does not assume unequivocal submission to the will of elders, legitimises their dissociation from the older generation (Starodubrovskaya 2015: 87):

> In matters of religion, there are no older and younger generations. There are young people now, 16–18 years old, who know everything, they have learned everything, but an old man, who is maybe sixty years old, he has not opened a single book, he has heard something about religion from his grandmother somewhere. (Salekh)

A sense of their rightness, based on knowledge rather than tradition, negates the moral cost of disobedience in the eyes of young people. Often conformist in matters that concern the profane aspects of life, they consistently resist the pressure of parents and older relatives in matters that concern their religious beliefs:

> I became a Sunni, but my relatives are all Shias. My ancestors in Derbent built a mosque and imposed Shiism in this city. I am a Sunni, and for Shias, Sunnis are enemy number one. Although for me, they [my relatives] are not enemy number one as long as I do not declare them enemies. Anyway, I had problems with my father, with my mother, with my brothers. (Mamuka)

Inequality and Discrimination

Identity processes in Russian megacities are complicated by stigma, inequality and discrimination. Young Caucasians are regularly confronted with hate speech, Islamophobia and racist stereotypes. These circulate in everyday communication, including at work as illustrated by Khabib:

> I realise that in the firm where I work, my ethnic background often plays against me. Even my supervisors ... talk about things or make

jokes in front of me that might be offensive or directed against me. But I don't want to ruin relations with them, so I can't respond to them how I would like to. (Khabib)

Such stigmatisation is encountered frequently also in public discourse, through the media or government communications, as described by Hamzat:

Our media manages to present even good news related to North Caucasians or Central Asians in such a way that people are more likely to feel a sense of disgust rather than a positive feeling [towards us]. (Hamzat)

This group of young people is often disproportionately targeted by law enforcers, among whom profiling based on xenophobic stereotypes is widespread:

Interviewer: Do you think police, law enforcement agencies in Russia, pay particular attention to North Caucasians or Muslims?
Respondent: Yes, of course. We are of particular interest to them.
Interviewer: Why do you think that is?
Respondent: If something happens – a murder, robbery, terrorist attack – there is already a stereotype that any North Caucasian is a potential criminal. (Jafar)

There is also extensive discrimination against people from the North Caucasus when applying for jobs and renting housing. One respondent recalled how, when looking for accommodation, he had sometimes called landlords and, when he said he was from the Caucasus, they replied, 'No, we don't want to rent to people from the Caucasus' (Jafar). Another respondent described his experience in seeking employment:

I applied for a job at the Tax Office and the offices of an energy company were right next to it. So I put in my CV to them too but got rejected. Later, talking to some people who worked in that company, when I told them I had hoped to get a job there at one time, they explained that I hadn't been taken on because I was a Dagestani. (Khabib)

Despite the state's declared freedom of religion, some employers also violate the right of observant Muslims to practise their religion:

Like some people go out for a smoke and we are not allowed to pray. In my last job I was told I was not allowed to go out (to pray). I said, 'How can't I go out?' You smoke, I say, cigarettes, I need five minutes, too, in short. No, they say, you are not allowed to go out. (Adam)

In the academic literature, horizontal inequality – the unequal social, economic or political position of groups based on ethnicity and religion –

is considered a key factor in radicalisation (Uslaner and Brown 2005; Wilkinson and Pickett 2010). Second- and third-generation migrants experience their otherness and alienation acutely – from both their host societies and the homelands with which their parents associate (Khosrokhavar 2009). Discriminatory barriers make it difficult for young people, even from relatively wealthy families, to emancipate themselves from their parents and build independent careers, leading to status frustration (Cottee 2010). The resulting sense of injustice of the existing economic and political order, which is reinforced by dissatisfaction with one's social position, generates resistance, which can take on terrorist and extremist forms (Ahmad 2017: 119). The narratives of respondents in this study about acquaintances who left, or were about to leave, for the war in Syria paint a similar social portrait of the (potential) jihadist as a young man from a wealthy family but employed in unskilled and low-paid service work (typical employment for ethnic minorities) and continuing to live with his parents:

> He worked as a security guard at McDonald's, lived with his sister, his mother sort of, yeah, he was a young handsome guy, twenty years old, went there. And straight away, he was killed there [in Syria]. ... His grandfather was a banker, he came from a very wealthy family, I wouldn't say he was poor. He had a good life. (Salekh)

This suggests a situation of status tension characterised by a gap between high family status and low individual status and associated with the inability to build an independent trajectory of professional fulfilment not least due to the barriers stemming from horizontal inequalities.

Radicalisation also reinforces inequalities (Boyle and Songora 2004; see also Franc, Poli and Pavlović, this volume). The activities of extremist groups contribute to a negative image of Muslims who are stigmatised as 'terrorists' and 'extremists'. As one respondent put it, 'When people say extremist, they mean Muslim' (Idris). This means that, especially in the media but in everyday life also, Muslims appear as collectively responsible for acts of terrorist violence: 'On TV we are always bad, here even in everyday life some people say, "It's a Muslim, it's a Muslim who blew up, it's a Muslim who did it". On TV we are always bad' (Adam). Guided by the same logic of collective responsibility, in which Muslims as a whole are considered a risk group, the state deploys disproportionate violence in the fight against terrorism. The impact of this is described by the following respondent: 'A number of radical groups provoke the state but the state no longer makes a distinction, it tars everyone with the same brush. Of course, it would be better if they distinguished us, ordinary Muslims, from them' (Salekh). This situation amplifies the isolation experienced by the second urban generation and leads to a sense of being besieged in a state that, by default, is set against Muslims. The consequences are an intensification of intra-group solidarity, in which commonalities of origin and religion are cemented by shared experiences of inequality and discrimination, and a corresponding hostility towards social and state institutions. These attitudes can serve as 'fuel' for radical sentiments.

Fathers and Sons, Brothers and Sisters

Intergenerational tensions observed in families of North Caucasian origin are intertwined with a deficit of trust in relations between the older and younger members of these families. This is seen in relations between fathers and sons, in which, according to traditional North Caucasian cultural norms, communication is 'business-like' and excludes mutual displays of intimacy and affection:

> Our family relations are quite traditional, as is customary in Dagestan. I call my father now and we communicated also when I was living in Dagestan. We always had a good relationship, but my father never used baby talk with me, never talked to me if it wasn't necessary. Somehow, we always talked about important things. (Khabib)

Emotional aloofness extends to relations with other older male relatives such as uncles and elder brothers. It is intended to emphasise the inviolability of the foundations of traditional patriarchy; to ensure the social distance necessary to maintain the power of the elders and underline the importance of controlling emotions for 'proper' male socialisation.

The closest, 'warmest' relationships with older family members among second-generation urban youth are with their mothers, who tend to take on all the emotional work associated with upbringing. However, this closeness often does not imply trust. Respondents understood that a son's love for his mother implies an obligation to 'protect' her from information that could be emotionally damaging to her.

In general, parents are not perceived as those with whom one can have a heart-to-heart talk or share worries and problems. The excessive hierarchy of intergenerational communication also does not encourage speaking out and asserting one's point of view. As one respondent explains, 'I could not allow myself to have a conflict with my parents because my upbringing was such that I could not object to my father, probably until I was about seventeen, I could not say anything to him' (Magomet Ali).

The dominance of relationships that are based primarily on obedience rather than trust results in the family often being unable to trace or reverse the radicalisation of its younger members:

> My brother is in [the police]. When he found out about my interests, he almost killed me. At that point, I had already realised [that there was no point in communicating with radicals]. He was too late [to notice it]. I mean it's never too late. If I was already there [in Syria], it would have been too late. (Mamuka)

Parents or other older relatives often become aware of radicalisation at a fairly late stage, when, according to the respondents, it is no longer possible to influence their sons. Moreover, their arsenal of deradicalisation methods is in line with their authoritarian parenting style. For example, they may forbid contact with friends who share radical views or send their son to another city or region. It is also possible that they do not react in any way to information about perceived radicalisation, demonstrating what Sikkens (2018) calls parental uncertainty.

A finding of our study was that within the family, the second urban generation builds the closest and most trusting relationships with their sisters and cousins, with whom they were in close contact before marriage. One respondent explains that, 'Until my sister got married, she and I were very close in spirit, we shared everything. If I had something going on, I would tell her, ask her advice, if she had something going on she would do the same' (Anvar). These relations are not entirely egalitarian, as there is always an age asymmetry, which, following Caucasian traditions, is the basis of authority. However, the age gap is not significant, usually less than four years. These relationships take on a particular hue in relation to religiosity where, interviews suggest, it is not uncommon for older sisters or cousins to introduce young people to Islam and become their first religious mentors:

> I started fasting while I lived in Dagestan. I have a female cousin – the situation is that our house burned down in 1997, and so we were left homeless, and our aunt, my mother's sister, took us in, she even raised us, called me her son. And so it was her daughter who brought me to Islam and showed me how to do *namaz* [Islamic prayer] and taught me everything, and from that moment to this day I am in Islam. (Idris)

There are also examples of the opposite scenario, in which the respondents themselves – as a rule in secular or ethnically Muslim families – acted as guides to Islam for their younger sisters. In one way or another, solidarity develops between brother and sister, facilitating a trusting communication on sensitive religious topics, including those touching on radicalism and extremism. The following interview excerpt illustrates how this solidarity works for non-radicalisation within family networks. It relates to a small Moscow-based Salafist group (*jamaat*) of which the respondent was the founder. Having been born into a secular family and lived most of his life in Moscow, he converted to Salafi Islam when he was an adult. He introduced his sister (three years younger than him) to it and introduced her to a friend who later became her husband. His trusting relationship with his sister enabled him to learn that there were people with radical beliefs in her social circle, and his authority as an older brother was enough to break this bond:

> My sister, before she got married, was in touch with a girl who had very scary beliefs. I took her [the girl's] phone from my sister, started talking to her, and afterwards I told my sister, 'That's it! You don't know that person anymore, basically, I don't want any trouble because of her'. (Salekh)

It is logical to assume that both trust and authority, which engender this solidarity, can also work in the opposite direction and facilitate radicalisation. Examples of this were not encountered in this study, however.

Peer Groups

In the big cities in which respondents resided, peer communities, providing space for young people to take part in cultural activities and explore their identity, were important. The discrimination and exclusion experienced by members of the second urban generation, however, often led them to prefer to join networks of people from their 'home' region.

Sports Crews

Interest in, and practice of, contact martial arts – mainly freestyle and other types of wrestling – often brought young men of shared ethnic and religious background together. In the North Caucasus, power wrestling has become a form of alternative institution for men's socialisation. In Dagestan, for example, almost all boys and adolescents participate in freestyle wrestling and other martial arts (Solonenko 2012). Our case study shows that this interest in contact martial arts persists among young people living outside the North Caucasus (Kapustina 2014). All respondents had trained actively for a number of years and around half of them were either current or former athletes with many years of experience. A pragmatic explanation for this interest is that a teenager or young person who regularly faces hostile attitudes from the local population or far-right groups has a better chance of defending themselves if they have self-defence skills and can count on the help of a close-knit group of physically developed athlete friends. As one respondent explains, 'When I was at school, I was always having problems with all sorts of skinheads harassing me, and so I had to do sports. I did freestyle wrestling, and when you do sport, you have a lot of athlete friends, it's not so scary – you can fight back' (Ramzan).

Maintaining an interest in sport is also influenced by popular culture, which has been shaped by the success of North Caucasian wrestlers in prestigious sporting events. In the context of horizontal inequality, this culture is an important symbolic resource for the second urban generation in constructing a relevant North Caucasian male identity, which is associated with success and popularity. Key aspects of this identity are violence and religiosity. As Crone (2016) notes, radicalisation processes involve the transformation of physical abilities and the acquisition of habitus, which enables the perpetration of violence. Contact martial arts, more than other sports, aim to shape the body-as-weapon (Messner 1990), a body insensitive to pain, predisposed to violence and capable of using it. In the 2010s, sporting communities in the North Caucasus actively radicalised, as a consequence of which demonstrative Islamic piety has become an obligatory attribute of the North Caucasian wrestler (Poliakov 2021). For some respondents, born outside the North Caucasus into secular or ethnically Muslim families, a passion for religion thus became an act of 'prestige imitation' (Crone 2016) as they sought to replicate the behaviour of those who had achieved success in their sporting career. As one respondent explained, 'I became consciously interested in religion at the age of sixteen because moving through sport, I found it very interesting to look at our freemen, they tend to be all religious people' (Musa).

Dagestan's recent history is replete with examples of prominent North Caucasian fighters as initiators, mobilisers and active implementers of religiously motivated violence directed against cultural practices they considered contrary to the norms of Islamic morality. In the narratives of the second urban generation one can also find direct references to the responsibility of sports idols in spreading the 'fashion' for radical Islam among North Caucasian youth:

> When I studied at university, from 2007 to 2012, it was such a terrible time in Dagestan, and it was all so openly propagandised in some mosques. All the athletes there were walking around with beards. It was transmitted to the youth, but some to a greater, some to a lesser extent. (Khabib)

Sports halls and arenas are also spaces for the formation of intense interpersonal bonds and emotional attachments, which often take on the character of a quasi-kinhood – a sports 'brotherhood' (Solonenko 2012). Thus, the starting point of religious conversion can be not only the desire to imitate the practices of successful sportsmen but also the desire to be together with 'brothers', to share with them relevant collective experience:

> One guy trained with me, he's my best friend now, and I saw him praying, going out and praying in training, I liked it. He taught me how to pray, I got interested in religion. Then I took up the Qur'an and was reading in Russian, and I came across a *sura* [chapter] from the Qur'an that the Almighty created people and *jinn* [spirit] to worship him. And I realised that I had to dedicate my life to the worship of the Almighty. (Mamuka)

This does not imply a predisposition of sports communities to radicalisation. Rather, that they constitute one cultural and social context in which radical ideas can emerge, circulate and become part of group discourse. Sports communities may be characterised also by a system of mutual obligations and loyalties that compel members to provide support and protection to their radicalised 'brothers', even if they do not share their views. However, there was evidence in this study that inclusion into the 'brotherhood' may be more flexible than imagined. For example, Ramzan recounted how one young woman, not of North Caucasian heritage, had been radicalised after becoming integrated into a North Caucasian sports community:

> I used to know a girl, her father is a colonel here in Saint Petersburg. She was involved in sports, and since the dominant groups in sports are specifically North Caucasians, they formed a close bond and through them, she converted to Islam. I think you can understand. Her father was a colonel ... His daughter converted to Islam – it could have affected his job. He threw her out of the house. She had nowhere to go. She turned to her friends, they turned to their friends and she ended up going to Dagestan and was studying there. As I have friends who work in the security service there, they let me know straight away that if you have such acquaintances, you should not communicate with them often. (Ramzan)

Niche Communities

Communities in which radical views are disseminated can emerge in structural niches that are occupied by members of the second urban generation in education, employment and residency.

In the labour market, young people with a migrant background are pushed into low-paid and low-prestige sectors of the market. However, this works to generate ethnic and regional solidarities as a mechanism of adaptation. This can be seen in the housing rental market also where young natives of the North Caucasus try to circumvent discrimination by renting from compatriots and practising collective accommodation. Islam is also an important factor in both labour and residential segregation. Respondents in this case study who position themselves as observant Muslims shun jobs that would involve charging interest or producing and trading alcohol or pork meat products. There is a vast market for Muslim goods and services in which religious affiliation is a key hiring criterion. The presence of a mosque or prayer room within walking distance may be a significant factor also in choosing where to live. Educational choices also focus on those fields of study considered to be prestigious higher education in the North Caucasus region – law, economics, petroleum, construction and medicine. At the same time, applicants often prefer to enrol at institutions where their relatives, acquaintances or compatriots already study, have studied or work, believing that they will be less likely to encounter bias, xenophobia and discrimination and have more opportunities to find support and understanding.

The evidence from this study on how radicalisation and non-radicalisation processes unfold in such niche communities is partial, but allows a number of tentative suggestions to be made. First, the experience of living and working together creates a space of trust in which radical views can be articulated and discussed. The communities of compatriots and fellow believers are seen by participants as a fairly safe communicative environment in which they can speak freely about their interests and sympathies:

> Respondent: I dissuaded one young guy [from joining ISIS]. He said he had to join, and cut them all [non-believers]. Such were his convictions. He just started holding such views, and then he didn't...
> Interviewer: You say that you convinced this guy. Is he from your circle?
> Respondent: He came here, got a job. We rented him a room. He lived with his family, somehow we communicated. He strongly supported [ISIS], it was at the height of it, when they had expanded there, they had an army, and they had everything there, in short. They thought they were the coolest there. (Salekh)

Secondly, the circulation of radical beliefs in higher education institutions is hindered by a system of cross-control involving the university administration, student compatriot-based associations, often created and overseen by the rector, regional and ethnic organisations, structures of official Islam and the relevant police and security service departments responsible for preventing extremism and terrorism. One of the interviewees, at the request of senior representatives of the Dagestani community, was himself conducting outreach to Dagestani students in one of the universities in Saint Petersburg, from where more than twelve students had previously left for Syria. The director of the compatriot group, which was institutionalised as a cultural and educational centre, was regularly invited to talk to young people who had been taken off flights to Turkey on suspicion that they intended to join ISIS or other terrorist organisations. Some of them were persuaded to change their minds and some were handed over to their relatives. However, without grounds for detaining them longer, it is likely that others continued their journey to Syria after release.

Virtual Communities

The scholarly literature (Yarlykapov 2016; Awan 2017; Piazza and Guler 2021) highlights the important role of modern communication technologies in recent waves of radicalisation. The compression of space due to the rapid development of such technologies contributes to the formation of virtual *jamaats*, whose members may live at significant distance from one another and be united only by a commonality of views, interests or religious authorities. Our data suggest that members of the second urban generation are critical of official religious institutions and prefer to obtain their basic knowledge of religion from the Internet and social networks. Virtual means of communication reduce the distance between ideological radicalisation and behavioural radicalisation. They provide a wide range of activities and occupations with relatively low risk and resource costs that do not require full dedication but create a sense of belonging to a common cause such as participation in the distribution of video and audio content, debate with opponents of radical ideas in public forums and fundraising for warring militants. Thanks to social media, young people have (or believe they have) the opportunity to communicate directly with recruiters and participants in terrorist organisations. Mamuka described contact he had had via the social media platform VKontakte: 'They wrote to me, "I am in Syria" and so on. I asked, "What are you doing there?" They told me they were fighting but explained their actions in a positive light' (Mamuka).

Virtual communities have the basic features of postmodern socialities: instability, fluidity, heterogeneity and the permeability of boundaries. The free nature of membership, implying no strict individual obligation to the group, allows young people to join several virtual communities at once and to be consumers of messages and cultural products, often

of competing ideological orientation. In this way, the milieu is characterised by immersion in ongoing discussions and conflicts between different movements and parties with the Islamic Ummah, a postmodern
take on the centrifugal forces at work in Islam since its inception. Virtual
space serves as a field of constant ideological and doctrinal struggle between schools, doctrines, sects and groups of followers of various Islamic
celebrities:

> There are groups on VKontakte where ordinary Muslims are mem-
> bers, and the Khawarijites [the respondent uses this term to denote
> ISIS followers] come there and propagate the views of their lecturers.
> We go there and start to say that these people should not listen, that
> they are harmful to Muslims, that they are not from Islam. A similarly
> harmful current is the *tariqa* – a misguided movement. They are not
> Khawarijites but we treat them the same way. Then their fans, follow-
> ers of these media imams, start writing to us. (Salekh)

As this case study shows, members of the second urban generation
are reflexive about the information they receive about Islam from the networks. The dominant view among them is that the assimilation of religion
should take place not through following specific authorities or doctrines,
but through individual study and reflection on religious experience in
constant comparison with the Qur'an and Sunnah. In practice, this means
that individual religiosity is assembled as a 'bricolage' of multiple discourses and ideologies.

Communication Problems in Deradicalisation

Narratives that illuminate the role of friendship networks do not support the popular representation of radicalisation as a virus that spreads
through social networks and small-group interactions. While these stories point to the significant influence of the social environment, respondents emphasise that radicalisation is an individual choice that is made at
one's own risk. The question arises as to how the community responds to
this choice, in particular the efforts it makes to deradicalise its members.

In some cases, a veil of silence is maintained; the topic of radicalisation is deliberately ignored or avoided by talking about distracting topics
(see also Pilkington and Hussain 2022: 20–21). Most often, this is due
to a desire to protect oneself and friends from harassment by law enforcement agencies. In other cases, the community attempts to persuade
friends or acquaintances, but respondents emphasise that such efforts
can only be effective at the initial stage of radicalisation when passion for

radical ideas is combined with openness to other views and perspectives. Thus, one respondent suggests:

> Some people are young and dumb. They are not mature, they do not have any arguments, they simply do not have any arguments, so we can still talk to them. But, those, for example, Jahmites and Asharites, others that I have met, these are people who have knowledge, who have some kind of evidence – this is another level. For example, in a mosque, when I know that they are Kharijites, I do not even sit next to them, let alone talk to them. (Salekh)

As this respondent indicates, those whose passion has already developed into a strict conviction are seen as incapable of communication and, at the same time, as posing a danger to the community. Towards them, a strategy of distancing and exclusion is adopted:

> So what would I do if I came across compatriots who were more extremist? I would first try to explain to them that it's wrong, try to make them see ... but not more than that because, for the most part, when you explain to someone, when you try to change their mind, for the most part, it doesn't work. If a person is committed to something, is convinced of something, it is very difficult to change their mind and of course, in such a situation it is easier not to engage, not to let your paths cross, so it doesn't lead to problems. (Anvar)

This communicative disjuncture – reflected in the sense that 'you can't change their mind' – is, I suggest, due to the lack of a common 'language' (understood as a system of meanings, categories and arguments) available to both partners in the dialogue. An indirect indication of this is the fact that those prepared to engage in dialogue with radicalised youth tend to be members of the Salafi *jamaats*, who do share a common 'language' with radical Islamists. Salafi Islam, as Atran (2011: 46) notes, is 'the host on which this viral Takfiri[1] movement rides'. This interpretation might be supported also by Wiktorowicz's (2006) finding that conservative fundamentalists (Salafis) and jihadists share the same doctrine but differ in their interpretation of how religion is connected to the actual political context.

Conclusion

This chapter has explored the role of family and kinship networks in radicalisation processes by situating them in the context of the ongoing process of erosion of the traditional multigenerational North Caucasian family and concomitant shift towards the nuclear family under the impact of urbanisation and modernisation. This transformation is most intense in cities outside the North Caucasus where families cannot rely on kinship or neighbourhood networks to control their members' behaviour. In megacities, identity processes of 'self-discovery' are also triggered, especially among the younger generation. The discussion in this chapter has focused on the second urban generation and identified two patterns of radicalisation. Radicalisation may arise, first, as a result of intergenerational tension within the family, caused by the younger generation's desire to emancipate themselves from parental family pressures in determining their life trajectories. At the same time, discrimination and horizontal inequalities faced by those from the North Caucasus living in Russia's megacities can channel that emancipation process into conflict, provoking their hostility towards social and state institutions. Secondly, radicalisation pathways may be influenced by relationships of affection, friendship and trust. Within the family, the second urban generation has the closest and most trusting relationships with their sisters, which can potentially both encourage and discourage radicalisation. Peer networks around martial arts activities and niche communities that emerge in universities, workplaces or communities of residence also have radicalisation potential. Inclusion in virtual communities of ideological or religious orientation can facilitate encounters with radical discourses and accelerate the transition to behavioural radicalisation by offering relatively safe forms of virtual participation. In virtual communities, young people from the North Caucasus can meet and communicate with members of jihadist organisations.

As our case study shows, a serious barrier to deradicalisation is the state's indiscriminate anti-terrorist policy, which promotes a veil of silence around 'dangerous' topics and thus hinders communication with radicalised and radicalising youth (see also Pilkington and Hussain 2022). There is also a widespread belief that friends and acquaintances who hold radical convictions are already lost to society and the only possible behaviour towards them is to break off social contacts. I have suggested that this is explained by the lack of a common 'language' – a system of concepts, categories and arguments – that is understandable to both parties. Such a language, I argue, could be formed 'from below', by the youth communities themselves, in conditions of more transparent and honest communication, not distorted by fear of a repressive state or Islamophobic society.

Acknowledgements

This chapter is written based on data from the DARE (Dialogue about Radicalisation and Equality) project, which received funding from the European Union's Horizon 2020 Research and Innovation Programme under Grant Agreement No. 725349. It reflects only the views of the author; the European Commission and Research Executive Agency are not responsible for any information it contains.

Sviatoslav Poliakov is a Researcher at the Centre for Youth Studies of the National Research University Higher School of Economics. His research interests focus on youth in post-Soviet Russia. He is currently working on issues including youth cultures and solidarities of contemporary Russia, Islamic radicalisation among young people in the North Caucasus and youth policy in the Russian and global context.

....

NOTE

1. *Takfiri* is a term denoting a Muslim who excommunicates a co-religionist, that is, who accuses another Muslim of being an apostate, and is often used to refer to followers of radical Islamist organisations.

....

REFERENCES

Ahmad, Irfan. 2017. 'Injustice and the New World Order: An Anthropological Perspective on "Terrorism" in India', *Critical Studies on Terrorism* 10(1): 115–37.

Albogachieva, Makka, and Irina Babich. 2010. 'Krovnaia mest' v sovremennoi Ingushetii' ['Blood Vengeance in Modern Ingushetia'], *Etnograficheskoe Obozrenie* (6): 133–40.

Asal, Victor, C. Christine Fair and Stephen Shellman. 2008. 'Consenting to a Child's Decision to Join a Jihad: Insights from a Survey of Militant Families in Pakistan', *Studies in Conflict & Terrorism* 31(11): 973–94.

Atran, Scott. 2011. 'Who Becomes a Terrorist Today?', in Charles Webel and John A. Arnaldi (eds), *The Ethics and Efficacy of the Global War on Terrorism: Fighting Terror with Terror*. New York: Palgrave Macmillan, pp. 45–58.

Awan, Imran. 2017. 'Cyber-extremism: ISIS and the Power of Social Media', *Society* 54(2): 138–49.

Bakker, Edwin. 2007. *Jihadi Terrorists in Europe.* The Hague: Netherlands Institute of International Relations, Clingendael.

Benedek, Tibor Wilhelm. 2018. 'Islam and Russian Power Politics', *New Eastern Europe* 1(30): 188–91.

Bobrovnikov, Vladimir. 2007. '"Islamskoe vozrozhdenie" v Dagestane: 20 let spustia' ['"Islamic Renaissance" in Dagestan: 20 Years On'], *Tsentral'naia Aziia i Kavkaz* 50(20): 161–72.

Boyle, Elizabeth Heger, and Fortunata G. Songora. 2004. 'Formal Legality and East African Immigrant Perceptions of the "War on Terror"', *Law and Inequality* 22(2): 301–36.

Cottee, Simon. 2010. 'Mind Slaughter: The Neutralizations of Jihadi Salafism', *Studies in Conflict & Terrorism* 33(4): 330–52.

Crone, Manni. 2016. 'Radicalization Revisited: Violence, Politics and the Skills of the Body', *International Affairs* 92(3): 587–604.

Dobaev, Igor. 2009. 'The Northern Caucasus: Spread of Jihad', *Central Asia and the Caucasus* 50(1): 49–56.

Drambyan, Mikhail. 2009. 'Islam kak faktor obshchestvennoi zhizni v Respublike Dagestan' ['Islam as a Factor of Societal Life in the Republic of Dagestan'], *Etnograficheskoe Obozrenie* 4: 42–50.

Hafez, Mohammed, and Creighton Mullins. 2015. 'The Radicalization Puzzle: A Theoretical Synthesis of Empirical Approaches to Homegrown Extremism', *Studies in Conflict & Terrorism* 38(11): 958–75.

Kapustina, Ekaterina. 2014. 'Sobstvennost' na sever: migranty iz Dagestana i osvoenie gorodskogo prostranstva v Zapadnoi Sibiri (na primere situatsii v g. Surgut)' ['Property to the North: Migrants from Dagestan and the Development of Urban Space in Western Siberia (Case Study of the Situation in Surgut)'], *Zhurnal Sotsiologii i Sotsial'noi Antropologii* 17(5): 158–76.

Khosrokhavar, Farhad. 2009. *Inside Jihadism: Understanding Jihadi Movements Worldwide*. Boulder, CO: Paradigm Publishers.

Kisriev, Enver. 2009. 'Fenomen stremitel'noi reislamizatsii Dagestana' ['The Phenomenon of the Rapid Re-Islamisation of Dagestan'], *Rossiia i Musul'manskii Mir* 12: 83–94.

Kurbanov, Ruslan. 2004. '"Raspolzanie" dzhihada: pervichnie faktory i masshtaby radikalizatsii islama na Severnom Kavkaze' ['The "Sprawl" of Jihad: Key Factors and Extent of the Radicalisation of Islam in the North Caucasus'], *Tsentral'naia Aziia i Kavkaz* 6(36). Retrieved 29 March 2022 from https://ca-c.org .ru/journal/2004/journal_rus/cac-06/05.kurrus.shtml.

Markedonov, Sergey. 2010. 'Radical Islam in the North Caucasus', *Center for Strategic & International Studies*. Retrieved 2 November 2021 from http://csis.org/ files/publication/101122_Markedonov_RadicalIslam_Web.pdf.

Matsuzato, Kimitaka, and Magomed-Rasul Ibragimov. 2006. 'Tarikat, etnichnost' i politika v Dagestane' ['*Tariqat*, Ethnicity and Politics in Dagestan'], *Etnograficheskoe Obozrenie* 20: 10–23.

McCauley, Clark, and Sophia Moskalenko. 2010. 'Recent US Thinking about Terrorism and Counterterrorism: Baby Steps towards a Dynamic View of Asymmetric Conflict', *Terrorism and Political Violence* 22(4): 641–57.

Messner, Michael. 1990. 'When Bodies Are Weapons: Masculinity and Violence in Sport', *International Review for the Sociology of Sport* 25(3): 203–20.

Mkrtchyan, Nikita. 2019. 'Migratsiia na Severnom Kavkaze skvoz' prizmu nesovershennoi statistiki' ['Migration in the North Caucasus through the Prism of Imperfect Statistics'], *The Journal of Social Policy Studies* 17(1): 7–22.

Piazza, James A., and Ahmet Guler. 2021. 'The Online Caliphate: Internet Usage and ISIS Support in the Arab World', *Terrorism and Political Violence* 33(6): 1256–75.

Pilkington, Hilary, and Ajmal Hussain. 2022. 'Why Wouldn't You Consult Us? Reflections on Preventing Radicalisation among Actors in Radical(ising) Milieus', *Journal for Deradicalization* 30: 1–44.

Poliakov, Sviatoslav. 2021. 'Wrestler Masculinity in Dagestan as a Local Hegemony', *Sotsiologicheskie Issledovaniia* 11: 212–18.

Polyakov, Evgenii. 2015. 'Terrorizm v sovremennoi Rossii (1994–2014): faktory dinamiki, struktura, etapy razvitiia' ['Terrorism in Contemporary Russia (1994–2014): Dynamics, Structure and Stages of Development'], *Vestnik Severo-Osetinskogo Gosudarstvennogo Universiteta Imeni Kosta Levanovicha Hetagurova* (1): 65–69.

Polyan, Pavel. 2001. *Ne po svoei vole… Istoriia i geografiia prinuditel'nikh migratsii v SSSR* [Not of Their Own Volition: The History and Geography of Forced Migration in the USSR]. Moscow: Ob"edinennoe gumanitarnoe izdatel'stvo – Memorial.

'Prichiny radikalizatsii chasti molodezhi i protivodeistvie ideologii IGIL na Severnom Kavkaze' ['Reasons for the Radicalisation of Some Youth and Counteracting ISIS Ideology in the North Caucasus']. 2016. Memorial Round Table Report, 23 August. Retrieved 3 November 2021 from https://memohrc.org/ru/news_old/otchet-po-itogam-kruglogo-stola-prichiny-radikalizacii-chasti-molodezhi-i-protivodeystvie.

Ratelle, Jean-François, and Emil Aslan Souleimanov. 2017. 'Retaliation in Rebellion: The Missing Link to Explaining Insurgent Violence in Dagestan', *Terrorism and Political Violence* 29(4): 573–92.

Sageman, Marc. 2004. *Understanding Terror Networks*. Philadelphia: University of Pennsylvania Press.

Sikkens, Elga. 2018. 'Relating to Radicalism: Family and Upbringing Experiences in Radicalization and De-radicalization', PhD diss. Utrecht University.

Solonenko, Mikhail. 2012. 'Bortsy za vlast': sportivnie soobshchestva i ikh rol' v politicheskoi zhizni Dagestana' ['Fighters for Power: Sports Communities and Their Role in the Political Life of Dagestan'], in Yuri Karpov and Evgenia Zakharova (eds), *Obshchestvo kak ob"ekt i sub"ekt vlasti: Ocherki politicheskoi antropologii Kavkaza* [Society as object and subject of power: Essays on the political anthropology of the Caucasus]. Saint Petersburg: Petersburg Oriental Studies, pp. 91–110.

Starodubrovskaya, Irina. 2015. 'Kak borot'sia s radikalizmom molodezhi na Severnom Kavkaze?' ['How Can We Fight Against Youth Radicalism in the North Caucasus?'], *Obshhestvennie Nauki i Sovremennost'* 6: 84–96.

———. 2016. 'Sotsial'naia transformatsiia i mezhpokolencheskii konflikt (na primere Severnogo Kavkaza)' ['Social Transformation and Intergenerational Conflict (Case Study of the North Caucasus)'], *Obshchestvennie Nauki i Sovremennost'* 6: 111–24.

———. 2019. 'Krizis traditsionnoi severokavkazskoi sem'i v postsovetskii period i ego sotsial'nie posledstviia' ['Crisis of the Traditional North Caucasian Family in the Post-Soviet Period and Its Social Consequences'], *The Journal of Social Policy Studies* 17(1): 39–56.

Starodubrovskaya, Irina, and Konstantin Kazenin. 2014. 'Severokavkazskie goroda: territoriia konfliktov' ['North Caucasus Cities: An Area of Conflict'], *Obshchestvennie Nauki i Sovremennost'* 6: 70–82.

Starodubrovskaya, Irina, et al. 2011. *Severnii Kavkaz: Modernizatsionnii Vyzov* [The North Caucasus: The Challenge of Modernisation]. Moscow: Delo.

Tekushev, Islam. 2012. 'Triumf Imarata Kavkaz: Imarat Kavkaz kak Unikal'naia Fundamentalistskaia Model'' ['The Triumph of the Caucasus Emirate: The Caucasus Emirate as a Unique Fundamentalist Model'], *Islam, Islamism and Politics in Eurasia Report* 50: 2–22. Retrieved 2 November 2021 from https://csis-website-prod.s3.amazonaws.com/s3fs-public/legacy_files/files/publica tion/120125_Hahn_IIPER50.pdf.

Uslaner, Eric M., and Mitchell Brown. 2005. 'Inequality, Trust, and Civic Engagement', *American Politics Research* 33(6): 868–94.

Wiktorowicz, Quintan. 2006. 'Anatomy of the Salafi Movement', *Studies in Conflict & Terrorism* 29(3): 207–39.

Wilkinson, Richard G., and Kate E. Pickett. 2010. 'Inequality: An Underacknowledged Source of Mental Illness and Distress', *The British Journal of Psychiatry* 197(6): 426–28.

Yarlykapov, Akhmed. 2006. '"Narodnii islam" i musul'manskaia molodezh' Tsentral'nogo i Severo-Zapadnogo Kavkaza' ['"Popular Islam" and Muslim Youth of the Central and North-West Caucasus'], *Etnograficheskoe Obozrenie* 2: 59–74.

———. 2010. 'The Radicalization of North Caucasian Muslims', in Roland Dannreuther and Luke March (eds), *Russia and Islam: State, Society and Radicalism*. London: Routledge, pp. 137–54.

———. 2016. 'Rossiiskii islam v kontekste situatsii na Blizhnem Vostoke' ['Russian Islam in the Context of the Situation in the Middle East'], *Valdaiskie Zapiski* 48: 1–11.

Youngman, Mark. 2016. 'Between Caucasus and Caliphate: The Splintering of the North Caucasus Insurgency', *Caucasus Survey* 4(3): 194–217.

Zelkina, Anna. 2002. 'Jihād in the Name of God: Shaykh Shamil as the Religious Leader of the Caucasus', *Central Asian Survey* 21(3): 249–64.

PART III

✦ ✦ ✦

Situational and Interactional Dynamics of (Non)Radicalisation

CHAPTER 6

Situational and Interactional Dynamics in Trajectories of (Non)Radicalisation

A Micro-Level Analysis of Violence in an 'Extreme-Right' Milieu

Hilary Pilkington

Introduction

Radicalisation is generally understood as the process by which actors come to engage in, or support, the use of violence to achieve their political aims. However, only a small proportion of those who hold radical, or even extreme, ideas go on to commit acts of violence and not even all of those who engage in violent behaviour have radical beliefs (Borum 2011a: 9; Horgan 2012). This leaves the nature of the relationship between the radicalisation of ideas and behaviours unclear (Neumann 2013: 873) and means the term radicalisation is used to conceptualise the process of shift (towards extremism) in aims, attitudes and perceptions *or* in forms of activism/action *or* both (Malthaner 2017a: 371). While classic models of radicalisation have envisaged cognitive radicalisation as largely preceding behavioural extremism, recent interventions suggest this may be misplaced; prior experience with violence, rather than extremist ideological views, may be the key precondition for engaging in terrorist acts (Crone 2016). Others have suggested that there is a relatively 'weak relation between attitude and behavior', meaning we should think about radicalisation in terms of separate pathways of radicalisation of 'opinion' on the one hand and 'action' on the other (McCauley and Moskalenko 2017: 211).

It is somewhat paradoxical that the shift in attention to the *process* by which people move towards violent extremism facilitated by the study of radicalisation has also re-affirmed the primacy of the endpoint in determining what constitutes a radicalisation pathway. Once violent extremism has been manifested, radicalisation studies have sought to chart, retrospectively, the stages through which individual actors progress towards terrorism (Horgan 2008) or identify important transitions or turning points in radicalisation (or deradicalisation) journeys (Sieckelinck et al. 2019). By seeking to explain involvement in terrorist violence by studying only those who have committed such acts while excluding those who move in the same milieu but do not become violent extremists – that is, by selecting on the dependent variable (Schuurman 2020: 16) – violence always appears as the radicalisation endpoint or apex of the pyramid (Pilkington 2017). Exploring pathways through radical milieus where the threshold into violent extremism has not been crossed – that is, by considering trajectories of 'non-radicalisation' (Cragin 2014; Cragin et al. 2015) as well as radicalisation – allows us to envisage a more fluid and multidirectional movement both towards and away from extremist ideas and/or violence. This also brings into our field of vision those still active in radical milieus. Moreover, adopting an ethnographic approach means we can draw on milieu actors' own understandings of how radical ideas and actions are connected – or not – as well as observation of interactions and situations in which violence is present, imminent or averted. This allows the study of radicalisation not only *as* but *in process*, that is, how pathways are navigated contemporaneously rather than constructed retrospectively.

The notion of radicalisation is mainly applied in the study of actors (individuals or groups) and/or forms of action; situations and patterns of interactions are seen rather as governed by processes of escalation (or de-escalation) and have been studied primarily at the meso level (between groups and the state, police or other movements) (Malthaner 2017a: 371). However, interactional and situational theory, it is suggested here, can be employed also to analyse dimensions of individual trajectories or to understand, at a micro level, the interactions and situations which lead actors to engage in violence. In this chapter, a micro-level analysis is employed to understand the role of participation in collective violence – directly or indirectly connected to the political cause – in individual trajectories through the milieu. Four contrasting cases from the study of an 'extreme-right' milieu in the UK are selected to illustrate trajectories in which high levels of political engagement are accompanied by violence or non-violence and in which routine participation in violence takes place in parallel with, but not directly connected to, political participation. In this way, the chapter aims to enhance our understanding of the relationship between radical ideas and radical behaviour (specifically participation in violence) and the role of situational and interactional dynamics in shaping individual trajectories and their outcomes.

Understanding the Role of Violence in Radicalisation Pathways

The micro-analysis undertaken here is underpinned by theoretical discussion on: the relationship between ideas and action in radicalisation pathways; the role of interactional and situational dynamics in the escalation, and diffusion, of confrontation; and the characteristics and dynamics of violent situations more broadly.

Classic models of radicalisation, such as that of Wiktorowicz (2005) or Mogghadam (2005), show how a combination of material, psychological, environmental and organisational/situational factors interact in shaping individual pathways to violent extremism. They envisage this process in the form of pyramid or staircase structures in which space is progressively closed down as individuals pass through distinct stages of socialisation or cross thresholds that implicitly or explicitly allow no 'turning back'. While it would be wrong to caricature these early conceptualisations as presenting a simple, linear model of radicalisation (Malthaner 2017a: 386), they share a broad premise that cognitive readiness for, or belief in, the legitimacy of the cause (and use of violence for the cause) precedes the taking of violent action. However, ideological commitment does not always precede engagement with radical groups or the undertaking of radical actions; while, for some, personal conviction and commitment to the cause is crucial to their willingness to take subversive action, for others, engaging in such action strengthens personal conviction and commitment (Bjørgo and Horgan 2009: 3; Borum 2011b: 58). Not even all terrorists, Borum (ibid.) suggests, 'radicalise'.

This has led some to envisage radicalisation that leads to violence, and radicalisation that does not, as distinguishable phenomena (Bartlett and Miller 2012: 2). This is most extensively elaborated in the 'two pyramids' model, charting separate pathways of radicalisation of 'opinion' on the one hand and 'action' on the other (McCauley and Moskalenko 2017).[1] McCauley and Moskalenko (ibid.) state explicitly that they are not presenting a 'stairway model' – individuals can skip levels in moving up and down the pyramids – and that there is no 'conveyor belt' from extreme beliefs to extreme action. However, the endpoint envisaged in both cases is violent extremism and, since at the apex of the 'opinion pyramid' are those who not only justify violence but feel a *personal moral obligation* to take up violence in defence of the cause, this extreme commitment appears to lay the ground for extreme action. However, importantly for the analysis below, the separation of pyramids allows for a potential imbalance between the degree of ideological commitment and the action engaged in; a separation that also, theoretically, accommodates Crone's (2016: 591) argument that ideological radicalisation is not a necessary precondition for engaging in terrorist acts.

A relational approach to radicalisation, while not resolving the question of how to understand the connection between cognitive and behavioural radicalisation, allows for the possibility that ideological commitment develops in the process of engagement, as a result of interactions with others (Malthaner 2017a: 387), and evolves over time (Fillieule 2010: 11). Most importantly for the discussion here, it opens the way to a micro-level analysis of how situational interactions may 'precipitate, consolidate or dissipate extremist attitudes and behaviour' (Malthaner 2017b: 1). 'Situation' might be understood broadly as the 'immediate setting in which behavior occurs' (Birkbeck and LaFree 1993: 115) and thus comprises the individual – including their personality traits – and the environment. Stenner (2005: 19) argues that situation – specifically the perception of normative threats – is a key catalyst for activating authoritarian predispositions and their expression in intolerant attitudes and behaviours associated with right-wing extremism. Understanding behaviour as a function of a dynamic interaction between person and situation, she argues (ibid.), helps explain why personality seems to manifest itself 'inconsistently' in different situations. At the micro level, moreover, the continuous interaction between individual and environment within a given situation means that situational cues influence behaviour but behaviour also shapes the situational cues (Magnusson 1976: 267). As situations have both objective (situations 'as they are' in terms of physical and social variables) and subjective (situations as they are interpreted) dimensions (ibid.: 266; Birkbeck and LaFree 1993: 119–20), this means situations can be a variable affecting an individual's behaviour *and* a product of the individual's behaviour, since an individual's response to the situation (based on their interpretation of it) partly constitutes the situation itself (Magnusson 1976: 266). Indeed, it is a shared definition of a situation, and the (struggle for the) maintenance of that single definition through social convention and ritual that shapes and structures interpersonal interaction (Goffman 1990: 246; Collins 2004: 24).

Central to the analysis presented below is the role micro-situational interactions in face-to-face encounters play in the escalation, and diffusion, of confrontation (see also Malthaner 2017b: 6; Busher, Holbrook and Macklin 2018). In this context, the situation consists of the local sites of interactions and encounters, which have both agency and structure (Collins 2004: 6). For Collins (ibid.), agency is not the property of the individual but should be understood 'as the energy appearing in human bodies and emotions and as the intensity and focus of human consciousness', which emerges in interactions in local, face-to-face situations or as part of chains of situations. When a shared emotion spreads within a group (in social movement action, for example) and becomes its focus of attention, it generates feelings of solidarity and morality; it is by appropriating the centre of attention in an emotionally engaged group that violence is also energised (Collins 2001: 28). Thus, Collins' (2008: 1) micro-sociological theory of violence is concerned not with violent *individuals* (their background, culture or motivation), but the characteristics and dynamics of violent *situations*. For Collins (ibid.: 449), violence is a relatively rare outcome – 'an interactional accomplishment' – of situations structured by emotions of confrontational tension and fear, which are difficult to overcome regardless of the weight of grievances, moral convictions or material incentives that might provide the motive for violence (ibid.: 442). It is thus always limited to 'the few' and situations of potential violence are more likely to produce social rituals of gesturing towards violence (such as verbal acrimony or blustering and boasting) rather than actual violence (ibid.: 338).

Governing the dynamics of these situations are emotions of fear, anger and excitement and their management in an interactional process involving all actors present (Collins 2008). Where those gathered become emotionally unified by their focus on a single confrontation generating feelings of excitement and solidarity, a smaller group of 'fighters' may accomplish 'group-located hot-emotion violence' (ibid.: 451). In contrast, 'cool technical violence', which involves a cluster of (learned) practices or techniques, may appear to be enacted individually (ibid.). Johnston (2014) also sees emotions – of fear and anger – and their mechanisms of management as central to explaining how individual states are translated into collective action and violence. Long-term anger – the emotional component of injustice that simmers in the background – can quickly become volatile, passion-fuelled anger in the face of police confrontation and counter-movements, while fear can be overcome by a surge of excitement and passion from situationally experienced group affirmation (ibid.: 40–41). Thus, emotions are essential to processes of radicalisation and, in particular, anger is often a trigger for escalation not least because it 'enables ordinary people to cease to fear reprisals for their actions' (Crenshaw 2014: 298).

The empirical analysis conducted below draws on Collins' micro-sociological theory of violence to consider the situational and interactional dimensions of how and why actors in a radical milieu move towards and away from violence. However, rather than exclude what Collins (2008: 21) calls 'background conditions', it combines attention to situational dynamics with an individual-focused understanding of how actors seek out, find themselves in and respond to violence-engendering settings (see also Bouhana 2019: 15–19) in order to explain why they might become entrained in, or, conversely, resist violence. This recognises Collins' (2004: 5) argument that situations have 'laws or processes of their own' and that individuals are an ingredient in, not the determinant of, any given situation. At the same time, it proposes individuals bring to those situations their experiences, influences, fears and desires from past interactions in the sphere of activism but also from formative experiences prior to, outside or adjacent to it. These experiences shape the different meanings individuals invest in violence (Pilkington, Omel'chenko and Garifzianova 2010: 121–42). Thus, in attempting to understand the relationship between situational dynamics and responses of violence or non-violence in the cases analysed below, factors shaping previous interactions and the interpretation of situations are considered crucial to understanding by whom, how and with what meaning violence manifests in radical milieus.

Milieu and Method

This article draws on the study of an 'extreme-right' milieu in the UK conducted by the author as one of nineteen case studies undertaken for the Horizon 2020 Dialogue about Radicalisation and Equality (DARE) project (see Introduction, this volume). The milieu studied in this case consists of individuals active in movements, organisations or campaigns in the UK associated in public discourse with the 'far right'. Research participants reported contact with a wide range of movements (thirty-two in total) but all had been active in, affiliated with or attended events of at least one of: the English Defence League (EDL),[2] the Democratic Football Lads Alliance (DFLA),[3] the British National Party (BNP),[4] Britain First,[5] Generation Identity (GI)[6] or Tommy Robinson support groups.[7] While what is referred to here as a milieu does not consist of a single organisation or network, all research participants had some connection to at least one other participant (see Pilkington 2020: 15–18).

I engaged in the milieu and with its participants from December 2017 to March 2020, undertaking participant observation and conducting one or more semi-structured interviews with twenty individuals. Field research commenced after an informal meeting with the research participant referred to below as Dan,[8] first encountered as an EDL activist. I followed Dan into his milieu – attending events, meeting some of his friends, following him on social media and making new contacts in the course of this. Two further 'snowballs' were started subsequently by direct messaging (via Twitter) a core member of a movement of interest, in one case, and via a 'gatekeeper' known from earlier research in the other.

Key socio-demographic characteristics were recorded for all participants (Pilkington 2020: 180–82). Due to the focus on 'youth' of the overall project, participants were younger than the wider 'extreme-right' scene; three quarters were under the age of thirty, with the rest in their thirties. Fifteen participants were men and five were women, which broadly reflects the gender composition of the wider scene. At the time of interview, most research participants were in employment, nine full-time and three part-time. Three were occupied in an unpaid capacity (in activism, volunteering or caring). Four were unemployed, of whom two had been unable to find employment since release from prison and one for health reasons. One was in full-time education. Ethnic homogeneity was high; all participants were born in the UK and all were white. Five said they had 'no religion'. Of the fifteen who declared a religion, five were Protestant, five were Catholic, four declared an 'other' Christian faith and one said they were pagan.

The final data set consists of one hundred sources including: sixty-one field diary entries; twenty-five audio and five video interview transcripts; and nine text documents received at observed events. Twenty-five of the field diary entries pertain to participant observations at events related to what milieu activists call 'patriotic' causes.

While privileged access to the group ensues from my shared whiteness with research participants, this is not an 'insider' ethnography; in terms of age, gender, occupational status and political viewpoint, I was an outsider. Of these aspects of positionality, my university employment was the most troubling for milieu members as it placed me within the dominant and ideologically hostile liberal elite. For those who agreed to participate, the most important factor in maintaining their involvement was that they felt listened to without prior judgement. While self-selection is inevitably an issue here, no claims are made to the representativeness of the respondents of 'extreme-right' activists more generally. Indeed, as outlined below, much of the focus of the analysis in this chapter draws on an even smaller selection of respondents in order to allow the exploration of very particular, micro-situational contexts through which we can better understand how, and when, violence manifests. As Johnston (2014: 44) notes, analysis of participant accounts is essential to understand more fully why, in some cases, long-term anger develops into violence. This ethnographic study thus provides an important supplement to existing research that has followed individual paths to terrorism through open source material (see for example Lindekilde, Malthaner and O'Connor 2019) and is empirically limited by the material available and the impossibility of interrogating those accounts directly. At the same time, a study of active radical milieu members carries its own methodological limitations since trajectories through the milieu remain in progress and the forms of violence in which individuals engage are diverse.

Two Pyramids, One Red Line?
Attitudes towards Violence in Pursuit of Political Aims

Research participants in this study largely reject the use of violence in support of the causes they pursue (for more detailed discussion, see Pilkington 2020: 34–47). In relation to the two pyramids model (see note 1), most might be categorised on the 'opinion pyramid' as 'sympathisers' (who believe in the cause but not that it justifies violence) and, on the action pyramid, as either 'activists' (who undertake legal action for the cause) or 'radicals' (who undertake illegal action for the cause). For many, the use, or support for the use, of violence constitutes a red line which marks the difference between their own positions and the 'real extremists', from whom they dissociate themselves. Central to this distinction is the unlinking of holding extreme beliefs from acting violently to impose them:

> . . . opinions aren't extremism. But they [extremists] try to bring about their opinions, and they try to express their opinions through violence, through terror. . . . You can believe in an absolute Islamic caliphate. That's not really extremism. Extremism is going out and blowing somewhere up, because you believe in the caliphate. I can believe in, you know, you can have people who believe in the Third Reich or Adolf Hitler. Now that's not extremism until you start attacking people and imposing your will on others. (Paul)

Will and Billy – both associated with Generation Identity at the time of interview – considered not only violence but also actions that might intimidate others as undermining the objectives of the movement 'as well as being morally wrong' (Will). Moreover, the strategic case for violence, identified in an earlier study of English Defence League activists (Pilking-ton 2016: 51, 183–85), was widely dismissed in this milieu; while violence might temporarily gain media attention, respondents felt it 'backfires every time' (Jacob) and, at best, would only succeed in attracting the wrong kind of people – 'people that want to fight' – to the movement (Will). As Mikey concludes, 'When you start using violence unnecessarily, unless it's obvi-ously in self-defence, then basically, you just become a thug, you know, you become rent-a-mob and ultimately, you're not gonna achieve anything'.

The most frequently mentioned circumstance in which it might be justified to use violence was in order to protect oneself, one's family or those weak and in need of protection. Mikey thus distinguishes between violence such as that committed by 'far right extremist groups and Mus-lim extremist groups' as well as among youth gangs, which is 'out of order', and violence in the context of military service or a 'just cause' such as self-defence or the protection of the weak, which, in contrast, is 'quite a noble thing'. In relation to political activism, Billy does not think violence achieves anything but, if attacked, you should have the right to self-defence. Robbie takes a similar view and, recalling an incident when a group of fellow DFLA activists had been 'cornered' by counterprotes-tors, he says, 'Yeah, if you get cornered, you can't just lay there and take it. 'Cause they won't stop, I don't think. They are the thugs really. They want to hurt you a lot more than you want to hurt them. . . . 'Specially if there's ten times more of them than there is you'. Dan also says that he would only ever 'join in' violence in a protest context in retaliation to aggression on the part of the police: 'If I was sitting there, doing nothing wrong and a policeman come over and hit me with a baton, then I would start. But until that happens, then. . .' (Dan). Outside the context of po-litical activism, respondents also talk passionately about protecting their family, especially siblings (Paolo), even if this necessitated 'using your fists' (Gareth).

As Cragin et al. (2015: 16) note, however, the relationship between ex-pressions of support for political violence and a willingness to engage in violence is not straightforward. While their concern is primarily with the implications of this for employing the survey method to measure radical-isation, qualitative researchers must also be alert to dissonance between support for, and engagement in, violence. In this study, as discussed above, when respondents reflect on the morality and efficacy of political violence, they reject it but, in practice, around half had been involved per-sonally in violence or fighting. Eight respondents talked about their own involvement and another three were known to have engaged in fighting around political activism, albeit narrated as being at the receiving end. Below, the trajectories of four milieu actors are explored in detail.

Understanding Violence in the Trajectories of 'Extreme-Right' Milieu Actors

Situational approaches to the understanding of violence in general and political violence in particular suggest that neither predisposing socio-demographic characteristics nor individual motives explain how violence is precipitated (Collins 2009: 10). Violent interactions in face-to-face encounters, and particular settings, bring together a constellation of actors, roles and identities creating micro-situational interactions that have a logic of their own (Malthaner 2017b: 6). This would appear to be confirmed by the fact that more than half the respondents in this study had participated in violence even though, outside of an immediate situation, they thought violence was ineffective and sometimes counterproductive for the cause. At the same time, I suggest, individuals respond very differently to such situations not least because, as Collins (2004: 4) recognises, their pathways through interactional chains and the mix of situations they encounter across time differ from those of others. To understand and explain the different role violence plays in pathways of radicalisation and non-radicalisation, the cases of four 'extreme-right' milieu actors are discussed below. These capture some of the range and complexity of the relationships encountered (see Figure 6.1).

In the case of Lee, engagement with the extreme end of the milieu is accompanied by violence at political events but with a relatively low level of ideological commitment. The dotted arrows in Figure 6.1 also indicate Lee's trajectory, at the time of interview, away from both violence (to non-violence) and political activism (to community activism). In the case of Dan, in contrast, a high level of political commitment is accompanied by consistent non-engagement with violence. In the cases of Robbie and Paolo, routine participation in violence (in relation to football) takes place in parallel with political activism, being connected only indirectly, in as much as the political activism is organised through the mobilisation of football firms. The findings suggest involvement in violence does not necessarily indicate a process of radicalisation of ideas or even action; violence may precede engagement in the radical milieu and individuals may take positions of violence and non-violence simultaneously, depending on the situation, the interactions that play out there and the meanings invested in the performance of violence or non-violence.

'Looking for a Scrap': Violence before Politics in Lee's Trajectory

As indicated in Figure 6.1, Lee's trajectory combines a high level of political participation, in groups at the most extreme end of the milieu stud-

Violence ― ― ― ― ▶ **Non-violence**

'violence is golden'

'I'm not interested in a fight'

'looking for a scrap'

Robbie

'I'm always the first one in'

Dan

Lee

Paolo

Political activism ― ― ➡

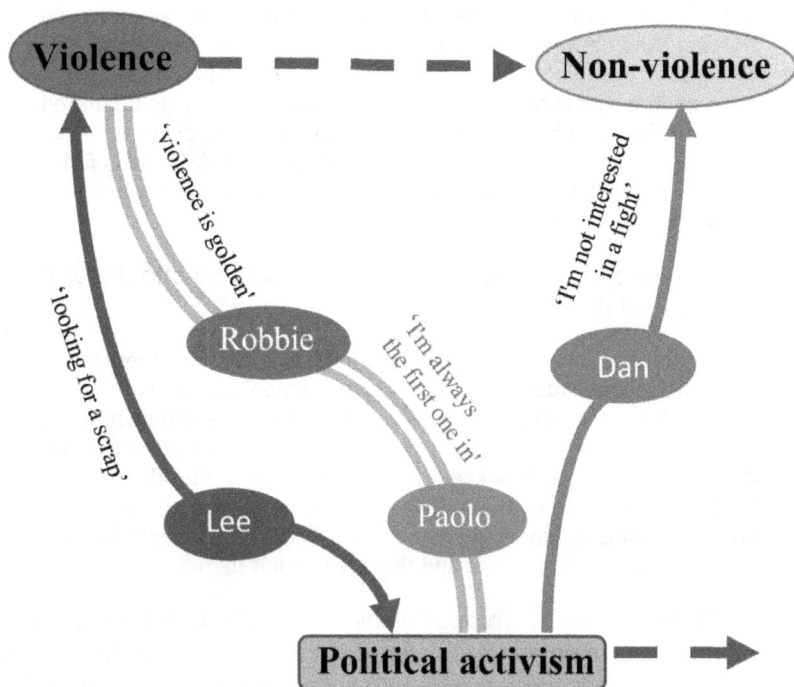

Figure 6.1. The relationship between violence and political activism: four case studies. Created by Hilary Pilkington.

ied, and regular participation in violence related to his political views. At thirty-eight, he is one of the oldest research participants in the study and, at the time of interview, had been recently released from his third prison sentence for violent disorder related to his political activism. Upon release, he had committed to disengaging from the 'extreme-right' milieu and thus the analysis below draws from interview data; I was not able to observe Lee's situational behaviour directly.

Lee grew up on a notorious housing estate in a town in the north of England. He mainly lived with his grandparents due to an absent father and his mother's drug use. He failed to finish college – a vocational course he didn't enjoy – and skipped classes to 'get pissed'. He had six of his own children as well as a caring role for his partner's children. Lee described growing up in a town that was ethnically segregated and in which racialised violence was deeply embedded in everyday life:

> . . . one of my main memories from being at school are, I think I were a first year, high school. And there was this, this lad . . . in my form and he were a Muslim lad, and well, waiting to go in, into the form

room in the morning, and we ended up bickering, and we ended up
fighting. And he were quite a bit bigger than me, but I ended up bat-
tering him and that were my first ever clash, kind of thing. But . . . I
got a good buzz out of it to be honest, you know. . . . 'cause I battered
him and that, and he were bigger than me. But then every time . . .
anything happened at school where there were like Asian lads fighting with white lads, we'd be there at the front of it all and, you know,
it was just the buzz.

These fights were so endemic that they were factored into the organisation of the school day:

We'd fight with them at dinnertime with the lads and then there were,
their uncles and dads would come up after school. . . . They'd turn up
with cricket bats and everything, so . . . So it got to the point where . . .
about twenty minutes before school had finished, they'd come and
collect the lads that they knew were involved in it. And they'd have
the [police] vans down the middle of the yard and they'd say, 'Right,
you go down that way, and you go down that path. And you Muslim
lads, go that way, your dads and that are waiting there'.

As part of a fight-seeking group (Collins 2008: 275), Lee did not just encounter situations of potential violence, he was invested in creating them.
The in-school clashes were turned into a weekend leisure practice: 'We,
we used to make a point of going into their area, 'cause we, we used
to get pissed and that and go looking for them and go, go looking for
a scrap and that' (Lee). In his later teens and early twenties, Lee was
drinking heavily and using drugs and a violent attack perpetrated against
a man owing money to a friend – an incident Lee says he cannot even
remember due to the drink and drugs consumed – led to his first prison
sentence when he was twenty years old. It was three years after release
from prison that he became politically active. After attending an EDL (see
note 2) demonstration in a nearby city, he was involved in setting up a
local division of the movement. Thus, in Lee's case, engagement in violence preceded ideological radicalisation; ideology appears to provide a
narrative to the violence rather than motivate it. Establishing the local
movement secured an arena 'to scrap', a way to generate situations in
which he could get the 'buzz that I used to get when I were a kid fighting
and that'.

Lee's interpretation of political activism as a point of access to situations for violence, however, led to conflict within the EDL, which was trying to dissociate itself from its representation as a movement of drunken,
racist thugs. As Lee puts it, 'We wanted a scrap . . . but they weren't
happy with that, so we used to break off. Like we'd go to the demo and
then we'd like sneak out of the demo and then get into the other, opposi-

tion demo. But they weren't happy with that . . . they kept pulling us up on it. . .'. There was also a dispute over a video that emerged of Lee and others 'doing Nazi salutes'. Intra-movement escalation of confrontation came when Lee was told he would not be allowed to give a speech at an EDL demo in his home town, leading to members of his group starting a physical confrontation with those in the EDL inner circle. Lee and others were expelled from the movement and, in a process similar to that described by Lindekilde, Malthaner and O'Connor (2019: 24) as the formation of a 'radicalizing micro-setting', in which radical cliques drift away from broader milieus, they decided, 'We're going full neo-Nazi now us lot. We're going, Combat 18,[9] no, National Front'.[10] However, relations with the National Front broke down and approaches by the BNP were rejected because, as Lee says, 'I weren't into political side of it; I was there for the scrap'. Instead, Lee and his immediate circle created their own movement[11] focusing on direct action and picking fights with what he calls 'militant left' groups and those supporting Irish republicanism.

This would appear to usher in a period of radicalisation of both ideas and actions, which, despite a series of prison sentences, Lee describes as 'some of the best time in me life'. To convey the emotional energy – and ensuing sense of solidarity and strength – experienced from 'kicking off with them', Lee shows me video clips on his phone from some of the clashes he describes. Part of the buzz, he says, was that 'they'd always outnumber us', as is evident from his description of the dynamics of one such situation in which he found himself, in which 'four or five people were fighting their way through groups of thirty people and that'. He goes on to recount how, after missiles were thrown, the police had been forced to 'build a cordon round us' to escort them through hundreds of counterprotestors, concluding that 'we buzzed off it. We loved it'. In this post-EDL period, he would also appear to radicalise ideologically. He starts to maintain contact with neo-Nazi groups such as the (subsequently proscribed) National Action[12] and only through circumstance missed the meeting at which Jack Renshaw revealed his plans to murder the Labour Party MP Rosie Cooper, as a result of which Renshaw was arrested, convicted under the Terrorism Act and subsequently sentenced to life imprisonment (Dearden 2018). Renshaw's plot was exposed by an attendee at that meeting, who felt compelled to blow the whistle after hearing what was being planned. When I asked Lee what his own reaction would have been had he been there, however, he replied, 'I probably would have let them do it, with mind-set that I were in then, yeah. I wouldn't have grassed them up or owt. It's like honour, innit?'.

These events suggest a connection between cognitive and behavioural radicalisation, but the relationship remains complex. In Lee's narrative, it appears that political activism did not motivate violence but was a vehicle in his search for 'a scrap', a deeply imprinted, interaction ritual chain underpinning his participation in collective violence from early teenage years. He consistently 'buzzed off' the emotional energy and feelings of solidarity he experienced from fighting and, following the split from the EDL, he could get that buzz more often. However, his engagement with the 'extreme-right' milieu was not by chance. The teenage fighting in which he was involved was racialised and although he did not become politically active himself until later, he grew up in an environment with a strong BNP (see note 4) presence and, as a teenager, recalls having leafleted for the party on behalf of a relative of a friend. Thus, while he might not see himself as 'into political side of it', his violence is intrinsically connected to his political views. Moreover, while violence is constant throughout his trajectory, ideologically, Lee appears to radicalise in the process of engagement with others in the milieu (see also Malthaner 2017a: 387). He recognises that as his new movement brought together individuals from more extreme parts of the milieu, so their ideological position became more extreme – 'anti-immigrant', 'anti-Jew' and sectarian – as 'what we basically tried to do was accommodate everyone in our mission statement'. His growing proximity to National Action, whom he describes as 'very, very antisemitic', was critical in this radicalisation process and in a demonstrative moment, after being banned from Facebook, he moved over to VKontakte (the Russian social media platform) and appeared to be on the verge of joining them, declaring, 'Right, that's it. I'm joining you'.

To understand this complex interaction, it is important to take into account not only the situation, however, but also its interpretation. It was not any situation with potential for violence that Lee embraced; when attending football or being on a night out in town, he says, if 'someone started getting mouthy and that, I'd walk away from it. . . . But in that other situation, where it's political views were at stake, we. . .'. The 'we' with which he fails to finish the sentence is indicative here. At the crucial moment when Lee declares he is ready to join National Action, it is loyalty to his own movement – to those who fight alongside you – that prevents him. However, he retains an 'unspoken relationship' with National Action to support each other's events. Thus, when Lee imagines, in relation to Renshaw's plan to murder a Labour Party MP, that he would have 'let them do it', his interpretation of the situation is not one in which he is being asked for ideological commitment (support for this act as part of a cause) but for loyalty (not to 'grass them up'). Thus, on one level, his response appears to signal a move to the apex of the 'opinion pyramid' (McCauley and Moskalenko 2017), that is, from justifying violence to feeling a moral obligation to take up violence for the cause. However, for Lee, this is not an exceptional but a routine response governed by a personal moral compass shaped by chains of previous interactions and situations ritualised in an etiquette of honour, loyalty and the principle that you 'never run'.

'I Get a Bit Mad . . . But I Don't Do Anything': Managing Anger in Dan's Trajectory

Dan's trajectory appears to illustrate empirically the importance of Mc-Cauley and Moskalenko's (2017) argument for the separation of the radicalisation of ideas and of actions. Dan became politically active following the murder of Lee Rigby (May 2013) and was taken to his first EDL demonstration by his dad. He went on to be a speaker at EDL events before striking out on his own, not affiliating with any particular group but being highly active across the 'extreme-right' milieu including organising his own actions. When I first met him, he was twenty-three years old but already a seasoned activist, earning him the designation by an anti-hate politics campaign organisation as one of the UK's leading 'faces of hate'.[13]

In sharp contrast to Lee, Dan feels a strong political motivation for his activism, stating, 'I want to make a difference, you know what I mean. I want to live for something. Even if people don't agree with me, you know, what I feel is right, I want to do something'. At the same time, he is not interested in fighting; on the contrary, he is proud that he has attended myriad demonstrations but never been arrested or involved in violence:

> Dan: . . . Touch wood, I've never been arrested on a demo. Never, ever.
> Hilary: Why do you think that is?
> Dan: 'Cause I don't do anything to. . . All right, I get a bit mad. I shout a few things and that. But I don't do anything. . . I don't go for a fight, know what I mean. . . .
> Hilary: So you're not interested in goading the other side?
> Dan: I'm not interested in a fight and things. I'm just interested. . . I love all that where you shout, and both sides are shouting at each other. Because that is democracy.

This evokes Collins' (2008: 339) observation that 'blustering' – or gesturing towards violence – rather than actual violence is the usual outcome of confrontational tension and was encountered first hand when attending protests and other events alongside Dan. It is illustrated below, drawing on observation at a Tommy Robinson European Parliament

Figure 6.2. Police line between rally participants and counterdemonstrators, 2019. © Hilary Pilkington.

election rally (Bootle, 19 May 2019), where confrontational tension was high due to the situation at the rally on the previous day (in Oldham), which had ended in significant violence. Counterprotestors – members of the Muslim Defence League – had appeared unexpectedly, having been initially escorted to the rally site by police. Missiles, including bricks, were thrown and twenty participants (mainly counterprotestors) were subsequently prosecuted for violent disorder (Dearden 2020; GMP 2020). At the Bootle rally, therefore, a strong sense of injustice and simmering anger (Johnston 2014: 41) was palpable. It was fuelled by a large counterprotest, whose participants outnumbered those attending the rally by around three to one and prevented many seeking to attend from reaching the rally site (see Figure 6.2). The mood is quite ugly, with a lot of gesturing and shouting between the two sides; counterprotestors chant 'Nazi scum off our streets' and *'No pasaran'* and are met with return taunts of 'Tommy's going to be, your MEP', 'Oh Tommy' and 'Paedos'. Dan climbs onto a low wall, showing his flag and attracting the requisite abuse back (Fieldwork diary, 19 May 2019). His gesturing gains him what Collins (2008: 362) calls an appreciative audience; next to me a middle-aged woman comments on how proud she is of 'young uns' like him. Most young ones, she says, are 'brainwashed' by the likes of 'them' (indicating the counterprotestors), so 'it is nice to see the odd one actually understanding' (Fieldwork diary, 19 May 2019). Tension rises further when the

Figure 6.3. Caught on film, 2019. © Hilary Pilkington.

Tommy Robinson campaign van approaches and the counterprotestors first stand and then sit in front of it, blocking its passage. Police scuffle with counterprotestors and eventually the van gets through, although it is another forty minutes before Tommy Robinson and the rest of his entourage arrive. In that time, there is a critical moment when another key figure in the 'extreme-right' milieu appears on the other side of the police line, from where Dan had also been trying to access the venue earlier. From his position on the wall, Dan can see that this figure has been identified by the counterprotestors, who start to chase him down the street. This sends a wave of emotion through those attending the rally, who rush towards the police cordon (Fieldwork diary, 19 May 2019).

The situational dynamics of the previous day are not repeated, however, and violence between protestors and counterprotestors is largely avoided. This is partially explained by the physical containment – including metal fences and police lines – put in place, which meant that, although rally participants and counterprotestors were in very near proximity, the opportunity for violence was limited. Events from the previous day also played an important role, not only creating simmering anger but also heightened awareness of the potential costs (physical and legal) of being caught up in violent disorder. Twenty police vans were visible from the rally site and police cameras, pointed at rally participants, left no doubt that any violence would be documented (see Figure 6.3). While anger might trigger escalation, to do so people must 'cease to fear reprisals for their actions' (Crenshaw 2014: 298).

A further significant factor, I suggest, is that the interactional and situational dynamics of this event were routinised, even ritualised confrontations – the chanting and gesturing rehearsed between these groups many times – and thus stabilising 'at the level of bluster' (Collins 2008: 361). For Dan, who relishes situations where 'both sides are shouting at each other', these ritualised interactions allow him to engage in the battle for 'conversational space' in the knowledge (gained from previous such interactions) that 'the longer the insulting and shoving goes on, the less likely a fight is to actually take place' (ibid.: 362–64). Indeed, it is as the crowds disperse and ritualised barriers to violence are dismantled that, as Dan puts it, 'a few scuffles' ensued during which 'punches was coming at me so I started hitting back – that's when I just got picked up in the air and slammed against a wall' (Fieldwork diary, 19 May 2019).

Dan is not immune to the emotional energy generated in collective action that can provide the ground for violence. Like respondents who do engage in violence, Dan feels that 'whoa' moment when 'you've got the adrenaline kicking in':

> No, no. Like I said, it is hard, because you've got the adrenaline kicking in and you think 'Whoa'. And I'm only young, know what I mean. And you know . . . you can't say when you're young, you don't like that sort of stuff. But like I said, I've got a bit of a brain for me age like. I don't want to be arrested for something stupid.

However, in contrast to Lee, who navigated these situations guided by the experience of previous interactional dynamics, which imprinted upon him the imperative 'never run', Dan is guided by the compulsion to not get 'arrested for something stupid'. Thus, when fighting kicks off, his strategy is to stand and 'observe' and he has no objection to others running. Reflecting on a previous situation, he remembers, 'I've seen a lad running away from the violence at a demonstration, and someone grabbed him, and went, "What the fuck are you doing? Stop running". Which you know, to be fair, if he wants to run, let him'. The situation Dan is referring to took place at a Support Tommy Robinson rally (London, June 2018), after which fourteen demonstrators were prosecuted for violent disorder. Dan shares the sense of anger of those around him on the day, explaining, 'You can't blame them for being angry. 'Cause I was angry meself. I'm very angry at what's going on in this country'. However, the emotional energy generated is not sufficient in Dan's case to overcome the fear in confrontational situations that transforms them into violence.

Indeed, for Dan the depth of anger is experienced as 'scary', not only in relation to the immediate situation, but because it presages a potential civil war, about which he expresses his fears on numerous occasions. At a more immediate and personal level, it conjures up the possibility of arrest and prison, to which Dan also refers during interview as a cause of dread for him. Like Robbie, discussed below, transferred experience from his dad – who he says has dozens of criminal convictions – may focus him on keeping his brain engaged during situations of imminent violence rather than succumbing to the adrenaline he undoubtedly feels.

Despite his long-standing commitment to ideologically motivated activism, Dan consistently opposes violence in the pursuit of the cause, in principle and, in situations of confrontation, employs strategies to avoid becoming entrained in collective emotion that might result in violence. Whilst backing down from violence might illustrate what Collins (2008) describes as the incapacity to overcome confrontational fear, the interactional dynamics of situations are not the only important factor. Dan's biographical trajectory suggests a greater degree of ontological security than either Lee (see above) or Paolo (see below), which allows him to stand his ground (observe, not run but let others run if they wish) without fearing this would undermine 'respect' for him. Although Dan, like Lee, grew up largely with his grandparents rather than his parents, he recounts this as not being a result of broken family bonds but because his grandmother doted on him as the only male grandchild (of eight). He had, he said, gained a lot of 'life experience' from this upbringing, especially from having travelled abroad (including to Muslim majority countries) frequently with his grandparents. Thus, a sense of secure personal (if not collective) identity, a reflexive awareness that anger is divisive as well as solidarising, and a capacity to experience the positive collective energy of fighting with words rather than fists, appear to keep Dan on a clearly delineated path of non-radicalisation of action no matter how loudly he shouts.

Violence as Fun? The Parallel Universes of Fighting and Politics in Robbie's and Paolo's Trajectories

The cases of Robbie and Paolo appear to confirm Crone's (2016) warning that the assumption that cognitive radicalisation precedes behavioural extremism is misplaced. In both their cases, political activism in the Democratic Football Lads Alliance (see note 3) was preceded by extensive engagement in football-related violence. However, exploring their journeys shows that, in these cases at least, violence outside political activism is not a gateway to political violence. Rather, their participation in football violence runs parallel to, but separate from, their engagement in non-violent political activism. Moreover, their life trajectories reveal they had very different introductions to violence and attach different meanings to it in the formation of identities and bonds with others, especially other men.

Robbie was twenty-two at the time of interview and had grown up mainly with his mum. However, he bonded closely with his dad over football, and at the age of seventeen he moved to live with him:

> It's always been what me and my dad do – go to football at weekend. That was our time together. But he was a hooligan in the seventies and eighties as well. So that's probably where I got it from. He was always telling me these war stories. I thought, as a young impressionable child, I think that's cool like, I want to do that. But he, silly as it sounds, he was all right with it. Because he knows what it's like. It is fun, to be honest.

Once he was old enough to attend the football with his own friends, Robbie also got into 'casual'[14] culture and fighting:

> Robbie: And obviously, the people I went to football with after my dad, I'd met at football, so they had the same mentality as me. And just went from there. It's chance meeting in a service station or summat like that. Got a big buzz.
> Hilary: . . . So you say chance meeting, so it wasn't organised?
> Robbie: Not always, no. Sometimes it was, if you knew that they were bringing some people. You know, 'cause everybody knows everybody from other teams, with the DFLA, everybody knew who we were before we started. But yeah. Sometimes you'd just be walking through town and they'd be coming out of a pub, and you think, 'Here we go, we're on'. Sometimes it would be, 'Meet here. No coppers. No cameras. Sorted'.

Robbie experiences football-related fighting as 'fun' and the 'buzz' it generates is amplified when the situation arises unexpectedly: 'The chance meetings are the best ones, at football. Where you walk round a corner and you're outside a pub. "Get him." And there's no coppers around because they don't know it's gonna happen. No one knows it's going to happen. And you steam into 'em and it's just. . .' (Robbie). The word that completes the sentence is 'chaos'; for those involved, they are participating in a liberating chaos – a term used also by another respondent, Jermaine, to talk about what attracted him to both football and EDL demonstrations – rather than violence.

Football hooliganism allows fans to experience the excitement of collective solidarity and dramatic tension and release associated with modern sports away from the game itself, and thus dissociated from the success or failure of the team they support (Collins 2008: 331). In this way, football hooligans are able to achieve their own, independent narrative gratification and place that, rather than team performance, at the centre of ritual attention (ibid.). This is evident in Robbie's case as he explains that football fighting also brings 'bragging rights' if 'you turn someone else over'. Between the adrenalin of the fights, past encounters are a source of 'entertaining stories, battle scars and things like that' (Robbie). A tattoo on his arm reads 'Violence is golden'.

Although actively engaged in football violence, Robbie fully endorses the DFLA's stance of non-violence in political activism:

> . . . One of the reasons I like the DFLA is because. . . my dad said this to me and I thought it was spot on. He says, 'Ever since any of these sort of groups have started – National Front, BNP, EDL – it's always descended into violence'. . . . The public don't want to be a part of that. That's why the DFLA is good in that respect, because we march in silence sometimes. We're always courteous to the police, you know. Even when there's a counterprotest from like Antifa or Stand Up To Racism, they goad us and they goad us, but no one ever bites. And that's the good thing.

This reinforces the importance of the interpretation of situations to the behaviour that emerges from the engagement between environment and individual (see Magnusson 1976: 266; Birkbeck and LaFree 1993). Where a situation of imminent violence such as an antagonistic or aggressive counterprotest is understood as deliberate provocation, designed to 'goad' movement actors and make them look like the aggressors, this hardens the resolve not to 'bite'. Thus, for Robbie, in football situations, violence is sought and relished both for the 'buzz' of the moment and narrative gratification that nourishes the group in between actual fights. In contrast, in situations of political activism, non-violence is gratifying since it allows the group 'to prove a point – that we don't need to be violent to try and make a change in sort of that situation' (Robbie).

In coming to this interpretation, Robbie mobilises less his own previous experience than that imparted by his dad. Like Dan, Robbie had attended his first DFLA demonstration with his dad, who, in his younger days, had been active in the BNP and the National Front but left them because he realised violence never solves anything (Fieldwork diary, 29 March 2019).[15] This transferred experience of the non-efficacy of violence steers Robbie towards a non-radicalisation pathway. When, at thirteen, older friends joined the EDL, he did not, despite the fact that 'it looked like a buzz'. Later, when a close friend joined the National Front, he started hanging out with a punk crowd and moved into a phase of heavy drinking and drug use. Most recently, he stated his rejection of violence in a social media post, after attending a DFLA mobilisation called to 'guard memorials' in London following the toppling of the Edward Colston statue in Bristol during a Black Lives Matter protest (7 June 2020). In it, Robbie berates 'the piss heads' who had started a confrontation with the police at the event and states he 'left straight away. That wasn't why I went' (Fieldwork diary, 13 June 2020). Thus, except in the case of self-defence, when cornered by those attacking you, violence is an interaction ritual chain in which Robbie engages in a particular setting – football – but rejects in relation to political activism.

Paolo is also active in the DFLA but considers himself first and foremost a football hooligan with a trademark reputation for 'head-butting'. He was twenty-six at the time of interview and had been released from prison a few days earlier (a conviction related neither to his political nor his hooligan activity). Paolo's active involvement in football violence alongside a non-violent approach to political activism mirrors Robbie's story but their routes to these positions are quite different and illustrate why the dynamics of micro-situational interactions alone cannot explain engagement in violence by actors in radical milieus.

In contrast to Robbie's intimidating physical stature, Paolo says of himself, 'I'm tiny. I admit that myself. I'm not the hardest bloke in the world; you can pick me up with one hand'. He mentions this a number of times in the course of the interview and says, especially when younger, he got badly hurt when he fought. His narrative of football violence is thus not one of 'having fun' but gaining 'respect'. By being always 'up' for a fight – in the knowledge that he will almost certainly get 'battered' – he turns this physical disadvantage into a marker of courage:

> You hit me, I'm always getting back up. And that's why I'm loved by the [names football firm] lot. My lot. . . I'm always the first one in. I'm always the one that's gonna always, always do something. I'm not gonna say I'm gonna do something and then not do it. They know full well if I say it, it's gonna happen. I mean, it's not that I enjoy fighting, but the respect and the notoriety that comes with it – that is more appealing than the actual giving a kicking bit.

Paolo does not 'enjoy fighting'; it had been a necessity for navigating the world growing up:

> . . . Well, to be fair, school was hard. Because there wasn't many white kids. And there wasn't many black kids. It was mainly Asians. And if you had a dispute with one lad, you had it with another sixty lads. I mean, I remember one day, I was about thirteen. And I asked

somebody just a basic question. And me and him used to get the same bus. And I was, 'What was your mum reading on the bus earlier?' The next thing I know . . . apparently that's an insult to the Qur'an. I've got sixty Asian kids trying to kick my head in, because I asked a simple question . . . So, I learned early on that I'm gonna have to learn to fight, I'm gonna have to learn to look after myself. And then going to the football, that kind of helped.

Paolo grew up in an area where the street code meant you had to carry a weapon because, as he put it, 'It's better to have and not need, than need and not have'. He regularly carried knuckledusters and coshes, although he had a personal aversion to knives, associated with the experience of his school friend who, at the age of sixteen, had stabbed and killed another young person (who had stabbed his cousin) during a fight and was now serving a life sentence. Nonetheless, Paolo says, if 'somebody hurt my brother, I'd do life happily with a smile on my face'.

In this sense Paolo shares much with Lee whose teenage years were also spent developing fighting techniques to navigate the racialised urban space of inner-city neighbourhoods characterised by dense networks of relationships and what Collins (2008: 369) calls 'the goldfish bowl of audience and individual reputation'. He also shares with Lee the disadvantage of small stature, which in Paolo's case makes fighting an obligation rather than a pleasure: 'I'm the smallest guy in the crowd, skinniest guy in the crowd. . . . That's why I'm always the first one in. Because I feel I've got to. . . . Doesn't matter how many times I prove myself in the past, still got to do that'. This obligation has weighed on Paolo since childhood; he recounts how his stepfather had insisted he fight back when he had been hurt by another boy, whom he had challenged for throwing a stone at his sister. When he had come home, crying, with what felt like a broken nose, he says, 'Me stepdad gave me a slap round the ear and told me to go back out. I wasn't allowed to come home until I'd basically chinned him. So that was kind of my upbringing'. In Paolo's trajectory, violence became part of a repertoire of action for the presentation of self and gaining respect (from other men) both at home and on the street. Even though now he feels 'looked up to' by some of the younger lads in the firm, because of what he has done in the past, this is also a burden because 'part of me then feels like I have to keep that up. Because that's what they know you for'.

The importance of such respect was noted also by Lee who found that once he had established his own movement, the intense collective experiences of fighting were a source not only of emotional 'buzz' but also of respect and recognition; as Lee put it, 'people putting you on a pedestal, telling you you're the best thing since sliced bread'. It is also documented in other studies of right-wing extremism where, in the context of feeling 'I'm just a nobody' at home, gaining authority on the street and the respect and adoration of younger milieu members can become the driving force of participation in skinhead violence (Pilkington 2014: 77). For Paolo, football hooliganism and the DFLA network also created a sense of support and meaning that was otherwise lacking. His tenuous relationship with his family – maintained through his grandmother – had been further weakened when his grandmother died. He repeatedly used the term 'family' to describe his football and DFLA crowd (Fieldwork diary, 2 January 2019), most poignantly when talking about a period of his life when he and his partner lost a baby and their relationship ended:

> I went completely off the rails. Massively off the rails; attempted suicide, I just. . . yeah, everything you can imagine . . . I tell you what, it was football hooligans that got me through it. Everyone can say what they want about us being this, that and the other, but they're my family. . . . I spoke to my mum maybe five or six times this year.

While in prison, Paolo says, he also got letters and phone calls from DFLA lads from rival clubs from all over the country: 'That's heart-warming. Because you see people that usually would want to kick your head in, just wanting to know that you're all right'.

Both Robbie and Paolo regularly engaged in violence in the form of football hooliganism and their football firm activism had brought them into the DFLA, which, at the time of research, was a new player in the 'extreme-right' milieu. The movement declared itself to be against 'all forms of extremism' and both Robbie and Paolo adhered to this line, rejecting the use of violence for the pursuit of political aims. Indeed, for Paolo especially, it is the DFLA's message that fellow activists are 'your new family, these are the people who will stand with you and support you' (Speaker at DFLA demonstration, Manchester, Fieldwork diary, 2 June 2018) that appears at the forefront of his 'ideological' commitment. Football violence was deeply embedded in both of their lives but carried very different experiences and meanings. For Robbie, it was an extension of the bond with his dad and provided rich material for narrative gratification; observational data confirmed the family's story-telling culture. His physical capacity, moreover, facilitated his experience of fighting as 'fun'. In sharp contrast, for Paolo, fighting was a necessity growing up and was used to gain respect that he could not command purely physically. While in the case of neither Robbie nor Paolo does this prior experience of violence lead to violent extremism, their trajectories confirm that the body, its physical capacities and social construction, is a dimension of (non) radicalisation pathways that is often forgotten (Crone 2016: 588).

Conclusion

This chapter brings a micro-analytical lens to the question of the relationship between radical ideas and radical action, specifically the participation in various forms of violence by actors in an 'extreme-right' milieu. Although it is widely acknowledged that most people who hold radical ideas do not go on to commit acts of violent extremism, most studies of radicalisation continue to consider, empirically, only those cases where this is the outcome and thus chart radicalisation as a process by which actors come to engage in, or support the use of, violence to achieve their political aims. The micro-analysis of individual pathways considered here includes a broader range of trajectories through the radical milieu and traces in detail those of four milieu actors. These selected cases cannot speak for the wider milieu but indicate how participation in violence may drive political activism, take place in parallel to it, or be consciously resisted, rather than constitute the apex of a radicalisation trajectory (see Figure 6.1).

Lee is the closest to a classic case of radicalisation, a term he himself attaches to his journey, in which he became routinely engaged in violence directed at oppositional groups driven, he says, by the search for the 'buzz' associated with fighting during his teenage years. However, while he became politically active only in his twenties, his earlier violence is imprinted with racialised (anti-immigrant and anti-Muslim) attitudes widespread in the neighbourhood, and the formation of his own group was accompanied by association with more extreme ideological agendas and movements. Now, as Lee seeks to move away from the radical milieu, he is engaged with local community projects, from which, he says, he is also 'getting a buzz'. Dan might be considered a classic case of nonradicalisation, in that he had been active in the 'extreme-right' milieu for several years without any significant radicalisation in terms of ideas or actions. Indeed, his trajectory through the milieu had brought him into contact with other groups and individuals whom he felt were 'too extreme' ideologically and situations encountered during activism had led to conscious choices not to engage with them and the development of strategies to avoid succumbing to the 'adrenalin' of situations that might lead to violence. Robbie and Paolo's political activism also brings them into situations where violence is present or imminent but in which they could envisage their involvement only in a situation of self-defence. However, both regularly engage in football-related violence as a kind of siloed experience of heightened collective emotion (see Collins 2008: 243). As Robbie reflects, 'It's like Monday to Friday, I'm this nice, sweet lad that's always kind and polite. But on a Saturday, you know, he changes like that [snaps fingers]'. For both Robbie and Paolo, the political cause is linked to football in as much as the DFLA originated in, and remains organised through, networks of football firms. However, they both support the movement's insistence on non-violence at events and feel their political message is stronger by showing how the DFLA's 'against all extremism' cause unites football 'lads' whose interactions in other settings might be violent.

To understand how, when and why violence happens, or does not, in the four selected cases, the analysis employed a micro-situational approach, which views the process of overcoming fear or tension to accomplish violence to be a 'structural property of situational fields, not a property of individuals' (Collins 2008: 19). This proved illuminating, especially in invoking the emotional dimensions of political activism (fear, tension, anger, but also the buzz of potentially violent situations), but did not fully explain when and where radical milieu actors engage in violence. The findings suggested that similar situations may lead to violence but also non-violence (comparing the cases of Lee and Dan), while overcoming the fear required to engage in violence (as shown in the cases of Robbie and Paolo) may occur in some situational fields (related to football) but not in others (related to political activism). To understand these dynamics, and their outcomes, it is argued, we must also attend to the role of the actor in micro-situational dynamics. While Collins understands that actors bring with them emotions and consciousness ensuing from chains of previous encounters – each 'situation' does not stand alone – his characterisation of individuals as no more than 'a moving precipitate across situations' about whom we can derive everything we want to know by starting with the dynamics of situations (Collins 2004: 4) is insufficient. Indeed, interactions observable through situational dynamics might obscure quite different pathways to an apparently similar role in those encounters.

The findings of this analysis – visualised in Figure 6.4 – suggest that, in order to understand behaviour ensuing from a situation and its dynamics, we need also to take into account experiences and encounters outside the immediate situation of interest. Such 'background conditions' (Collins 2008: 21) provide essential insight into family situation, childhood experiences and trauma, body esteem, life experiences and horizons as well as transferred experience (from parents, siblings or other trusted figures) and negotiation of local contexts (including territories, gangs, political and criminal groups) that profoundly shape individual journeys into current situations and responses to the interactions encountered there. These background conditions also shape previous interactions and situational encounters which govern how individuals interpret a given

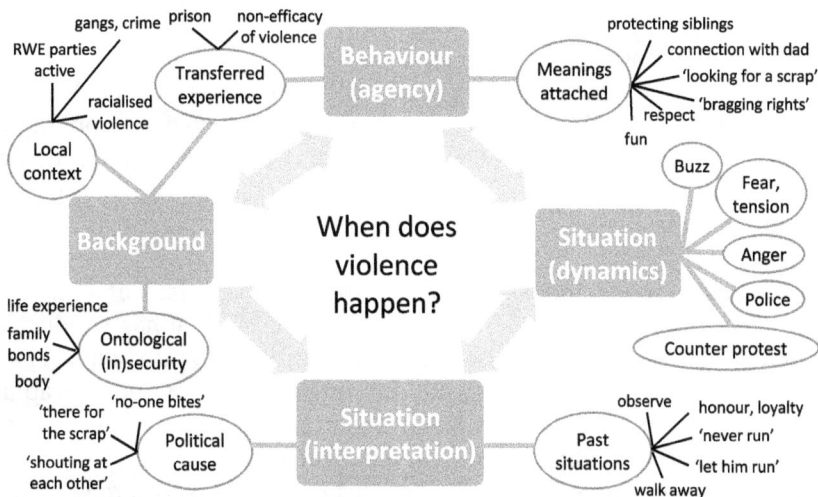

Figure 6.4. The role of situational dynamics in the occurrence of violence. Created by Hilary Pilkington.

situation; not only personality but perception of a situation is a crucial factor in understanding how individuals respond differently to situations and variation in responses by an individual in different situations (see also Stenner 2005: 19). Through the trajectories analysed, not only the dynamics of the situation but how situations are interpreted – as opportunities for 'a scrap' or for 'shouting at each other' (and then walking away) or proving oneself able to resist violence – are crucial to explaining individual and collective behaviour. These interpretations are profoundly shaped, moreover, by past interaction chains often rooted in childhood or teenage experiences, such that violence may become part of a repertoire of action for the presentation of self well before political activism commences. Finally, since an individual's response to the situation (based on their interpretation of it) partly constitutes the situation itself (Magnusson 1976: 266), the meanings attached to situations by individuals (whether they invest in it for narrative gratification, to gain respect, to secure a bonding relationship with family members or peers or just for 'fun') also shape the dynamics of situations and the interactions that take place there. Thus, violence and non-violence are deeply tied up with not only the situation but the formation of the subject, or subjectivation (Wieviorka 2003: 43), and the meanings violence takes on for individuals in this process.

Acknowledgements

The research drawn on in this chapter is part of the Dialogue about Radicalisation and Equality (DARE) project, which received funding from the European Union's Horizon 2020 research and innovation programme under Grant Agreement No. 725349. It reflects only the views of the author; the European Commission and Research Executive Agency are not responsible for any information it contains.

Hilary Pilkington is Professor of Sociology at the University of Manchester and Fellow of the Academy of Social Sciences. She has conducted ethnographic research on youth and youth subculture, youth political participation, activism and extremism and published also on ethnographic research methods and meta-ethnographic synthesis. She was coordinator of the H2020 DARE (Dialogue about Radicalisation and Equality) project (The University of Manchester, 2017–21). She is a member of the Academic-Practitioner Countering Extremism Network of the Commission for Countering Extremism and served as independent Commissioner on the GMCA Preventing Violent Extremism and Promoting Social Cohesion Commission.

NOTES

1. The 'opinion pyramid' starts, at the base, with those who pursue no political cause (*neutral*) and climbs through those who believe in the cause but do not justify violence (*sympathisers*), those who justify violence in defence of the cause (*justifiers*) to the apex where people feel a *personal moral obligation* to take up violence in defence of the cause. At the base of the 'action pyramid' are those not active in a political group or cause (*inert*), followed by those who are engaged in legal political action for the cause (*activists*), those who carry out illegal action for the cause (*radicals*) and, at the apex, those whose illegal action targets civilians (*terrorists*) (see McCauley and Moskalenko 2017).
2. The EDL was founded in 2009 as a response to Islamist (al-Muhajiroun) activism in Luton. Drawing on the football hooligan network, it initially mustered 2–3,000 at demonstrations (2009–13) and held smaller, regional rallies throughout the fieldwork for this study.
3. The DFLA emerged in April 2018 after a split in the Football Lads Alliance (FLA) over alleged misappropriation of funds by the FLA leader. The movement formed after a series of Islamist-inspired terrorist attacks in the UK (March–June 2017) and its first two marches in London attracted tens of thousands of demonstrators.

4. The BNP was founded in 1982 by former National Front leader, John Tyndall. In the 1990s, it became the UK's main extreme-right party, having success in local elections and the 2009 European Parliament elections. The party imploded following the 2010 general election.

5. Britain First was founded in May 2011 by former BNP activists including current leader, Paul Golding. Golding has faced a series of prosecutions and convictions for public order offences and religiously aggravated harassment.

6. GI is part of the wider European Identitarian movement rooted in the French *nouvelle droite* intellectual tradition. The UK branch was established in 2017 but has suffered repeated infiltrations and internal ruptures.

7. Tommy Robinson (Stephen Yaxley-Lennon) was co-leader of the EDL until October 2013. He currently styles himself as a 'citizen journalist' conducting campaigns on issues such as Child Sexual Exploitation (CSE). In 2018, he was imprisoned on charges related to live streaming outside a court during a CSE case leading to numerous local and national support rallies.

8. Written informed consent was obtained prior to commencing fieldwork and revisited informally throughout the research. Pseudonyms were assigned to all respondents, chosen by research participants themselves in many cases, and are used here throughout.

9. Combat 18 (C18) was initially founded by the BNP as a 'stewards group' to protect its activities but became an entity in its own right and the most violent of groups on the far right. It was publicly disavowed by the BNP in 1995.

10. The National Front (NF) was formed in December 1966 from an amalgam of smaller far right groupuscules. It had two peaks of electoral support during the 1970s but its poor showing in the 1979 general election led to splits in the movement and decline in efficacy.

11. The name of this group, along with some other details of Lee's trajectory, are withheld to preserve anonymity.

12. National Action was formed by Alex Davies and Ben Raymond in 2013 as a new nationalist youth movement seeking to establish Britain as a 'white homeland'. In 2016, it became the first extreme-right organisation in the UK to be proscribed as a terrorist organisation.

13. This source is not referenced to protect the anonymity of the research participant.

14. Casual culture revolves around a combination of football hooliganism and designer wear.

15. This conversation with Robbie's dad took place in a bar after a demonstration both he and Robbie attended and was one of two occasions where I was able to talk to them together.

REFERENCES

Bartlett, Jamie, and Carl Miller. 2012. 'The Edge of Violence: Towards Telling the Difference between Violent and Non-Violent Radicalization', *Terrorism and Political Violence* 24(1): 1–21.

Birkbeck, Christopher, and Gary LaFree. 1993. 'The Situational Analysis of Crime and Deviance', *Annual Review of Sociology* 19: 113–37.

Bjørgo, Tore, and John Horgan. 2009. 'Introduction', in Tore Bjørgo and John Horgan (eds), *Leaving Terrorism Behind: Individual and Collective Disengagement*. London: Routledge, pp. 1–14.

Borum, Randy. 2011a. 'Radicalization into Violent Extremism I: A Review of Social Science Theories', *Journal of Strategic Security* 4(4): 7–36.

———. 2011b. 'Radicalization into Violent Extremism II: A Review of Conceptual Models and Empirical Research', *Journal of Strategic Security* 4(4): 37–62.

Bouhana, Noémie. 2019. *The Moral Ecology of Extremism: A Systemic Perspective*. London: Commission for Countering Extremism. Retrieved 22 December 2021 from https://www.gov.uk/government/publications/the-moral-ecology-of-extremism-a-systemic-perspective.

Busher, Joel, Donald Holbrook and Graham Macklin. 2019. 'The Internal Brakes on Violent Escalation: A Typology', *Behavioral Sciences of Terrorism and Political Aggression* 11(1): 3–25.

Collins, Randall. 2001. 'Social Movements and the Focus of Emotional Attention', in Jeff Goodwin, James M. Jasper and Francesca Polletta (eds), *Passionate Politics: Emotions and Social Movements*. Chicago: University of Chicago Press, pp. 27–44.

———. 2004. *Interaction Ritual Chains*. Princeton, NJ: Princeton University Press.

———. 2008. *Violence: A Micro-Sociological Theory*. Princeton, NJ: Princeton University Press.

———. 2009. 'Micro and Macro Causes of Violence', *International Journal of Conflict and Violence* 3(1): 9–22.

Cragin, Kim. 2014. 'Resisting Violent Extremism: A Conceptual Model for Non-Radicalisation', *Terrorism and Political Violence* 26: 337–53.

Cragin, Kim, et al. 2015. 'What Factors Cause Youth to Reject Violent Extremism? Results of an Exploratory Analysis in the West Bank', Rand Corporation. Retrieved 5 January 2022 from https://www.rand.org/pubs/research_reports/RR1118.html.

Crenshaw, Martha. 2014. 'Conclusion', in Lorenzo Bosi, Chares Demetriou and Stefan Malthaner (eds), *Dynamics of Political Violence: A Process-Oriented Perspective on Radicalization and the Escalation of Political Conflict*. Farnham: Ashgate, pp. 293–303.

Crone, Manni. 2016. 'Radicalization Revisited: Violence, Politics and the Skills of the Body', *International Affairs* 92(3): 587–604.

Dearden, Lizzie. 2018. 'National Action Trial: "Neo-Nazi" Admits Terror Plot to Murder Labour MP Rosie Cooper with a Machete', *The Independent*, 12 June.

Retrieved 10 January 2022 from https://www.independent.co.uk/news/uk/ crime/national-action-terror-plot-rosie-cooper-murder-labour-mp-jack-ren shaw-nazi-a8395026.html.

———. 2020. 'Tommy Robinson: 20 Suspects Charged with Violent Disorder at Oldham European Elections Rally', *The Independent*, 3 March. Retrieved 9 January 2022 from https://www.independent.co.uk/news/uk/crime/tom-my-robinson-rally-charged-muslim-defence-league-oldham-a9372516.html.

Fillieule, Olivier. 2010. 'Some Elements of an Interactionist Approach to Political Disengagement', *Social Movement Studies* 9(1): 1–15.

Goffman, Erving. 1990. *The Presentation of Self in Everyday Life*. London: Penguin Books.

GMP (Greater Manchester Police). 2020. 'Twenty People Have Been Charged Following a Large Scale Disturbance in Oldham in May 2019', Greater Manchester Police, 5 March. Retrieved 9 January 2022 from https://www.gmp.police. uk/news/greater-manchester/news/news/2020/march/twenty-people-have-been-charged-following-a-large-scale-disturbance-in-oldham-in-may-2019/.

Horgan, John. 2008. 'From Profiles to Pathways and Roots to Routes: Perspectives from Psychology and Radicalization into Terrorism', *The Annals of the Academy of the Political & Social Sciences* 618: 80–94.

———. 2012. 'Discussion Point: The End of Radicalization?' National Consortium for the Study of Terrorism and Responses to Terrorism (START). Retrieved 5 January 2022 from https://www.start.umd.edu/news/discussion-point-end-radicalization.

Johnston, Hank. 2014. 'The Mechanisms of Emotion in Violent Protest', in Lorenzo Bosi, Chares Demetriou and Stefan Malthaner (eds), *Dynamics of Political Violence: A Process-Oriented Perspective on Radicalization and the Escalation of Political Conflict*. Farnham: Ashgate, pp. 27–49.

Lindekilde, Lasse, Stefan Malthaner and Francis O'Connor. 2019. 'Peripheral and Embedded: Relational Patterns of Lone-Actor Terrorist Radicalization', *Dynamics of Asymmetric Conflict* 12(1): 20–41.

Magnusson, David. 1976. 'The Person and the Situation in an Interactional Model of Behavior', *Scandinavian Journal of Psychology* 17(1): 253–71.

Malthaner, Stefan. 2017a. 'Radicalization: The Evolution of an Analytical Paradigm', *European Journal of Sociology* 58(3): 369–401.

———. 2017b. 'Processes of Political Violence and the Dynamics of Situational Interaction', *International Journal of Conflict and Violence* 11: 1–10.

McCauley, Clark, and Sophia Moskalenko. 2017. 'Understanding Political Radicalization: The Two-Pyramids Model', *American Psychologist* 72(3): 205–16.

Moghaddam, Fathali M. 2005. 'The Staircase to Terrorism: A Psychological Exploration', *American Psychologist* 60(2): 161–69.

Neumann, Peter. 2013. 'The Trouble with Radicalization', *International Affairs* 89(4): 873–93.

Pilkington, Hilary. 2014. '"My Whole Life is Here": Tracing Journeys through "Skinhead"', in David Buckingham, Sara Bragg and Mary Jane Kehily (eds),

Youth Cultures in the Age of Global Media. Basingstoke: Palgrave Macmillan, pp. 71–87.

———. 2016. *Loud and Proud: Passion and Politics in the English Defence League*. Manchester: Manchester University Press.

———. 2017. 'Radicalisation Research Should Focus on Everyday Lives', *Research Europe* 9: 7. Retrieved 31 December 2021 from https://www.research research.com/news/article/?articleId=1366511.

———. 2020. *Understanding 'Right-Wing Extremism': In Theory and Practice*. DARE Research Report. Retrieved 28 August 2022 from https://documents .manchester.ac.uk/display.aspx?DocID=58702.

Pilkington, Hilary, Elena Omel'chenko and Al'bina Garifzianova. 2010. *Russia's Skinheads: Exploring and Rethinking Subcultural Lives*. London: Routledge.

Schuurman, Bart. 2020. 'Non-Involvement in Terrorist Violence', *Perspectives on Terrorism* 14(6): 14–26.

Sieckelinck, Stijn, et al. 2019. 'Transitional Journeys into and out of Extremism: A Biographical Approach', *Studies in Conflict & Terrorism* 42(7): 662–82.

Stenner, Karen. 2005. *The Authoritarian Dynamic*. New York: Cambridge University Press.

Wieviorka, Michel. 2003. 'Violence and the Subject', *Thesis Eleven* 73: 42–50.

Wiktorowicz, Quintan. 2005. *Radical Islam Rising: Muslim Extremism in the West*. Oxford: Rowman & Littlefield.

CHAPTER 7

Trajectories of (Non)Radicalisation in a French Prison

Bartolomeo Conti

The role that prisons play in the radicalisation process remains the subject of academic debate (Béraud, De Galembert and Rostaing 2016; Khosrokhavar 2016; de Galembert 2020). In both the collective imagination and within French institutions, however, prisons have already come to be seen as one of the main sites of the propagation of Islamist radicalisation (Kepel 2015; Micheron 2020; Rougier 2020). In France, the gradual development of a state model for countering terrorism that focuses on the prevention of radicalisation (Sèze 2019; Conti 2020) has led to the considerable expansion of the field of the fight against radicalisation.[1] In this process, prison has become the object of specific measures that have come to structure the prison space and the relationships therein.[2] While in France, like other European countries, prison is seen as an environment where radicalisation occurs more frequently than elsewhere in society – which would appear to be confirmed by the large number of people who have passed through the prison system prior to committing acts of terrorism – one might wonder whether the image of prison as a 'terroristogenic' place is not, at least partially, the result of its construction as such through academic and political discourse. In reflecting on this, three observations are worth noting. First, in response to a strong institutional and societal demand, the social sciences have mainly focused on those prisons where there is a concentration of prisoners with terrorist convictions, that is, where the discourse of radical Islam was not only more accessible, but also stronger and more visible. Secondly, like the prison administration, researchers have focused almost entirely on prisoners convicted of terrorism or who have been 'radicalised' or 'suspected of being radicalised', rather than looking at a broader spectrum of prisoners. Finally, the primary objective of much of this research has been to produce profiles that might, among other things, be useful for prevention or even detection of radicalisation (Crettiez and Sèze 2017; Micheron 2020).

Taking these observations as a starting point, the research upon which this contribution is based provides a novel perspective due to three distinguishing features of the methodological approach adopted. First, it focuses on a prison considered to be 'peripheral' or designed for 'radicalisation dispersion' (Chantraine, Scheer and Depuiset 2018), that is, a prison where the size of the population judged to have been 'radicalised' or 'suspected of being radicalised' is limited. Secondly, it is concerned with prisoners with a range of profiles and trajectories in relation to the offences committed, their attitude in detention and their affiliations, as well as their religion and/or religiosity. This allows the study of not only radicalisation trajectories but also those that might be defined as trajectories of 'non-radicalisation'. Finally, the research was based on a dialogue with the respondents concerning inequalities, injustices (real or perceived) and prisoners' responses – including a turn to radical Islam – to them. It is through this shift in perspective that this chapter aims to illustrate how prison – a place of confinement which tends to promote de-socialisation and the breakdown of the prisoners' social and affective ties – is a milieu that can give rise to highly varied, even opposing, outcomes and narratives, which more often than not manifest in a rejection of the radical Islam narrative.

Data Collection and Methodology

This contribution is based on ethnographic research conducted, primarily, in a correctional centre, far from any large city and housing a population of around 450 male inmates. This centre was selected as the site for ethnographic research because it had already been the subject of participatory action research on 'Contesting knowledge in the prison milieu', which was carried out in response to a request from the prison's teaching staff, who are increasingly confronted with challenges to their educational activity, in particular by incarcerated students who contest knowledge and/or use the idea of God to explain the world.

A range of data sources, collected between 2017 and 2019, are drawn on. In-depth interviews were conducted with a total of eighteen respondents. In several cases, three to four interviews were carried out with participants, sometimes spaced out over the course of the fieldwork. Data are also drawn from interviews conducted with prison staff (management, teachers, the warden, guards etc.), with the Muslim chaplain and with other inmates. A third source of data is a series of observations conducted during scheduled classes, on organised walks, in the corridors and exercise yards and during staff meetings. The final source of data comes from three group discussions. Two of these were conducted within the context of the action research 'Contesting knowledge in the prison milieu', where two groups of inmates participated in approximately ten group sessions. The third such discussion took place in the form of the DARE project Community Dialogue Event, which brought together a dozen prisoners for a day of collective reflection on the relationship between inequality, injustice, radicalisation and violence.

The methodological approach adopted in this study distinguishes it from the majority of French research to date on radicalisation in as much as the entire prison is considered as a 'negotiated' social space (Khosrokhavar 2016) in which it is possible to generate a situational and interactional understanding of what is perceived as injustice and inequality and how these relate to extremism and radicalisation. This means that we employ a micro-sociological approach, where the researcher actively participates in the construction of an individual and collective narrative in which dialogue and contradictions can emerge between different stakeholders. The extended timeframe also gave us the opportunity to observe the evolution of phenomena and individuals and to avoid reducing them to their initial discourse or outward posturing.

This research was conducted with eighteen respondents, including one woman whom we met twice in a women's prison. The respondent set included three minors (at the time of the first interview one was sixteen and the other two were seventeen) and four individuals over thirty (thirty-seven, thirty-nine and forty-one respectively). The decision to include older individuals was based on the initial research results, which revealed the importance of the interaction between individuals of different ages, as the oldest individuals may be seen as (and claim to be) charismatic leaders who provide meaning to the juvenile rage that is acted out. The respondent set was composed of fifteen Muslims and three non-Muslims. Two were converts to Islam, both convicted of terrorism-related offences. The decision to include non-Muslims in the study came from previous studies, which illustrated how radical Islam can offer itself as a possible path for non-Muslims, in particular within the prison environment. The eighteen people in the respondent set were incarcerated for a variety of offences and crimes. Approximately one-third had been imprisoned for acts of terrorism, a third had been charged with, or convicted of, theft or armed robbery and the remaining third were in prison for drug trafficking.

The Desire for a Rewarding 'Elsewhere'

Inequality permeates the respondents' daily lives. It is engendered by structural relations within French society (at the macro level), the assigning of individuals to and/or identifying them with social groups (meso) and subjective experience (micro). Inequality at these three levels intersects in the lives of individuals, producing a widely shared feeling of injustice to which the responses are varied. The lives of the respondents are marked, above all, by a sense of physical, social and symbolic confinement, generally producing a shared feeling of being unable to move forward and, ultimately, to control one's life.

Spatial Marginalisation and Collective Identification

This experience manifests, firstly, in the form of physical and spatial confinement, as the majority of respondents grew up and lived in disadvantaged and marginalised neighbourhoods. The latter are mainly inhabited by immigrants and people of immigrant origin and are characterised by low-quality social services and a lack of social and economic mixing. They are neighbourhoods where there are very few people of French origin. This is the case for, among others, Steven:[3] 'Well, where we live, and even at school, almost all of us are black, Arab and so on, or gypsies, and at my school there were only two French kids. So I'd never talked to them, never, not a word.' Anissa, who grew up in a small-town neighbourhood, described how her spatial horizon was limited to two high-rise buildings that embody the ghetto in which she lives. Her marriage allowed her to move from one high-rise to the other, in a kind of parody of the social mobility to which she, like most other prisoners, might aspire. Characterised by poverty and economic marginalisation – as well as the weak presence of the state, whose coercive branches are the most visible – these spaces are seen as the expression of a deliberate policy of exclusion. Anissa explains: 'Yeah, they do it on purpose . . . putting all the Arabs in the ghettos. So that we keep to ourselves and so that the shit stays in the shit.'

In a process of ghettoisation, in which a world is gradually and collectively built away from the outside world (Lapeyronnie 2008), childhood memories and forms of solidarity and bonds between groups nonetheless help shape a spatial identity, one that is rooted in the social and physical space where the individual lived and grew up, so much so that, for some, segregation engenders a sense of total separation, operating within a binary framework that pits what is inside, 'Us', against what is outside, 'Them'. This is expressed by Paul, a seventeen-year-old in prison for homicide:

Where we live, nobody comes and hassles us, we're chilled, we don't bother anyone, we're with our own people, we know everyone ... We're in our little village, we've got everything we need in our village . . . Why would we leave? To do what? . . . They don't want to mix with us, why should we go mix with them?

Stigmatisation, Labelling and Discrimination

All of the respondents were born and/or raised in France. Most of them are French nationals who went to French schools and were educated in the values of the French Republic. Yet nearly all of the respondents of foreign origin underline how they are constantly reminded of their foreign roots and, in this way, rendered alien. They denounce a society, the media and institutions that deny them their Frenchness by preventing them from writing their story within the national narrative. The words of sixteen-year-old Griezmann, who has a French father and an Arab mother, serve as a brutal reminder: 'Since they always called me a "dirty Arab" and all that, I didn't think of myself as French anymore. I mean, I tell myself "I'm in France, I was born in France, I'm French and they treat me like a foreigner".' These are dilemmas associated with 'double absence' (Sayad 1999), that feeling of not belonging anywhere, of being second-class citizens, the 'illegitimate children' of French society. It is essentially a sense of rejection and non-recognition (Pilkington and Acik 2020), which often become reciprocal through the rejection of French society, as expressed by, among others, Paul: 'I don't feel French. Because for them, for French people – real French people, white French people – for them, we're not French. And I don't like this country. I was born here, but I don't like it.'

The respondents' experiences of discrimination, which play a major role in their life, are tied to background and belonging, ethnic-racial origins or religion, especially Islam. Within the prison, Islam is described by detainees as a 'refuge', 'helping them to escape it' and 'the only resort' enabling them to confront the conditions of detention, as well as social discredit and stigma. While Islam – like other religions – may be a mobilising source that detainees use to cope with prison, unlike other religions, and inside prison even more than in the rest of the society, Islam is perceived as a threat (Hajjat and Mohammed 2013), a source of stigmatisation and discrimination. This is vividly illustrated in the words of one prison officer: 'There are lots of Muslims in prison and they're all the same, they make incarceration hell . . . Neither side wants to live together. We are trying to integrate people who don't want to be integrated. Islam is an intrusive religion and it's scary.'

The untenable gap between the perception of Islam as a resource on the one hand, and the institutional and societal discourses and practices that present Islam as a danger on the other, represents a clash of perceptions which shatters relationships of trust (Conti 2020). But in prison, this clash goes beyond Islam. As one detainee explained, it is present in the form of a feeling or certainty that you are being punished 'for who you are and not what you did': 'Here you have religious, ethnic and social racism. In prison, discrimination is everywhere. There is one law for white people and another law for everyone else. This is where people become anti-French. This is a jihadist factory. Push youngsters too far and you turn them into extremists.' This line of thinking reveals the strong feeling of a double standard whereby the people most likely to be convicted come from categories that dominant society and elites define as 'at risk' or as 'dangerous' (Kundnani 2014). This leads to the widespread perception of being victims of a stigmatising process that relegates individuals to 'dangerous' categories or groups and which, as a consequence, already finds them guilty. Following an interactionist logic, discrimination becomes a form of interaction between people on both sides of the prison bars who have been reduced to a category that labels them: Arabs, foreigners, Muslims, Whites, French people.

A Conflictual Relationship with the State

The respondents' stories portray an almost warlike relationship with law enforcement resulting from riots, police brutality, disputes, provocation, beatings and insults. For some, the story of violence is told through the scars on their bodies, which stem from conflict escalations or even cumulative violence and become spaces of memory that symbolise hatred towards the state, where the state is often reduced to its repressive institutions: the police, the justice system and prison.

This relationship of distrust and violence towards state institutions translates into (and is the reflection of) the absence, in the lives of respondents, of civic engagement and community-based and political culture. One by-product of this is the decision not to vote. Hardly any of the respondents had ever voted or joined political movements or associations. They are, and feel, simply removed from democratic life and their lives are characterised by non-participation. For the respondents, this is primarily the consequence of deliberate measures taken by decision makers to exclude certain segments of the population from spaces of power and decision-making bodies. On this subject, Adil, arrested after spending four months with Islamic State (IS) in Syria, expresses his feeling of exclusion and his contempt for politics: 'Yes, people have opinions and they express them, but then what? Expressing one's opinion doesn't achieve anything. People's opinions are simply not taken into account . . . The voice of the people is like a sound, with no impact.'

What becomes especially apparent for these young people is the absence of intermediary bodies allowing them to collectively challenge their sense of injustice and to create fulfilling social connections – a role previously filled by workers' unions or political parties. The absence of resources needed to transform inequalities and the feeling of injustice into a political discourse and thus to establish oneself as a socio-political actor engenders fatalistic attitudes and feelings, and hence the perception that action is futile because everything is pre-determined. This fatalism is widespread among the prisoners, who feel that they have no control over their lives, a feeling which reinforces the conditions leading not only to recidivism,[4] but also to victimisation, disempowerment and violence. The consequence is summed up in the words of one prisoner during a group session: 'I don't fit in with society . . . it is not a society for us.'

Socio-Economic Exclusion and the Desire for Social Mobility

Almost all of the respondents belong to the working class. Like them, their families are often 'stuck' in low-skilled, low-paid and sometimes degrading work. In certain cases, they and their parents are unemployed, in unstable jobs, or even involved in illegal activities. As the supervising prison officer bitterly says, '80% of those in prison have had family members in prison. So prison becomes a family legacy'. The delinquency in which certain young people are involved aligns with family history and practices and a 'know-how' that passes from generation to generation as a resource allowing one to climb the social ladder or simply to take what one does not have.

What is lacking, however, are not simply economic resources; indeed, some respondents have become accustomed to 'earning' large amounts of 'dirty' money through illegal activities. We therefore need to examine the social conditions of our respondents more broadly, in terms of economic, cultural and social capital (Ilan and Sandberg 2019). From this perspective, the dynamics of the street may be seen as a path towards social mobility and hence towards the type of success that most respondents have never found in their studies or in the workplace. Marco, a 21-year-old man who grew up around gang wars in a French overseas *département*, is one example of how deviance makes it easy to obtain what one desires and compensate for the lack of social mobility:

> There's no such thing as easy money on the streets. With someone who doesn't have experience, you're going to put him on the side of the road to sell the 100 grams of weed or cocaine he's carrying. It's not easy, you know. Standing there for hours with the police passing by, it's not easy. The risk he has to take, the risks that other people

have to take in a job as a psychologist or school teacher or whatever,
it's not the same, you know?

The Crisis of the Family Institution

At the micro level, it is in particular the breakdown of the family institution that affects respondents' perceptions and lived experiences. The
accounts, as well as the silences, generally relate to a family model that
no longer works, that of the traditional patriarchal family built on a rigid
division of roles between father, mother and children. Parental authority
and its associated normative framework are generally absent, weakened
or openly contested, clearing the way for transgression, dysfunctional
or reckless behaviour and violent outbursts. Among the respondents,
we identified different configurations of what Khosrokhavar (2018: 278)
has termed the 'headless patriarchal family'. The first configuration is
that of those who essentially grew up without either parent, like Paul
and Romain, who were both raised by their grandmothers. The second
configuration, which applies to approximately half of the respondents, is
that of single-parent households, in which, usually, it is the mother who
struggles to bring up the children alone. In some cases, it is the death of
the father that leads to this situation and the concomitant disruption of
emotions and domestic norms, sometimes leading to delinquency and
violence. In most cases, however, it is because the father is estranged
from the family or has simply abandoned the household; this relinquish-
ing of paternal duties is a consistent feature of the upbringing of those in
prison. The third configuration is the reversal of generational roles, with
sons replacing their fathers as authority figures within the fragmented
family. The final configuration involves the symbolic death of the father
(representing parental authority) in line with clearly jihadist frameworks
(Ferret and Khosrokhavar 2022). In these cases, parental authority is replaced by that of a strict reading of religious texts, by the authority of the
peer group, or of the imaginary community of believers (the *Ummah*).
This is the case for Adrian, who had been affiliated to IS. After adopting a strict vision of Islam at the age of sixteen, he took on the role of
moraliser in the family and adopted a controlling attitude towards his
parents, whom he accused of being infidels.

What emerges from the respondents' accounts, above all, is the lack
of intergenerational sharing and the consequent lack of knowledge of
one's own origins, which makes it quite difficult for these individuals to
tell their stories and thus understand where they come from (Yuval-Davis
2006). As Teodoro, who was engaged in a profound self-examination,
said during a collective session on family trajectories: 'My story is similar
to that of all the others in here. We are all uprooted people.'

Detachment: The Paradigm of Radicalisation

Taking a widely shared feeling of injustice as our starting point, we consider here the options presented to young people already feeling a sense of detachment from the rest of society. We show how, in some cases, this leads to a complete rupture with society while, in others, individuals are able to mobilise resources to avoid cutting themselves off completely from the world.

Momo's trajectory allows us to see both the ambivalence of such trajectories – propelled by conflicting desires to break away and to put down roots – and how the 'tipping point' into violent extremism is often the consequence of a chain of events and interactions that are not always predictable and are sometimes barely controllable. Momo, twenty-one years old, is incarcerated for the fifth time. Since the age of sixteen, he has spent just two years on the outside and four years in prison, which feeds the feeling of being stuck in a never-ending vicious circle. At the origin of his delinquent trajectory is the desire for money, because 'with money you can do everything, without money you can't do anything'. Growing up without a father, Momo has been involved in all kinds of violence, both inter-gang and against the police, who are, for him, the symbol of a repressive state. The nonchalance with which he speaks demonstrates this trivialisation of violence, which is by no means exclusive to him: 'I liked that. Going around town, getting it on with other neighbourhoods . . . Yeah, in a group. But sometimes I did it on my own. And I'd find myself surrounded by ten guys. But no worries, I really liked that.'

Violence and disorder aside, hatred was also part of Momo's trajectory. Although on the outside Momo's hatred was essentially directed at the police, in prison it is directed at the guards, in an 'us' vs 'them', or even warlike, relationship:

> In this place the guards are heartless . . . Forgive my language, but they are total bastards. They do whatever they can to break you. If you're not strong enough mentally, you're screwed . . . they can do whatever they want, they'll never break me. That said, the only thing that frightened me was that one day I'd get hold of one or two of them and rip them apart.

Momo is a Muslim but his faith is not embedded in official Islam. Rather, Momo's Islam follows a discourse of distrust and contempt against the prison chaplain and against Imams in general, whom he accuses of perversity:

> No problem, I'm well informed about my religion . . . I don't need to go and see an Imam, I know tons of people, they know a hundred times better than the Imams. And I get information about my religion

every day. About what to do and what not to do . . . Imams aren't necessarily knowledgeable! I've known Imams who prostitute their daughters. They put their daughters on the street.

More than anything else, his discourse reflects a broader phenomenon of the emergence of new figures of authority in Islam as well as of individualisation in the production of religious knowledge (Roy 2002). It also reflects a dehumanisation of the Other, which encompasses Imams, police officers, supervisors and more generally a society described as deeply unjust and racist. First and foremost, his response to the feeling of injustice demonstrates the weakness of social ties, but also brings out the last available ties, to which Momo clings in order not to become part of a jihadist vision:

I hate France. I don't like France. And if someone asked me: 'Why do you stay in France?', I'd say 'I don't like France but I like what people have done with it, and that basically these people are all immigrants' . . . And I'm happy to have grown up in a neighbourhood. That's the atmosphere I like. . .
Interviewer: And what don't you like about France?
Momo: Everything! The only good thing is the social security. That's all! . . . It's a country full of big fat sons of cowards. The French – they are big fat sons of cowards! They prefer rapists to thieves, they prefer rapists to drug dealers . . . There's no justice. There's no justice! There's no liberty, no equality, no fraternity. It's a lie . . . I have nothing in common with this country.

Momo has a radical discourse that mixes hatred with an extreme vision of Islam, one that is marginal and oppositional, in the sense that it is positioned outside or even against the traditional Islam of families and mosques. Its discourse is that of a dehumanisation of the Other, identified with evil, filth and disorder. Nevertheless, while breaking his links with French society, Momo desperately tries to hold onto those that remain, in order to avoid crossing the line. This emerges from the full interview with him, in which he imagines a mythic return to Algeria, a country 'that drove out the French'. He goes on to describe his neighbourhood as a social and physical space of identification, the last bastion of a wounded identity. Finally, he evokes the family, in particular his mother to whom he feels he owes a debt and who, in spite of everything, is still there to offer him a path to salvation through emotion.

Momo's trajectory introduces us to the importance of 'detachment' in radicalisation trajectories. Following a narrative of radical Islam, or even jihadism, means breaking one's emotional, social and political links in this world, that is, of taking the uprooting process even further.

In this sense, radicalisation appears as a process of detachment (de-socialisation) from the already fragile links that connect each individual to social, affective or territorial spaces, accompanied by a process of resocialisation into a new entity, the group or the neo-*Ummah*, the community of Allah remade in the image of the heroic period of Islam under the Prophet. For some, radical Islam thus extends a process that is already at work, with most of the young people in our respondent set being 'uprooted', as Teodoro puts it.

Anomie and Family Chaos: The Neo-Ummah as Substitute Family

Born into a Protestant family in a French overseas *département*, Romain is a 21-year-old convert who was imprisoned on suspicion of planning a terrorist attack and of wanting to reach Syria to join jihadist groups. His adherence to violent extremism is rooted in his family trajectory, one that is chaotic and marked by wounds that he finds difficult to put into words. He told us about an absent mother and an unknown father, an adopted brother and a grandmother who raised him until the age of sixteen. During his teens, he finally found his mother in France, a far-off country in his eyes: 'For me, France meant snow. That's all.' He moved in with his mother in a small town in the east of the country. He did not know anyone and spent his time doing nothing; he was alone and bored. It was during this phase, which might be described as anomic, that he converted to Islam. He undertook his conversion alone and thus his Islam was built in solitude, discovered exclusively on the Internet, and offered a way out of his isolation and a connection with what appeared to be an imaginary community. His conversion and adherence to radical Islam took place at the same time, without any contact with the traditional Islam of the mosques. As Romain recounts, 'I only went to the mosque twice. Then the police came and arrested me'. He seized this new ideology, first on social networks, then in prison. This new community cradles him, protects him and makes him feel part of a larger community, the neo-*Ummah*. For Romain, this community has become a substitute family:

> Muslims are like a family. As far as I'm concerned, Muslims are family . . . I didn't know them, but I don't need to know them . . . Simply by reading the Qur'an I already know them. From the moment someone makes a declaration of faith, I will stand by him. For me, a Muslim, whether he is French, American or whatever, is dearer to me than any unbeliever from my country even if he is my own mother's son.

Romain took his uprooting to the extreme, sweeping aside all pre-existing ties, and being reborn in a new identity that calms him. The idea of detachment, expressed in the doctrine of *al-walā' wa-l-barā'* (loyalty and disavowal), which encourages the believer to make a categorical break with all dimensions deemed unbelieving in contemporary society, provides Romain with the explanatory and strictly ideological framework to replace ineffective and disappointing family ties with new ones, in a society that presents itself as an epiphany of a new subjective and social order. It is in the neo-*Ummah*, an immaterial space that knows no boundaries, and which is not anchored in real cultures (Roy 2002), that the isolated and anomic individual can reinvent himself and be reborn in a new, valorising identity.

Countering Injustice with Commitment and Rejection

Adrian's case illustrates the link between radicalisation and the feeling of confinement and rejection. Adrian became a refugee in France at the age of nine, initially living with his family in reception centres for migrants, sometimes on the streets. He was eventually housed in a working-class neighbourhood, inhabited by an immigrant population and known for its marginalisation, which was a source of stigmatisation for its residents. When he arrived, Adrian did not speak French but he quickly learned the language and proved to be a good student. His success gave him a sense of worth and the hope that he might find a way out of the ghetto and improve his social standing, in what seemed to be the fulfilment of the family's migratory experience. But his origin and his place of residence became an obstacle. Against his wishes, he was sent to a vocational high school, a choice imposed by his origin, just as it was for many other young people from minorities in France. Later, when it came to finding an internship to complete his course, he found that all doors were closed due to his place of residence, which stigmatised him as dangerous. This, Adrian says, was 'hard to take' because it signals 'a kind of rejection, a complete rejection'. He found refuge in a fundamentalist vision of Islam, which gave him an opportunity to counter the rejection he had suffered with his own spectacular rejection: 'As soon as I quit school I jumped straight into religion. Direct. Everything that was prayers, and all that. I found solace in my religion. I dived directly into religion in fact . . . I instantly felt hatred.'

Coming from a non-practising Muslim family, Adrian did not attend the mosque. His Islam was that of a quietist Salafism that he learned mainly on the Internet and which gave him a reason to detach himself from the society that had rejected him. But quietist Salafism was only a brief chapter, because he wanted action, rather than a rigorous and restrictive practice. The revolts in Syria, the repression that followed and the creation of jihadist groups offered him a new possibility, a chance to respond to the rejection he had suffered and to a growing feeling of injustice. It was a second event which pushed him to take a step further and join the Islamic State, however:

> There were terrorist attacks on the 16 November, and they came to our home, armed and wearing balaclavas. They kicked the door down, ran in and grabbed me . . . I've never felt such anger . . . It was like the first time I had felt rejected by society. So that was the second rejection.

This event, experienced as a profound injustice and humiliation, was the turning point for Adrian, who now sought 'revenge' and to take action. The ideology of the Islamic State supported his actions and gave a broader meaning to his subjective anger. Thus, with every instance of perceived injustice Adrian took a step further towards shutting himself inside an increasingly rigorist vision of religion and an extremist attitude that legitimised violence. Several years after his arrest, while we were talking, Adrian managed to put his trajectory into words:

> It's a need for justice, a search for justice . . . but it's also in relation to the life I'd had . . . I mean I'd always grown up with injustice. I think that things like that are unfair to me . . . I feel as though I'm damned forever, until the end of my life. So yeah, obviously when faced with this feeling of injustice and . . . when there are things that happen like the Islamic State, you know, to restore justice in the world and all that, well . . . That's why I did it, I mean, I wanted to do it because of the anger I felt.

Adrian's trajectory is one of cumulative rejections over time and of the impossibility of escaping from the stigmatising condition in which he was confined. At every stage of his life, the doors had been shut and the rejection to which he was subjected in turn provoked a rejection, in a cumulative relationship. Adrian constructs his identity, his representations and his belonging based on the stigmas at the heart of his exclusion. As in the case of Romain, and all those who followed radical Islamist ideas, his commitment is built around the powerful notion of a persecuted and humiliated Muslim community across the world – one with which he identifies. The defence of Muslims is combined with the idea of the birth of a new society, where justice will finally reign and where differences will be erased, whether they be class-related, economic, racial or territorial. It is this dream of an (imaginary) egalitarian society that promises to sweep away the inequalities and injustices that have shaped the lives of these young people whilst failing to recognise its own roots in other forms of inequality including that of gender and between 'true believers' and 'unbelievers'.

Commitment and Self-Worth: The Ideal

Adil's trajectory illustrates the subjective need to achieve self-esteem through a rewarding commitment. As a young man with little religious experience who 'lives life to the full', as he puts it, Adil left a large French city and headed for Syria with his brother and a dozen friends. Some died in Syria, others returned to France, where they were convicted in one of the biggest trials related to jihadism. The last of them was to blow himself up during the 13 November 2015 terrorist attacks in Paris.

Adil's commitment is based on a fierce criticism of the democratic system, which he describes as hypocritical and dedicated exclusively to defending the interests of a minority. In his opinion, the voice of the people simply goes unheard and French society is governed by the stigmatisation of minorities, starting with Muslims. In what appears, again, as a reciprocal, cumulative process of rejection, Adil responds to marginalisation by placing himself outside the society that has rejected him. Like many others, radical Islam offers him the possibility of a rewarding commitment: 'I'd never had any opportunity to engage, and then it happened in a natural and spontaneous way. A natural commitment to go and help Muslim people. I had to take responsibility.' In this way, taking responsibility becomes a way to break free and claim a new role in society, a way to exist by stepping up to responsibility. Adil explains that this commitment was the result of the interaction between this personal need to commit to a cause, and an ideal of building an authentically Islamic society:

> If you want to understand, you mustn't start with the details . . . And ask yourself how differences between people have been erased by a common element; they are attracted by an idea! . . . It's the ideal to reproduce their original religion. Rebuilding the original Islam is an idea that transcends differences, the differences between the rich and the poor, between people from different countries; it includes everyone, because it is an idea that has no boundaries.

The subjective need to commit oneself in the name of justice, and in particular against the injustice done to Muslims, goes hand in hand with a desire to write history and to take part in the construction of an authentically Islamic society based on the model of the ancestors. This is an ideal that also fulfils the desire to participate in something 'great' and 'just', accomplishing a self-affirmation that these young people cannot find in French society. In his approach, Adil pushes the doctrine of al-

walā' wa-l-barā' to the extreme through the idea of a voluntary exit from French society.

Becoming the 'Chosen Ones':
Changing Status through God's Forgiveness

Radical Islam offers a way out for young people who are failing, lost, anomic, alone, searching for an ideal through which to engage or even reinvent themselves. It offers them a change of status as long as they break the pre-existing political, social and emotional ties in order to be reborn into a new identity. Jeremy is a convert in his forties, convicted of recruiting young people whom he had allegedly encouraged to leave for Syria. His narrative provides insight into how reinvention through radical Islam appeals to young people.

Jeremy describes himself as someone who knows religion and introduces two important aspects of the radical Islam narrative: being 'chosen', and the condition of detachment, that is, the need to detach oneself from everything, including one's own personal desire and affects, in order to be able to follow the divine path. Clarifying this notion of detachment, he offered the following example: 'If you choose your wife because you love her, you are giving in to what you love. And not to that which allows you to progress. It is God who must decide. Not us . . . Our ally is God, our enemy is the soul, the Devil, this lowly world.' He explains that even his incarceration is simply an expression of the divine will, and that for him 'prison is heaven!' as it allows him to 'bring those who are lost to the right path'. In particular, Jeremy is talking to those who carry a burden of guilt and significant, even crushing, social disapproval. He offers them a way out that will erase the past and open up new perspectives, God's forgiveness. All is forgiven when one follows the will of God, or of those who speak in his name, when one detaches oneself from this lowly world and from the desires of the soul. The individual leaves a world of sin, to be reborn in purity. For young people caught up in the feeling that their condition offers no way out, this idea of a new status is fascinating in that it allows them to escape the humiliation they feel; they thus become the all-powerful 'chosen ones', as Jeremy or Romain put it, 'after a lifetime of being losers'.

Safeguards to Resist, Reject and
Counter the Narrative of Radical Islam

This narrative of radical Islam, which aims to sever ties with 'this lowly world' or with this society of 'unbelievers', as a response to the feeling of injustice, does not go unchallenged. Alternative narratives mobilise other resources, which we might describe as capital, which provide a response rooted in the maintenance, rediscovery or strengthening of ties, not in their breaking.

The Temporalities of Radicalisation

In order to illustrate the resources (emotional, memory, relational, social) that are mobilised to resist, reject and counter the path of total withdrawal offered by radical Islam, we begin, at the macro level, by considering the declining attraction of what is being offered.

During a particular period, roughly between 2012 and 2017 (i.e. during the construction of the Islamic State in Syria), we witnessed what Adil refers to as a 'social movement', namely young people drawn to the great adventure of building a new, authentically Islamic society. This was a phase of exaltation that mobilised a broad cross-section of young people beyond their social origin, political involvement or even religious practice. Within the prison system, this meant that the narrative of radical Islam was particularly attractive and that the 'radicals' basked in a special aura, as a sort of 'vanguard' who were 'models' of ethical integrity and great courage. They bore testament to an emancipation that was (and is) highly sought after among ghettoised, marginalised or imprisoned youth.

Just a few years later, that period simply appears to be over. The narrative of radical Islam is no longer as enchanting as it was before, either in prison or outside. There are three main reasons for this.

Firstly, the ideal was never attained, above all because IS lost the territory it had gained. In addition, the 'returnees' brought back a feeling of disappointment, as evident from Adil's experience: 'I have no regrets about the intentions. There might be regret about how things played out, the way, the method – that was disgusting. The intentions were noble, but the method was despicable . . . I came back following this disappointment.' In Syria, where the ideal was supposed to be achieved, the French fighters ultimately 'imported their *jahilya* (pre-Islamic religious ignorance) of the hood' (Thomson 2016: 174), by reproducing the frameworks, the power relations and the injustices of the ghetto/neighbourhoods (and society) that they wanted to escape. Secondly, the violence, which was largely mediatised by IS, was a problem in relation to confrontations with other prisoners. As jihadist discourse became less and less audible in prison, even those who expressed a certain fascination with the perspectives offered by radical Islam openly stated their opposition to a violence 'taken out on children' or a 'blind' violence that some describe as clearly 'contrary to Islam'. Thirdly, the phase of exaltation, where 'radicals' were seen as 'models', seems to have come to an end, because the trajectories of the 'radicals' (almost) always ended badly, leaving no models to follow.

Without claiming to be exhaustive, in this peripheral prison we identified four major outcomes of the trajectories of those labelled in prison as 'radicals' or 'terrorists'. Firstly, one that might be described as a take-it-to-the-limit attitude, like Adil, whose trajectory has alienated him, cutting him off from society, from his feelings and even from his memory. Such individuals may fascinate by their defiant attitude towards the prison administration, or a society they deem to be unjust, but (almost) none of the other prisoners wishes to follow their path. A second outcome, which, in some ways, takes things to the limit also, is that of a 'between-self' that flirts with madness. As in the case of Romain, this involves a process of immersion in the religiously normative. Madness is similarly unappealing, however; on the contrary, it is evidence of a path that leads to failure. Another way out is that of the development of a critical or even guilt-based appraisal, like that of Adrian. Here, with the passage of time, the individual can take the path of rationally structuring the commitment, which is often accompanied by the remobilisation of previously neglected links. Finally, we encountered those for whom the outcome is disappointment and admission of failure. This was the case for Blaise and Jeremy, both of whom were around the age of forty. Tired, caught up in a life of successive disappointments, with a bleak future, these individuals now only dream of withdrawing from the world and/or of settling down, forming a family and renewing neglected ties. As Blaise said: 'I plan to go back to Algeria and even to have a job there that will let me remain outside society . . . For example, living like a peasant, like my grandfather did . . . The farm, life in nature, that's what the Prophet recommends . . . And also, with my grandfather, it's important to remember where you come from, you have to go back to your roots.' Here Blaise depicts familial roots instead of religious ones, a farm in the mountains instead of the utopian homeland where religious law would rule.

Affective Ties: The Family

Despite the breakdown of the family, at a micro level family ties remain a resource that the respondents can mobilise. While the narrative of radical Islam pushes family dysfunction to the extreme, by cutting emotional and normative ties, the detainees who resist, reject and counter the discourse of radical Islam try 'desperately' to renew or reinvent such bonds. Family thus presents itself as a space which can have three main functions: identity construction, forgiveness and looking ahead.

Identity construction is evident, first of all, in the creation of a personal narrative, being able to articulate a wounded identity, which occurs when family history is put into words. These family histories occupy a central place in the trajectories of the young people who are constantly trying to bring coherence to their lives in order to rebuild themselves. This task of bringing order to one's biography operates in particular through family memory and through the (re)discovery of familial sentiments and bonds. Teodoro, who is thirty years old, imagines an escape from delinquency by rebuilding a family history. Griezmann, who is sixteen, constructs his identity in the image of his grandfather, who, as a role model, helps him to respond to the feeling of injustice and the pain of double absence.

Secondly, with its affective ties, the family also presents itself as a place for forgiveness and hence salvation. Marco, Saïd and Ousmane all speak of a family that did not abandon them, despite the suffering caused by their delinquent paths. Not abandoning an imprisoned son, brother or husband proves to be a gift of the self, which engenders self-esteem and entails a moral obligation, even a moral debt, in that one also wants to give. We must stress that blood and family ties also retain a place for those who adhere to a radical vision of Islam and who spent time severing social and emotional bonds. In such cases, the original family is seen as an emergency exit, leading towards salvation. As Adrian states, 'If someone really wants to see me change, the only way to do it is through my parents . . . For me, they're the solution.'

Finally, family represents a space in which one can plan for the future. Some of these young people are now parents themselves, which changes their status. Such is the case of Anissa, whose sole dream is to leave her ghetto to ensure a better future for her three children. Here, we again find the need to construct oneself by giving of oneself, which becomes a source of attributing value and building a particular ethic. The responsibility towards others in some way constitutes the key to escaping a vicious circle of disdain, uselessness and failure.

So, while the narrative of radical Islam accelerates the destruction of the family in crisis, by replacing it with an ideal (but also ephemeral) family, those who refuse or resist adherence to the narrative of radical Islam still cling to their families (or what remains of them) and to what family can represent.

Islam as a Shield against Radicalisation

Islam is mobilised by individuals who identify with radical Islam. They claim to speak in the name of 'true Islam', that which is created by scholars. As the prison chaplain says, 'Those whom they call "scholars" are able to simplify the world, making things easier to grasp: "God said", "the Prophet said". What they are seeking is simplicity . . . For this radicalised youth, there's a real problem of knowledge.' Before turning to radical Islam, few of these young people had practised regularly or had much religious knowledge. Some, like Adil, continued to relegate religious practice to second place, even after carrying out *jihad*. None of the respondents situate themselves in the Islam they associate with French mosques, traditional Islam or family traditions surrounding religious practice. Their Islam is instead one of separation, disconnected from concrete reality – what we call a PDF Islam (Conti 2022).

Other respondents employ Islam to counter the narrative of radical Islam, in what appears to be a mutual act of excommunication regarding what constitutes 'true Islam'. First, there are those like Saïd and Ousmane, who practise Islam regularly and rigorously, settling into religion, which represents peace and stillness, not action and movement like it does for the jihadists. Most importantly, by setting down norms and structuring their lives, Islam offers a means of establishing order. For others, and younger inmates in particular, Islam primarily represents an escape route, a last resort to which they can turn to save themselves, a refuge that must be preserved. Islam is thus described as a resource that allows one to become calm, find stability and conform to a particular ethical framework. It is, therefore, a way to escape from illegality, while at the same time constituting a resource with which, for example, to build a family. This vision contrasts with radical Islam precisely because the discourse and actions of 'radicals' deprive young inmates of this 'last' resource that is Islam. Radical Islam is an Islam of revolt, which uproots and breaks the bonds that these young people struggle to renew.

Becoming a Socio-Political Actor

Other identifications and loyalties allow for more direct responses to feelings of injustice. We observed a variety of what Truong (2017) refers to as 'safeguards' that shield one from the temptation of totally breaking away from society. These 'safeguards' can become a reality at different levels (local, national and transnational) and require different types of loyalty and identification, as well as forms of engagement.

At the local level, safeguards appear in the form of relationships that are forged daily within the living spaces of these individuals. These include friendships, relationships with neighbours and professional relationships, along with support that is provided by institutions such as schools, the social security system, hospitals and so on. These relationships primarily take shape at the neighbourhood level, which can become a place of identification, not a place to escape.

Narratives of identification and loyalty can also be constructed at the national level. The nation essentially remains a powerful agent of identification around which certain individuals build their identities. Such is the case of Nabil, who refers to Morocco, where he was born, as the place that allows him to integrate and which serves as a shield against the potential allure of radical Islam. Some of those who were born and raised in France openly assert their attachment to the country and clearly lay claim to their French identity. As Anissa states, 'I love France. We're happy here, we're safe and we get a lot of assistance'.

Finally, socio-political engagement may also act as a safeguard where narratives rooted in social history and the collective imagination make it possible to turn the sense of injustice into a conflict. By being part of a grand mobilising narrative, one finds a source of valorisation. This is what happened to Teodoro, who is rebuilding himself through the social movement of the fight against racism and through getting involved (or aspiring to) in helping young people from disadvantaged urban neighbourhoods. For Teodoro, engaging with young people has become a way to cultivate rewarding commitments and become politically active.

Criminal Logic

There is an ambiguous relationship between criminal logic and radical Islam. Within the prison system, there is no shortage of cases involving alliances, convergences or transitions from one to the other (Basra, Neumann and Brunner 2016). This is, firstly, because, as Ilan and Sandberg (2019) point out, street capital can be an added value in the jihadist career and therefore facilitate recruitment into extremist groups. Adherence to radical Islam may offer a way out of criminality and the possibility to have 'everything forgiven', as Jeremy says. However, the trajectory can also be inverted, as criminality (and criminal forms of loyalty and morality) can also act as an alternative to a radical ideology. As Marco explains: 'We, the bandits, the thugs, we're not like that (extremism). We have values. We would never kill a child. We'd never take out a kid.' This is a discourse shared by others, such as Griezmann and Anissa, for whom criminal morality imposes boundaries that must not be crossed. Finally, the hedonistic aspect of delinquent or criminal practice may exclude radical Islam. As Paul explains, when young people who do not hide their love for money, drugs, trafficking, alcohol, uninhibited sexuality and so on are confronted with the jihadist offering – rooted in sacrifices and renunciation – they simply prefer the 'lowly' world, built on passion, desire and pleasure, which functions according to a strictly criminal logic, with its own rules, objectives and modalities: 'Personally, I'm not into this whole terrorism thing and all that stuff . . . I'm just fine doing my own thing, hashish, drugs. There you have it . . . I'll stick with that rather than go kill people or whatever.'

Conclusions

How do we explain the now axiomatic observation that 'all extremists have grievances, but not all people with grievances become extremists' (Berger 2018: 129)? Based on the findings of research drawn on in this chapter, it appears that there is, in fact, a very thin line between becoming radicalised and not becoming radicalised. Everything is held together by a tiny thread, a tiny connection that prevents one from shifting from 'Us' to 'Them'. Such affective and social connections, these 'tiny threads' that hold everything together, can snap without a major reason or event, but simply as a result of one small thing: encounters at a particular moment in life; a small injustice that accumulates on top of those already experienced; a hurtful word that was never taken back; the boredom of an existential void for young people searching for an identity. Just one small thing can change everything.

Most of the young people we met in the course of this research tread the perilous edges of this limbo, where such a 'small thing' can precipitate events, break links and erase the last remaining attachments. From one moment to the next, a link can be broken, which, when one has to put it into words years later, is difficult to explain but, at the time, seemed logical. An epiphany of a new order. All-encompassing. And there, to help, even to provoke this properly individual, subjective, sometimes intimate process, there is the offer, the narrative of radical Islam, and the forms of sociability (groups, networks) that link the individual to the macro level. Ideology has exactly this power of explaining everything, of eliminating doubts and uncertainty, of 'being in the truth', as Romain puts it, in that which presents itself as a state of grace. The offer proposes a new (ephemeral) family (Ferret and Khosrokhavar 2022), a distant and imaginary world where (divine) justice will reign, a change of status, an escape from shame, a reversal of humiliation and the overcoming of alienation. To be the chosen ones. To restore justice in this world, if necessary through violence, generating a new order (and untold new injustices).

If everything can be turned upside down by just 'a small thing', everything can be held together by it too. Safeguards are at work. These links, even though they are fragile, prevent one from falling and are ultimately the cornerstone of the non-radicalisation of a youth that shares inequalities and a feeling of injustice. Family ties, living space, personal memories, desires, the trust of a close friend. Or a model grandfather, a mother who is always there, a friend who helps, the desire for a son, a teacher or a guardian who has the 'courage' to listen. Then there is the mobilising force of other major narratives, which help to explain, to let one feel part of something bigger, which allow one (to have the illusion) of participating in the construction of this world. As a result, the encounter between the offer of radical Islam and the subjective dimension is not linear, but is made up of back-and-forths, of the combination of events, encounters and situations. It is based on structural factors, such as injustice, inequality, non-recognition, stigmatisation, exclusion and can be caused by just 'a small thing', by a severing of ties that can occur very suddenly. This interconnectedness suggests the importance of examining these phenomena through what, like Dawson (2017), we might call an 'ecological approach'. By adopting such a holistic approach, we are able to take into account the 'small things', which may prove, in fact, to be the 'huge things' that are decisive in following or countering trajectories of radicalisation.

Acknowledgements

The research drawn on in this chapter is part of the Dialogue about Radicalisation and Equality (DARE) project, which received funding from the European Union's Horizon 2020 research and innovation programme under Grant Agreement No. 725349. It reflects only the views of the author; the European Commission and Research Executive Agency are not responsible for any information it contains.

Bartolomeo Conti is a sociologist at the Ecole des Hautes Etudes en Sciences Sociales (EHESS) in Paris, where he obtained his PhD in Sociology (2011) with a thesis on the rise of Islam in the Italian public sphere. From 2013 to 2015, he was associate researcher at the European University Institute (EUI), where he studied conflict over the construction of mosques in Italian cities. In 2015, he participated in a research project on Islamist radicalisation in French prisons, with the aim of elaborating methods and tools for the social reintegration of radicalised young people. Following a fellowship at the University of California, Berkeley, he worked on the H2020 DARE project (2017–21) and is currently engaged in a cross-national project on the shifting nature of identities and representations of Muslims in four European contexts.

NOTES

1. Recent years have seen a considerable broadening in the scope of the fight against radicalisation; it no longer relates to just jihadists or 'radicals', but also includes persons who are 'potentially radicalised' or 'in the process of being radicalised'. This evolution in vocabulary demonstrates a security shift that now encompasses an increasingly broad spectrum of inmates.
2. The prison administration distinguishes between two profiles of prisoners associated with radical Islam. The first are those incarcerated for terrorist acts relating to radical Islam (known as TIS); these inmates numbered 511 in 2019 compared to just ninety in 2014. The second category are those incarcerated for common law offences but who are flagged for radicalisation (DCSR); there were approximately 1,100 such inmates in 2019. To the latter, we should add 635 individuals, in open custody, monitored by the French Penitentiary Integration and Probation Department (SPIP) for radicalisation. On this, see https://www.assemblee-nationale.fr/dyn/15/rapports/cion_lois/l15b2082_rapport-information.
3. Place names and interviewees' first names have been changed to ensure anonymity. Participants in group discussions and institutional employees interviewed, such as prison officers, are not given pseudonyms but referred to by their role or status (e.g. 'prison officer', 'detainee').
4. According to a report by the French Ministry of Justice, 31% of prisoners released in 2016 were sentenced for a new offence committed during the year of their release. See http://www.justice.gouv.fr/statistiques-10054/info stats-justice-10057/mesurer-et-comprendre-les-determinants-de-la-recid ive-34044.html.

REFERENCES

Basra, Rajan, Peter Neumann and Claudia Brunner. 2016. *Criminal Pasts, Terrorist Futures: European Jihadists and the New Crime-Terror Nexus.* London: The International Centre for the Study of Radicalisation and Political Violence.

Béraud, Céline, Claire De Galembert and Corinne Rostaing. 2016. 'Islam et prison: liaisons dangereuses?' ['Islam and Prison: Dangerous Liaisons?'], *Pouvoirs* 3(158): 67–81.

Berger, John M. 2018. *Extremism.* Cambridge, MA: The MIT Press.

Chantraine, Gilles, David Scheer and Marie Aude Depuiset. 2018. *Enquête sociologique sur les 'quartiers d'évaluation de la radicalisation' dans les prisons françaises* [A Sociological Study on 'Radicalisation Assessment Units' in French Prisons], Rapport DAP. Retrieved 21 February 2022 from https://hal.univlille.fr/hal-02458977/document.

Conti, Bartolomeo. 2020. *Case Studies of Interactive Radicalisation: France*, DARE Research Report. Retrieved 28 August 2022 from https://documents.man chester.ac.uk/display.aspx?DocID=58683.

———. 2022. 'Rise and Fall of a Jihadist Neo-Family: The Cannes-Torcy Cell', in *Jérôme* Ferret and Farhad Khosrokhavar (eds), *Family and Jihadism: A Socio-Anthropological Approach to the French Experience*. London: Routledge, pp. 111–50.

Crettiez, Xavier, and Romain Sèze. 2017. *Saisir les mécanismes de la radicalisation violente: pour une analyse processuelle et biographique des engagements violents* [Understanding the Mechanisms of Violent Radicalisation: Towards a Process-based and Biographical Analysis of Involvement in Violence]. Retrieved 21 February 2022 from http://www.gip-recherche-justice.fr/wp-con tent/uploads/2017/08/Rapport-radicalisation_INHESJ_CESDIP_GIP-Jus tice_2017.pdf.

Dawson, Lorne. 2017. 'Sketch of a Social Ecology Model for Explaining Home-grown Terrorist Radicalisation', ICCT Research Note. Retrieved 21 Febru-ary 2022 from https://icct.nl/publication/sketch-of-a-social-ecology-model-for-explaining-homegrown-terrorist-radicalisation/.

De Galembert, Claire. 2020. *Islam et prison* [Islam and Prison]. Amsterdam: Am-sterdam Eds.

Ferret, Jérôme, and Farhad Khosrokhavar (eds). 2022. *Family and Jihadism: A Socio-Anthropological Approach to the French Experience*. London: Routledge.

Hajjat, Abdellali, and Marwan Mohammed. 2013. *Islamophobie: Comment les élites françaises fabriquent le 'problème musulman'* [Islamophobia: How the 'Muslim Problem' Is Manufactured by French Elites]. Paris: La Découverte.

Ilan, Jonathan, and Sveinung Sandberg. 2019. 'How "Gangsters" Become Jihad-ists: Bourdieu, Criminology and the Crime-Terrorism Nexus', *European Jour-nal of Criminology* 16(3): 278–94.

Kepel, Gilles. 2015. *Terreur dans l'Hexagone: Genèse du Djihad français* [Terror in the *Hexagon*: The Genesis of French Jihad]. Paris: Gallimard.

Khosrokhavar, Farhad. 2016. *Prisons de France. Violence, radicalisation, déshuma-nisation: quand surveillants et détenus parlent* [Prisons of France. Violence, Radicalisation, Dehumanisation: When Guards and Prisoners Speak]. Paris: Robert Laffont.

———. 2018. *Le nouveau jihad en Occident* [The New Jihad in the West]. Paris: Robert Laffont.

Kundnani, Arun. 2014. *The Muslims Are Coming! Islamophobia, Extremism, and the Domestic War on Terror*. London: Verso.

Lapeyronnie, Didier. 2008. *Ghetto urbain: Ségrégation, violence, pauvreté en France aujourd'hui* [The Urban Ghetto: Segregation, Violence and Poverty in Today's France]. Paris: Robert Laffont.

Micheron, Hugo. 2020. *Le jihadisme français: Quartiers, Syrie, prisons* [French Jihadism: Neighbourhoods, Syria and Prisons]. Paris: Gallimard.

Pilkington, Hilary, and Necla Acik. 2020. 'Not Entitled to Talk: (Mis)recognition, Inequality and Social Activism of Young Muslims', *Sociology* 54(1): 181–98.

Roy, Olivier. 2002. *L'islam mondialisé* [Globalised Islam]. Paris: Seuil.

Rougier, Bernard (ed.). 2020. *Les territoires conquis de l'islamisme* [Islamism's Conquered Territories]. Paris: PUF.

Sayad, Abdelmalek. 1999. *La double absence: Des illusions de l'émigré aux souffrances de l'immigré* [The Double Absence: From Emigrant Illusions to Immigrant Suffering]. Paris: Seuil.

Sèze, Romain. 2019. *Prévenir la violence djihadiste: Les paradoxes d'un modèle sécuritaire* [Preventing Jihadist Violence: The Paradoxes of a Security Model]. Paris: Seuil.

Thomson, David. 2016. *Les revenants: Ils étaient partis faire le jihad, ils sont de retour en France* [The Returned: They Left to Wage Jihad, Now They're Back]. Paris: Seuil.

Truong, Fabien. 2017. *Loyautés radicales: L'islam et les «mauvais garçons» de la nation* [Radical Loyalties: Islam and the Nation's 'Bad Boys']. Paris: La Découverte.

Yuval-Davis, Nira. 2006. 'Belonging and the Politics of Belonging', *Patterns of Prejudice* 40(3): 197–213.

CHAPTER 8

Responses to Radical(ising) Messages and Their Messengers by Young Marksmen and Their Clubs
From Rejection to Normalisation

Benjamin Kerst

Introduction

This chapter explores how young marksmen and markswomen[1] engage with, and respond to, radical(ising) messages and their messengers in concrete, everyday situations and interactions. It draws on situational descriptions and narratives of encounters with radical(ising) messages and those who convey them from interviews with young people from a German marksmen's club milieu, together with observations from the field, to illustrate the spectrum of responses. These range from their outright rejection, suggesting 'resilience' to radicalisation or 'non-radicalisation', to their normalisation, indicating the potential for radicalisation. Alongside the analysis of individual responses, the chapter considers the responses encountered within the milieu of the marksmen's clubs to which interviewees belong and from the clubs themselves. While, today, marksmen's clubs (*Schützenvereine*) may be considered part of the political mainstream or the social centre of society (*Mitte der Gesellschaft*), the milieu has attracted right-wing or extreme-right actors who have sought to influence and appropriate certain aspects of it. In this contribution, responses at both individual and milieu levels are analysed to explore the interactive, contextual and situational dimensions of radicalisation and non-radicalisation, on the one hand, and factors of resilience to radicalisation, on the other. This dual-analysis approach also allows insight into how resilience of the marksmen's club milieu might impact on the resilience and non-radicalisation of individual milieu actors.

Non-Radicalisation as Process and the Concept of Resilience

While there may remain 'no agreed definition' (Neumann 2013: 874) of radicalisation, it has become widely understood as a process (ibid.; Khalil, Horgan and Zeuthen 2019: 2–3) in which 'people become increasingly motivated to use violent means against members of an out-group or symbolic targets to achieve behavioural change and political goals' (Doosje et al. 2016: 79). However, in some formulations a distinction between 'attitudinal' or 'cognitive' and 'behavioural radicalisation' is drawn (McCauley and Moskalenko 2017; Gøtzsche-Astrup 2018), which recognises that 'radicalisation of opinion' may take place without 'radicalisation of action' (McCauley and Moskalenko 2017). This may explain why only a small proportion of those who have radical or extreme ideas engage in political violence and not all of those who engage in violence have radical or extreme ideas (ibid.: 211; Moghaddam 2009: 280; Horgan 2012; Neumann 2013: 879–80). In terms of the endpoint of the radicalisation process, it suggests a person might be considered radicalised if they support political violence in their attitudes and/or in their actions.

Together, these understandings of radicalisation offer a means to shift the perspective away from the violent individual at the 'sharp end of radicalization' (Schuurman 2020: 16) and towards an understanding of radicalisation as a process of 'becoming more radical' (Malthaner 2017: 371). The latter is indicated by a transformation of aims, attitudes and perceptions and/or changed forms of activism and actions (ibid.: 372) on a spectrum between non-radicalisation and radicalisation. Moreover, if radicalisation is a process, then non-radicalisation is also; this offers the possibility of exploring the process not only of becoming more radical, but also of partial, stalled or partially reversed radicalisation (see Introduction, this volume) or remaining non-radical. It is with this process of remaining non-radicalised that this contribution to the volume is primarily concerned. It understands this as an interactive, contextual and situational process in which individuals, or communities and organisations – specifically marksmen's clubs – engage with radical(ising) messages and their messengers but reject the support for attitudinal or behavioural violence. This is largely in line with Cragin's (2014: 342) concept of 'non-radicalization', understood as the 'rejection of violence' by individuals exposed to radical ideologies or violence, envisaged as involving a process evolving in a 'series of stages with multiple choices along the way' (Cragin et al. 2015: 11).

In contrast to Cragin's studies, however, this chapter draws explicitly on the concept of *resilience* to, at least partially, explain the rejection of radical(ising) messages and their messengers at the level of both individual respondents and the marksmen's clubs or communities to which they belong. The concept of resilience, with disciplinary genealogies and applications in physics, material science, ecology, psychology and political science, has become a key concept in Counter Terrorism (CT) and Preventing and Countering Violent Extremism (P/CVE) research, discourses and policy. Reviewing its use in CT and P/CVE, Grossman (2021: 295) notes how resilience refers to *prevention of* violent extremism and *resistance to* violent extremism (akin to Cragin's use of non-radicalisation) but also to *adaptation* or *recovery* (ibid.: 297). In this sense, resilience in CT and P/CVE draws on social-ecological resilience models (ibid.: 298), which broadly understand resilience as '...processes of recovery, adaptation, or systemwide transformation before, during, and after exposure to adversity' (Ungar 2021: 6). Thus resilience, like violent extremism, terrorism and radicalisation or non-radicalisation, can be understood as a multi-systemic and interactive process that takes place within and between several nested or co-occurring interdependent systems (e.g. an individual child and their family), their parts and across different scales (e.g. spatial scales, time scales, organisational scales) and various systemic contexts and situations (Ungar 2018, 2021; Bouhana 2019; Grossman 2021). Drawing on these conceptualisations, in this chapter, resilience is used to understand a process manifest primarily as resistance – to encounters with radical(ising) messages and their messengers – in situations of the exposure (of individual marksmen, marksmen's clubs and their umbrella organisations) to adversity. In some situations, however, it will be shown also how such resilience leads to the adjustment of behaviour or learning (adaptation) or even more comprehensive and radical change of the system exposed to adversity (transformation) (Ungar 2018: 7–9; 2021: 20).

Existing studies of non-radicalisation are set in the context of civil or military conflict (e.g. Cragin 2014; Cragin et al. 2015) or concerned with the non-practice of political or terrorist violence (Schuurman 2020) or the more general differentiation between violent and non-violent extremism (Holt et al. 2018; Becker 2021; Pritchett and Moeller 2021). In contrast, this contribution focuses on the everyday engagement with radical(ising) messages, and those who convey them, of individuals who are non-radicalised or weakly radicalised. Specifically, it considers how such messages and messengers are either rejected or normalised by individuals and in the context of the marksmen's club milieu.

German Marksmanship and German Marksmen's Clubs

The history of German marksmanship is centuries old (see Leineweber et al. 2020: 19–51),[2] dating back to the Middle Ages, when marksmen's clubs first appeared in the form of marksmen's guilds and brotherhoods and provided security, protection and order within medieval towns. Today it is recognised as an 'intangible cultural heritage'; according to the German UNESCO Commission, 'in many regions, marksmanship is an important and vibrant part of the regional or local identity. It incorporates many customs and traditions, which manifest themselves in different ways' (Deutsche UNESCO-Kommision n.d.). The marksmen's club milieu, with its over one million marksmen throughout Germany, is characterised by a strong sense of community and a Christian and middle-class or civic self-understanding. In the public perception, marksmen's clubs are considered to be rather conservative (Burger 2014). This is reflected in the importance placed by many clubs on values, history, customs and traditions,[3] and their often hierarchical or military organisational structure. While some clubs focus on so-called 'cultivation of tradition and customs' (*Traditions und Brauchtumspflege*), celebrated in particular at annual marksmen's festivals,[4] others emphasise shooting sports;[5] this split began in the Weimar Republic when the number of club memberships and newly founded clubs increased sharply (Leineweber et al. 2020: 30).

Regarding their political positioning, marksmen's clubs in general can be understood as a milieu of the political mainstream or the social centre of society (*Mitte der Gesellschaft*), which is also reflected in the milieu's self-understanding. Thus, in selecting the marksmen's milieu for research, it is not suggested that the wider milieu, or individual clubs, are either radical or extreme right-wing in a classically defined sense. Rather, it recognises that the milieu exhibits various characteristics attractive to right-wing and extreme right-wing agents, which makes it a target for such actors, who may seek to influence or appropriate elements of it. These characteristics include its membership profile (being predominantly white, male and Christian) as well as the traditionalist orientation of many marksmen's clubs and strong attachment to 'home' (*Heimat*) (so-called '*Heimatverbundenheit*'). The marksmen's club milieu is also known for its structures and rituals borrowed from the military, training in the use of firearms and the practising of shooting sports. Indeed, one of the few means to legally acquire and possess small firearms and ammunition in Germany is through engagement in shooting sports, through the issuing of a 'gun ownership card' (*Waffenbesitzkarte*). A number of racist and right-wing terrorist attacks and killings have been perpetrated by members of marksmen's clubs. These include the murder (in 2019) of the district president of Kassel, Walter Lübcke, and the racist attack in Hanau (in 2020), in which the perpetrator killed nine people of immigrant background as well as his own mother (Lohr, Meyer and Thiele 2019; Weber 2020). Field research in a number of marksmen's clubs for this study has suggested, moreover, that the marksmen's club milieu is a site of encounter with radical(ising) messages and those who promote them. In selecting the marksmen's milieu, however, it was also envisaged that some characteristics of this milieu – including (Christian) values, a strong sense of community and a set of democratic and participatory structures – might work to prevent young people from becoming radicalised, at least to the point of violent political extremism. Thus, the milieu appeared a promising site to explore not only radicalisation but also trajectories and pathways of non-radicalisation (Kerst 2021a, 2021b).

Empirical Approach and Dataset

This chapter draws on empirical data collected during field research conducted between December 2018 and August 2019 as part of the Dialogue about Radicalisation and Equality (DARE) project. Of these data, twenty-three semi-structured interviews (audio recorded, transcribed and analysed) with young members of German marksmen's clubs have been used for this chapter alongside data from ethnographic observation in the milieu. The interviews were conducted with informed consent and were carried out either in the author's office or at a location chosen by the respondents, such as local pubs or clubhouses. All respondents gave informed written consent prior to the interview in line with the ethical guidelines of the project.

The marksmen's clubs to which the respondents belong are located in urban areas, in medium-sized and large cities, or particular districts of these cities, in a western German region where marksmanship is relatively strong. Most respondents live in the cities or districts of the city where their clubs are located. In total, respondents from five clubs were interviewed; thirteen respondents came from a single club, six from a second club and the remaining four respondents were drawn from three other clubs. The respondents were on average 23.5 years old, and the median age was twenty-five. At the time of the interviews, the youngest respondent was sixteen years old, and the oldest respondent was thirty-two. Twelve respondents were male, and eleven respondents were female. It is worth noting that the gender and age profiles of research participants do not reflect the average gender and age profile of membership of the marksmen's clubs, which have a high proportion of male[6] and older members (Deutscher Schützenbund 2019; Leineweber et al. 2020: 58–59). The age profile of the study was dictated by the overall DARE project, which focused on young people (between twelve and thirty years old). The project also encouraged including women's views and experiences in the milieus even where they were a minority. The study's sample does closely correspond with wider marksmen's club membership distribution in relation to religious affiliation and ethnic background. Twenty respondents were of German origin, and twenty-three respondents were Christian (although not all of them were practising) and white. This corresponds to a study by the Federal Institute for Sports Science, which showed that in 2009, only 5% of members of marksmen's clubs had an immigration background (Breuer and Wicker 2011: 151 ff.), but also to the accounts of respondents and field observations.

Ethnographic field data were collected through participation in numerous events in the marksmen's milieu, especially marksmen's festivals and other events such as summer parties or shooting competitions. The clubs I researched, or key marksmen in these clubs, were informed about my research from the outset. I carried out my research as a 'participant observer' but also as an 'observing participant', that is, through involvement in the activities and practices engaged in by others, including my respondents, at these events (Hitzler and Gothe 2015: 10–12). I recorded my observations and experiences in the field in over a hundred pages of field diary.

In the following empirical sections, respondents' situational descriptions and narratives of their encounters with radical(ising) messages and their messengers, field observations and documentary research material are drawn on to illustrate respondents' trajectories as well as the strategies of engagement and response to radical(ising) messages and their messengers by individuals, the marksmen's clubs to which they belong and one of their umbrella organisations.

Encounters with Radical(ising) Messages and Their Messengers

The term 'radical(ising) messages' is used to refer to messages whose radical content can give rise to attitudes, feelings or actions that constitute or facilitate attitudinal/cognitive and behavioural radicalisation processes. Such content might be of a racist, anti-human, anti-democratic or neo-Nazi nature and, whatever its specific content, is more radical than the attitudes currently held by those exposed to it. It is delivered

Internet	Close Family and Friends	
- Anti-Muslim racist images in Whats App friends groups - (Extreme) right-wing people among FB 'friends' - Racist discussions in FB neighborhood groups - Far-right party FB posts	- (Grand-) parents with anti-Muslim views - Ex neo-Nazi sibling - Right-wing oriented friends - Friends with anti-Muslim views - Far-right voting family members	**Leisure Time** - Racist comments in the park Neo-Nazis and extreme right-wing hools in the football stadium - Right-wingers in local pub

Examples of encounters with radical(ising) messages and their messengers

Marksmen's Clubs		Public Spaces
- Racist/right-wing attitudes of older marksmen - Past, and continued unofficial use of racist term in club - Disussions of refugees in a racist and dehumanising way - (Radical/extreme) right-wing posts on FB by marksmen		- Right-wing extremist group and neo-Nazis in the neighbourhood - Extreme right-wing or Islamist stickers - 'Heil Hitler' shouts from drunks on the street

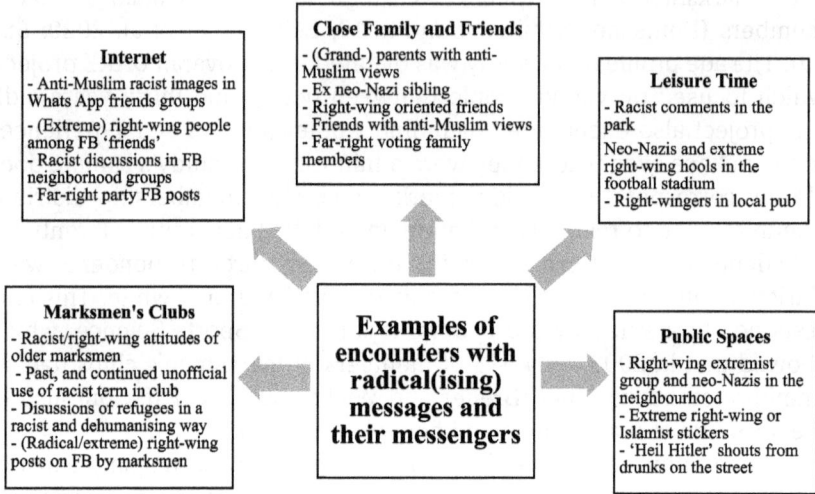

Figure 8.1. Examples of encounters with radical(ising) messages and their messengers. Created by Benjamin Kerst.

in 'messages' that may take a wide range of forms including statements, utterances, slogans, arguments, appeals, jokes, flyers, posters or social media posts. Certain ways of dressing, adorning the body or acting may also be said to constitute a form of radical(ising) message.

Those who convey these messages do not necessarily have to be radical or extreme to trigger or fuel radicalisation processes through the messages they disseminate, or through other interactions, and, in this way, become agents of radicalisation. Radical(ising) messages and messengers can manifest in different systemic contexts, such as the immediate social environment (family or circle of friends), within different milieus (such as the marksmen's club milieu), in public spaces or on the internet. The dataset revealed more than forty encounters with radical(ising) messages and their messengers among respondent narratives, mostly in the systemic context of their family, friends and acquaintances, at school, at work, or in the marksmen's clubs as well as in their neighbourhoods, local pub, city districts, public spaces, football stadiums or online environments. Respondents encountered such messages in situations such as discussions with friends, during everyday activities in the neighbourhood or at the marksmen's festival. Some respondents reported only occasional encounters while, for others, these situations were more frequent; regular encounters were experienced, for example, by respondents who had right-wing friends and acquaintances and by members of one particular club, who regularly came across 'racist' or 'right-wing' jokes and remarks (see Figure 8.1).

Situations and Factors of Resilience: The Individual Level

At the individual level, rejection of radical(ising) messages and/or their messengers was evident in a range of situations narrated by respondents while their reflections on these responses suggest a number of important factors that build resilience to radicalisation.

Rejecting Radical Messages and/or Their Messengers

At the individual level, the research data reveal a variety of degrees, and ways, of rejecting radical(ising) messages. This illustrates the interactive, contextual and situational character of resilience towards radical(ising) messages and their messengers and of pathways of non-radicalisation.

The complete rejection of such messages and those who convey them is illustrated in the case of Anne, who rejects what she considers unacceptable right-wing content shared online by deleting the responsible person from her Facebook (FB) 'friends' list. She explains her decision thus:

> I kicked him off, because, at some point, his political opinion became too extreme for me. He regularly stirred up hatred . . . And he also shared many articles from the AfD [Alternative für Deutschland] party and so on. So, I thought to myself, 'No. I don't want to have that kind of thing in my list' . . . Maybe that's also intolerant of me, undoubtedly – because actually I should accept his political opinion – but I don't want to be confronted with it every day. (Anne)

Anne's response not only displays resilience as resistance but enacts a form of adaptation; by removing this individual, she has changed her online environment in such a way that the likelihood of future encounters with radical(ising) messages and their messengers is reduced.

Jana is more inclined to engage in 'heated debates' with 'right-wing oriented' friends but also seeks to stop the flow of those political views she does not agree with when they become too much. At a certain point, she tells these 'right-wing' friends, 'I like being friends with you, but I don't want to talk about politics with you in that case' (Jana). In this sense, like Anne, Jana's strategy is to try to change her social environment, in this case her friends' behaviour, so that she is less confronted with radical(ising) messages. Unlike Anne, however, she only rejects the messages and not the messengers. She continues to engage in argument and dialogue with her friends, partly with the aim of changing their views; she sometimes succeeds.

Vanessa also struggled with some of her friends' views on immigration and immigrants, expressed in comments such as 'bloody foreigners' and 'they have no business here' or blanket generalisations like 'Muslim equals terrorist'. Her response was to challenge such statements, arguing that 'you can't lump them all together' and pointing out that, following such logic, another friend in their group, who had an immigration background from a Muslim majority country, would be made to leave the country. Like Jana, Vanessa thinks that she has dissuaded friends from their views as a result of such discussions. Jana's and Vanessa's encounters and responses to radical(ising) messages and those who convey them within their circle of friends appears to involve an interactive process of non-radicalisation, in which both show an adaptive form of resilience to these messages by challenging (as well as suppressing) these views and entering into dialogue with those who promote them. Given that this strategy, at least sometimes, leads to a shift in views among their friends, Jana and Vanessa's disputative and dialogical interactions might also be interpreted as contributing to the development of a certain resilience among their friends in that they prevent their progression to more radical views or attitudinal or behavioural support for violent extremism. Data from this study cannot demonstrate whether this is likely to result in any long-term or comprehensive change in the political views within these circles of friends. However, it suggests that milieu actors are engaging in what might be called a kind of informal radicalisation prevention or non-radicalisation practice (for further discussion, see Kerst 2021b).

Not all respondents are so decisive in their rejection of radical(ising) messages and may find their resilience weakened by messages they encounter through their immediate social environment or on social media. Camilla considered herself politically neutral or leaning towards the 'left-wing'; she had never voted 'right-wing' and could not imagine ever doing so. She thinks it is 'dangerous' that many people vote for far-right parties and says some of those close to her had done so and have critical or negative attitudes towards refugees, immigrants and immigration policy. However, discussions with these friends and family, as well as AfD and other right-wing content on social media, had made Camilla doubt her decision not to vote for the AfD and influenced her political views:

> . . . I have discussed this with my colleagues at work, I have discussed it with my friends and family. There are many people who say that we

should vote for the AfD party or The Right [a small German, neo-Nazi, extreme right-wing party], because then you are more likely to be heard and some change in politics would be more likely to happen. And at one point, I started to hesitate and think, 'yes, hmm, hmm, they are not wrong'. And, after the elections, there was really a moment, very briefly, where I thought, 'wow, did you vote correctly or should you have also. . .'. (Camilla)

Camilla's narrative provides insight into the interactions, contexts (family, romantic relationship, work, social media) and situations (discussions, reading social media content) in which her political views shifted towards a more radical position. However, her reflections also indicate how this relative radicalisation, itself as much an emotional as an ideological process, is interrupted by moments of resilience:

Well, I do read some [online] articles [referring to online content from right-wing parties] and catch myself thinking: 'Wow. Are you really clicking on that now? If anyone saw you looking at this.' Then, I am really thinking: 'What would others think. . .?' But you read it anyway and you always think: 'Wow, they are actually right. . . . We let everybody in and why didn't we register [those entering the country] somehow differently? But then . . . I catch myself feeling ashamed of the fact that I sometimes think like that. Because I don't think all people are the same. . . . Even if my boyfriend or my work colleague [do think like that] . . . Lots of people [have negative attitudes towards refugees and immigrants] . . . Like being quick to say, 'wow, them [refugees or immigrants] again' or 'they are getting something again'. That often happens when you are overwhelmed by emotions. And then, when you think about it again, I think, 'wow, what did I just say?' Or, 'was that so right?' And, 'if you were in that situation, you wouldn't want to be treated like that either'. That's the point [of reflection] when I just don't get it. Not at all. Because, at that moment, it seems that it's just not human. (Camilla)

At these moments, feelings of shame, empathy and the reflection they invoke furnish Camilla with a resilience to radical(ising) messages, and those who convey them (even when they are very close to her), and stall potential radicalisation.

Individual Factors of Resilience

Alongside insight into the processual, interactive, contextual and situational character of non-radicalisation and resilience that can be gleaned from how individuals respond to encounters with radical(ising) messages and their messengers, the data also allow the identification of a number of factors of resilience to these messages. These may be individual factors, such as experiences, desires or views, which participants 'charged up with emotions and consciousness' (Collins 2004: 3) bring into the interaction, but can also be properties of higher-level systems such as groups and communities. In both cases, these 'background conditions' (Collins 2008: 21–22) shape and are shaped by the interaction.

In Camilla's case (see above), while negative sentiments towards refugees and immigrants[7] appeared to make her susceptible to radical(ising) messages, a sense of shame about those feelings also worked as a factor of resilience to, or protection from, such messages (Kerst 2021b). Camilla also feels a certain, at least residual, trust in established parties and politics, stating, 'It is still the case that I think there is definitely a solution and that politics is there for that'. This is reflected also in her belief that it is important to vote in order to 'express your opinion'. The belief that it is possible to change something by democratic means is also shared by other respondents and potentially confirms that 'democratic citizenship' may work as an individual factor of resilience against violent extremism (Sieckelinck and Gielen 2017; Council of Europe 2018: 114). Camilla's engagement also demonstrates her ability to empathise, a capacity that has been identified by P/CVE researchers as an individual factor in resilience to extremism (Feddes, Mann and Doosje 2015; Lösel et al. 2018; Grossman 2021: 298) and which explains respondents' rejections of radical(ising) messages and their messengers. Camilla's reflection that not all people are the same, mirrored by other respondents' statements that it is wrong to generalise when considering issues of immigration and multicultural coexistence, also indicates adherence to a fundamental idea of humanity. This is found also among respondents who base their understanding of equality on the fact that 'human is human' and 'it doesn't matter how someone looks or whatever. . .' (Vanessa). These principles all reflect Schwartz's (1992) basic value of 'universalism', which also includes understanding, appreciation and tolerance (see also Schwartz and Boehnke 2004: 239).

Camilla's response to the adversity of radical(ising) messages and their messengers demonstrates a wider ability to reflect, differentiate, question her own views and tolerate ambiguity. Together, these suggest a certain open-mindedness, including the willingness to engage in dialogue (see also Pilkington 2020: 49–51; 2022; Kerst 2021b: 114–15). Such open-mindedness is also identified as a possible factor of resilience in the context of preventing violent extremism (BOUNCE n.d.; Sieckelinck and Gielen 2017; Council of Europe 2018; Stephens and Sieckelinck 2021: 4). Moreover, this open-mindedness is contrasted by Camilla, and other respondents, to the closed-mindedness that they associate with those who convey radical(ising) messages, who are described as right-wing individuals who 'do not think outside the box. They only look inside themselves instead of looking out to the world' (Julian). As discussed extensively in the literature, such closed-mindedness is characterised by a 'need for closure' (Kruglanski 2004), the need for clear-cut knowledge, the avoidance of uncertainty, and intolerance of ambiguity and challenges to one's worldview and considered a key cognitive disposition associated with extremism, especially right-wing extremism (Kruglanski 2004; Kruglanski and Orehek 2012; Schmid 2013; for a critique of this association, see Pilkington 2022).

As is evident from respondents' differentiation of themselves from closed-minded, right-wing individuals, many viewed negatively what they perceived as right-wing, and especially as radical or extreme right-wing. Most respondents associated the terms 'radical' or 'extreme' with the 'right-wing camp', far-right parties, like the AfD, 'aggressive neo-Nazis' or actions and attitudes such as right-wing violence, 'racial hostility' and 'xenophobia'.[8] Anton used 'incomprehension', 'grief' and 'suffering' when describing what the terms 'radicalism' and 'extremism' meant to him, while Alexander associated them with 'fear' and said that he tried to avoid and (mentally) distance himself from anything radical or extreme. Ronja explained that she had not voted for the far-right AfD party, even though she agrees with the party's assertion that too many refugees have been received, 'because they are presented as right-wing'. Many other respondents rejected the AfD at least partially because they viewed it as a right-wing or right-wing radical/extremist party, while Frederik, who considers himself 'somewhat right-wing', rejected the party because it was 'more right-wing than me'. As demonstrated by Camilla (see above), the high level of stigma attached to right-wing radicalism or extremism in Germany means that many respondents feel, or would feel, ashamed of having thoughts that might be considered right-wing (Kerst 2021b). This might be considered another possible factor in the resilience of respondents to radical(ising) messages and their messengers and, thus, also as part of the explanation for their non-radicalisation.

The highly negative association with extremism, especially right-wing extremism, is evident among the broader German population.[9] It is a stigma rooted in German history as refracted through the highly critical approach to the German National Socialist past and current phenomena of right-wing extremism conveyed through civic or political education. Such education may be understood as another dimension to the 'democratic citizenship' noted above that acts to promote resilience to (violent) radicalism/extremism. This is reflected in Peter's rejection of violence as a means to reach political goals: '. . .whenever I have an opportunity to vote, to participate, to change something, I think it's unrealistic [to use violence]. I do not need violence in Germany' (Peter). Such a rejection of (political) violence was found among the majority of the respondents, while two-thirds of the respondents connected terms like (right-wing) 'radical', 'extreme' or related phenomena to physical (political) violence (and sometimes also to verbal violence and closed-mindedness). Thus, the data suggest that respondents evaluate (right-wing) radical/extreme phenomena as negative, in addition to rejecting phenomena across the right-wing political spectrum, because they evaluate (verbal/political) violence associated with these phenomena as negative.

When considering individual factors of resilience to radical messages and their messengers, therefore, in addition to personal capacities for open-mindedness, empathy, shame, trust in democratic institutions and adherence to universal principles of humanity, negative associations with (violent) right-wing radicalism or extremism can be considered an important factor also.

Situations and Factors of Resilience: The Milieu Level

The rejection of radical(ising) messages and/or their messengers was identified in this study not only at the individual level but also at the level of the milieu (in individual marksmen's clubs as well as marksmen's clubs' umbrella organisations). Such rejections are facilitated by a number of milieu-specific factors of resilience that became evident during field research. Exploring rejections of radical(ising) messages and resilience factors at this level reveals how resilience can develop in extra-individual systems such as organisations and communities (Grossman 2021: 299–300). It also allows insight into how resilience at the milieu level impacts on the resilience and non-radicalisation of individual milieu actors and vice versa.

Rejections of Radical(ising) Messages and/or Their Messengers in the Marksmen's Club Milieu

One of the most striking examples of the rejection of radical(ising) messages and their messengers encountered during fieldwork were the declarations made by the Catholic 'Historic German Marksmen's Brotherhood'[10] (Bund der Historischen Deutschen Schützenbruderschaften, BHDS) umbrella organisation and its youth organisation 'Federation of the St. Sebastianus Marksmen's Youth' (Bund der St. Sebastianus Schützenjugend, BdSJ). These declarations stated the incompatibility of membership of the AfD party with membership of the BHDS/BdSJ (Staudenmaier 2020; Kirche und Leben 2021) and were issued following attempts by the AfD to influence and appropriate Catholic marksmen's clubs, for example by distributing flyers to the BHDS, and their clubs, which sought to appeal to the reservations of sports shooters and hunters about a tightening of gun control laws (Staudenmaier 2020). In an interview on this issue, the first president of the BHDS responded to the overtures made by the AfD by stating, 'For us, home is not only the place where I was born and grew up. Home is not defined by origin, nationality, skin colour or religion. For us, home is the place where I feel at home and secure. Our Christian view of humanity is clearly different from the ideas and statements of the AfD'[11] (Zerback 2020). This case might be understood as an illustration of the resilience of systems such as organisations and communities consisting in a multi-systemic interactive process that takes place between different systems and subsystems (BHDS, BdSJ, member clubs of the umbrella organisation, political organisations like the AfD party, the press, individuals such as the first president of the BHDS etc.) and at different scales (e.g., following a change of rules, declarations of incompatibility with the AfD party are now allowed by clubs). In this way, the resilience of the BHDS and the BdSJ can be understood not only as resilience in the sense of a process of resistance, but also as a process of adaptation and transformation as these organisations implement far-reaching changes in the wake of the AfD's attempts at influence and appropriation.

At the level of individual marksmen's clubs, the field research also revealed processes of resilience that we might consider as episodes of resistance of these clubs to radical(ising) messages and their messengers. For example, in two cases where individual marksmen made statements or comments reflecting xenophobic or extreme right-wing sympathies, the club's management responded by speaking to those concerned. Even if it is not clear whether these conversations led to a real shift in attitudes, the conversations stopped these behaviours. Another example is the case of two marksmen who posted right-wing content on Facebook, as a result of which they were excluded from their clubs. Anton, from whose club a marksman was expelled, alongside those fellow marksmen who defended him, supports such strict measures:

> Because it's just not tolerable. I think the marksmen's club is very clear on that point. I think it is right and symbolic to say. Because we can't claim that, 'Everyone is welcome here, no matter what skin colour, no matter what cultural background' while, on the other hand, tolerating that. Or to say, 'Hey, you – don't do that again'. It's not appropriate. (Anton)

Factors of Resilience in the Marksmen's Club Milieu

As at the individual level, such examples of responses to radical(ising) messages and their messengers can be used to identify possible background conditions that work as factors of resilience in the milieu or individual clubs within it. These examples suggest that certain values associated with the club milieu are evoked in rejecting radical(ising) messages.

In the example of the statement of incompatibility of the BHDS umbrella organisation with the AfD party above, the first president of the organisation directly referenced the importance of Christian values in taking this stand. The prevalence of these Christian values in his marksmen's club was also cited by Peter when explaining how he had become conflicted about the 'extremist ideas' within a neo-Nazi group of which he had been a member at that time. In his marksmen's club, he said, he learned also to help and stand up for other people, challenge bullying and voice his views in a democratic way. This suggests that Christian values, as well as democratic structures and a strong sense of community in the marksmen's clubs (Kerst 2021b), can also contribute to the individual resilience of marksmen in resisting radical(ising) messages and their messengers and ensure pathways of relative non-radicalisation, or, as in the case of Peter, deradicalisation.

The field research also revealed a certain culture of openness in some marksmen's clubs – as indicated by Anton's reflections above. This was reflected also in the positions stated by members of marksmen's clubs' management boards, when speaking for example at marksmen's festivals. In addition to openly speaking out against racism, right-wing populism and right-wing extremism, they also emphasised cosmopolitan values, open-mindedness, diversity, tolerance and multicultural coexistence. This culture of openness corresponds to the open-mindedness of respondents noted above and, as such, shapes, or at least reinforces, such a disposition among individual club members. That this culture of openness is a factor that protects young people in her club from radicalisation is articulated directly by Lara:

> Because the club already conveys such an open image. We accept everyone and if then maybe people from other cultures come to the club and you live near each other and then you get to know something about their culture, but you can also show them the marksmen's club and your own culture, this helps. . . . So, it was not explicitly said that it was open to everybody. That was just somehow clear, because nobody was ever looked at in a strange way or . . . it was always out of the question that people from other cultures or nationalities couldn't come into the club. That was somehow irrelevant. It was other things

that mattered – whether people were nice or so on, not their origin or accent or anything. (Lara)

In this way, a culture of openness appears to constitute a factor of resilience towards radical(ising) messages and their messengers at the club level and act as an effective non-radicalising force.

Normalisations of Radical(ising) Messages and Their Messengers

Alongside the widespread rejection of radical(ising) messages and their messengers discussed above, this study also revealed examples of where such messages were received uncritically or were played down, tolerated, accepted, perceived as normal, or evaluated as benevolent and positive; to a degree at least, they became normalised. Such normalisation was found both inside and outside the marksmen's club context and is explored below drawing on two particular examples and focusing on the interactive, contextual and situational dimensions of the normalisation of such messages and its implications for radicalisation.

The first example concerns the attitude among some respondents towards a violent right-wing extremist group active in the district of one of the researched marksmen's clubs. These respondents appeared forgiving or accepting of this group, members of whom were also visibly present at their club's marksmen's festival. Not only did their presence go unchallenged but I observed interactions, such as greetings and conversations, between some marksmen and members of the group. One respondent with whom I spoke even felt that the presence of this group helped maintain safety at the festival:

> Researcher: And what do you know about them [the right-wing extremist group]?
> Steven: [breathing noticeably and pausing a few seconds before answering] They are also ordinary people [tinged with laughter] like you and me. Right? Well, really calm, they don't come here [to the festival] and play up or whatever. I have never seen that. They don't want that either. They really do keep law and order here [at the festival] because their presence is a bit of a deterrent, I think.

Other respondents told me that, when walking past them or chatting to them, members of the group had not acted in a hostile way to them or others; their members were 'nice' or 'harmless'. Although considering the group to be 'far-right', Anne believed that they would not act violently: 'They might say, when a person [with foreign appearance] had gone, they

might get upset about the person or say, "shame on Germany" or whatever. But I don't think they're really that extreme. Or even radical enough
to attack someone who walks past them. I don't believe that' (Anne). The
group may have been accepted at the festival because respondents, and
other marksmen, were, to various degrees, acquainted with the group.[12]
Of course, the respondents in this study also encountered the group primarily in everyday situations in which they did not behave violently and
this might also explain why the group was not considered radical.

The second example concerns a number of young male members
of another marksmen's club, who are 'right-wing' and frequently make
racist and right-wing jokes and statements within the club milieu itself.
Mona, another member of this club, explained that she responded to
such jokes and statements with a gently disapproving 'come on, boys'.
She accepts their behaviour as 'all right', explaining that, '. . .they only
talk among themselves. They don't have a go at anyone or anything. . . .
But uhm, as long as they just talk, I don't care'. She would only intervene,
she said, 'if they were really yelling at someone and attacking someone
or whatever'. When I asked Mona, like other respondents, if she thought
that her marksmen's club could do anything to counter radicalisation, she
felt that, on a small scale, they could talk critically, for example, to AfD
voters. However, she does not believe that anything could be done to stop
radicalisation in the group of young marksmen she mentioned:

> Because we are also among ourselves, because we are also predom-
> inantly German. If someone has something against something or
> somebody, then he says, 'yes, for this and that reason'. And uhm then
> you talk more about it and then it is often the case that you say, 'oh
> yes, that's right and so on'. And then you just have this one-track
> thinking again. . . . Well, there are also discussions, but that is a bit
> difficult and it is quite rare to be divided, for example, when it comes
> to foreigners. (Mona)

Mona's descriptions of the contexts in which the normalisation of radi-
cal(ising) messages and their messengers manifests indicates the proces-
suality, interactivity, contextuality and situativity of such normalisations.
These situations are ones in which club members feel 'among ourselves',
in which, due to the relative ethnic homogeneity of the group, she thinks,
others, such as 'foreigners', are spoken about and discussed in a uniform manner, leading to individuals confirming, rather than challenging,
each other's opinions. In addition, as in the case of the acceptance of the
right-wing extremist group, racist and right-wing jokes and statements
of fellow marksmen are perceived as relatively unproblematic because
they did not involve acts of physical violence. This view was encoun-

tered among other respondents with right-wing persons in their close social environment, who, like Mona, would only find that a real problem if they were (verbally) violent towards others or openly right-wing extremist. Thus, Maria, another member of this club, considered the jokes and statements of her fellow marksmen as 'a bit radical' but not extreme; they would become the latter only if they started 'to distribute flyers or conduct propaganda in the right-wing direction. . . . Or if they were beating up people, which fortunately they don't'. 'As long as it stays with some drunken jokes', she continues, 'I think you can still tell them to take a break'. Thus, within the respondent set, radical(ising) messages and their messengers were rejected, among other things, when they were perceived as right-wing and especially as radical/extreme right-wing or as radical/extreme in general or accompanied by (political) violence. If this was not the case, and radical(ising) messages and their messengers did not cross the line into the attitudinal or behavioural support for political violence and/or were not associated with organised (violent) radical/ extremist right-wing behaviour, like neo-Nazism, they were, in contrast, normalised by some respondents.

The implications of the normalisation of radical(ising) messages and their messengers are two-fold. First, such normalisation facilitates the expression of hostile attitudes towards certain groups, expressed as anti-Muslim racism or right-wing extremist attitudes. This is a cause for concern since such attitudes correlate significantly with the acceptance of, and willingness to use, violence (against immigrants and other groups) (Zick, Küpper and Hövermann 2011: 118–21; Küpper, Berghan and Rees 2019: 194; Zick et al. 2019: 99–102) or with the intention to vote for anti-immigrant parties or to discriminate against immigrants (Zick, Küpper and Hövermann 2011: 115–18, 121). Second, this normalisation can provide an entry point and fertile soil for extreme right-wing closed-mindedness or trigger entry into corresponding milieus across the right-wing political spectrum. Thus, such attitudes can be elements of, or facilitate, attitudinal/cognitive and behavioural radicalisation processes. When radical(ising) messages and their messengers are normalised, they can also lead to a social climate in which, as was visible in the case of the right-wing extremist group at the marksmen's festival and in Mona's situational descriptions, no need for interventions, counteractions or distancing seems necessary and in which critical opinions are not challenged or are even confirmed. This increases the risk of non-radicalised individuals being radicalised or radical and extreme individuals having their views and behaviours confirmed, as, it might be assumed, was the case in the marksmen's club in which the murderer of Walter Lübcke was a member. In a television interview about this case, the chairman of the marksmen's club in which the perpetrator and his alleged accomplice (who has since been acquitted of this charge) were members reportedly claimed that neither of these individuals had been noticed as a 'right-wing extremist'. He is also quoted as saying that 'politics, however, had been discussed . . . After all, many people did not like the immigration policy'[13] (Feldmann and Seidel 2021). This does not mean that disagreement with immigration policy is always radical or extreme, but in this case, it is possible that the individuals mentioned felt confirmed or at least not contradicted in their radical or extreme views.

Arguably, the tendency towards the normalisation of negative and prejudicial attitudes towards (minority) groups and radical or extreme right-wing views, or at least the tendency to see them as problematic only when they are linked with far-right parties or right-wing extremist organisations or when they cross the line into political violence, is evident in German society more widely. Such attitudes are not only found on the radical/extreme and violent fringes of society but exist in what has been called 'extremism of the centre' (Decker, Kiess and Brähler 2016), in the political mainstream, or in the social centre of society (*Mitte der Gesellschaft*) (Schröter 2019b; Zick, Küpper and Berghan 2019; Zick, Küpper and Schröter 2021). Over recent years, this normalisation of radical(ising) messages and their messengers across the right-wing of the political spectrum has become more permanent or even increased in the social centre due to the mainstreaming of the extreme and a corresponding shift to the right (Brähler et al. 2016; Melzer 2016; Decker and Brähler 2018; Schröter 2019a; Kerst 2021a; Zick, Küpper and Schröter 2021). Ultimately, such normalisation of radical(ising) messages and their messengers can weaken and erode possible resources to prevent and counter radicalisation in the marksmen's club milieu and society as a whole.

Conclusion

This chapter has explored how young members of selected marksmen's clubs in Germany, as well as the clubs themselves and their umbrella organisations, engage with, and respond to, radical(ising) messages and their messengers in concrete, everyday situations. It identified the existence of a spectrum of responses from outright rejection to the normalisation of such messages and those who convey them. Drawing on the latest developments in the theorisation of resilience to radicalisation, it has been suggested that these findings support a multi-systemic, processual and interactional understanding of resilience and non-radicalisation. This is reflected in the concrete processes identified of *resistance* to radical(ising) messages and their messengers but also *adaptation* to such messages and messengers in individuals' immediate social circle. The empirical research also identified processes by which radical messages were halted (by suppressing political discussion in friendship circles or removing those conveying them from one's communicative circle) or disputed, through dialogical engagement. In this way, individuals in these milieus either remained non-radicalised, or showed partial radicalisation, often interrupted by episodes of resilience (for example expressed in feelings of shame or reflection), or even engaged in informal radicalisation prevention by challenging the views of those conveying radical(ising) messages.

Alongside the importance of the situational dimensions of the encounter with radical(ising) messages, the study allowed the identification of a number of factors of resilience to radicalisation. At the individual level, these included personal capacities for reflection, open-mindedness, empathy and the experience of emotions such as shame as well as the presence of certain values such as humanism and the negative evaluation of (right-wing) radicalism/extremism and (political) violence. At the level of the marksmen's club milieu, Christian values, democratic structures, a strong sense of community as well as a culture of openness were identified as factors that can also increase the resilience of individual marksmen towards the adversity of radical(ising) messages and their messengers. While these factors demonstrate resilience as *resistance*, the study also identified resilience as a process of *adaptation* and *transformation* in the example of the multiscale interaction of a marksmen's umbrella organisation with the far-right AfD party, following the latter's attempts to influence and appropriate parts of the milieu. Through this dual-level (individual and milieu) approach, the empirical data drawn on in this chapter not only demonstrate the interactive and processual nature of resilience, and its non-radicalising effects at intra- and extra-individual levels, but also provide insight into how extra-individual resilience processes at the marksmen's club milieu level can impact individual processes of resilience and non-radicalisation.

At the other end of the response spectrum, the interactive dynamics of the normalisation of radical(ising) messages and their messengers were explored. This discussion drew on empirical examples of encounters in the neighbourhood, or at marksmen's festivals, with right-wing extremists and of responses to racist and right-wing statements and jokes within a marksmen's youth group. Such normalisations appeared to take place first and foremost where the messages, and messengers, encountered were perceived as not supporting political violence (attitudinally or behaviourally), or as not associated with organised (violent) right-wing radical/extremist behaviour, such as neo-Nazism. Such normalisation, it was suggested, could counteract factors that prevent radicalisation and fuel radicalisation processes also on a societal level.

This study of young marksmen and markswomen, their clubs, and the broader marksmen's club milieu has identified factors that contribute to explaining resilience to radical(ising) messages (and thus to non-radicalisation and the prevention of radicalisation) but also to the normalisation of such messages and their messengers, that can undermine these factors. Encounters with radical(ising) messages and their messengers take place in everyday life and everyday situations where, in the course of interactions that take place there, such factors of resilience may develop or become activated or strengthened. As a consequence, individuals, and milieus, may reflect and adjust what they consider legitimate and what is too radical, what should be criticised and what should not, but are able to resist attitudinal or behavioural support for political violence and remain relatively non-radicalised. However, the encounter of radical(ising) messages and agents in such everyday situations may also lead to their underestimation, toleration, acceptance, perception as normal or evaluation as benevolent and positive; they become, in some sense, normalised. Thus, the study of such everyday situations, with their specific interactions and dynamics, is critical for understanding radicalisation, non-radicalisation and the prevention of radicalisation.

Acknowledgements

The research drawn on in this chapter is part of the Dialogue about Radicalisation and Equality (DARE) project, which received funding from the European Union's Horizon 2020 research and innovation programme under Grant Agreement No. 725349. It reflects only the views of the author; the European Commission and Research Executive Agency are not responsible for any information it contains.

Benjamin Kerst, M.A. Philosophy and M.A. Sociology, is a research assistant at the Hochschule Düsseldorf–University of Applied Sciences, Germany. He has worked on a number of projects including the DARE project from 2018 to 2021. His current research focuses on radicalisation and non-radicalisation as well as recent phenomena of the extreme right such as vigilante right-wing extremist groups.

....

NOTES

1. In the marksmen's club milieu, the terms 'marksman' (*Schütze*) or 'marksmen' (*Schützen*) are the terms generally used to refer to members even by female club members, i.e. markswomen (*Schützinnen*). Thus, unless referring explicitly to markswomen, this chapter will use these terms whilst recognising that they refer to people of two or more genders.

2. For a more detailed history of (German) marksmanship and its various stages of development, see: Reintges 1963; Sauermann 1983; Stambolis 1999; Crombie 2016; and Kreyenschulte 2017. On the interesting and complex history of German marksmanship during National Socialism, see Borggräfe 2010.

3. The high value attached to tradition is evident in one of the few empirical studies on marksmanship, which found that 69% of the surveyed marksmen (n=3,871) thought the term 'tradition' 'strongly' applies to marksmen's clubs, and 28% responded that it 'applies' (Leineweber et al. 2020: 60, 70).

4. Marksmen's festivals (*Schützenfeste*) are probably the most famous of the marksmen's customs. They are annual events organised by every marksmen's club. In many cases, marksmen's festivals are not merely club events but function as whole village, town or city fêtes or folk festivals.

5. The clubs I researched can be categorised more as clubs that focus on traditions, customs and sociability, although they also engage (to various degrees of professionalism) in shooting sports.

6. Traditionally, marksmen's clubs were largely men-only clubs, and although this has gradually changed, some marksmen's clubs still do not allow women as active members. This was the case in one of the clubs I researched.

7. Camilla reported a sense of injustice – articulated by other respondents also – about the perceived favouring of refugees and immigrants over herself or the German population, for example in terms of state support (Kerst 2021a: 38–44).

8. Some respondents did also mention 'left-wing extremists' and, less frequently, 'Muslims', 'Islamist terrorists' and the 'Islamic State' in connection with these terms.

9. Representative German long-term studies on right-wing extremist attitudes in Germany show that only a very small proportion of the German population has a 'closed right-wing extremist worldview' (1.7% in the most recent of these studies) and that there is a broad rejection of extreme right-wing ideological content in the German population (Küpper, Zick and Rump 2021: 84–91).

10. The BHDS was founded in 1928 and is the largest umbrella organisation for its so-called 'marksmen's brotherhoods' (*Schützenbruderschaften*). It claims to have 400,000 members distributed across almost 1,300 clubs (European Community of Historic Guilds n.d.).

11. Translated by the author.

12. However, no respondent was a member of this group and as far as I know neither were any marksmen of this club.
13. Translated by the author.

....

REFERENCES

Becker, Michael H. 2021. 'When Extremists Become Violent: Examining the Association between Social Control, Social Learning, and Engagement in Violent Extremism', *Studies in Conflict & Terrorism* 44(12): 1104–24.

Borggräfe, Henning. 2010. *Schützenvereine im Nationalsozialismus* [Marksmen's Clubs under National Socialism]. Münster: Ardey-Verl.

Bouhana, Noémie. 2019. *The Moral Ecology of Extremism: A Systemic Perspective*. London: Commission for Countering Extremism. Retrieved 25 March 2022 from https://www.gov.uk/government/publications/the-moral-ecology-of-extremism-a-systemic-perspective.

BOUNCE. n.d. *Resilience Training, Network and Evaluation: STRESAVIORA II (Strengthening Resilience Against Violent Radicalisation) 2015–2018*. Brussels, Belgium: European Commission with the Egmont Institute. Retrieved 2 March 2022 from https://www.bounce-resilience-tools.eu/sites/default/files/downloads/2018-04/.

Brähler, Elmar et al. (eds). 2016. *Die enthemmte Mitte: Autoritäre und rechtsextreme Einstellung in Deutschland* [The Disinhibited Middle: Authoritarian and Right-Wing Extremist Attitudes in Germany]. Gießen: Psychosozial-Verlag.

Breuer, Christoph, and Pamela Wicker. 2011. *Die Situation der Sportarten in Deutschland: Eine Analyse der Sportvereine in Deutschland auf Basis der Sportentwicklungsberichte* [The Situation of Sports in Germany: An Analysis of Sports Clubs on the Basis of Sports Development Reports]. Cologne: Sportverl. Strauß.

Burger, Reiner. 2014. 'Was die Basiswelt zusammenhält' ['What Holds the World Together'], *FAZ.NET*. Retrieved 30 August 2021 from https://www.faz.net/aktuell/politik/inland/schuetzenvereine-was-die-basiswelt-zusammenhaelt-13088243.html.

Collins, Randall. 2004. *Interaction Ritual Chains*. Princeton, NJ: Princeton University Press.

———. 2008. *Violence: A Micro-Sociological Theory*. Princeton, NJ: Princeton University Press.

Council of Europe. 2018. 'Chapter 6: CDC and Building Resilience to Radicalisation Leading to Violent Extremism and Terrorism', in Council of Europe (ed.), *Reference Framework for Democratic Culture: Vol. 3. Guidance for Implementation*. Strasbourg: Council of Europe Publishing, pp. 101–23.

Cragin, R. Kim. 2014. 'Resisting Violent Extremism: A Conceptual Model for Non-Radicalization', *Terrorism and Political Violence* 26(2): 337–53.

Cragin, R. Kim, et al. 2015. 'What Factors Cause Youth to Reject Violent Extremism? Results of an Exploratory Analysis in the West Bank'. Santa Monica. Retrieved 24 March 2022 from https://www.rand.org/pubs/research_reports/RR1118.html.

Crombie, Laura. 2016. *Archery and Crossbow Guilds in Medieval Flanders, 1300–1500*. Woodbridge, UK: The Boydell Press.

Decker, Oliver, and Elmar Brähler (eds). 2018. *Flucht ins Autoritäre: Rechtsextreme Dynamiken in der Mitte der Gesellschaft: die Leipziger Autoritarismus-Studie 2018* [Escape into Authoritarianism. Right-Wing Extremist Dynamics in the Social Centre of Society: The 2018 Leipzig Authoritarianism Study]. Gießen: Psychosozial-Verlag.

Decker, Oliver, Johannes Kiess and Elmar Brähler. 2016. '"Fertile Soil for Ideological Confusion"? The Extremism of the Centre', in Johannes Kiess, Oliver Decker and Elmar Brähler (eds), *German Perspectives on Right-Wing Extremism: Challenges for Comparative Analysis*. London: Routledge Taylor & Francis Group, pp. 83–103.

Deutsche UNESCO-Kommision. n.d. 'Nationwide Inventory of Intangible Cultural Heritage: Marksmanship in Germany'. Retrieved 10 June 2021 from https://www.unesco.de/en/marksmanship-germany.

Deutscher Schützenbund. 2019. 'Mitgliederstand der Landesverbände des Deutschen Schützenbundes per 31.12.2019' ['Membership of Regional Branches of the German Shooting Association as of 31.12.2019']. Retrieved 27 September 2021 from https://www.dsb.de/fileadmin/_horusdam/4873-DSB_Mitgliederstand_31.12.2019.pdf.

Doosje, Bertjan, et al. 2016. 'Terrorism, Radicalization and De-radicalization', *Current Opinion in Psychology* 11: 79–84.

European Community of Historic Guilds. n.d. 'Bund der Historischen Deutschen Schützenbruderschaften e.V.' ['Historic German Marksmen's Brotherhoods']. Retrieved 6 March 2022 from https://schuetzen.erzbistum-koeln.de/Europa/Regionen/Region_1/sdarstellung_BHDS.html.

Feddes, Allard R., Liesbeth Mann and Bertjan Doosje. 2015. 'Increasing Self-Esteem and Empathy to Prevent Violent Radicalization: A Longitudinal Quantitative Evaluation of a Resilience Training Focused on Adolescents with a Dual Identity', *Journal of Applied Social Psychology* 45(7): 400–411.

Feldmann, Julian, and Nino Seidel. 2021. 'Ein Mörder, viele Ermöglicher' ['One Murderer, Many Enablers']. Retrieved 27 April 2021 from https://daserste.ndr.de/panorama/aktuell/Ein-Moerder-viele-Ermoeglicher,luebcke208.html.

Gøtzsche-Astrup, Oluf. 2018. 'The Time for Causal Designs: Review and Evaluation of Empirical Support for Mechanisms of Political Radicalisation', *Aggression and Violent Behavior* 39: 90–99.

Grossman, Michele. 2021. 'Resilience to Violent Extremism and Terrorism', in Michael Ungar (ed.), *Multisystemic Resilience: Adaptation and Transformation in Contexts of Change*. New York: Oxford University Press, pp. 293–317.

Hitzler, Ronald, and Miriam Gothe. 2015. 'Zur Einleitung: Methodologisch-methodische Aspekte ethnographischer Forschungsprojekte' ['Introduction: Methodology and Methods in Ethnographic Research Projects'], in R. Hitzler and M. Gothe (eds), *Ethnographische Erkundungen*. Wiesbaden: Springer Fachmedien Wiesbaden, pp. 9–16.

Holt, Thomas J., et al. 2018. 'Examining the Utility of Social Control and Social Learning in the Radicalization of Violent and Non-Violent Extremists', *Dynamics of Asymmetric Conflict* 11(3): 125–48.

Horgan, John. 2012. 'Discussion Point: The End of Radicalization?'. Retrieved 24 October 2021 from https://www.start.umd.edu/news/discussion-point-end-radicalization.

Kerst, Benjamin. 2021a. *Marksmen's Clubs in Germany in the Context of Mainstreaming the Extreme*. DARE Project Report. Retrieved 28 August 2022 from https://documents.manchester.ac.uk/display.aspx?DocID=58695.

———. 2021b. 'Shame, Norms and Values as Possible Resources in Preventing and Countering Radicalisation', *Journal for Deradicalization* 29: 92–128.

Khalil, James, John Horgan and Martin Zeuthen. 2019. 'The Attitudes-Behaviors Corrective (ABC) Model of Violent Extremism', *Terrorism and Political Violence*: 1–26. Published online 18 December 2019.

Kirche und Leben. 2021. 'Mitgliedschaften in katholischen Bruderschaften und der Partei seien nicht vereinbar: Katholische Schützenvereine mit einem deutlichen Nein zur AfD' ['Memberships in Catholic Brotherhoods and the Party Are Not Compatible: Catholic Marksmen's Clubs Give a Clear "No" to the AfD']. Retrieved 30 January 2022 from https://www.kirche-und-leben.de/artikel/katholische-schuetzenvereine-mit-einem-deutlichen-nein-zur-afd.

Kreyenschulte, Sebastian. 2017. 'Genese und Entwicklung des Schützenwesens im Nordmünsterland' ['Genesis and Development of Marksmanship in Nordmünsterland'], in Forschungsgemeinschaft zur Geschichte des Nordmünsterlandes e. V. (ed.), *Nordmünsterland: Forschungen und Funde*. Lage, pp. 138–95.

Kruglanski, Arie W. 2004. *The Psychology of Closed Mindedness*. New York: Psychology Press.

Kruglanski, Arie W., and Edward Orehek. 2012. 'The Need for Certainty as a Psychological Nexus for Individuals and Society', in Michael A. Hogg and Danielle L. Blaylock (eds), *Extremism and the Psychology of Uncertainty*. Malden, MA: Wiley-Blackwell, pp. 3–18.

Küpper, Beate, Wilhelm Berghan and Jonas H. Rees. 2019. 'Aufputschen von Rechts: Rechtspopulismus und seine Normalisierung in der Mitte' ['Fuelling the Right: Right-Wing Populism and its Normalisation in the Centre'], in Franziska Schröter (ed.), *Verlorene Mitte - feindselige Zustände: Rechtsextreme Einstellungen in Deutschland 2018/19*. Bonn: Dietz, pp. 173–202.

Küpper, Beate, Andreas Zick and Maike Rump. 2021. 'Rechtsextreme Einstellungen in der Mitte 2020/21' ['Right-Wing Extremist Attitudes in the Social Centre 2020/21'], in Andreas Zick, Beate Küpper and Franziska Schröter (eds),

Die geforderte Mitte: *Rechtsextreme und demokratiegefährdende Einstellungen in Deutschland 2020/21*. Bonn: Dietz, pp. 75–111.

Leineweber, Jonas, et al. 2020. *Das Schützenwesen in Westfalen als Immaterielles Kulturerbe*: *Tradition im Wandel*: *Entwicklungen, Kontinuitäten und Zukunftsperspektiven* [Marksmanship in Westphalia as Intangible Cultural Heritage: Tradition in Transition: Developments, Continuities and Future Prospects]. Münster: Verlag für Regionalgeschichte ein Imprint von Aschendorff Verlag GmbH & Co. KG.

Lohr, Matthias, Kathrin Meyer and Thomas Thiele. 2019. 'Mutmaßlicher Lübcke-Mörder: Stephan Ernst schoss in weiterem Verein' ['Alleged Murderer of Luebke, Stephan Ernst, Linked to Another Marksmen's Club'], *HNA online*. Retrieved 6 April 2021 from https://www.hna.de/kassel/luebcke-mord-stephan-ernst-schoss-bei-kassel-in-weiterem-verein-13282884.html.

Lösel, Friedrich, et al. 2018. 'Protective Factors against Extremism and Violent Radicalization: A Systematic Review of Research', *International Journal of Developmental Science* 12(1–2): 89–102.

Malthaner, Stefan. 2017. 'Radicalization: The Evolution of an Analytical Paradigm', *European Journal of Sociology* 58(3): 369–401.

McCauley, Clark, and Sophia Moskalenko. 2017. 'Understanding Political Radicalization: The Two-Pyramids Model', *American Psychologist* 72(3): 205–16.

Moghaddam, Fathali M. 2009. 'De-Radicalization and the Staircase from Terrorism', in David Canter (ed.), *The Faces of Terrorism*: *Multidisciplinary Perspectives*. Chichester, UK: Wiley-Blackwell, pp. 277–92.

Neumann, Peter R. 2013. 'The Trouble with Radicalization', *International Affairs* 89(4): 873–93.

Pilkington, Hilary. 2020. *Understanding 'Right-Wing Extremism'*: *In Theory and Practice*. DARE Research Report. Retrieved 28 August 2022 from https://documents.manchester.ac.uk/display.aspx?DocID=58702.

———. 2022. 'Why Should We Care What Extremists Think? The Contribution of Emic Perspectives to Understanding the "Right-Wing Extremist" Mind-Set', *Journal of Contemporary Ethnography* 51(3): 318–46.

Pritchett, Sarah, and Kim Moeller. 2021. 'Can Social Bonds and Social Learning Theories Help Explain Radical Violent Extremism?', *Nordic Journal of Criminology*: 1–19. Published online 24 February 2021.

Reintges, Theo. 1963. *Wesen und Ursprung der spätmittelalterlichen Schützengilden* [Nature and Origins of Late Medieval Marksmen's Guilds]. Bonn: L. Röhrscheid.

Sauermann, Dietmar. 1983. 'Geschichte des Schützenwesens im Kurkölnischen Sauerland und am Hellweg' ['History of Marksmanship in Kurkoelsch Sauerland and on the Hellweg'], in Dietmar Sauermann, Friederike Schepper and Norbert Kirchner (eds), *Schützenwesen im kurkölschen Sauerland*. Arnsberg: Strobel, pp. 9–60.

Schmid, Alex P. 2013. *Radicalisation, De-radicalisation, Counter-Radicalisation*: *A Conceptual Discussion and Literature Review*. ICCT Research Paper. The

Hague: International Centre for Counter-Terrorism. Retrieved 10 June 2021 from http://www.icct.nl/download/file/ICCT-Schmid-Radicalisation-De-Radi calisation-Counter-Radicalisation-March-2013.pdf.

Schröter, Franziska (ed.). 2019a. *Verlorene Mitte - feindselige Zustände: Rechtsextreme Einstellungen in Deutschland 2018/19* [The Lost Centre – Hostile Conditions: Right-Wing Extremist Attitudes in Germany 2018–19]. Bonn: Dietz.

———. 2019b. 'Vorwort der Herausgeberin' ['Editor's Foreword'], in Franziska Schröter (ed.), *Verlorene Mitte - feindselige Zustände: Rechtsextreme Einstellungen in Deutschland 2018/19*. Bonn: Dietz, pp. 11–14.

Schuurman, Bart. 2020. 'Non-Involvement in Terrorist Violence', *Perspectives on Terrorism* 14(6): 14–26.

Schwartz, Shalom H. 1992. 'Universals in the Content and Structure of Values: Theoretical Advances and Empirical Tests in 20 Countries', *Advances in Experimental Social Psychology* 25: 1–65.

Schwartz, Shalom H., and Klaus Boehnke. 2004. 'Evaluating the Structure of Human Values with Confirmatory Factor Analysis', *Journal of Research in Personality* 38(3): 230–55.

Sieckelinck, Stijn, and Amy-Jane Gielen. 2017. 'RAN Issue Paper: Protective and Promotive Factors Building Resilience against Violent Radicalisation'. Amsterdam, The Netherlands: RAN Centre of Excellence. Retrieved 2 March 2022 from https://ec.europa.eu/home-affairs/document/download/19378f29-dd34-4a33-9379-0e9cd091f0a3_en.

Stambolis, Barbara. 1999. 'Schützenvereine in der Gesellschaft des 19. und 20. Jahrhunderts. Interdisziplinäre Arbeitsmöglichkeiten am Beispiel historischer Vereine' ['Marksmen's Clubs in Nineteenth and Twentieth Century Society. Interdisciplinary Opportunities in the Study of Historical Associations'], *Rheinisch-westfälische Zeitschrift für Volkskunde* 44: 171–213.

Staudenmaier, Rebecca. 2020. 'Schützenvereine gegen Vereinnahmung durch die AfD' ['Marksmen's Clubs against Appropriation by the AfD'], *DW.COM*, 12 March. Retrieved 10 June 2021 from https://www.dw.com/de/sch%C3%BCtzenvereine-gegen-vereinnahmung-durch-die-afd/a-52745214.

Stephens, William, and Stijn Sieckelinck. 2021. 'Resiliences to Radicalization: Four Key Perspectives', *International Journal of Law, Crime and Justice* 66: 1–14.

Ungar, Michael. 2018. 'Systemic Resilience: Principles and Processes for a Science of Change in Contexts of Adversity', *Ecology and Society* 23(4): 1–17.

———. 2021. 'Modeling Multisystemic Resilience', in Michael Ungar (ed.), *Multisystemic Resilience: Adaptation and Transformation in Contexts of Change*. New York: Oxford University Press, pp. 6–32.

Weber, Holger. 2020. 'Waffenbesitz: Diese Regularien müssen erfüllt werden' ['Gun Ownership: Regulations That Must Be Observed'], *Hanauer Anzeiger online*. Retrieved 6 April 2021 from https://www.hanauer.de/hanau/waffen besitz-diese-regularien-muessen-erfuellt-werden-13568351.html.

Zerback, Sarah. 2020. 'Schützenbruderschaften und AfD: „Ich nehme für unseren Verband politische Neutralität in Anspruch"' ['Marksmen's Brotherhoods and the AfD: "I Claim Political Neutrality for Our Association"'], *Deutschlandfunk*, 12 March. Retrieved 10 June 2021 from https://www.deutschland funk.de/schuetzenbruderschaften-und-afd-ich-nehme-fuer-unseren.694. de.html?dram:article_id=472314.

Zick, Andreas, Beate Küpper and Wilhelm Berghan. 2019. 'Zerreißproben und Normalitätsverluste der Gesellschaft: eine Hinführung zur Mitte-Studie' ['Stress Testing and Loss of the Sense of Normality in Society: An Introduction to the Centre-Study'], in Franziska Schröter (ed.), *Verlorene Mitte - feindselige Zustände: Rechtsextreme Einstellungen in Deutschland 2018/19*. Bonn: Dietz, pp. 15–39.

Zick, Andreas, Beate Küpper and Andreas Hövermann. 2011. *Intolerance, Prejudice and Discrimination: A European Report*. Berlin: Friedrich-Ebert-Stiftung, Forum Berlin.

Zick, Andreas, Beate Küpper and Franziska Schröter (eds). 2021. *Die geforderte Mitte: Rechtsextreme und demokratiegefährdende Einstellungen in Deutschland 2020/21* [The Demanded Middle: Right-wing Extremist and Democracy-Threatening Attitudes in Germany 2020/21]. Bonn: Dietz.

Zick, Andreas, et al. 2019. 'Gruppenbezogene Menschenfeindlichkeit in Deutschland 2002–2018/19' ['Group-Focused Enmity in Germany 2002–2018/19'], in Franziska Schröter (ed.), *Verlorene Mitte - feindselige Zustände: Rechtsextreme Einstellungen in Deutschland 2018/19*. Bonn: Dietz, pp. 53–116.

Has Radicalisation Research Reached Its Endpoint?

Hilary Pilkington

The contributions to this volume have provided insight from the study of a wide spectrum of 'Islamist' and 'extreme-right' radical(ising) milieus in very different national and regional contexts across Europe and its neighbouring territories. These ethnographic studies capture a cacophony of conflicting, and often uncomfortable, voices, attitudes and ideas swept along by a maelstrom of emotions – from anger, fear and isolation to familial warmth, belonging and 'buzz'. In this concluding chapter, we elaborate a number of themes that emerge across these very different case studies and critically reflect on their implications for the theoretical models and debates that shape contemporary radicalisation research. Building on existing critical engagements in the field (see Introduction, this volume), as well as the findings from across the DARE research project, we formulate these cross-cutting conclusions as five propositions. First, radicalisation research, if understood as the tracing of social profiles in order to identify those at risk of radicalisation, has reached its endpoint. If we are to continue to study radicalisation, we must see it as a relational concept reflecting a societal phenomenon that is the product of interactions between all involved actors (including institutional and state actors) and between individual psychological dispositions, ideological and intergroup attitudes and context. Secondly, such interactions may facilitate but also constrain radicalisation and it is vital we study their impact complexly. Thirdly, to avoid over-determining our understanding of the journeys people take through radical(ising) milieus through the exclusive study of their relatively rare endpoint in violent extremism, radicalisation must be studied not only *as* process but *in* process. This means studying not only radicalisation but partial radicalisation, stalled radicalisation and non-radicalisation, and the interactional dynamics that shape this process. Fourthly, we should not study the 'how' of radicalisation and non-radicalisation at the expense of the 'why'. Indeed, understanding the concerns that drive people to activism may help explain why so few journeys through radical(ising) milieus end in violent extremism. Finally, we need to study radicalisation journeys that do not end in violent extremism not simply to fill a gap in knowledge, but for what they tell us about the protective factors, resilient qualities and individual agency that combine to establish the 'red lines' that milieu members choose not to cross. This situated knowledge of milieu actors, indeed, is important in informing work to strengthen resistance to violent and anti-democratic responses to individual and collective grievances (see also Pilkington and Hussain 2022).

Radicalisation as a Relational Concept

The findings of our research confirm recent scholarship that views 'radicalisation' and 'extremism' as intrinsically relational constructs (Malthaner 2017; della Porta 2018). Radicalisation is an attributed shift towards something defined as 'extreme' or 'radical', while what constitutes extreme or radical is determined in relation to an external continuum or marker, which differs over time, place and sphere of concern (see Figure 9.1). Thus, radicalisation must be seen as the outcome of interactions *between* 'us and them', not something *in* 'them' (see also McCauley and Moskalenko 2011).

Shifts towards the radical or extreme may be identified by milieu actors themselves but are more usually externally attributed by institutional and societal actors whose concern is to identify those who radicalise others or who are 'at risk' of being radicalised. The relationship between those who 'label' and those who are 'labelled' is infused with power and experienced as a form of relational inequality by actors in both 'Islamist' and 'extreme-right' milieus (see discussion below and Figures 9.2 and 9.3). As illustrated by Conti (this volume), Muslim inmates in French prisons find themselves subject to an increasingly elastic, yet forensically graduated, risk categorisation not only as radicalised or non-radicalised but also as 'potentially radicalised' or 'in the process of being radicalised'. 'Extreme-right' milieu actors, in contrast, complain that the lack of differentiation within the right-wing political spectrum in public discourse results in the indiscriminate application of the descriptors 'extreme' or 'radical' such that 'anyone right of Lenin seems to be a radical' (respondent in UK milieu cited in Pilkington 2022: 331).

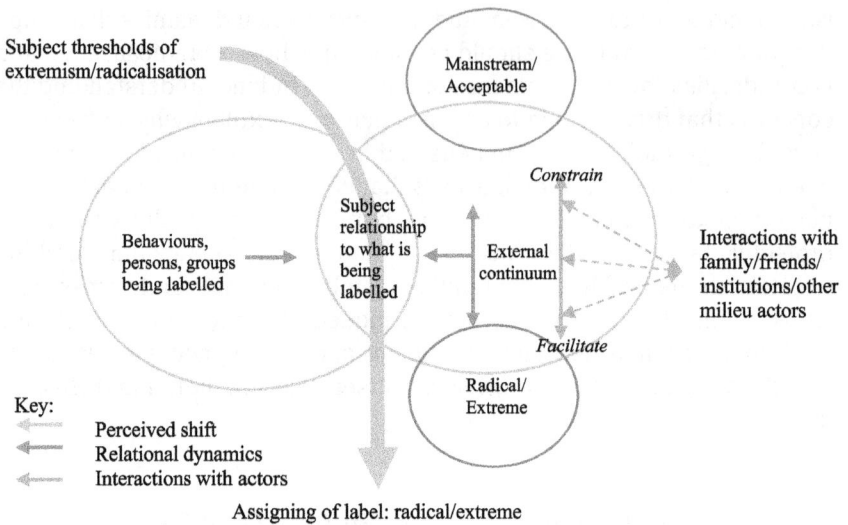

Figure 9.1. The relational nature of radicalisation. Created by Hilary Pilkington.

These 'insider' perceptions illustrate also the very different continuums or markers of what constitutes 'radical' or 'extreme' that underpin the concept of radicalisation; continuums that, as Sedgwick (2010) warns, shift historically, in relation to national or regional context and across different policy spheres and types of radicalisation. Recognising the 'confusion' that the failure to recognise the very different applications of the term brings (ibid.), the case studies drawn on in this volume are situated in relation to the spectrum of attitudes and behaviours considered 'radical' or 'extreme' in that context.[1] Looking across our case studies, we might note that, while 'radical' and 'extreme/extremist' are applied to both 'Islamist' and 'extreme-right' milieus, 'radicalisation' remains used primarily in relation to 'Islamist' actors (on how this is reflected in academic literature, see Introduction, this volume). Within each strand of radicalisation, moreover, we see the threshold and spectrum of concern vary significantly across countries and contexts. For example, in the French prison context noted above or in the Turkish case, located close to the Syrian border, radicalisation refers to a journey into support for, or participation in, violent *jihad* at home or abroad. In contrast, in the Greek context of historically rooted animosity towards, and sense of threat from, its Turkish neighbour, even to demand an official mosque in which to practise one's faith might be considered a potential sign of radicalisation. In relation to right-wing radicalisation, the continuum referenced is generally ideational rather than behavioural, with the main concern being the potential for the socially divisive mainstreaming of hate towards minority groups in society. Thus, milieus such as the marksmen's clubs in Germany or the Democratic Football Lads Alliance in the UK, whose participants' views may not diverge radically from the conservative end of the 'mainstream', and whose leaders publicly adopt anti-extremism positions, may arouse significant public concern. At the same time, in the Greek context, the past electoral success of neo-Nazi parties such as Golden Dawn mean that small, extreme-right para-military groups active within the milieu studied may attract surprisingly little attention.

Our studies not only confirm that 'radicalisation' is applied within academic and policy debates to an inconsistent and wide spectrum of behaviours and attitudes but demonstrate that etic characterisations and conceptualisations of extremism, radicalism and radicalisation are widely disputed by those active themselves in radical(ising) milieus. The stigmatisation of Muslim communities through radicalisation discourse has led to profound critique of the concept of radicalisation and reluctance to engage with counter-extremism interventions. In this volume, we have taken a critical position in this debate but not disengaged from it. Rather, we suggest, a relational understanding of radicalisation can inform a critical approach to academic and policy (etic) debates (see, *inter alia*, Schmid 2013) through engaging with radical milieu actors' own (emic) understandings of attitudes and behaviours associated with radicalisation (see Introduction, this volume; Pilkington 2022). In both the UK and Dutch 'Islamist' milieus studied here, for example, respondents recounted how praying 'five times a day' was a simple expression of being a Muslim for them but was interpreted as a sign of 'extremism' or 'radicalism' by others (Pilkington, Patel and Jones 2021: 11; Pilkington and Hussain 2022: 17). Similarly, to meet external criteria of being a 'moderate' Muslim meant, for them, having to behave in a non-Muslim way (drinking alcohol or going to nightclubs) (ibid.).

While actors' own accounts must be subjected also to critical reflection (see Introduction, this volume), we argue that taking emic understandings of extremism, radicalism and radicalisation seriously is important. The lack of recognition of self in the descriptors applied to actors in radical(ising) milieus can lead to the emptying of meaning of terms such as 'extremism' and 'radicalisation', such that they become, as one French respondent put it, no more than 'a semantic device to discredit people' (Pilkington et al. 2021: 6). The significance of this is evident in the central role played by feeling unfairly labelled – by media, state and societal institutions – as 'right-wing extremist' or 'Nazi' in 'extreme-right' grievance narratives (Pilkington and Vestel, this volume) and in what is characterised as the 'traumatic' impact of the labelling of particular city districts as 'hotbeds' of Islamist radicalisation (Dechesne, this volume). There is already evidence that such disjuncture between etic and emic understandings can have counterproductive effects in terms of the prevention of violent extremism among 'radical' Muslim milieus (Lindekilde 2012). In our study, actors in 'extreme-right' milieus also suggested that what they saw as indiscriminate labelling of milieu actors as 'far right' or 'right-wing extremists' can make individuals feel they have nothing left to lose; they might as well become extremist since they are already labelled as such (see Pilkington and Vestel, this volume). In this way, the contraction of the space of what is considered 'moderate' – such that those deemed 'radical', but who do not see themselves as such, are excluded from normal public and political processes – runs the risk of exacerbating rather than reducing the security threat since exclusion from such processes encourages a search for alternative means of action (Sedgwick 2010: 491; Pilkington and Hussain 2022: 21–22).

Interactional Dimensions of Radicalisation

Central to the relational approach to radicalisation outlined above is its understanding as a dynamic social phenomenon (Alimi, Bosi and Demetriou 2012) shaped by 'complex and contingent sets of interactions among individuals, groups, and institutional actors' (della Porta 2018: 463). Social networks, pre-existing social ties and influential figures have been widely identified as key routes into activism, including in extremist groups (McAdam and Paulsen 1993; Sageman 2004; Wiktorowicz 2005). The close-up engagement with individuals on their journeys through radical(ising) milieus in our study allows important insight into how interactions with others – family, friends, influential figures in the milieu or institutional actors – may shift people towards extremism but also away from it (see Figure 9.1). These complex relational dynamics are explored in several contributions to the volume and their role in facilitating but also stalling trajectories of radicalisation is captured in Figure 9.2 and Figure 9.3.

Family relationships are found to be highly significant in young people's journeys through radical(ising) milieus. Amongst respondents in the 'Islamist' milieus, Dechesne (this volume) finds that the absence of one or both parents growing up, lack of parental moral guidance or the failure to develop an emotional relationship with one's father may heighten vulnerability to radicalisation while a supportive family environment can contribute to the rejection of radical messaging. In both Poliakov's (this volume) consideration of young people of North Caucasian heritage liv-

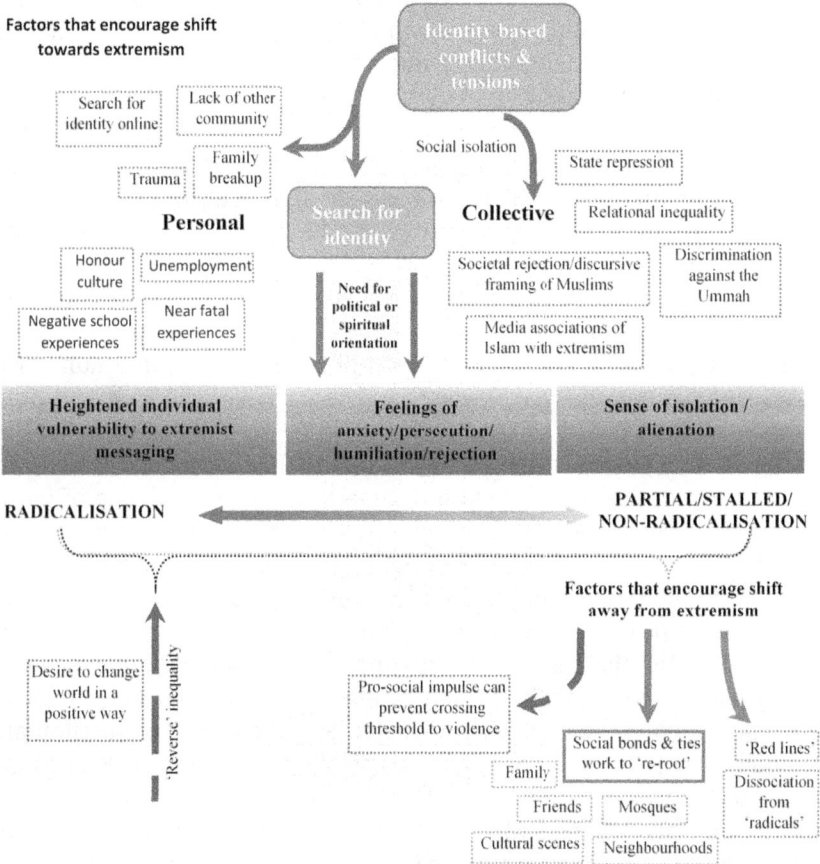

Figure 9.2. Trajectories through 'Islamist' milieus. Created by Hilary Pilkington.

ing in northern Russian cities and Conti's (this volume) interviews with French prison inmates, the fracturing of the institution of the traditional patriarchal family following migration to new cultural contexts emerges as important to radicalisation in the narratives of respondents. As parents' attempts to hold on to traditional values in new contexts clash with young people's desire to free themselves from parental pressure in choosing life trajectories, Poliakov argues, intergenerational tension within the family can facilitate radicalisation. Alternatively, this emancipation process can lead to external conflict directed at societal and state institutions as young people simultaneously encounter the discrimination and horizontal inequalities faced by ethnic minority groups from the North Caucasus.

Conti (this volume) finds that respondents who have grown up without either parent, or in single-parent households, suffer from a sense of being 'uprooted' resulting from an absence of intergenerational sharing, consequent lack of knowledge of one's own origins and, in some cases, a reversal of generational roles whereby sons replace their fathers as authority figures within the fragmented family. While such experiences, he suggests, facilitate radicalisation, family can be a key resource also for young people rebuilding their lives – acting as a site of identity construction, of forgiveness and a base from which to anticipate one's future after prison.

Among 'extreme-right' milieus, families are also found to be important in both facilitating and constraining radicalisation (see Figure 9.3). Families can be a first site of exposure to radical messages; in a number of cases studied, parents were reported to be sympathetic to 'extreme-right' views and fathers and siblings active in 'extreme-right' milieus had introduced respondents to these environments (Pilkington and Vestel, this volume; Kerst, this volume). At the same time, the experience of family members in the movements led to the sharing of strategies, and practices of care, designed to protect or divert respondents away from the most radical or violent segments of the milieu. In this way, they worked to build resistance or protect against further radicalisation. As in the 'Islamist' milieus, moreover, the absence of supportive or bonding relationships with family was found to facilitate engagement in radical(ising) milieus. Such individuals experienced low self-esteem, a sense of social isolation and a longing for community or belonging, which led them to seek a positive sense of family or community in activist groups (Pilkington and Vestel; Pilkington, this volume). Shifts away from extremism in 'extreme-right' milieus were also often associated with family; family was frequently referenced in decisions to reprioritise life over activism or as the site of new responsibilities (see Figure 9.3).

Friends were found to be less significant than family members in radicalisation and non-radicalisation trajectories (see also Cragin et al. 2015: 15). However, among 'Islamist' milieus, social isolation was identified as a key factor in radicalisation (Conti, this volume), while having good friends and a feeling of belonging in one's neighbourhood were found to ameliorate experiences of inequalities that might otherwise lead to grievances and their resolution through radical action (Dechesne, this volume). In 'extreme-right' milieus, friends acted as organic influencers towards extremism – as identified in the French and Maltese milieus where individuals had accompanied friends into, or formed with them,

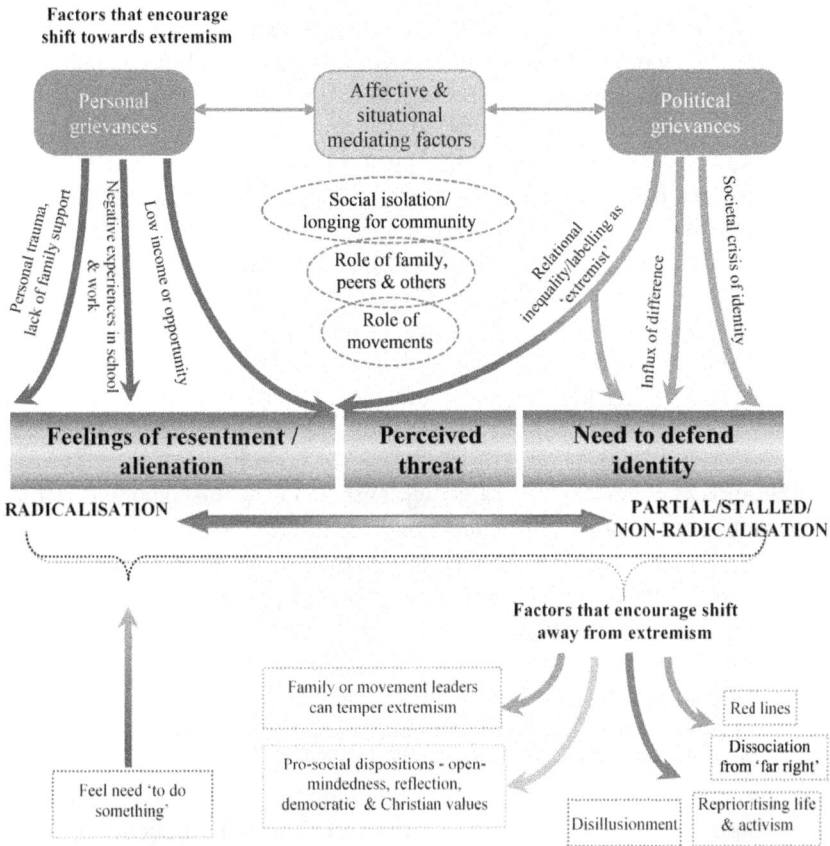

Figure 9.3. Trajectories through 'extreme-right' milieus. Created by Hilary Pilkington.

radical nationalist groups. However, individuals, especially in the UK milieu, were found also to consciously decide against following friends into more radical environments or movements (Pilkington and Vestel, this volume). As discussed below, moreover, such moments constituted points of reflection leading some research participants to draw their own 'red lines' in terms of what they believed or how they chose to act.

The recognition that social ties may constrain as well as encourage activism is not new (see, for example, McAdam and Paulsen 1993: 645). Perhaps less well established, however, is that this constraining role might be played within milieus including by movement leaders or influential figures. In our study of 'extreme-right' milieus, individuals talked positively about the familial warmth, sense of purpose or belonging to a like-minded community that they experienced from joining a movement, group or scene. The search for such belonging or purpose may be exploited by movements looking to recruit to their cause but we also found examples of influential milieu figures or organisational leaders who consciously sought to constrain radicalisation (Pilkington and Vestel, this volume). They did this by steering young people away from the more extreme fringes of the milieu and/or from engagement in violence (Pilkington, this volume) and actively engaging in counter-extremism campaigns or messaging and disciplining milieu members whose behaviour was inappropriate (Kerst, this volume). Similar examples were encountered in the studies of 'Islamist' milieus. One respondent from Norway explained how he had been deterred from leaving for Syria (having lost a number of friends there already) only after advice from an important figure in the milieu who, he says, 'helped me to understand and see the bigger picture, and not only parts of it. He made me realise what is right and wrong' (Pilkington et al. 2021: 11). More widely, actors in the 'Islamist' milieus emphasise the importance of social bonds and ties with institutions such as mosques and other cultural scenes in their neighbourhood which act to ground and re-root them in a way that protects them from radical(ising) messages. Mosques – if they feel inaccessible – can encourage young people towards the formation of religious identity based on internet sources and religious 'bricolage' but also protect young people from such; as one respondent from the Netherlands put it, 'going to mosque and taking classes, that is a shield against radicalisation' (Dechesne, this volume; Pilkington et al. 2021: 10). Alongside the resilience to extremism that respondents say is gained from correct religious education, actors in a number of the 'Islamist' milieus noted that, in a more general sense, Islamic faith serves as a bridge to social involvement and belonging since being a Muslim means taking on a role of responsibility in society (Dechesne, this volume). As Sakellariou (this volume) explores, in Greece, Muslim communities and their official organisations have used a range of dialogic and other means to 'absorb' grievances associated with the subjection of Muslim communities to violence, racism, surveillance and stigmatisation and thus prevent reciprocal radicalisation.

Radicalisation *as* Process and *in* Process

As evident from Figure 9.2 and Figure 9.3, in this study, we locate journeys through radical(ising) milieus on a continuum – from non-radicalisation, partial radicalisation, stalled radicalisation to radicalisation. In the Introduction to this volume, we argued that it was somewhat paradoxical that a consensus around the value of radicalisation as a concept that offered an understanding of violent extremism as the outcome of a process – rather than as embedded within specific ideologies or beliefs – remains accompanied by approaches to its study defined by a single point in time (the endpoint of that process). While, as Malthaner (2017: 387) warns, it would be wrong to caricature classic models of radicalisation as adopting a wholly unidirectional understanding of the relationship between extremist beliefs and violent extremist behaviour, nonetheless, the exclusive concern with studying trajectories that do end in crossing the threshold into violence means that engagement with radical ideas all too easily appears as a gateway to terrorism. Throughout the contributions to this volume, we have argued that this endpoint focus obscures what we can learn about radicalisation as a process from the multitude of different trajectories through radical milieus that end not in violent extremism but in some form of partial, stalled or non-radicalisation. Tracing such pathways is facilitated by the milieu approach adopted in our study, which focuses on young people's encounters and responses to radical(ising) messages and agents and thus to trajectories *in process* – as they unfold in situ. The concept of non-radicalisation as 'resistance to violent extremism' introduced by Cragin (2014: 342), alongside discussion of 'resilience' to radicalisation and extremism in the literature on P/CVE (see Introduction, this volume; Kerst, this volume), help identify factors that protect those in situations of regular encounter with radicalisation from progression to violent extremism. By following individuals over an extended period of time, using an ethnographic method, our study allows us to go further and construct a complex picture in which extremism is not simply embraced or resisted but trajectories through radical(ising) milieus are characterised by multiple shifts and turns both towards and away from extremism shaped by situations, interactions and individual agency.

Based on the findings of the ten 'Islamist' milieus studied, Dechesne (this volume) identifies a set of factors which distinguish individuals who adopt pathways of non-radicalisation rather than radicalisation. These factors relate to: positive societal participation and connectedness; having a mind-set that understands difference or 'others' through a cooperative rather than conflict frame; and being in a societal setting characterised by stability, lack of violence and non-access to radical networks. The factors identified from this synthesis intersect with Cragin's (2014) model of non-radicalisation but the milieu approach points to pathways of radicalisation and non-radicalisation being not singular, planned behaviours as Cragin's model might suggest, but constructed in a dynamic and interactional way. The synthesis of findings from the nine 'extreme-right' milieus studied illustrates the complex interweaving of grievances – po-

litical and personal (see McCauley and Moskalenko 2008: 417–19) – and
affective and situational factors that shape individual pathways of milieu
actors (Pilkington and Vestel, this volume). Pilkington and Vestel argue
that the process by which personal grievances become political grievances and political grievances take on profoundly personal meaning is
shaped by a range of situational or affective factors such as feelings of
isolation, dislocation and frustration which, for some, contribute to a
sense of collective existential insecurity and the perception of the need
for radical action. Such affective and situational dimensions of participation in radical milieus, however, may also work to constrain engagement.
Family members, friends and movement leaders or influencers may temper extremism or steer individuals away from more extreme movements
while individual capacity for reflection, psychological dispositions (such
as open-mindedness) and core values (related to democratic or religious
ideals) may foster resilience to radical(ising) messages. Situation is thus
crucial to understanding why and how people move towards (violent)
extremism, but also why most do not.

Understanding the dynamics of situations, and the interactions that take
place there, in propelling people towards or away from extremism is the focus of a number of contributions to this volume (see Pilkington; Conti; and
Kerst). This is not to suggest that radicalisation is no more than 'being in
the wrong place at the wrong time and in the wrong company' (Dalgaard-
Nielsen 2010: 805). Following Birkbeck and Lafree (1993: 115), we understand 'situation' not as a one-off or chance occurrence but the immediate setting in which behaviour occurs and to which participants bring
the emotions and consciousness generated from previous interactions
and situations (Collins 2004: 3). In her comparison of four individual
pathways through a UK 'extreme-right' milieu, Pilkington (this volume)
employs a micro-situational approach to understand when and how radical milieu actors engage in violence. She finds that participation in violence may drive, take place in parallel to, or be consciously resisted
in, political activism rather than constitute the apex of a radicalisation
trajectory. However, she also argues, in contrast to Collins (2004: 4), that
the study of the dynamics of situations is insufficient to explain how violence happens; we need also to take into account a range of 'background
conditions' (Collins 2008: 21) that profoundly shape individual journeys
into current situations and responses to the interactions encountered
there. These background conditions also shape previous interactions and
situational encounters which govern how individuals interpret a given
situation, which, Pilkington argues, is crucial to explaining individual and
collective behaviour.

Kerst (this volume) also draws on a processual and situational under-standing of resilience and non-radicalisation to explore a wide range of responses among members of the German marksmen's club milieu to encounters with 'extreme-right' messages and those who convey them. These messages – statements, slogans, appeals, jokes, flyers or social media posts with racist, anti-democratic or neo-Nazi content – are met by young marksmen and markswomen with responses ranging from out-right rejection through to toleration or trivialisation. While acceptance – or normalisation – of such messages might facilitate shifts towards more radical positions, encounters with them, and their messengers, can also lead milieu actors to resist and adapt to such situations of adver-sity, thereby activating underlying factors of resilience. These different responses, Kerst suggests, are explained by the situational contexts in which the messages are encountered, the interactions with others (fam-ily, friends, partners, other milieu members) that surround them, indi-viduals' emotional and psychological capacities and dispositions (of empathy, open-mindedness etc.) and the response to such messages and individuals of the marksmen's club or wider milieu to which they belong. These findings confirm Franc, Poli and Pavlović's (this volume) sugges-tion that future radicalisation studies might focus on the interactive effect of psychological dispositions and context in order to generate a complex understanding of pathways to (violent) extremism.

While prison, as an immediate setting of behaviour, might appear to be cut off from the rest of society, and thus impervious to grievance nar-ratives and ideologies that circulate in radical(ising) milieus, there has been much discussion of prison as a key site of radicalisation, especially Islamist radicalisation. Micheron (2020) argues that prisons remain in constant interaction with the neighbourhoods from which jihadism in France has emerged, and convicted jihadists see prison sentences not as the end of the line but part of the journey, time they can use to grow, ed-ucate themselves, build networks and enhance their authority. However, while prisons may be sites of both conversion to, and intensification of, Islamic faith, intensive religious change can be associated with radical-isation towards an 'Us' versus 'Them' Islamist worldview but also with heightened commitment to rehabilitation (Wilkinson et al. 2021). Con-ti's (this volume) extended engagement with Muslim prisoners in France demonstrates how interactions in prison can lead to both radicalisation and non-radicalisation. Against the background of multiple pre-existing factors – experience of injustice, inequality, non-recognition, stigmatisa-tion and exclusion – for some young Muslim prisoners, already feeling a sense of detachment from the rest of society, just one 'small thing' can lead to the severing of all ties and passage into radical Islamism. However, he demonstrates how other inmates are able to mobilise emotional, relational and social resources, inside and outside prison, in a way that allows them to resist, reject and counter the path of total withdrawal offered by radical Islam.

Relational Inequality:
Why People Radicalise (and Why They Don't)

The fourth proposition we arrive at from our study is that focusing on 'how' radicalisation takes place – especially the situational and interactional factors that illuminate how processes of radicalisation and non-radicalisation unfold in time and place – should not come at the expense of understanding 'why' it does. Listening to actors, with very different agendas, in radical(ising) milieus across Europe reveals the consistent expression of deeply held grievances that underpin their engagement in such milieus. Taking these grievances seriously, we argue, helps explain radicalisation trajectories but is also crucial to understanding what stalls, stops or reverses that radicalisation process as young people make choices not to cross the threshold into violent extremism. Such explanations must include consideration of both the structural drivers of radicalisation – referred to here as relational inequalities – and the role of individual agency in trajectories of radicalisation and non-radicalisation.

Franc, Poli and Pavlović (this volume) find that the evidence to date in published research on radicalisation points to subjective inequality – the perception of being disadvantageously positioned in relations of power, regardless of whether this is associated with an objective situation or not – as superseding objective variables of inequality in triggering a path towards radicalisation. Moreover, they find that perceived socio-political inequality could be more important than economic inequality in shaping a sense of injustice and discrimination. The ethnographic research largely confirms this (Patel, Pilkington and Jones 2021). The objective socio-economic circumstances of the 'extreme-right' milieus studied were mixed and material insecurities were expressed by respondents only in a minority of milieus (most notably the Greek milieu). The majority of fieldwork sites in the study of 'Islamist' milieus, in contrast, were districts where social exclusion, poverty, low-skilled and precarious employment prevail and material deprivation was mentioned by respondents in these milieus more frequently. However, in both sets of milieus, perceived socio-political injustices resonated in narratives of milieu actors more consistently than socio-economic injustices.

Perceived inequality appears in milieu actors' narratives as *relational*. In terms of horizontal inequality this is expressed as being treated differently and unfairly because of who you are, or who you are thought to be. In relation to vertical inequality, it is experienced as feeling subordinated to institutions and powers whose authority you do not recognise, such as global elites, politicians, state and law enforcement bodies, teachers and parents. This sense of relational inequality, although differentially experienced among actors in 'Islamist' and 'extreme-right' milieus, is articulated in both. For those in 'extreme-right' milieus, injustice is expressed as a vertical inequality – some have 'money on their side' while others are 'living in poverty' – but one that is attached, horizontally, to groups of people. Thus, 'people like us' live in poverty while 'they' ('the elites') are 'living in complete luxury' (Pilkington and Vestel, this volume). Research participants from the 'Islamist' milieus (in the non-Muslim majority countries studied) had grown up feeling that being of immigrant background and resident in particular districts meant they would be subject to the arbitrary brutality of the state, and its law enforcement agencies, which perceive 'terrorists' and 'Muslims' as one and the same (Dechesne, this volume). This confirms the danger that policies and measures aimed at 'tackling' radicalisation and terrorism could backfire by increasing perceived injustice and discrimination among those communities they target. It also points to the bi-directional relationship between inequality and radicalisation; while inequality produces radicalisation, radicalisation also plays a role in producing inequality through injustice and discrimination (Franc, Poli and Pavlović, this volume).

Of course, no one grievance propels individuals towards extremism and, in our study, most research participants engaged with radical ideas or beliefs partially or temporarily rather than completing a process of radicalisation to violent extremism. Moreover, grievances are central motivations for participation in radical(ising) milieus because such participation offers some prospect of challenging, or at least escaping, relational inequality. In the case of 'Islamist' milieus, radical Islamism appears to offer a reversal or way out of relational inequality; as one French respondent put it, 'we have to create much more equality' (Pilkington et al. 2021: 14). In the case of 'extreme-right' milieus, becoming politically active is a statement of the unwillingness to stay silent just because your 'truth' is rejected and the expression of the need 'to be able to say I've fought and done my part to try and make this world a better place' (ibid.). While these impulses lead research participants into radical(ising) milieus, they indicate the retention of a social connectedness – a pro-social orientation – that is also central to what pulls them back from crossing the threshold into violent extremism (see Figures 9.2 and 9.3). Indeed, our study shows the importance of not conflating even extended presence in such milieus with eventual radicalisation into violent extremism.

Reflection, Critique and Thresholds: Agency in Radicalisation and Non-Radicalisation

Finally, we propose that studying journeys through radical(ising) milieus can help develop a more complex understanding of the role of agency than evident in much of the literature on radicalisation to date, which tends to envisage radicalisation as something 'done to' an individual (Pilkington 2016: 3, 8; McDonald 2018: 10). This tendency is exacerbated in the case of young people, who, especially in the P/CVE and safeguarding literature, are often seen to be inherently vulnerable to radicalisation either by external agents ('recruiters') or through over-exposure to extremist messages. Our findings suggest that young people are, on the contrary, far from passive objects of radicalising influences but are actively seeking ways to address the injustices they perceive, including through the formation of new social ties, whilst critically engaging with a range of radicalising messages (see also Lindekilde, Malthaner and O'Connor 2019: 23–24).

An important site of critical engagement and reflection is online space. Our research shows online spaces to be a significant source of encounter with radical(ising) messages in both 'Islamist' and 'extreme-right' milieus (Hall, Pilkington and Jones 2021). Moreover, information accessed online is often viewed as more 'trustworthy' and online forums experienced as spaces in which alternative or stigmatised knowledge can be accessed and 'people like us' can communicate our ideas and 'be heard'. However, across the milieus studied, research participants also emphasise their critical approach to what they see or hear and pride themselves on using, and checking, multiple sources to get as near to 'the truth' as possible (ibid.). We also found milieu actors to be aware, and critical, of the tendency for milieus to be self-affirmative and, in a number of cases, respondents talked about moving away from movements because they constituted 'a typical echo chamber' (see Pilkington and Vestel, this volume).

The engagement with emic perspectives facilitated by the ethnographic approach taken in our study shows that milieu actors themselves deploy a relational understanding of extremism and that this is central to the choices they make as they navigate through radical(ising) milieus. Young people's encounters with views or individuals within or on the edges of the milieu served to formulate a sense of those groups or worldviews that they considered 'too extreme' (Pilkington, Patel and Jones 2021). 'Too extreme' for respondents in the 'extreme-right' milieus studied was most often described as 'Nazi', 'neo-Nazism', 'white supremacism', 'racism' and 'antisemitism', while among 'Islamist' milieu actors the most frequent references were to *takfiris*, *jihadis* and *kharijites*. These were people and ideas from which respondents, with some notable exceptions, dissociated themselves. While such dissociation was often declaratory in nature, respondents also provided examples of how they observed these 'red lines', including resisting recruitment attempts, not attending actions of movements they considered too extreme or refusing to carry placards or applaud a speech that carried messages they considered to be derogatory to others.

Such 'red lines' were drawn most consistently, and across milieus, in relation to the rejection of violence. Across the 'extreme-right' milieus studied, support for, or use of, violence in the interests of a political cause is the most frequently cited marker of extremism or radicalisation towards extremism. Actors in these milieus (with a few exceptions) seek to dissociate themselves from violence, seeing it as acceptable only in direct self-defence. Among the 'Islamist' milieus studied, the term 'extremism' is ascribed where violence is present and perceived to be indiscriminate and illegitimate. The use of violence is sometimes considered justified – in self-defence but also as a response to ongoing violence directed by western forces against Muslims. While participants in 'Islamist' milieus were more likely to justify violence than respondents in the 'extreme-right' milieus, they were also more likely to consider those adopting some ideological positions – such as *takfirism* and *jihadism* – as expressions of 'extreme' or 'radical' values, beliefs and behaviours, with or without their express support for, or involvement in, violence. In contrast, in 'extreme-right' milieus, relatively few milieu actors believed holding opinions or ideas, on their own, might be considered 'extremism' (ibid.; see also Pilkington, this volume).

There is a danger that the role of agency is amplified in our findings due to its engagement with active milieu participants who tend to narrate their journeys in relation to the choices they make and actions they take rather than the structural forces constraining horizons and opportunities for alternative action. However, our findings clearly point to radicalisation and non-radicalisation trajectories as shaped by milieu actors themselves and the choices they make between violent and non-violent pathways (see also Cragin et al. 2015: 11). This is evident when, for example, an initial attraction to the community or brotherhood offered by an extremist group is resisted because it would demand willingness to engage in political violence, which is a moral 'red line' respondents could not cross

(Pilkington and Vestel, this volume). Over the course of our research, a number of participants made choices to move away from particular groups or from activism altogether. While, in some cases, this resulted from high expectations of the emotional dimensions of the new community leading to disappointment or even a sense of betrayal (see also Bjørgo 2011: 284), in others, it was the result of a decision to reprioritise other aspects of life over activism due to a change in life circumstances or responsibilities. An opening of horizons, following positive interaction with someone previously identified as 'other', was also cited by a number of respondents as a key moment in decisions to reflect on the untenable nature of their positions of hate and to redirect their pathways (see Dechesne, this volume; Pilkington and Vestel, this volume).

Has Radicalisation Research Reached Its Endpoint?

In this volume we have argued that research into radicalisation that is tied to tracing journeys to an endpoint of violent extremism may have reached its own endpoint. We have confirmed the value, however, of the shift in the field towards understanding radicalisation as a relational concept that can illuminate movement towards extremism as a dynamic and interactional process. We have emphasised that, if the value of the concept of radicalisation is its approach to extremism as not inherent in particular ideologies but emerging *as a process*, then we must also study it *in process*; in this way, the process is released from being bound to a single endpoint of violent extremism. By studying the plethora of journeys individuals make through radical milieus and their multiple outcomes (in partial, stalled or non-radicalisation), we are able to gain insight not only into 'what goes on before the bomb goes off' (Sedgwick 2010: 479) but what goes on when it doesn't. This brings crucial insight into what halts or reverses the process of radicalisation of those who engage with radical ideas and milieus. Of course, we must be alert to the risk that, by studying those who engage with such milieus but have not (yet) radicalised, we unintentionally extend the sphere of surveillance. Adopting a societal, as opposed to security-focused, approach is central to this, as is engagement with milieu actors not as 'targets' of CVE policy but as agents who can, and often want to, be engaged in a constructive, dialogic process that helps prevent pathways into violent extremism.

The research presented here is, empirically, neither comprehensive nor representative – cases are drawn predominantly from Europe, from mainly non-Muslim majority countries and in relation to only two strands of extremism. Even theoretical generalisability is complicated by the very different natures of the milieus studied and our interest in following the range of individual trajectories through them. We suggest that there is important insight to be gained, nonetheless, from problematising existing radicalisation models with the empirical study of the unfinished business of radicalisation processes. The messiness of radicalisation journeys, started, stalled or reversed, we argue, creates a more complex but more valid picture of the range of outcomes of engagement with radical ideas. Direct engagement with those still on these journeys, moreover, enriches our understanding through accessing emic as well as etic conceptualisations of what constitutes extremism and movement towards it. It is through listening to individuals' reflections on their everyday encounters with radical(ising) messages and observing their responses to them that we can begin to understand not only what drives radicalisation but also what prevents most actors in these milieus from crossing the red lines to 'extremism' that they mark for themselves. Such situated knowledge should not be treated uncritically but is essential if we are to ensure that radicalisation research facilitates P/CVE practice rather than perpetuating a stigmatising discourse that hinders it.

Acknowledgements

The research drawn on in this chapter is part of the Dialogue about Radicalisation and Equality (DARE) project, which received funding from the European Union's Horizon 2020 research and innovation programme under Grant Agreement No. 725349. It reflects only the views of the author; the European Commission and Research Executive Agency are not responsible for any information it contains.

The author would like to thank Sofia Patel and Rosie Mutton for their contributions to the development of Figures 9.1, 9.2 and 9.3.

Hilary Pilkington is Professor of Sociology at the University of Manchester and Fellow of the Academy of Social Sciences. She has conducted ethnographic research on youth and youth subculture, youth political participation, activism and extremism and published also on ethnographic research methods and meta-ethnographic synthesis. She was coordinator of the H2020 DARE (Dialogue about Radicalisation and Equality) project (University of Manchester, 2017–21). She is a member of the Academic-Practitioner Countering Extremism Network of the Commission for Countering Extremism and served as independent Commissioner on the GMCA Preventing Violent Extremism and Promoting Social Cohesion Commission.

....

NOTE

1. While extensive historical and political contextualisation is not possible in each of the contributions to this volume, each case study report includes a section situating the study in this way. The individual case study reports on 'Islamist' milieus can be found at https://sites.manchester.ac.uk/dare/home/research-reports/islamist-radical-milieu-studies/. The case study reports on 'extreme-right' milieus can be found at https://sites.manchester.ac.uk/dare/home/research-reports/extreme-right-radical-milieu-studies/.

....

REFERENCES

Alimi, Eitan Y., Lorenzo Bosi and Chares Demetriou. 2012. 'Relational Dynamics and Processes of Radicalization: A Comparative Framework', *Mobilization* 17(1): 7–26.

Bjørgo, Tore. 2011. 'Dreams and Disillusionment: Engagement in and Disengagement from Militant Extremist Groups', *Crime, Law and Social Change* 55(4): 227–85.

Birkbeck, Christopher, and Gary LaFree. 1993. 'The Situational Analysis of Crime and Deviance', *Annual Review of Sociology* 19: 113–37.

Collins, Randall. 2004. *Interaction Ritual Chains*. Princeton, NJ: Princeton University Press.

———. 2008. *Violence: A Micro-sociological Theory*. Princeton, NJ: Princeton University Press.

Cragin, Kim. 2014. 'Resisting Violent Extremism: A Conceptual Model for Non-Radicalization', *Terrorism and Political Violence* 26: 337–53.

Cragin, Kim, et al. 2015. *What Factors Cause Youth to Reject Violent Extremism? Results of an Exploratory Analysis in the West Bank*. Rand Corporation. Retrieved 22 December 2021 from https://www.rand.org/content/dam/rand/pubs/research_reports/RR1100/RR1118/RAND_RR1118.pdf.

Dalgaard-Nielsen, Anja. 2010. 'Violent Radicalization in Europe: What We Know and What We Do Not Know', *Studies in Conflict & Terrorism* 33(9): 797–814.

Della Porta, D. 2018. 'Radicalization: A Relational Perspective', *Annual Review of Political Science* 21(1): 461–74.

Hall, Natalie-Anne, Hilary Pilkington and Charlotte Jones. 2021. *How Important Are Online Spaces to Radicalisation?* DARE Research Briefing. Retrieved 28 August 2022 from https://documents.manchester.ac.uk/display.aspx?DocID=58629.

Lindekilde, Lasse. 2012 'Neo-liberal Governing of "Radicals": Danish Radicalization Prevention Policies and Potential Iatrogenic Effects', *International Journal of Conflict and Violence* 6(1): 109–25.

Lindekilde, Lasse, Stefan Malthaner and Francis O'Connor. 2019. 'Peripheral and Embedded: Relational Patterns of Lone-Actor Terrorist Radicalization', *Dynamics of Asymmetric Conflict* 12(1): 20–41.

Malthaner, Stefan. 2017. 'Radicalization: The Evolution of an Analytical Paradigm', *European Journal of Sociology* 58(3): 369–401.

McAdam, Doug, and Ronnelle Paulsen. 1993. 'Specifying the Relationship between Social Ties and Activism', *American Journal of Sociology* 99(3): 640–67.

McCauley, Clark, and Sophia Moskalenko. 2008. 'Mechanisms of Political Radicalization: Pathways toward Terrorism', *Terrorism and Political Violence* 20(3): 415–33.

———. 2011. *Friction: How Radicalization Happens to Them and Us*. New York: Oxford University Press.

McDonald, Kevin. 2018. *Radicalization*. Cambridge: Polity.

Micheron, Hugo. 2020. *Le jihadisme français: Quartiers, Syrie, prisons* [French Jihadism: Neighbourhoods, Syria and Prisons]. Paris: Gallimard.

Patel, Sofia, Hilary Pilkington and Charlotte Jones. 2021. *How Important Are 'Perceived Inequalities' to Trajectories of (Non)Radicalisation?* DARE Research Briefing. Retrieved 28 August 2022 from https://documents.manchester.ac.uk/display.aspx?DocID=58713.

Pilkington, Hilary. 2016. *Loud and Proud: Passion and Politics in the English Defence League*. Manchester: Manchester University Press.

———. 2022. 'Why Should We Care What Extremists Think? The Contribution of Emic Perspectives to Understanding the "Right-Wing Extremist" Mind-Set', *Journal of Contemporary Ethnography* 51(3): 318–46.

Pilkington, Hilary, and Ajmal Hussain. 2022 'Why Wouldn't You Consult Us? Reflections on Preventing Radicalisation among Actors in Radical(ising) Milieus', *Journal for Deradicalization* 30: 1–44.

Pilkington, Hilary, Sofia Patel and Charlotte Jones. 2021. *A Common Language? Emic Perspectives on 'Extremism', 'Radicalism' and 'Radicalisation'*. DARE Research Briefing. Retrieved 28 August 2022 from https://documents.manchester.ac.uk/display.aspx?DocID=60813.

Pilkington, Hilary, et al. 2021. *Radicalisation: Critical Reflections*. DARE Research Briefing. Retrieved 28 August 2022 from https://documents.manchester.ac.uk/display.aspx?DocID=60812.

Sageman, Marc. 2004. *Understanding Terror Networks*. Philadelphia: University of Pennsylvania Press.

Schmid, Alex P. 2013. 'Radicalisation, De-Radicalisation, Counter-Radicalisation: A Conceptual Discussion and Literature Review'. *ICCT Research Paper*. The Hague: International Centre for Counter-Terrorism.

Sedgwick, Mark. 2010. 'The Concept of Radicalisation as a Source of Confusion', *Terrorism and Political Violence* 22(4): 479–94.

Wiktorowicz, Quintan. 2005. *Radical Islam Rising: Muslim Extremism in the West*. Oxford: Rowman & Littlefield.

Wilkinson, Matthew, et al. 2021. 'Prison as a Site of Intense Religious Change: The Example of Conversion to Islam', *Religions* 12(3): 162.

Overview of Milieus Studied

This appendix provides a brief description of each of the ethnographic case studies referred to in the contributions to this volume along with details of the case study reports where a fuller contextualisation of the studies as well as their findings can be found.

'Extreme-Right' Milieus

The nine 'extreme-right' milieus studied fall into two broad clusters of cases (see Figure A.1). These are: those where the milieu consists of activists in nationalist, radical- or extreme-right or 'new right' movements (France, Malta, Norway, Netherlands, UK); and those where the milieu is focused around a non-political interest (e.g. football, shooting, religion) but there are strong ideological connections between this milieu and nationalist, radical- or extreme-right movements and ideologies (Germany, Greece, Poland, Russia).

Case Studies of Activists in Nationalist, Radical- or Extreme-Right or 'New Right' Movements: France, Malta, Netherlands, Norway and the UK

In **France**, the case focuses on youth involved in, or close to, Corsican nationalist movements accessed either via prisons or via anti-immigrant groups. Participants in the study are mostly middle class or upwardly aspirant members of the working class frustrated at their perceived treatment as a low-status minority group by the French state. They see Christianity as an important identity marker in the struggle against a perceived Islamic takeover in the West and take inspiration ideologically from the French new right. Thus, the Corsican case is not exceptional

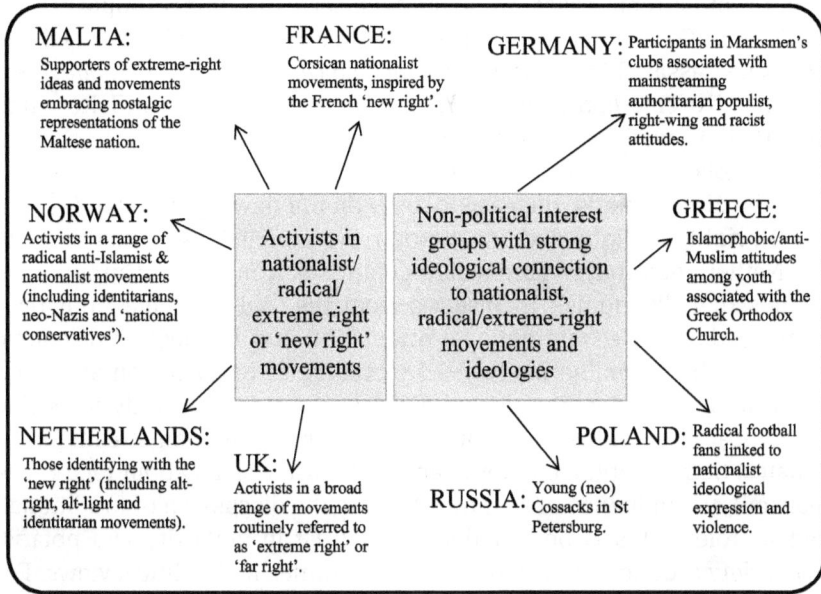

Figure A.1. 'Extreme-right' milieus studied. Created by Hilary Pilkington.

in France but can be seen as an example of the kind of radicalisation on the Right observed elsewhere in the country. Actors in this milieu have sought contact with a number of European radical or extreme right-wing groups but reject the ascription of labels of racism, fascism or Nazism. For further details, see Terrazzoni, Liza. 2020. *Youth Involved in, or Close to, Corsican Right-Wing Nationalist Movements*. DARE Research Report. Retrieved 28 August 2022 from https://documents.manchester.ac.uk/display.aspx?DocID=58694.

The **Maltese** case considers young people's online and offline experiences of engaging with extreme-right ideas, individuals and groups. Narratives were collected from young people currently or formerly affiliated with extreme-right groups as well as young people living in areas subject to social upheaval and potentially susceptible to extreme-right narratives. In a broader sense, the case explores how young people make sense of, and engage with, their place and individual identities in the context of Malta's insularity from mainland Europe, its geopolitical position between Europe and Africa and the transformations brought about by EU membership and new migration dynamics. Its findings suggest that an absence of belonging and social cohesion drives young people to embrace nostalgic, and contested, representations of the Maltese nation, or, in extreme cases, to define themselves in unified opposition to the 'other'. For further details, see Said, Maurice, Jean-Pierre Gauci and Christine Cassar. 2020. *Mapping Online and Offline Spaces of Engagement with the Extreme-Right among Young Maltese People*. DARE Research Report. Retrieved 28 August 2022 from https://documents.manchester.ac.uk/display.aspx?DocID=58697.

In the **Netherlands**, the case focuses on the new right milieu (including alt-right, alt-light and identitarian movements) as it manifests in the Netherlands today. This milieu comprises a mixture of groups and strands that distinguish themselves from the 'old' extreme right by a more modern style, international orientation and intellectual discourse as well as by its online methods of recruitment, organisation and communication and, ideologically, an anti-Islam focus. The study finds that the radical ideas of the milieu are seeping through to mainstream public debates, being identifiable, for example, in discussions about race ('race realism'), the influence of race on IQ and in the discussion of (traditional) gender roles. This is both undermining trust in authority and polarising society around ethnic and religious identities and political views. For further details, see van der Valk, Ineke, Natalie-Anne Hall and Mark Dechesne. 2021. *The New Right in the Netherlands*. DARE Research Report. Retrieved 28 August 2022 from https://documents.manchester.ac.uk/display.aspx?DocID=58698.

The **Norwegian** case explores the political trajectories and motivations of individuals within a milieu involved in, or with links to, groups and networks from a wide spectrum of radical anti-Islamist and nationalist ideologies including identitarians, neo-Nazis and 'national conservatives'. Participants in the study share a common purpose in 'defending the nation' – its assumed unique values, history and culture – in the context of the perceived threat posed to Europe and the West more widely by immigration. Most participants support 'remigration', inspired by the ideology of 'ethnopluralism' and 'traditionalism' associated with the thought of Julius Evola. For further details, see Vestel, Viggo. 2020. *Globalisation, Identity and Nationalism: The Case of Radical Right-Wing Youth in Norway*. DARE Research Report. Retrieved 28 August 2022 from https://documents.manchester.ac.uk/display.aspx?DocID=58699.

The **UK** case explores the trajectories of young people affiliated with a wide range of movements, parties or political campaigns in the UK routinely referred to as being part of the 'extreme-right' or 'far right'. While not co-located, physically or ideologically, these individuals inhabit a common milieu and are connected either personally or through shared activism. The study identifies the growing influence of identitarianism and the alt-right, not least in the perceived threat posed to white identities from demographic change and the commitment to multiculturalism among the liberal establishment. However, this co-exists with a continued discomfort in talking about race and awareness that the naturalisation of racial difference underpins racism, which most participants in the study see as unacceptable. The study pays particular attention to the dissonance between the conceptual descriptor ('far-right', 'extreme-right') applied to the views and behaviours of those in the milieu and the rarity of anti-democratic or pro-authoritarian positions or the legitimation of violence in the pursuit of political goals among participants. For further details, see Pilkington, Hilary. 2020. *Understanding 'Right-Wing Extremism': In Theory and Practice.* DARE Research Report. Retrieved 28 August 2022 from https://documents.manchester.ac.uk/display.aspx?DocID=58702.

Case Studies of Non-Political Interest Groups with Links to Radical or Extreme-Right Ideologies and Movements: Germany, Greece, Poland and Russia

In **Germany**, the study explores the particular milieu of Germany's 'marksmen's clubs' in the context of the mainstreaming of authoritarian populist, right-wing and racist, including anti-Muslim, attitudes in wider German society. The marksmen's clubs have their roots in a centuries-old tradition and millions of people participate nationwide in these ideologically conservative clubs. Their attraction for protagonists on the far right is evident in attempts by such actors to influence the marksmen's clubs milieu and to appropriate aspects of it. This study considers the responses of young people participating in marksmen's clubs to these developments. For further details, see Kerst, Benjamin. 2020. *Marksmen's Clubs in Germany in the Context of Mainstreaming the Extreme.* DARE Research Report. Retrieved 28 August 2022 from https://documents.manchester.ac.uk/display.aspx?DocID=58695.

In **Greece**, the case focuses on Islamophobic or anti-Muslim attitudes, behaviours and sentiments among young people associated with the Greek Orthodox Church. The milieu is characterised by a synthesis of the ideological and identity characteristics that bring together Orthodox zealots (who see themselves as 'soldiers of Christ'), Greek Orthodox far-right activists, militarists and neo-Nazi Golden Dawn supporters. They view themselves as participants in a common struggle for the protection of 'faith and fatherland' from the threat of 'Islamification' and for the propagation of nationalist and authoritarian far-right political programmes necessary to resist perceived threats and injustices faced by the Greek

Orthodox majority due to globalisation, multiculturalism, immigration and secularism. Attention is paid to comparing and contrasting attitudes between participants in the study belonging to more, and less, radical groups within the milieu. For further details, see Lagos, Evangelos, et al. 2020. *Young Orthodox Greeks with Islamophobic/Anti-Muslim Views and Attitudes*. DARE Research Report. Retrieved 28 August 2022 from https://documents.manchester.ac.uk/display.aspx?DocID=58696.

The **Polish** case focuses on the milieu of radical football fans as a site of radical nationalist ideological expression and violence directed not only against rival supporters but other perceived 'enemies'. The expression of ideological symbolism in football culture is a significant element of the contemporary construction of national identity in Poland and connections between the football fan movement and the Catholic Church (epitomised by the annual pilgrimage of Polish football fans to Czestochowa) are indicative of the fan milieu's engagement with the social mainstream. Nationalist ideology and symbolism are deployed in the radical fan milieu as a tool for constructing not only the nation but also a vision of the enemy, excluded from the imagined community, and subject to vilification. This study of radical fan milieus in a number of Polish cities analyses examples of such expressions and argues that football culture has been used as a cultural resource and political tool by nationalist movements promoting particular versions of national 'memory' and 'identity'. For further details, see Kuczyński, Paweł, et al. 2021. *Radical Football Fans*. DARE Research Report. Retrieved 28 August 2022 from https://documents.manchester .ac.uk/display.aspx?DocID=58700.

The **Russian** case considers the right-wing milieu of the young (neo) Cossacks of Saint Petersburg. Originally a free military formation originating in the sixteenth century, the Cossacks gradually became an ethno-social community performing the function of protecting and defending the increasingly militarised state and its political and social order. Today the Cossack movement is characterised by a rigid hierarchical structure, which, supported by the state, performs an informal policing function including the deployment of violence against the civilian population in the event of protest and disorder. Ideologically, the Cossacks see themselves as defenders of Orthodox Christianity but also share xenophobic and anti-immigrant positions, 'traditional' and neo-patriarchal values. These positions, alongside a sense of perceived injustice, regarding rights and access to resources, act as a basis of radicalisation within the (neo) Cossack milieu. For further details, see Sablina, Anastasia, and Alena Kravtcova. 2020. *(Neo)Cossacks in St. Petersburg, Russia*. DARE Research Report. Retrieved 28 August 2022 from https://documents.man chester.ac.uk/display.aspx?DocID=58701.

'Islamist' Milieus

The ten 'Islamist' milieus studied might be very loosely grouped into two clusters (see Figure A.2). These are: those conducted in urban districts or neighbourhoods associated with 'Islamist' activism, migrants from Muslim majority countries and, often, social deprivation (Belgium, Germany, the Netherlands, Norway, Tunisia, UK); and those focusing on particular sites or channels (family and informal networks, non-official prayer houses, civil society organisations, prisons) of potential 'Islamist' radicalisation (France, Greece, Russia, Turkey).

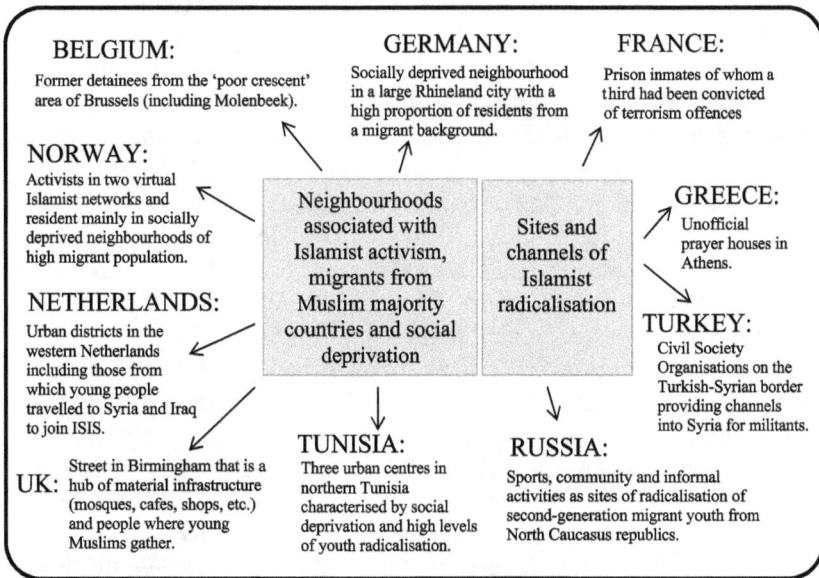

Figure A.2. 'Islamist' milieus studied. Created by Hilary Pilkington.

Case Studies of Neighbourhoods Associated with 'Islamist' Activism: Belgium, Germany, Netherlands, Norway, Tunisia and the UK

The **Belgian** case study focuses on the 'poor crescent' area of Brussels – comprising a crescent-shaped collection of deprived inner-city neighbourhoods, including the infamous Molenbeek district – which have become associated with jihadism at home and abroad. The district is home to a significant proportion of young descendants of Moroccan immigrants who have experienced a variety of social challenges growing up and have often been engaged with criminal activity as well as with 'Islamism'. The research focuses on biographical interviews with young men in prison for terrorism-related offences contextualised in a wider engagement with the neighbourhoods from which they come. For further details, see Benaïssa, Chaïb. 2021. *Radicalisation from the 'Poor Crescent' Area*. DARE Research Report. Retrieved 28 August 2022 from https://documents.manchester.ac.uk/display.aspx?DocID=58681.

In **Germany**, research was conducted with young Muslims living in a socially deprived district of a large city in the Rhineland, with an established neo-Salafist network. A significant proportion of the population is of migrant background and many face racist discrimination in their daily lives. The area suffers from issues with drugs and crime and carries an externally imposed stigma that is reproduced by local and national media. The study focuses on the identity struggles of young Muslims in this area, most of whom are from migrant backgrounds but some of whom are converts to Islam. Those in this milieu varied in terms of their current or former connectedness with radical neo-Salafist networks and their physical and mental proximity to radical neo-Salafist narratives. However, none had closed worldviews or opinions that were not open to challenge. For further details, see Nanni, Sara. 2021. *Neustadt and Beyond*. DARE Research Report. Retrieved 28 August 2022 from https://documents.manchester.ac.uk/display.aspx?DocID=58684.

The **Dutch** ethnographic research concerned a number of urban areas in the western part of the Netherlands, focusing on a district in The Hague, which in recent years has witnessed a considerable outflow of young people travelling to Syria and Iraq to join ISIS. Research participants were individuals, groups and organisations with first-hand experience of issues related to 'Islamist' radicalisation in the Netherlands either because they themselves were part of the radical scene (recently or when home-grown terrorism had emerged following the 9/11 World Trade Centre attacks) or because they knew people in their vicinity who participated in such scenes. For further details, see Dechesne, Mark, and Ineke van der Valk. 2021. *Islamist Radicalisation in the Netherlands*. DARE Research Report. Retrieved 28 August 2022 from https://documents.manchester.ac.uk/display.aspx?DocID=58688.

The **Norwegian** case study focuses on individuals, most of whom had grown up in the high-rise suburbs on the east side of Oslo, involved in two 'Islamist' networks – The Prophet's Ummah and Islam Net. These emerged as virtual networks but developed into physical groups that partially overlap. The milieu studied consists of young people who surround the cores of these groups and who have considered going to Syria, or have connections with other young people who have travelled to participate in the Syrian conflict, either as combatants or through humanitarian work. For further details, see Vestel, Viggo, and Qasim Ali. 2021. *Globalisation, Identity and Islam: The Case of Radical Muslim Youths in Norway*. DARE Research Report. Retrieved 28 August 2022 from https:// documents.manchester.ac.uk/display.aspx?DocID=58689.

In **Tunisia**, the ethnographic study focuses on three urban centres in northern Tunisia: Tadhamon (a suburb of Tunis), Bizerte and Menzel Bourguiba. The areas are characterised by unemployment, lack of prospects, poverty and ineffective local governance. Moreover, while many Tunisians living along the coast consider themselves primarily Mediterranean, embracing freedom of religion, Tunisians living in the interior of the country as well as those who have migrated to the urban areas studied here typically adopt more orthodox forms of Islam. This has led to the areas being viewed as prone to high levels of radicalisation among young people in a period in which Tunisia became one of the main recruiting sites of youth for ISIS. Whilst a Muslim majority country, in Tunisia, 'Islamism' and Salafism remain under scrutiny by the authorities. For further details, see Memni, Chokri. 2021. *Young People's Trajectories through Radical Islamist Milieus: Tunis (Tadhamon), Bizerte, Menzel-Bourguiba*. Unpublished DARE Research Report.

The fieldwork in the **UK** focuses on what is referred to as 'Muslim street' in Birmingham, characterised by a rich Islamic infrastructure and resources for living out 'Islamist' lifestyles. It has a plethora of commercial enterprises and formal and informal organisations that cater to the needs of young Muslims and was seen by research participants as a hub where young Muslims gather, connect and pass through. However, the area is also characterised by high rates of multiple deprivation, and recent media and policy attention to the street and broader neighbourhood has led to its representation as a space where extremism is fostered. The street is a focus of attention for counter-extremism agencies, which operate in partnership with a number of prominent mosques in the area. 'Islamist' activists are also attracted to the area because of its combination of resources, in the form of spaces, and individuals potentially receptive to their message (often framed in a negative perception of South Asian Islam and folk practices and its traditional authorities). For further details, see Hussain, Ajmal. 2021. *Muslim Street*. DARE Research Report. Retrieved 28 August 2022 from https://documents.manchester.ac.uk/display.aspx?DocID=58692.

Case Studies of Sites and Channels of Islamist Radicalisation: France, Greece, Russia and Turkey

The **French** ethnographic study was located in a prison, where a third of the young Muslims participating in the study had been convicted for crimes related to radicalisation and terrorism. While the socio-economic conditions of the *banlieues* where many young Muslims grow up and live point to the link between inequality and radicalisation, in France, prison has been seen as a particular catalyst for radicalisation. This is because of the experience of confinement, the sense of isolation, guilt and lack of future prospects combined with the often humiliating behaviour and omnipresence of guards, which can create an openness to radical 'Islamist' narratives. The ethnographic study captures experiences and attitudes related to personal history, society and radicalisation of the inmates to elucidate the complex interrelationship between socio-economic circumstances, psychological processes and radicalisation and non-radicalisation. For further details, see Conti, Bartolomeo. 2020. *Trajectories of (Non)Radicalisation in a Prison Milieu*. DARE Research Report. Retrieved 28 August 2022 from https://documents.manchester.ac.uk/display.aspx?Doc ID=58683.

The **Greek** study focuses on a specific milieu in a central area of Athens where young Muslims attend, and gather socially in, non-official places of worship. Although there has been a small Muslim minority community in Greece from the Ottoman Empire, a significant influx of Muslim immigrants in recent years has increased the Muslim population to around 5–10% of the total population of Athens. However, historical animosity and suspicion towards Turkey and Islam, combined with the powerful presence of Greek Orthodox Christianity as the official state religion, means that the capital city has had no official mosque (until November 2020). In this context, non-official prayer houses are often portrayed as potential incubators of radicalisation while stigmatisation of Muslim refugees and immigrants, as well as the active campaign by extreme-right groups to prevent the construction of the Athens mosque, has fuelled the potential for radicalisation of young Muslims in the city. For further details, see Sakellariou, Alexandros. 2021. *Young Muslims in Unofficial Prayer Places of Athens*. DARE Research Report. Retrieved 28 August 2022 from https://documents.manchester.ac.uk/display.aspx?DocID=58686.

The ethnographic fieldwork in **Russia** is focused on young men with a North Caucasian regional background currently living in two Russian megacities – Saint Petersburg and Moscow. The research participants come mainly from Dagestan, the largest and most Islamised republic in the North Caucasus and the main arena of confrontation between regional and federal authorities and jihadists. These young people are second-generation city dwellers but the first generation to be born after the beginning of the post-Soviet re-Islamisation of the North Caucasus. Thus, unlike their parents and older relatives, who tend to be adherents of traditional Sufi Islam, they are more likely to opt for fundamentalist versions of Islam. Their religious views are characterised by a high degree of protest politicisation and those from this social milieu reportedly predominate among young people who have gone to fight in Syria on the side of the Islamic State. For further details, see Poliakov, Sviatoslav, and Yulia Epanova. 2021. *Urban Second Generation Muslims from the North Caucasus in St Petersburg and Moscow, Russia*. DARE Research Report. Retrieved 28 August 2022 from https://documents.manchester.ac.uk/dis play.aspx?DocID=58690.

In **Turkey**, the focus of the research was on the role of civil society organisations (CSOs) in providing a space for 'Islamist' and Salafist influences to take root among young Turkish men and women living along the Turkish-Syrian border at the time of significant conflict (2015–18). Many young men and women engaged with the humanitarian efforts and benefitted from substantial aid and support provided by these 'Islamist' CSOs, in the process adopting more conservative norms and finding legitimation for radical views and ideals that engaged with the ongoing conflict and war within and beyond the Turkish borders. These were sites also of targeted recruitment of young people by Salafi individuals and organisations as well as, in some cases, being an instrument of the government, allowing it to exert influence across the border in Syria and provide channels into the country for militants. For further details, see Kurt, Mehmet. 2020. *When the Salt Stinks: The Syrian War, Kurdish Question and Borderline Radicalisation in Turkey*. DARE Research Report. Retrieved 28 August 2022 from https://documents.manchester.ac.uk/dis play.aspx?DocID=58691.

INDEX